REED, JOHN

# THE NATURAL HISTORY OF
# H.G. WELLS

# The Natural History of

# H.G. WELLS

"Through his familiarity with science, he [Wells] recognized those strands of thought which were weaving a new image of man and his place in nature."

John R. Reed

# The Natural History of

# H.G. WELLS

by
# John R. Reed

 Ohio University Press: Athens, Ohio

**Library of Congress Cataloging in Publication Data**

Reed, John Robert, 1938—
    The natural history of H. G. Wells.

    Includes bibliographical references and index.
    1. Wells, H. G. (Herbert George), 1866-1946
—Philosophy. 2. Wells, H. G. (Herbert George),
1866-1946—Criticism and interpretation. 3. Phil-
osophy in literature. I. Title.
PR5778. P5R4   1981    823'.912    81-11261
ISBN 0-8214-0628-0          AACR2

Book Design by
William Kevin McCarty

For Ruth

# Acknowledgements

I owe much to the anonymous reviewers of my original manuscript whose challenges and recommendations have, I believe, greatly improved the final text. I am indebted to Ms. Helen Gawthrop, who tended the manuscript through its editorial stages with thoroughness and care. Little original work can be done on Wells without recourse to the splendid collection at the University of Illinois Library's Rare Book Collection, and I wish to thank the professionals there for their assistance, in particular Frederick Nash and Louise Fitton.

Parts of this text appeared in different form in *The Journal of Modern Literature* and *The North American Review*.

# Contents

# Preface

There has been a good deal of sound writing on H. G. Wells. I am grateful for that work and have drawn upon it; but because my own study seeks to develop matters neither mentioned before nor treated in detail, I do not often refer to many general sources of information, especially the fine biographies of Wells from Geoffrey West's and Vincent Brome's to Norman and Jeanne MacKenzie's. Their studies have been essential to my framing a picture of Wells's nature, and I wish to state my debt to them here. Rosylnn D. Haynes's *H. G. Wells: Discoverer of the Future* (1980) appeared after I had completed my manuscript, and therefore I have not made much use of that study even though Professor Haynes and I obviously share many basic assumptions about Wells and his works.

Although my efforts depend upon a detailed picture of Wells's life and character, I have little to say about either except insofar as they illuminate Wells's intellectual and esthetic attitudes. In this book I argue that Wells had a world view that, while it developed and evolved over the half century of his career, remained coherent and mainly consistent—more so than with most men of letters. This world view was rooted in Wells's private fears and desires and found expression in powerful sets of images which, when studied with care, reinforce Wells's intellectual constructions.

There have been quarrels about whether Wells was an optimist or a pessimist, whether he changed radically from the time of the early romances to the time of the realist novels. I do not wish to engage in these quarrels, for my impression of Wells is of a man of immense intellectual energy and almost painful emotional craving who could envision marvels for humanity that he knew he would never himself witness. Inevitably, the tension of this condition generated shifts of mood, sudden despairs, abrupt reliances. In his calmer moments he recognized one essential point—that despair and confidence were equally false. The only rational faith was a provisional faith. Wells described illusions both dark and bright, but he had none.

By describing some of Wells's central beliefs and his ways of presenting them, I hope to provide a clearer picture of his accomplishment. In choosing to quote Wells himself, I realize that I have sometimes sinned in repetitiveness; but since one of Wells's great gifts was to vivify dry ideas with saucy phrases, I felt that the sin was venial. I have drawn fewer examples from *Kipps, Tono-Bungay*, and *The History of Mr. Polly* than some readers might expect, but that is simply because these novels have elsewhere enjoyed more discussion than the others. Often Wells's clearest expressions of his opinions and his intentions do not appear in his best novels.

I have often repeated the dates of Wells's works in the text when I have felt that a sense of temporal location was necessary. Wells wrote so many books over so long a period of time that it is important for a reader not familiar with his canon to have a sense of chronology constantly suggested.

There is no standard edition of Wells's works. The Atlantic Edition is far from complete. As a result, I have chosen to include all citations to Wells's books within the text, using an abbreviated title followed by volume, book, chapter, or section divisions as necessary; *The New Machiavelli*, book I, chapter I, section 1 thus becomes (*Machiavelli*, bk. I, chap. I: 1). I have given no citations for short stories unless they have internal divisions. Almost all of these are quoted from *The Famous Short Stories of H. G. Wells*, Doubleday, 1938.

I have used the revised rather than the serial version of *When the Sleeper Wakes, The Euphemia Papers* from the Atlantic Edition rather than *Certain Personal Matters*, the Atlantic Edition version of *First and Last Things*, and the American title, *Social Forces in England and America*, for the collection of essays often referred to as *An Englishman Looks at the World*.

Unless otherwise stated, all italics in quoted matter appear in the original text.

# Introduction

Think of H. G. Wells as a Victorian and your admiration for the man increases, for you realize that he was one of the first literary figures of any stature in England to shape himself into a Modern. This becoming self-consciously modern had been going on in France for some time, but it was a novelty in England. Not even George Moore or the Decadents were modern as we now understand the term.[1] But Wells, while appreciating accumulated cultural tradition, conceived of the literary artist as the shaper of a plastic future, not merely as a rebel against the inertia of the past, though he was surely that. At least one critic has described Wells as an early existentialist, an argument with merit.[2] As we shall see later, Wells had mixed feelings about the term *art* because he did not isolate it from action. In any case, ideas came first with him—ideas that moved to action. He believed that man's will could initiate and control change. Moreover, through his familiarity with science, he recognized those strands of thought which were weaving a new image of man and of his place in nature.

Despite his reputation for innovation, Wells discovered very little that was new. Despite his polemical writings, he had scarcely any effect upon the course of events. Despite the many tributes to his influence, he established no clear school of followers nor any party prepared to defend his reputation. Friends marveled at his stupendous energy, but energy alone does not ensure survival in the minds of succeeding generations. And although he is not honored as he once was, he has not been forgotten.[3] Indeed, all those who have been hiding him beneath a bushel of conventional assumptions are now surprised to see the light so brightly beaming as the bushel is lifted away. There is a reason why he has survived and will survive, a reason that his contemporaries recognized but which we have to some degree forgotten. Wells was a master of language, capable of shaping original and borrowed ideas and forms into vivid, memorable, and novel ar-

1

rangements.[4] He had a clear delivery, a trenchant style, and a sure grasp of nuance in most of his writing—certainly in his best writing. And because he could turn this capacity to almost any service, he created of himself a monument to the spirit of a wildly changing time. He kept abreast of the times by remaining in advance of them. If there was a new invention—physical or mental—abroad, Wells was sure to know it and tell it to his reader as though it had long been his own. Christopher Caudwell called him an "entrepreneur of modern theories"[5]; it was a hostile judgment.

Was Wells a great thinker? Some say yes, some no.[6] I shall not consider the question in those terms. If Wells was not a great or profound thinker, he was undeniably a great expositor of broad ideas and he was a superb polemicist.[7] Time and again he claimed the gift of grasping general concepts and of being able to convey these simple and—as he would say, "spacious"—notions to others.

Was Wells a fine novelist? The question may be beside the point. It is a question that arose at a time when theorists were just beginning to codify the novelist's art. Since then we have seen ample changes. In his own day he was accepted as a leading novelist.[8] That, of course, is not the same thing. He could certainly write thrilling, penetrating, or funny fictions when he chose. But he did not always choose, and undeniably, in his later career that power of choice was impaired as he became more concerned with fabulation than fiction. Wells wrote to instruct, and there has always been a danger to novelists and to fiction in that practice, as the unjustly ignored career of Bulwer-Lytton and the deservedly forgotten one of Robert Plumer Ward suggest.[9] Theodore Dreiser disapproved of Wells's didacticism, insisting that a novelist is best when he is without bias.[10] Edward Shanks more humorously described Wells's didactic novels as " 'not novels' but a sort of literary mules, doomed to sterility and bad tempers."[11] But Wells persisted in breeding hybrid novels because he believed they were made for work, not show. He wished to teach, not merely to entertain.[12] He felt an enormous respect for the only other man whose history he wrote—Sanderson of Oundle—because he saw him as a teacher of the first rank, a rank that included Wells himself. What was important about Wells was his ability to understand the currents of his time (in his case we must say times) and make of them, through his power over language, something striking, entertaining, and mainly edifying. He was able to do this over nearly the whole of his sixty-year career.

To understand what Wells was doing, one must have at least a general idea of what the circumstances were in which he developed. Science and social philosophy are two broad categories important to such an understanding. We shall return to both later, but a summary view is helpful at the outset. Thomas Henry Huxley was the major scientific influence on Wells. This influence is important because Huxley was much more than a scientist; he was a gifted writer, willing to take up difficult, wide-ranging questions. There is a strong echo of Huxley's essays, most notably *Evolution and Ethics*, throughout Wells's works. Thus, although Wells learned the Darwinism that was militant, if not yet secure, in the 1880s, he comprehended it in more than merely scientific terms. Science and philosophy were still near cousins in his student days. Today's commonplaces were matters for excited speculation then. Even the basic processes of human physiology were barely fathomed.[13] Atomic theory was in its infancy. Mendelian genetics had not been rediscovered. Hence, although such fields as geology, paleontology, archeology, and physics were offering more precise accounts of the natural world and man's place in it, the biological sciences were just beginning.

Wells delighted in this unsteady state of thought which allowed the maximum range for speculation. It was a pleasure to dispute the question of a fourth dimension or to discuss the huge issue of transformation of species or to ponder the infiniteness of a universe that Einstein had not yet contorted. Into this welter of speculation Wells introduced the questions of ethics and justice. It was not a new questioning. It was certainly part of the Huxleyian heritage, and both Herbert Spencer and Auguste Comte had offered their versions of moralized science.[14] They were not new questions, but they remained open ones. Wells matured in an atmosphere of philosophical speculation about science which accounts to some degree for his tendency to approach science in a broad, comprehensive manner. But there were personal reasons why intellectual issues of this kind should so have captured his imagination.

Wells hated things as he knew them. He felt a lifelong resentment against the social conditions that had made his early life a struggle and which had come close to killing him.[15] Although, like Huxley, he recognized the grim implications for man in the theory of evolution, he embraced it eagerly because it offered the only real hope for mankind. Without some such hypothesis, Wells would have found no justification for a belief in progress, for he had little faith in men as a whole and depended largely upon the actions of a gifted fraction of the race to bring about improvement. Darwinian theory suggested that chance mutations provided the mechanism for organic adaptability. Herein lay man's hope.

From his earliest writings it is evident that although Wells had a solid conviction of the uniqueness of all things, he saw the importance of concerted effort, from the massing of individual selves in the formation of an organism to the social cooperation of insect and animal communities.[16] There was much writing at this time to support his views. Near the end of his life Wells said that his "Rediscovery of the Unique" (1891), which stated one of his fundamental philosophical positions, was merely a revival of the views of Roger Bacon "in the light of modern observational science."[17] But John Ruskin had much earlier called for the acceptance of the unique in nature in *Modern Painters* (1843-1860), and Henry Thomas Buckle's *History of Civilization in England* (1857-1861) acknowledged an evolutionary impulse in human history.[18] Comte, Spencer, and Fiske all hypothesized the evolution of a finer world and an ideal man.[19] William Morris was calling for a world civilization and championing socialism as he understood it. Wells probably read Winwood Reade's *Martyrdom of Man* (1872) very early. This widely popular book gave an account of man's progress through stages of increasing organization and awareness toward a splendid future through science.[20] From the numerous favorable references he makes to the work throughout his career, there can be no doubt that Wells appreciated Reade's main argument.[21] Wells thus assembled a rudimentary belief from the many different theories flourishing in his youth which combined socialism, science, and evolutionary progress as basic ingredients.

In many ways the turning point for Wells's social attitudes came with his writing down of the astonishing collection of thoughts he published as *Anticipations* in 1901, for the book represented a significant departure from his role as a writer of fiction. When Arnold Bennett read the book, he wrote to Wells, "Either you have in a supreme degree the journalistic trick of seeming omniscience, or you are one of the most remarkable men alive."[22] In his reply, Wells playfully confessed to greatness. But Bennett had perceived a double truth, for Wells was a remarkable man and he did have a journalist's knack for powerful expression. Of course he had had a good deal of experience as an essayist on social and scientific matters during his apprenticeship, but most of his early speculations on the future were channeled into the profitable acreage of fiction, as the publishing history of *The Time Machine* demonstrates.[23]

Wells was fully aware of the change that he was initiating in his own career.[24] He felt that his venture into futurology was important for himself and for mankind. He wished to weigh the history that had not yet taken place against the future that had died. The past was a fossil record by which men could read their steady advance, noting the dead-end experiments along the way. But the future was a projection of operating laws forward in time. After the success of *Anticipations* and the subsequent invitations to serious intellectual intercourse with informed and influential groups and persons, most notably the Fabians, Wells realized that he would now be able to revive his teaching career, but on a vastly extended scale. Moreover, he began to see his potential as a leader, a sort of exalted schoolmaster prepared to guide his enthusiastic scholars toward a civilization grander and finer than anything known before. There was much in his past that convinced him he had the necessary equipment for the task.

After having eluded the drapery trade, Wells germinated in an educational atmosphere for several years. He was a scholarship boy primed and encouraged along a new, rather than a traditional, route to intellectual distinction. His youthful mood, alluded to in many of his stories, but especially "A Slip Under the Microscope" (1893) and *Love and Mr. Lewisham* (1900), was one of hectic aspiration. Learning was not merely an acquired grace but a practical weapon in a series of skirmishes against a hostile society. Wells never forgot that his learning came to him outside the normal channels of achievement, and he never let the normal channels forget how little irrigation they provided for the likes of him and for mankind generally.

Because education was so liberating for him, Wells considered it the chief means for human advancement. He had taught in private schools and adult extension programs, but he had a notion of education that went far beyond these forms. He believed that education was a lifetime endeavor and that all forms of communication should be harnessed to that purpose. His private reading and experience with journalism may have helped him to form this view. It is certainly obvious that Wells's desire to teach and his desire to express himself were intimately associated. He considered himself a journalist rather than an artist because he recognized the didactic strain in himself from the outset.

Wells was making his way as a journalist at an early age, first with the *Science Schools Journal*, but soon after in such reputable periodicals as the *Saturday Review*, the *Pall Mall Gazette*, *Nature*, and the *New Review*. His training in science was valuable to him in this career not merely because it provided him with interesting and unusual themes but also because it taught him the perceptive acuity and logical extension of the scientific method.[25] But skill at observation and power to convey what is observed did not come to Wells from science alone. He himself credited the catchy journalistic techniques of the day for much of his ability to write effectively. To make a living at journalism of the *Tit-Bit* variety, he had to keep an eye out for eccentric and intriguing "copy." His inspiration seized what was at hand, a method that revealed how useful the minutiae of contemporary life could be in the formulation of plots or arguments. Nor did he hesitate to imitate or appropriate any method, manner, or style that had proved successful. The early stories show him practicing the adventure tale after Kipling, the ghost or occult tale in the manner of Poe or Stevenson, and so forth. He also exploited timely subjects such as anarchism, exotic exploration, literary aestheticism, or spiritualism and parodied familiar literary forms.[26] In his nonfiction, Wells was similarly eclectic, often taking issue with some current fashion, theory, or text, and thereby throwing his own opinions into strong relief in the role of antagonist. This skill in employing other ideas or works of literature as springboards for his own creations was to remain with Wells throughout his career and to serve as a convenient armature for much of his writing.

From the outset, Wells was a *writer*, not specifically a specialist in fiction. He did not try to form a single, identifiable style, nor did he aim at exquisiteness. When the question of literary elegance and fine taste came up, he was likely to mock it. Literature for Wells was purposive, not an end in itself. Though he made fun of writers who tried to teach the world, he respected above all else writing designed to move men to action or thought. The quarrel between Wells and James was inevitable, and even while Wells recognized how important James's skill with his craft was, how essential command of language was, he could not accept the ends to which James put his mastery.

So, in 1901, having amazed himself and the literary world with his success as a writer of science fables, Wells suddenly found himself back in the undisguised position of a lecturer to English-speaking peoples. Should he have rejected the role? Did his involvement in social and political discussion vitiate his literary talents? The question is unanswerable, I think, but one need only consider what might have happened to Wells if he had not turned schoolmaster to his age.[27] Despite their excellences, there is a certain unsubstantiality in even the most widely admired of his fictions from this time, and certainly, despite their spirited and charming manner, such novels as *The Wonderful Visit* (1895), *The Wheels of Chance* (1896), and *The Sea Lady* (1902) are trivial productions from a writer aspiring to eminence. The fact is that Wells wrote what he thought was striking but acceptable at the time. In a letter of 1897 he admitted that he had been "banging away with the idea of keeping myself before the public." He considered that it was wiser "to turn out a succession of striking if rather unfinished books and so escape from journalism than to let myself be forgotten again while I elaborated a masterpiece saving my limitations."[28] Although he wrote a fine traditional novel in *Tono-Bungay* (1909), there is no indication that he would ever have been patient enough to dedicate himself to the art of fiction. He exploited his gift to the utmost and was an opportunist, as so many hostile observers noted. But he was an opportunist of the finer kind, in the way of many respected politicians (for example, Lloyd George, whom Wells admired for a time). Unless he was prominent, his message was lost. Most of his early writing aimed at securing a livelihood, yet nearly all of it carries with it a purpose of instruction. There is a lamp in almost everything Wells ever wrote.

Instead of so belligerently denominating himself a journalist, Wells might more correctly have designated himself simply "writer," for that is what he was. He trained himself to an astonishing command of language and then utilized whatever form seemed most appropriate to communicate his fancies, ideas, and convictions. He had shaped this tool for a purpose and now, with strong faith in the power of his own will to use it, he set out to instruct his less fortunate fellows.

The most obvious feature of Wells's mature writing is its autobiographical cast. This is not to say, as some have, that Wells was a mere egotist. He enjoyed himself. He loved to talk about himself. He had the very human trait of seeing himself as the center of his universe. This habit of mind was not very Copernican, and he knew that; but it was unavoidable. When he described himself as a "very ordinary brain" in his autobiography, he may not have been entirely candid, but he was trying to express his sense of his own typicality. He declared that he saw his own history as the history of his time. For a man trained in science who knew the implications of the maxim "phylogony recapitulates ontogony," this was an important affiliation. No matter how indirectly, Wells was using himself as a specimen and testing himself for the benefit of the race.[29]

His early writings, especially "The Rediscovery of the Unique" (1891), show how conscious he was of the individuality of all organisms. He never lost confidence in the spontaneity of the individual and his fiction provides an array of lovable eccentrics. He fostered the picture of himself as just such another type. He did not go so far as George Bernard Shaw in theatricalizing himself and becoming a sort of self-manipulated marionette to convey a point, but he was inclined in the same direction. One might say he was a Shaw with a libido. That made all the difference. Whereas Shaw set himself above the humanity around him in order to instruct it, Wells insisted that he was qualified to lecture his fellow man because he was one with him.

In a manner more self-conscious and studied than one might expect from an apprentice journalist, Wells used himself and his own experiences freely. He drew upon his scientific background (as we have noted with "A Slip Under the Microscope") and his personal life, as in the light essays in *The Euphemia Papers* and *Select Conversations with an Uncle*. Like a good journalist, he was even willing to cannibalize his role as a journalist, as the essays "In a Literary Household" and "The Literary Regimen" show. This liberal use of himself as source and subject matter for his writing encouraged Wells's introspectiveness. Because he was an honest man, he discovered many inconsistencies within himself. Ultimately, it became evident that his highly aggressive, individualistic nature did not run well in harness with his theoretical assertions. Friends and adversaries were quick to point this out. Sheer bulk of evidence suggests that there was a granary of truth in their accounts of his waywardness. But contradiction of this sort is neither unusual nor surprising in a man of lively intellect and temperament. H. G. Wells was not John Stuart Mill. Like a philandering priest, he could work honestly and diligently for the faith he could not keep. Failing to harmonize the discords in his behavior, he was resolved to understand and exploit them.

Wells was aware of the conflict between the concept of uniqueness and individual assertion and communal subjugation. He was no fool. He identified the conflict within himself and offered many equations for it, principally the traditional opposition between passion and reason. He urged the suppression of animal impulse and the cultivation of intellect, but he was always conscious of the former's power and the tenuousness of the latter. He saw reason, self-control, self-denial, and the extension of the self beyond the self as clear advances upon man's basic animality. "A Story of the Stone Age" (1897) has this progression as its premise, with the proto-human Ugh-Lomi being distinguished not only by his power to think more consistently than others but also by his ability to escape his own desires in the interest of another, specifically his beloved Eudema.

Facing the essential struggle between passion and self-denial in himself prepared Wells for the germane conflict between self and society. Here too he asserted that the self must subordinate itself to the needs of the community. It was a broader version of what was evident within the individual. Little wonder then that he saw himself, or any man, as a microcosm of the struggle being played out on a cosmic scale. But there was a complication. From the first, Wells realized that human personality was not a simple lamination of animal passion and human reason. It was more like a complicated energy field or a cell structure in which multiple forces exerted themselves with varying intensity, creating now one entity, now another. For a good part of the time Wells presented this internal division as a simple bifurcation in the nineteenth-century tradition, but eventually he described it in its full complexity. His belief in a multiple self left him receptive to ideas about the reassembling of that self. Just as species were not fixed but dynamic in the Darwinian theory, so the individual was not bound by an imprisoning definition. He was an organism, an amalgam constantly in a state of mutation, and what set him apart from other organisms was his power to conceive of that which was not already existent. Voluntarily, in the power of the imagination, and involuntarily in dreams, man had a capacity to rise above the limitations of instincts and impulses that bound the animals to their causal rack.

Wells frequently refers to dreams in his writings. Often, as in *The Dream* (1924) or *The Shape of Things to Come* (1933), he employs the device as William Morris did in "A Dream of John Ball" (1888) and *News From Nowhere* (1890), and Edward Bellamy in *Looking Backward* (1888), as a convenient way to compose a fiction about another time or place. But it is clear from other instances, as in *The Happy Turning: A Dream of Life* (1945), that dreaming had a special significance for him. A key to this special meaning appears in "A Story of the Stone Age" (1897), where Ugh-Lomi's mind is freed in dreams to follow out a logic not always completed in his waking mind, which is subject to distraction. Nightmares are equally significant. After battling Uya, the ruler of his tribe, Ugh-Lomi is haunted by the old warrior in nightmares until he is compelled to seek out and murder the man in order to free himself from his obsession. Nightmares and dreams have functions. Nightmares keep fear alive in us, prompting the brave to action. It is backward looking, rooted in memory and pain. If nightmares are goads, dreams are guides. Through them the imagination creates ideal situations otherwise unknown to man.

Wells was quick to acknowledge the value of psychoanalytic approaches to the phenomenon of dreaming, for he had always valued dreams and nightmares as uncontrolled signals to behavior. He was much interested in his own dreams and nightmares as we shall notice in greater detail later; he reckoned that if his unconscious mind could project its aversions and attractions, so could the racial mind. He modified the tradition of prophetic dreams which suggested that a supernal power might grant glimpses of otherwise inaccessible knowledge in moments of importance or crisis.[30] To him dreams were visions without grace. He did not depend upon Jung or later theorists for this notion, since adventurous thinkers had proposed the idea of a common racial memory before. Samuel Butler had done so in his vivid, if somewhat playful, *Unconscious Memory* (1880), and William Butler Yeats was a contemporary spokesman of a similar conception.

Wells seemed to believe that dreams were instinctive responses to experience that should be attended to like any other responses. Dreams, like the sensation of pleasure, could serve as guides, and just as capriciously. Nightmares could warn like the sensation of pain, and just as mysteriously. Thus understood, the unconscious imagination became subject to the will as its operations became manifest. This was a useful perception regarding individual behavior, but overwhelmingly important for mankind, since it involved the paramount realization that mankind's dreams were the compositions of its imaginative writers. Wells had a slight appreciation for poetry, but one poet he was willing to credit was Shelley, for Shelley recognized that the fabricators of visions, whom he called poets, were indeed the legislators of the world.

If the dreams of the race were recorded in its literature, then it was man's duty to test those dreams in reality, just as Ugh-Lomi applied the vision of his sleep to the practical affair of surviving in Pleistocene times. This meant that the race, like the individual, must shape its purpose and discipline itself to test each new dream that promised usefulness. Comparably, all of the failed past became a nightmare to be exorcised. Wells did not picture progress as a passive advance down a distinguishable road; to him, it involved the careful inducing of a very real donkey down an unknown road with an imaginary carrot.

Wells expected the race to pull itself together. "Do you want to end up like the Megatheria?" he would threaten, as a nurse frightens children with a bogey. Remember the nightmare; apply the dream. That was the message. It had the same application at the racial as at the personal level, and it had to follow the same process: the suppression of personal lusts and needs to a larger objective. Behind everything was the consolidation of the self under the dominion of the will. Time and again Wells stressed the individual man's need to put down the ape and tiger in himself and discipline his will to high ends. Although he failed personally in this effort again and again, the standing account of his achievement proves that he was largely successful in his aim. He expected mankind to travel the same distance.

Like Nietzsche, whose ideas his frequently resemble, Wells insisted that mankind had to change its concepts about itself and about nature. Neither man's past nor his destiny was fixed. Nature was not his servant, but his antagonist. Though governed by measurable laws, existence was frighteningly open and unpredictable, not secure and explicable. Man himself was the least explicable feature of his world. But man could govern nature, had indeed proved this ability amply in the past. While despising its faults, Wells commended his race and advised greater effort toward control. It was not external nature that posed the greatest problem, but the nature within. Hence Wells demanded that men become as aware of the laws of their own beings as they were of the laws of the physical world. He was a relentless and ruthless student of his own inner cosmos. What he found there is what we all find—conflict, confusion, and contradiction. What is remarkable is that he could understand and exploit each weakness as well as each strength. His advice comes down to at least one important word—control. He knew there would be lapses, but he knew that these could be corrected while the will to command persisted.

Wells was an astonishingly self-aware man, and this self-awareness is perhaps what many of his critics—especially those of his own day—did not see. He used his acquaintances roughly in his fiction. He handled public figures roughly as well. But he was just as fierce with himself. Many of the so-called autobiographical heroes of his novels might more correctly be called trial specimens. Wells claimed to admire and employ a scientific method. I think he did. He boasted of his powers of broad generalization, but he was equally gifted in dissection. In what follows I shall examine in detail certain persistent motifs and recurrent ideas that demonstrate the underlying consistency and force of Wells's beliefs and his methods. His own awareness of these motifs, beliefs, and methods constitute part of the pleasure in reading what he so abundantly wrote.

# 1

# Liberation

Summarizing his friend H. G. Wells in his own autobiography in 1936, Frank Swinnerton, who cared little for Wells's utopian schemes, asserted that Wells's "true passion is for liberty."[1] Nothing is more evident in Wells's writings than the exaltation of human freedom; and for Wells, freedom meant liberation. Like Benham in *The Research Magnificent* (1915), his sentiment was "first, escape" (*Research*, chap. I: 12).[2] G. K. Chesterton described Wells as a "permanent reactionary" because whenever he met him "he seemed to be coming from somewhere, rather than going anywhere."[3] Although Chesterton is craftily unfair, there is a flake of accuracy in this gout of generalization, for Wells operated chiefly on the principle of response and reaction. Moreover, he was always outgrowing situations, friends, and ideas as though he had tasted his own Herakleophobia and increased his dimensions so greatly that he was obliged to strip old associations like old clothes. His sense of freedom relates more to escape from confinement, entrapment, and entanglement than to aspiration, though the impulses of flight and yearning are too mixed to separate entirely.

Wells candidly faced his need for freedom, and in his autobiography examined the "flight impulse" that came on him from time to time. His revolt against a life in the draper's trade was its first manifestation, but it recurred later. Sometimes escape was "completed in imagination if not in fact" (*Autobiography*, chap. IX: 8). One instance of Wells's urge to break loose was his elopement with Amy Catherine Robbins. Intimations of social and intellectual freedom, not sexual passion, led them to their adventure. Ultimately, Wells conceived of freedom as an intellectual achievement. "The truth remains," he said, "that to-day nothing stands in the way to the attainment of universal freedom and abundance but mental tangles, egocentric preoccupations, obsessions, misconceived phrases, bad habits of thought, subconscious fears and dreads and plain dishonesty in people's minds—and especially in the minds of those in key positions" (*Autobiography*, chap. IX: 9).

Most of Wells's narratives assume the need for a personal or broader liberation. "Life," says Capes in *Ann Veronica* (1909), "is rebellion, or nothing" (*Veronica*, chap. XVI: 1). V. S. Pritchett was struck by the sense of freedom evident in Wells's early tales.[4] It is a sense of someone bursting from bondage, but not necessarily going anywhere. Always there was the desire to escape; only gradually did Wells wrestle that urge into a coherent pattern of development. Chesterton, who shared Wells's love of freedom, was constitutionally unfit to appreciate one aspect of it; he admitted to a lifelong love of boundaries, always wanting things reduced to a smaller and smaller scale, whereas Wells wanted no boundaries at all.[5] He never saw the use of them. He called for a World State without frontiers and even that did not satisfy his appetite for expansion. His *Outline of History* (1920) made mankind's career a progress toward universal freedom, but it was first of all an escape from primitive entrapment. As we shall see later, human freedom depended finally upon man's capacity for self-suppression. But in order to place restraints upon himself, man had to escape the restraints imposed by others. First, escape. . . .

Though Wells believed that liberation and escape were chiefly mental adventures, he rendered conditions of entrapment and confinement in concrete terms, using images of entanglement and imprisonment to depict a psychological state because his own sense of constraint was rooted in physical experience. When he spoke of escaping from his early life, Wells meant a physical deliverance. Throughout his life he angrily recalled the cramping physical conditions of his youth, which became the vivid analogue for all that entrapment meant to him. He contrasted his pinched Bromley home and the airless draper's shop in which he was nearly snared with the spacious and grand house at Up Park.[6] In Bromley, he said, the family lived "mostly downstairs and underground" (*Autobiography*, chap. II: 2). His resentment is modified by sympathy for his parents, "economic innocents who, looking for stability and shelter in a world breaking away toward adventure, dropped into that dismal insanitary hole . . . in which I was born, and from which they were unable to escape for twenty-four dreary years" (*Autobiography*, chap. II: 3).

This piercing memory of the dank cellar of his childhood made Wells sensitive to the question of housing generally. In *Experiment in Autobiography* (1934), he indulges in a diatribe against the typical London house, which he felt led to "much massacre, degeneration and disablement of lives" (*Autobiography*, chap. V: 6). Although he had escaped the mold, Wells felt constantly obliged to resist new forms of physical or mental entrapment. Consequently, he regularly called attention to the crippling and inhibiting conditions he saw about him. They began as topographical but quickly extended to the psychic. In *Mankind in the Making* (1903), he asked of those who grew up in middle-class English homes, "Can one expect them to escape the contagion of its cramped pretentiousness, its dingy narrowness, its shy privacy of social degradation, its essential sordidness and inefficiency?" (*Mankind*, chap. V).

Wells began his complaints at a time when much attention was directed to the subject of unsuitable housing, but his attacks have the gusto of personal animus. He can sound objective in recommending more vigorous attempts "to re-house the mass of our population in a more civilised and more agreeable manner" if labor unrest is to be allayed (*Forces*, "The Labour Unrest": 4). But even when cloaked in the tone of objective history, as in *The Shape of Things to Come* (1933), his personal anger comes through as his narrator describes the Age of Frustration, when the great majority of lives "were passed laboriously in squalid or dingy surroundings, in huts, hovels, cottages, tenements and cellars almost as dismal as the ancestral cave and nearly as insanitary" (*Shape*, bk. I: 13). By 1940, he was fearlessly blunt, having already disclosed the personal sources of his rage.

We can now infer how truly torturous and emotionally and physically maiming Wells's early physical environment was. Shrewdly, as with many other similar sources of pain and distress, he used these experiences to advantage. In an early essay of the sprightly sort appearing in the *Pall Mall Gazette* entitled "House-Hunting as an Outdoor Amusement" (1894), Wells developed his contempt for English housing conditions in a fluffy, amusing style, though there is a ring of sincerity in his axiom: "All houses are taken in despair" (*Euphemia*).

Whether presented amusingly or ominously, the theme of improper housing appears regularly in Wells's fiction. It is significant in *Kipps* (1905), *The History of Mr. Polly* (1910), and *Marriage* (1913), and is a central concern in *Tono-Bungay* (1909), where the contrast between middle-class and upper-class housing conditions forms a part of the thematic structure of the book.[7] Elsewhere, housing and economic exploitation are closely identified. Mr. Brumley, in *The Wife of Sir Isaac Harman* (1914), reveals to Lady Harman the petty tyrannies under which her husband's employees are forced to live, and she responds by seeking to establish more rational living conditions for them. Resonating here and also in *Kipps* is the rage of young Bertie Wells who suffered not only the subterranean imprisonment of the house in Bromley but also the cramped barracks life and the petty tyrannies of the draper's shop.[8]

Wells utilized his detestation of confined places in obvious ways. In "The Red Room" (1896), the central figure is reduced to panic through confinement in a room alone with his own fear.[9] Sometimes he was subtly self-allusive, as in *The New Machiavelli* (1911), in which Remington wishes to keep free of the stultified worlds of Cambridge and Oxford that give him a feeling of "physical oppression, a sense of lowness and dampness almost exactly *like the feeling of an underground room where paper moulders and leaves the wall*, a feeling of ineradicable contagion in the Gothic buildings, in the narrow ditch-like rivers, in those roads and roads of stuffy little villas" (*Machiavelli*, bk. I, chap. IV: 3; italics mine). This is Wellsian short-hand to equate official centers of learning with the mentally and physically disfiguring milieu of his own childhood. Both maimed unmercifully and permanently.

Wells used his obsession to energize his early romances where underground oppression is associated with economic exploitation and physical degeneration. *The Time Machine* (1895) is a good example. With each revision of his tale, Wells made the Morlocks' situation clearer until, in the final version, the Time Traveller himself theorizes that through biological processes of differentiation the Haves have come to dominate the upper world while the Have-nots, the Workers, have adapted to a subterranean life among their machines. Soon he discovers that circumstances have been reversed; the once-exploited workers are now the predators, feeding upon the effete and helpless Eloi who wander through the useless garden that their world has become. Considering the labor unrest at the time when Wells was writing, this fable constitutes a grisly and ominous jest, which Wells intensified through the claustrophobic motif of the Time Traveller's descent among the Morlocks.[10] The same potent claustrophobia vivifies the anxiety of Bedford and Cavor when they find themselves prisoners in the subterranean world of the Selenites in *The First Men in the Moon* (1901), a world identified with unresisting subordination to authority.

The narrator of *The War of the Worlds* (1898) shares a few squalid days with a greedy, undisciplined curate, trapped in a ruined house on the edge of a pit occupied by Martians. The curate represents human weakness and vanity defended by hypocrisy and an unreasoned faith that collapses at the first genuine test. The cramped scullery of the ruined house resembles the one Wells played in as a child; consequently, it is an apt image of degenerate human civilization. Later in the novel, a bombastic artilleryman recommends an underground existence to ensure man's survival, but such a marginal buried life does not appeal to the narrator who prefers warfare in the open.[11]

Wells was not always so coy about indicating the significance of his lower depths. In *In the Days of the Comet* (1906), Leadford recognizes that Parload's seedy room, the dirty underground kitchen and scullery of his own dwelling, and all the tacky living conditions of his day were "the outward visible manifestations of the old world disorders in our hearts" (*Comet*, bk. I, chap. I: 1). The purified people of the world after the comet purge this human warren with fire.

Wells believed that minds would not be cramped and distorted if they developed in a setting conducive to expansion. His relief is almost palpable when he liberates his characters from oppressive quarters. In "A Story of the Days to Come" (1897), two struggling young lovers escape a life of painful, degrading labor, returning from their "cramped subterranean den" to a dwelling place that is high above the city—open and airy and with a "spacious view" (*Stories*, "A Story of the Days to Come": 5). It is only from this vantage that the young man can gain a long perspective over time analogous to the spatial vista before him and speculate upon the history and destiny of mankind. In a less-exalted manner Ann Veronica feels that she "walks out of a cell into a free and spacious world" when she leaves her restrictive suburban home for an independent life in London (*Veronica*, chap. V: 6). Later she discovers that she is still living in a pit because her sex prevents her from achieving true freedom. Finally she escapes with Capes to a truly free and courageous life that begins auspiciously in the high, open country of the Alps.

Wells was unequivocal about the value of congenial surroundings; they were essential to the improvement of man and the advance of his civilization. In *Experiment in Autobiography* (1934), he declared "that modern civilization was begotten and nursed in the households of the prosperous, relatively independent people" and was represented through the centuries by the spreading of "country houses and chateaux and villas over the continually more orderly countryside" (*Autobiography*, chap. III: 6). These great establishments were models for the coming Modern State. One great house of that kind is the fictional equivalent of Up Park in *Tono-Bungay* (1909) called Bladesover, which was notable for "its airy spaciousness, its wide dignity," and which "declared itself to be the land, to be essentially England" (*Tono*, bk. I, chap. II: 1).[12]

Wells's architectural requirements are met in his Utopias. The narrator of *A Modern Utopia* (1905) admires the clean, open, practical bedroom and clear and ordered workroom of his dwelling in Utopia. Like Leadford, he sees that the ugliness in his own world is a "gaunt and gawky reflection of our intellectual and moral disorder" (*Utopia*, chap. III: 9). Later, in *Men Like Gods* (1923), Mr. Barnstaple's Utopian quarters are similarly airy, open, and clean, with the bathroom a marvel of convenience and hygiene. For Wells, Utopia was characterized by openness of prospect as well as of mind, and throughout his career *spacious* remained one of his most honorific terms. His dream of amplitude arose out of a real, physical loathing. He knew in his bones what relentless confinement could do to mind and body alike. To him the converting of narrow chambers into shared open spaces was the equivalent of shared wealth. Spaciousness was his ideal because it freed the mind through physical discovery of perspective, just as learning freed it through mental discovery of perspective.

Wells's architectural vision was closely bound up with his social and moral views. In the delightful late fable *The Happy Turning* (1945), Wells disclosed that there is a lot of architecture in Dreamland, but "the architects of Dreamland lay out a whole new world" (*Turning*, chap. VI). At times architecture was his metaphor for the imagination—the shaping imagination that makes dreams usefully real. There was an intensely vivid personal reason for this. An entire treatise could be written on Wells's architectural references, but instead of following Wells into Dreamland and vastness, I shall say a few words about windows and doors.

One of Wells's most haunting short stories is "The Door in the Wall" (1906). In this Forsterian tale he tells the story of Lionel Wallace, a man of superior abilities and achievements, who, at the peak of his successful career, is tormented by a feeling that he has lost the most valuable possibility of his life by passing by, at critical moments, a door in a wall that he accidentally entered as a child to find an enchanted garden, gentle and happy playmates, and a wise and handsome woman who showed him the book of his life. Now he can think of nothing but the world beyond that door, and his yearning for it makes all of his ostensibly rich life pale and empty to him. Redmond, to whom he had confided this longing, reports that Wallace was found dead in a deep excavation, having entered a workman's door in the hoarding apparently by accident. Redmond speculates on his friend's fatal obsession.

> You may think me superstitious, if you like, and foolish; but, indeed, I am more than half convinced that he had, in truth, an abnormal gift, and a sense, something—I know not what—that in the guise of wall and door offered him an outlet, a secret and peculiar passage of escape into another and altogether more beautiful world. At any rate, you will say, it betrayed him in the end. But did it betray him? There you touch the inmost mystery of these dreamers, these men of vision and the imagination. We see our world fair and common, the hoarding and the pit. By our daylight standard he walked out of security into darkness, danger, and death.
> But did he see like that? (*Stories*, "The Door in the Wall": 4)

Since Wells frequently rendered his sense of entrapment and freedom in architectural terms, it is not surprising that his means to liberation should be architectural apertures. The image is highly charged, for it suggests not merely a practical release from entanglement, but a metaphysical manumission. We have already seen that Wells identified imaginative freedom and architecture in *The Happy Turning* (1945) and *Men Like Gods* (1923). In the latter, Mr. Barnstaple's passage from his ordinary world to

Utopia resembles the opening and closing of a door, and the Utopians know themselves to be a race "who can open the doors into such other universes or close them as we choose" (*Gods*, bk. I, chap. VI: 5).

This access to a visionary realm through door, window, or other aperture is consistent with Wells's larger pattern of movement from a confining chamber or circumstance to a spacious, purified atmosphere. In *The Salvaging of Civilization* (1921), Wells declared, "The air of our lives is a close and wrathful air; it has the closeness of a prison—the indescribable offence of crowded and restricted humanity." But there is a way out. "Up certain steps there is a door to this dark prison of ignorance, prejudice and passion in which we live—and that door is only locked on the inside. It is within our power, given the will for it, given the courage for it—it is within our power to go out." Even the initial step of controlling the spread of lies would be "like opening the windows upon a stuffy, overcrowded and un-ventilated room of disputing people" (*Salvaging*, chap. VII).

The image is so common and familiar that, in the polemical writings, its Wellsian overtones are sometimes obscured. Thus the deep poignancy of that sad and sickened last testament, *Mind at the End of Its Tether* (1945), is lost for those who do not recognize the code when Wells writes of the defeat of the human dream.

> Mind near exhaustion still makes its final futile movement towards that "way out or round or through the impasse".
> That is the utmost now that mind can do. And this, its last expiring thrust, is to demonstrate that the door closes upon us for evermore.
> There is no way out or round or through. (*Tether*, chap. I)

It is in his fiction that Wells exploits the aperture image most elaborately. There are many forms of fissures, gaps, and openings in Wells's tales. Though he sometimes used the biblical image of a rent veil to describe visionary experience, he preferred the architectural mode, which he employed with varying intensity. Often doors and windows signify escape from intolerable social conditions. Ann Veronica sees the world about her "in wrappers, like a house when people leave it in summer. . . . And there was no intimation that the blinds would ever go up or the windows or doors be opened" (*Veronica*, chap. I: 2). Young Edward Albert Tewler imagines that evening classes in business methods "would be like a great door opening upon unknown mysteries and freedoms" (*Careful*, bk. II, chap. VI). References to openness and release imply personal liberation, but the same images characterize a larger social craving. In *In the Days of the Comet* (1906), the great politician Melmount likens the world rulers before the comet to drowsing people "in a stifling room, too dull and sleepy and too base towards each other for anyone to get up and open the window" (*Comet*, bk. II, chap. I: 6).

Doors and windows opening may signify a visionary opportunity to glimpse one's destiny. When Rud Whitlow in *The Holy Terror* (1939) has a momentary view of what he might achieve, it is as though "a door opened in a hitherto impenetrable and unclimbable wall and revealed—the dark and indistinguishable landscape of some unknown land on which no sun had ever yet risen. And then it was as if the door slammed again" (*Terror*, bk. I, chap. II: 6). Rud's vision is not so sunny as some others, but that is the result of his inner darkness; nonetheless, like Wells, Rud yearns for airy openness because "his early upbringing in stuffy little rooms had given him a sort of architectural claustrophobia" (*Terror*, bk. IV, chap. I: 10). How better to escape than through a window or door and, failing escape, at least to glimpse a better world? And it is almost always a better world that lies beyond the barrier, even if that world is nothing more than a hopeful psychological projection as it may be in "The Door in the Wall."

In *The Dream* (1924), the visionary experience is reversed. Sarnac, a man of the spacious and free future, is deeply moved by Chopin's "Revolutionary Etude" and similar music played by a musician who "seemed to open shutters upon deep and dark and violent things that had long been closed to mankind" (*Dream*, pt. I, chap. I: 1). Later, Sarnac dreams an entire life from the lost past of the race in which he is one Henry Mortimer Smith, whose history is typical of all those cramped and tawdry careers that Wells so frequently described. Ignorance deprived men of freedom then. Thousands of youngsters realized that "the doors of practical illiteracy were closing in upon them, and yet did not know enough to find a way of escape from this mental extinction" (*Dream*, pt. I, chap. IV: 7). Smith and his family lived like troglodytes in a dark underground kitchen, where they became white and thin in the winter months. Wells repeats here the inevitable parallel between the wrong-headed architecture of the Victorian times and the intellectual and emotional confusion of the population. Smith's escape from this atrocious late nineteenth-century England comes when he is shot to death. But it is a welcome release reminiscent of Wallace's perhaps happy death in "The Door in the Wall." "This pistol shot had come like the smashing of a window in a stuffy room" (*Dream*, pt. II, chap. VII: 9).

In his history of mankind Wells likened the liberating function of writing to "a mere line of light coming through the chink of an opening door into a darkened room" until the onset of printing pushes the door so that it "swings wider, and the light behind grows brighter." Even so, the door is not half open (*Outline*, chap. XVI: 4). Wells believed that while spreading knowledge edged open one exit, a gust of religious emotion might "blow through life again like a great wind, bursting the doors and flinging open the shutters of the individual life" (*Outline*, chap. XL: 1).

"The Magic Shop" (1903) indicates playfully what those doors and windows meant to Wells. In this story Wells takes his son to a remarkable shop where magical devices are real and the shapes of the rooms and dispositions of doors and walls alter. "It's only the Right Sort of Boy gets through that door-way," says the magical proprietor, greatly resembling one of E. T. A. Hoffmann's fabulously gifted beings. The doorway is that of the imagination. Only through imagination can man enter a realm where magic is either real or the means of escape from a stifling prison to a beaming, spacious world.[13]

If commonplace life was a stuffy, dank chamber, then windows and doors offered the vision or reality of existence beyond it. But what precisely did the metaphor mean? You are self-imprisoned, Wells told his and later generations. But how was one to learn the way out? In that lively and curious novel *The Autocracy of Mr. Parham* (1930), which is crammed with insights about himself variously projected, Wells describes a scene in which the cultivated Mr. Parham guides the untutored, but sharp-witted Sir Bussy Woodcock through a few museums to instruct him on art. At one point Sir Bussy puts a direct question to Parham. "I don't see that this Painting gets you out to anything. I don't see that it gets you out of anything. It's not discovery and it's not escape. People talk as if it was a door out of this damned world. Well—*is* it?" (*Parham*, bk. I, chap. II). Parham cannot show that it is. And if painting is not the door out, neither is music. It is a pleasure, like smoking, Sir Bussy allows, but it doesn't "*let you out*" (*Parham*, bk. I, chap. V). By extension, no art can let you out of this world. Images of liberating doors and windows are illusions luring us to a freedom to which no immediate access is available. Yet through those windows and doors come glimpses, visions. Human history is not a chamber to be escaped, or if it is, escaped only through Wallace's door to death. Otherwise, it is an enclosure to be altered, to be transformed, a Dreamland in which universal architects are to be given their way. Apertural images are not a solution, but merely signs, like several others we shall study later. True release is not spatial and most certainly not permanent, but it is real and available.

I have examined one set of figures that Wells used to illustrate his desire for liberation from confinement. Later we shall examine another deeply rooted set. But now it may be worthwhile to consider how the pattern of release, escape, and liberation works in a more general way for Wells. From the first, Wells was a champion of freedom, even when he was not entirely serious. In an early essay entitled "The Amateur Nature-Lover" (1893), he gave a simple urbanite's view of a country walk, noting particularly the extensive use of barbed wire, which he calls the last product of civilization, and which he hates (*Euphemia*). Similarly, in *Select Conversations With an Uncle* (1895), he satirized his fellow man's bondage to custom in preparations for marriage, fashions in art, and other areas of civilized life, implying that most people, incapable of an original approach to life, remain ensnared in a humiliating net of unexamined conventions. They are like Mr. Polly before his liberation.

The *Wonderful Visit* (1895) is an inverted paean to release from the commonplace. In this fanciful tale the Reverend Hilyer shoots what he believes to be a rare bird, only to discover that he has wounded an angel. The rest of the story demonstrates how a narrow English community, unable to accept the *unlikeness* of the Angel, obliges him to assume the disguise of a mortal, a disguise which, in the manner of the rake's mask in Beerbohm's "The Happy Hypocrite," steadily becomes a reality. The pattern of confinement followed by freedom is reversed in this story, for the Angel comes from a land more open, unbounded, and orderly than earth. In the world of men, he is like an imprisoned bird. He considers his experience a dream, but the narrow passionate life of earth threatens to crush him. In an act of self-sacrifice and love he leaves the world again. His passing is accompanied by the same rush of music that ushered him into this world, beginning and ending "like the opening and shutting of a door" (*Visit*, chaps. I & L).

The *Wonderful Visit* is a fantasy and its message is somewhat garbled, but Wells was explicit elsewhere. In works such as *Anticipations* (1901) and *The Salvaging of Civilization* (1921), he commented openly upon the physical and intellectual congestion of the modern world. Wells deplored the human tendency to decline into complacency and accept regulation unthinkingly. G. K. Chesterton, who shared Wells's sentiment, praised him for teaching men to be reckless. He liked Wells for his willingness "to lark" and dispute decorum.[14] Wells saw life as a challenge and, in *The New America: The New World* (1935), declared himself an enemy of restraint. "A living creature or species that will not live more and more, will soon be living less and less and presently pass away. Restraint that concentrates vigour is always justifiable, but only if it amounts to a real net gain in vitality" (*New America*, chap. III). Wells asked if there was no escape from society's self-devised and entangling system. His answer was the lesson of *The Wonderful Visit*. Self-sacrifice in a greater cause was the way to freedom. Stated thus it is the answer of mystics, religious and political idealists, and others through the ages. But short of this grand escape, which we shall examine later, Wells offered more limited forms of release.

Wells regularly provided his characters with locomotive forms of deliverance. The bicycle served that purpose in *The Wheels of Chance* (1896) and the automobile in *Mr. Britling Sees It Through* (1916), *The Secret Places of the Heart* (1922), *Men Like Gods* (1923), and *The World of William Clissold* (1926). Bert Smallways's inadvertent escape by balloon in *The War in the Air* (1908) is a more sensational version of the same thing. Increasingly the airplane becomes a vehicle of liberation and control for Wells, and of course, there were his fanciful devices for traveling through time or to the moon.

More important than physical escape is psychological release. For R. A. G. Trafford, the world-besieged genius of *Marriage* (1912), work provides a temporary enfranchisement, just as the pursuit of ideas offers Benham a sense of escape in *The Research Magnificent* (1915). After the therapeutic passage of the comet in *In the Days of the Comet*, people are caught up by a religious fervor, "a great passion to escape from the jealous prison of themselves" (*Comet*, bk. II, chap. II: 7). But escape from the self is only a beginning. A further step in overcoming the dulling sense of restraint is transcendence of the self through fellowship with another human being. Marriage is the formal social embodiment of this alternative. Wells examined it thoroughly in *Marriage* (1912).

Trafford is an intelligent man capable of clear thought, but success in life has not brought him happiness. He is especially perplexed by the loss of candor between himself and his wife, Marjorie, with whom he had been able to speak freely during their courtship and honeymoon. Other forms of release failing, Trafford feels a growing need for physical escape to some genuine solitude where he can think things out. When Marjorie decides to accompany him to Labrador, Trafford feels like a man "who discovers after years of weary incarceration that the walls of his cell are made of thin paper" (*Marriage*, bk. III, chap. II: 9). His discovery is a reassertion of Mr. Polly's memorable revelation a couple of years earlier that life is open to change. Trafford and Marjorie are successful not in any ultimate sense, but only insofar as they realize that together they have a better chance of working toward emancipation through service in some larger purpose. They have helped one another to escape the narrowness of selfish individual life.

The whole range of what escape truly signifies for Wells is articulated by Job Huss, the supreme educator of *The Undying Fire* (1919). Without instruction, Huss declares, man is no more than an egotistical beast. Through teachers, man can escape from death and futility. An uninstructed man remains a beast, but "a man instructed is a man enlarged from that narrow prison of self into participation in an undying life, that began we know not when, that grows above and beyond the greatness of the stars" (*Fire*, chap. III: 4). Men can be freed from imprisonment by learning the truths of the world in which they live. This is the meaning behind Wells's call for redemption in *The Open Conspiracy* (1928). Religion, he says, depends upon the desire "for service, for subordination, for permanent effect, for an escape from the distressful pettiness and morality of the individual life" (*Conspiracy*, chap. III). The aim of the new man is to become objective, to lose himself in a greater cause. Although man has been released from the absolute struggle for subsistence, he has not taken the next step away from his animal nature. The present egoistic civilization ensnares the young, but Wells discerns in the young people of his time an inclination to "escape in some manner from the aimless drive and compulsion of accident and everyday" (*Conspiracy*, chap. XI).

The call that Wells makes in this and other works is to a life that is free because it is beyond the limitations of egoism and vanity. Wells said that the spirit of *A Modern Utopia* (1905) was one with "the undying interest of the human power of self-escape, the power to resist the causation of the past, and to evade, initiate, endeavour, and overcome" (*Utopia*, chap. I: 1). The utopianist narrator's detached manner is a model of this self-escape, for in his objectivity he sees the purposes of mankind unbiased by personal desire. He achieves this dispassionateness by reconceiving humanity in a new and neutral setting—Utopia, in fact. Later we shall see what complications develop from this impulse toward objectivity, but in *A Modern Utopia* Wells considers objectivity a clear virtue. The narrator acknowledges that men cannot live outside the flow of history since they are product and process of it. But they can take advantage of history. This was possible only through liberation from self, which remained a central requirement of Wells's program for salvation, looking forward to the day imagined in *The Shape of Things to Come* (1933) when the Modern State will have broken the "cramping circle of interests for every human being," freeing him to use his intellect in a way incredible to our own benighted generation (*Shape*, bk. V: 8).

In escaping oneself, one escapes an accumulated history, for no human is alone; although each person is unique, he is also a part of mankind and thus to escape oneself is to transcend one's inheritance. That inheritance is history. Peter in *Joan and Peter* (1918) is an aviator during the war; his preferred situation above the battlefield provides him with a way of understanding what he desires.

> He was convinced that high above the things of the past he droned his liquid way towards a new sort of life altogether, towards a greater civilization, a world-wide life for men with no boundaries in it at all except the emptiness of outer space, a life of freedom and exaltation and tremendous achievement. But meanwhile the old things of the world were trying most desperately to kill him. (*Joan*, chap. XIII: 14)

Later, the passionately radical novelist, Alfred Bunter, in *Brynhild* (1937) puts it more directly: "Man—all the sanity in man—has been struggling to escape from the past—continually" (*Brynhild*, chap. XI: 1).

A year later, Wells drew several of his familiar themes together in a new and interesting assemblage, for *Apropos of Dolores* (1938) treats escape as both an intimately personal and a broadly philosophical issue. The novel assumes that the unhappiness of life arises mainly from frustration occasioned by an increasing sense of confinement and restraint in a rapidly changing civilization.[15] Stephen Wilbeck, the narrator, wishes to be free from his harridan wife. Gloomily he broods, "There are times when I feel that all humanity lives in traps, gripped by obligations they have incurred, born caged from the first in the menagerie" (*Dolores*, chap. IV: 14). Having expected greater liberty with the freedom-loving Dolores, Wilbeck has found stricture instead. Now he sees himself and Dolores as representatives of two opposed attitudes in a contest of "shut and narrow against open and wide," reminiscent of the opposition between Remington and his wife in *The New Machiavelli* (*Dolores*, chap. IV: 16).

Wilbeck's frustration is not localized in sexual jealousy and private inconvenience. He is a dreamer who believes that a larger life is open to man beyond the pettiness of selfish desire. Though he escapes Dolores, he is doomed to new disenchantments because his dreams constantly ignore the human traits that hinder the realization of a new humanity. He will never be a part of that new world, but he can foresee it.

> Maybe human intimacy is escaping from the prison of the present and the visible, the prison of our current life, unlocking the door but still using the old cell for sleeping and eating. We'll still love sights and sounds and desire pretty people, but lightly and transitorily, not cruelly and insatiably, and our invisible tentacles will stretch through time and space to an altogether deeper and different fellowship. (*Dolores*, chap. VII: 5)

We have returned to the prison image quoted from *The Salvaging of Civilization* (1921) earlier. In that book Wells told his readers that there was an unlocked door waiting to be tested. Now the image has changed somewhat, has become more suitable to Wells's total doctrine. In fact, one does not actually leave the prison but makes it the habitable locus of a more adventurous life. The architecture of the world to come will be a vast, secure structure where all mankind may come and go at will, refining, cleansing, beautifying as it goes.

But how does man open that door? The question takes us back to Wallace and his mysterious door in the wall. Freedom is available to all who can conceive themselves free. The human imagination entraps itself or sets itself free. As Miss Thalassia Waters explains in *The Sea Lady* (1902), men live in dreams of their own making, but there are better dreams for men to create than any they now know (*Lady*, chap. VI: 2). Man's enlightened imagination is his principal means of liberation. When men see the world afresh, they can refashion it. Of the New Republicans he urges into being in *Mankind in the Making* (1903), Wells says, "They will in their own time take this world as a sculptor takes his marble and shape it better than all our dreams" (*Mankind*, chap. XI). It is dream still, but dream made real.

For Wells, writing was the key that opened the door out of the cramped cell of self and also out of the social prison of poverty and convention. He called writing the modern form of adventure.[16] It admitted him to that dangerous magic shop where marvelous toys were real. Believing himself free, believing at least the dream of freedom, Wells set about freeing the minds of others with that dream.[17] But standing between one man's mind and another's was the less manageable reality of the material world. Before he could deal with the airy architectural order of the future, Wells had to face the preliminary necessity of clearing the jungle of Nature.

# 2

# Nature

Chesterton said it well when he called Wells "a sportive but spiritual child of Huxley," for Wells was deeply influenced by the method and thought of T. H. Huxley, under whom he studied for a time at the Normal School of Science in 1884.[1] He continued to regard Huxley and Darwin as very great men throughout his life, and there is no doubt that he derived many of his basic ideas from both of them, but mainly from Huxley. He accepted, for example, Huxley's modification of the optimistic Darwinian view of evolution. The more Huxley defended Darwin's theory, the more he insisted that it did not offer automatic hope for mankind. Quite to the contrary, man had to consider himself as an antagonist of Nature. Huxley presented his view clearly in his important late lecture "Evolution and Ethics" (1893). "Let us understand, once and for all, that the ethical progress of society depends not on imitating the cosmic process, still less in running away from it, but in combating it."[2] In the "Prolegomena," written later to clarify his position, Huxley unequivocally declared that there is an inescapable conflict between the state of nature and the state of art, or between unaltered and fashioned nature.

Like Huxley, Wells put no faith in Nature, which he viewed as a hostile force to be controlled, though not in the individualist manner of Herbert Spencer, whose version of Darwinism emphasized the individual's, rather than the community's, struggle for survival. The great arguments about the design of Nature, the providential rightness of Nature, and even Huxley's earlier insistence on the morality of natural law were over when Wells arrived at South Kensington. He came, saw, and was conquered utterly; thereafter the only nature he trusted was human nature, and despite his hopeful utopianism, not that very much.[3] It is, however, the one thing man could count on toward his salvation and even survival. Wells's early works emphasize the hostility or indifference of Nature, and his last works return to this mainly negative view. In between is a courageous but by no means blind attempt to convince man that he need not be the animal he seems.

31

Wells's attitude toward Nature was direct and obvious, as a sampling of his opinions will show. In an early essay entitled "A Vision of the Past" (1887), Wells mocked man's confidence in his secure place in nature by having an imaginary amphibian species of the distant past boast: "During all the vast ages to come we shall continue upon this earth, while lower beings pass away and are replaced. This world is ours for ever, and we must progress for ever unto infinite perfection." Wells hammers his satire in by calling his amphibians Nem of Dnalgne—an obvious toying with "Men of England" (*Early Writings*, chap. V).

Man's fragility as a species is always the ground tone of Wells's argument.[4] Many of his early stories warned man that his hold on existence was not firm. After describing the near extermination of mankind by a wandering star, Wells ends "The Star" (1897) from the point of view of Martian astronomers who consider the damage to earth relatively slight. "Which only shows," he adds, "how small the vastest of human catastrophes may seem, at a distance of a few million miles." *The War of the Worlds* (1898) provides a vivid account of how swiftly "the fear and empire of man had passed away" (*War*, bk. II, chap. VI). Mankind's unwarranted confidence in its survival is underscored by the narrator's return to the manuscript he was writing before the descent of the Martians. "It was a paper on the probable development of Moral Ideas with the development of the civilizing process; and the last sentence was the opening of a prophecy: 'In about two hundred years,' I had written, 'we may expect——' " (*War*, bk. II, chap. IX). How near that interruption came to being permanent!

Nature is not man's friend, not the nurturing and protective mother so frequently assumed in the popular thought of the time. Man must be clearsighted precisely because Nature is not. The Utopians in *Men Like Gods* (1923) try to make this clear to their visitors from earth.

> These Earthlings do not yet dare to see what our Mother Nature is. At the back of their minds is still the desire to abandon themselves to her. They do not see that except for our eyes and wills, she is purposeless and blind. She is not awful, she is horrible. She takes no heed to our standards, nor to any standards of excellence. She made us by accident; all her children are bastards— undesired; she will cherish or expose them, pet or starve or torment without rhyme or reason. She does not heed, she does not care. She will lift us up to power and intelligence, or debase us to the mean feebleness of the rabbit or the slimy white filthiness of a thousand of her parasitic inventions. There must be good in her because she made all that is good in us—but also there is endless evil. Do not you Earthlings see the dirt of her, the cruelty, the insane indignity of much of her work? (*Gods*, bk. I, chap. VI: 5)

Man's survival depends upon this vision of alienation. Job Huss in *The Undying Fire* (1919) discovers this truth when he witnesses the relentless savagery that characterizes the apparently placid animal world. William

Clissold has a similar awakening when as a boy he wades into a pool to pick some beautiful blue flowers only to discover with horror that his legs have been viciously slashed by the sharp-edged sedge. But the evil is not confined to the animal and vegetable world as Richard Remington discovers in a childhood encounter with a band of roughs in *The New Machiavelli* (1911). "It was the first time I glimpsed the simple brute violence that lurks and peeps beneath our civilization," he recalls (*Machiavelli*, bk. I, chap. III: 3).

Not only is Nature blind and vicious, she is inept as well. When the sexual instinct first begins to disturb and confuse Theodore Bulpington in *The Bulpington of Blup* (1933), Wells remarks, "So slovenly old Mother Nature, presiding inexactly and inconsiderately over this Dame-School of hers which is our world, scribbled athwart Theodore's reluctant intelligence her intimations of what she has ever insisted upon as the main business of her children" (*Blup*, chap. III: 1). Nor can man expect that his refinement of his own nature will be easier or more lasting than his control of external nature, as Stephen Wilbeck learns in *Apropos of Dolores* (1938) when he sets out deliberately to overcome his impulses and advance from the egoistical to the communal life. "Mother Nature," he says, "who does not care to have evolution taken out of her hands, will dissent." Yet it is essential that man wrest control of his being from Nature (*Dolores*, chap. VII: 2).

Another perspective on Wells's attitude emerges in *Joan and Peter* (1918) where Oswald Sydenham, in his African adventures, sees Nature at her worst both in man and around him. But man has a choice. He need not behave as the jungle and the beings in it behave but may imitate "Nature in her better moods, that is to say after the manner of Nature ploughed and weeded and given light and air" (*Joan*, chap. VII: 2)—that is to say, Nature under the rule and order of man.

Through his brief history, man has gone far toward taming Nature but scarcely nowhere toward taming himself. Many of Wells's early fictions dwell upon the bestiality of man—"The Reconciliation" (1895), "Pollock and the Porroh Man" (1895), *The Time Machine* (1895), *The Island of Dr. Moreau* (1896), *The Invisible Man* (1897). The theme persisted as an undertone in his later writing, but rather than denounce man for his animality, Wells often tried a persuasive method. In *In the Days of the Comet* (1906), for example, he tempts his readers with a picture of how rapidly man could advance were he able to overcome his animal impulses. More directly in *Men Like Gods* (1923), the superb Utopians are models to the Earthlings who are frankly referred to as animals.

When his frustration at man's inability to control his animal nature was increasing, Wells wrote a vicious fairy tale called *The Croquet Player* (1936) in which a very dull narrator, whose principal interest is croquet, falls into conversation with a Dr. Finchatton, who describes the sense of archaic evil lingering like the ghosts of man's apelike predecessors at a place called Cainsmarsh. Dr. Finchatton's psychiatrist explains that his patient has created a fairy tale to symbolize the dreadful condition of the world. Archeological discoveries, he says, have enlarged man's scale of perception but at the same time have released the old evil upon him by showing that his civilization is a delusion and that the cave man has not passed away but has merely been in hiding. Man, unmasked and disillusioned, is still a beast, and soon he will have only two choices—to be a driven animal or a stern devotee of disciplined civilization (*Croquet*, "The Intolerable Psychiatrist").

Eventually time eroded Wells's hope that man would will to save himself. This was the dilemma: man was in a trap and yearned for freedom, but he was himself part of the trap. As we shall see, Wells employed constellations of recurrent images to convey his sense of man's enslavement and his own participation in that enslavement.

Before evolution became an accepted dogma, but when it was already implicit in the thinking of Western civilization, Alfred Tennyson provided one of the most enduring images of a god-bereft world dominated by "Nature, red in tooth and claw / With ravine . . . " (*In Memoriam*, lvi). Tennyson did not conclude *In Memoriam* (1850) on this note but offered instead a picture of man steadily advancing toward a more refined humanity. His lines of incitement toward this goal are almost as familiar as those describing Nature incarnadine.

> Arise and fly
> The reeling Faun, the sensual feast;
> Move upward, working out the beast,
> And let the ape and tiger die.
> (*In Memoriam*, cxviii)

This association of man's animal nature with apes and tigers was in the public domain, but Huxley gave the connection a more specific application when he employed Tennyson's scheme in "Evolution and Ethics" (1893) to argue that man's highest evolution would not be in his animal nature, but in his capacity as a cooperating member of an organized polity. Primordially the qualities man shared with ape and tiger were beneficial to him, but with the emergence of organized society they became defects and it was therefore in his best interests to overcome the vestigial impulses.[5]

Since Tennyson's poem was the best known of its century and Wells would have been familiar with Huxley's lecture, it might appear that in using the images of ape and tiger to signify man's bestial nature, Wells was merely appropriating a serviceable cliché. But there was a deep personal reason for his choices. Describing his youthful reading of Theodore Wood's *Natural History*, Wells wrote, "I conceived a profound fear of the gorilla, of which there was a fearsome picture" (*Autobiography*, chap. II: 5).[6] Wells adverted to this fear throughout his lifetime.

Similarly, Wells never felt comfortable with jungles, which serve him as a consistent metaphor for entanglement, confusion, and a threateningly abundant disorder. As obstructive undergrowth, the jungle represented an impediment to progress; as an environment for hostile predators it signified the dread characteristics of man's unenlightened state. Thus the jungle could be both an external condition signifying frustration and difficulty, and an internal condition of fear against the outbreak of fierce impulses and instincts. But while the jungle as barrier was daunting, as habitat of gorillas and gorillaism it was terrifying.

If the jungle represented human emotions out of control, the contrasting image of the garden, probably borrowed from Huxley's horticultural metaphor in the "Prolegomena" to *Evolution and Ethics*, represented Nature brought under control.[7] Although the image of the garden was commonplace, it had a particular meaning for Wells, whose father had been a gardener at country residences, one of which was the admired Up Park. Joseph Wells lost his place as a gardener to the rich, and the only garden he tended thereafter was the dreary little patch behind the house in Bromley. Wells credited his father as "a gardener of some resolution" for persuading a grape vine to flourish in that unpromising soil, but surely defeat was the prevailing sensation (*Autobiography*, chap. II: 1). By the time he began to write for a living, Wells must have looked back on his father's exile from the spacious parks of elegant estates to the barren rood of Bromley as a fall comparable to Adam's exit from Paradise. But whereas Adam was forced into a wide wilderness to make his way, Joseph Wells clamped his family into quarters more reminiscent of a medieval dungeon or a Neanderthal cave. Wells's struggle to escape that cave can be read in part as an attempt to reverse his father's history.

Wells's scheme of movement through an entangling, dangerous jungle toward a garden, upland, or other clear place, is one of his most persistently vigorous analogues for the human struggle.[8] It complements the pattern of architectural release we have already examined but implies a subtler note. He began by rendering wild beasts and settings directly but became largely metaphorical later. The short stories are filled with literal circumstances. Strange creatures threaten men in "In the Avu Observatory" (1894), "The Sea Raiders" (1896), "The Empire of the Ants" (1905), and the comic "AEpyornis Island" (1894). A lovely flower displays predatory inclinations in "The Flowering of the Strange Orchid" (1894), and jungles are appropriately ominous settings in "The Treasure in the Forest" (1894), "Pollock and the Porroh Man" (1895), and other stories already mentioned. "A Story of the Stone Age" (1897), which testifies to Wells's abiding interest in the primitive stages of man's history, is chiefly an account of one man's struggle against the elements, a bear, a tiger, and his fellow men.

The early novels exploit these same images. The Time Traveller's flight through the dark forest, defending himself and Weena from the apelike Morlocks by an untrustworthy flame in *The Time Machine* (1895) is a compelling example. This novel pitted a strong character against malign external conditions; *The Island of Dr. Moreau* (1896) exhibited the other face of the jungle's danger—the transformation of the inner self. Ostensibly a tale about animals changed into humanoids, it really dramatizes the constant threat of humanity's melting once more into bestiality. The near-human creatures that people Moreau's jungle island are hypostatizations of man's various appetites. After he has escaped the island and returned to England, Prendick realizes that his condition has scarcely changed, for he sees that man's animal instincts lurk always just beneath the thin veneer of that fragile civilization that makes men different from the beasts.

As Wells became more secure in the world and more hopeful for man, he clove to the sunnier side of doubt, reminding men that if they were animals, they were also something more. In two novels of midcareer he made this conflict graphic by confronting realistic characters with real beasts. Trafford of *Marriage* (1912), withdrawing into the wilderness of Labrador with his wife, Marjorie, to examine their problems beyond the entanglements of the civilized world, meets his nemesis in the form of a genuine lynx, which he kills but which wounds him badly. The scene presents in realistic terms what had surfaced earlier in Wells's tales as romantic or fantastic incidents. Trafford's journey into the wilderness is a psychological journey. In this "hinterland" he confronts and overcomes the symbol of his weakness—egotistical animal impulse. Having vanquished that danger, he is made whole by a vision of himself as part of a larger whole.

The lynx in this novel does not entirely fit Wells's usual metaphorical pattern, but in *The Research Magnificent* (1915), Wells corrected that oversight. In this novel, too, Wells argued that man has much to learn from the wilderness. Although the metaphorical jungle of disorderly civilization must be cleared away and replaced by a spacious and free existence, the real jungle constitutes a school for human effort. Like his creator, William Benham has an ineradicable fear of animals, which drives him to consider the nature of human nobility, the subject that leads him on his research magnificent. Benham's quest takes him to India, where, moved by the spirit of adventure, he goes with a friend into jungle country. One night he finds himself alone on a jungle path. Noticing the extreme alertness of his senses in this new and challenging environment, he reflects upon the nature of jungles.

> Was the jungle just an aimless pool of life that man must drain and clear away? Or is it to have a use in the greater life of our race that now begins? Will man value the jungle as he values the precipice, for the sake of his manhood? Will he preserve it?
>
> Man must keep hard, man must also keep fierce. Will the jungle keep him fierce?
>
> For life, thought Benham, there must be insecurity. (*Research*, Prelude: 11)

And then he sees a tiger. "At last the nightmare of Benham's childhood had come true, and he was face to face with the tiger, uncaged, uncontrolled" (*Research*, Prelude: 11). Remembering his previous thoughts on the jungle, he announces to the tiger, "I am Man . . . The Thought of the world," and after a moment the tiger goes on its way. It is as though Benham's humanness has faced down the animality so inimical to it. Although it may appear incredible or out of place in a realistic novel, this scene dramatizes the central conflict in man that so bedeviled Wells. Moreover, it is a reification of his own presiding fears and perhaps a temporary exorcising of them.

Wells exploits the negative connotations of the jungle throughout *Joan and Peter* (1918), which is saturated with jungle images that recall the frightening jungle and cleansing fire of *The Time Machine*.[9] Uncle Oswald, who has killed his tiger in his day, is a fitting guide for his two wards because he can warn them of the possible ambushes and hazards on their way. He knows what the jungle is, but Joan and Peter must fashion their own woodcraft to lead them to a clearing, for when it comes to dealing with the new world emerging, Oswald is as much in need of guidance as they. Wells did feel that such guides were to be found and described the great educationalist F. W. Sanderson as "a sweating, panting, burly leader pushing a way for himself and others through a thorny thicket" (*Schoolmaster*, chap. V: 2).

Some of the permutations on Wells's favorite metaphorical constellations are extremely subtle and engaging. In *The Secret Places of the Heart* (1922), Sir Richmond Hardy, nearing a nervous breakdown, seeks help from Dr. Martineau, who recommends a motor tour to locations in England associated with the infancy of the human race. The tour signifies Sir Richmond's journey into his troubled soul. Dr. Martineau informs him that man is still largely an ape and that the "souls of apes, monkeys, reptiles and creeping things haunt the passages and attics and cellars of this living house in which your consciousness has awakened" (*Heart*, chap. I: 4). To the casual reader this is merely a strong metaphor, but someone familiar with Wells's fiction will recognize that Wells has brought two self-conscious clusters of images together and transformed that real childhood fear of beasts lurking in a real house to an internal state. Man is his own house of fear and the beasts therein are traits of his own nature. Dr. Martineau's solution to Sir Richmond's quandary is the "conscious getting out of one's individuality" (*Heart*, chap. IV: 7). In fictionalizing his own haunting fears and giving them greater scope, Wells is attempting to do just that for himself. At the same time, the compressed image is a shorthand of frustration and anxiety by which Wells telegraphs a central dilemma he felt in himself and in mankind.

The *Secret Places of the Heart* recorded a realistic breakdown and recovery preceding a fatal collapse. A few years later, Wells combined the substance of this novel and touches of *The Island of Dr. Moreau* in another fable of mental collapse. *Mr. Blettsworthy on Rampole Island* (1928) is also a journey of discovery; but whereas the sinister primitive features of *The Secret Places of the Heart* were metaphorical, in *Mr. Blettsworthy* they are fabular. Arnold Blettsworthy matures under the tutelage of his uncle Rupert Blettsworthy, who believes that the real sins are weeds practically extinct and that no tigers are left to threaten man. Through betrayed love, Arnold learns "something of the meanness of trusted fellow-creatures, and something also of the vile cellars in [his] own foundation" (*Blettsworthy*, chap. II: 1). The tigers are alive and hungering.

At a doctor's advice Arnold sets off on a sea voyage, hoping for escape, though he finds the small, hostile world of the ship as uncomfortable as the life from which he flees. Blettsworthy is abandoned when the ship founders, but is picked up by savages and brought to live in their gorge where they enforce a "strict taboo upon all climbing or indeed upon all talk of climbing towards the sunlight of the uplands" (*Blettsworthy*, chap. III: 3). In a parody of Darwin's discovery of the bones of the Megatheria, which provided him with evidence for his theory of evolution, Blettsworthy's discovery of living Megatheria teaches him that evolution does not mean the survival of the fittest. An ostensibly triumphant human species may be converting is own habitat into an unlivable desert; "so far from Evolution being necessarily a strenuous upward progress to more life and yet more life, it might become . . . a graceless drift towards a dead end" (*Blettsworthy*, chap. III: 5). Blettsworthy's Megatheria, for example, represent institutions such as Christianity, which hinder progress toward freedom.

In what seems to be a self-conscious echo of *The Time Machine* and "A Story of the Stone Age," Blettsworthy rescues a maiden named Wena and flees from the tribal leader, Ardam, just as Ugh-Lomi fled from Uya. Then he wakes up in Brooklyn Heights, New York, tended by his lover,

Rowena, and Dr. Minchett. Gradually Blettsworthy returns to sanity, but his hallucination of Rampole Island is a constant parabolic reminder of mankind's underlying savagery. Near the end of the novel, he asks his friend and former betrayer, Lyulph Graves, "Do you believe mankind will ever leave the gorge?" (*Blettsworthy*, chap. IV: 14). Graves thinks so, but there is enough evidence of man's weaknesses in the novel to make any reader doubt such a facile assurance.

Wells developed the jungle/animal images elaborately in *Mr. Blettsworthy* and other novels, but often a mere reference was sufficient to indicate an appropriately pejorative association. Hence the moon's abundantly pullulating foliage in *The First Men in the Moon* (1901) turns from wonderful curiosity to sinister threat when we learn that it is a "dreamlike jungle" where mooncalves feast on narcotics. Sometimes Wells was overt. In *The Shape of Things to Come* (1933), presocial man is described as a tiger, and men rebuilding the world after the First World War attack "what seemed a perpetually recuperative jungle of mixed motives, tangled interests and cross-purposes, within themselves and without" (*Shape*, bk. V: 9 and bk. I: 9). Ironically, a plague that decimates mankind is called "maculated fever," a disease of "captive baboons" (*Shape*, bk. II: 10).[10] This is a typically Wellsian joke with a brutal Swiftian point. Mankind is a herd of captive baboons, succumbing to a disease that fortuitously purges the race and provides it with a new opportunity to redeem itself.

The conquest of this jungle is arduous because, as we have seen, man is not only in it, it is in him. Thus the whole mess of fundamental thought through the ages is a jungle through which Wells's surrogate, William Burroughs Steele, tries "to smite lanes of lucidity" (*Frustration*, chap. II) in *The Anatomy of Frustration* (1936). The agony of this effort could at any time overwhelm him—a suicidal ambush in the jungle within. "You may go out without your philosophy one day, as a man goes out into a jungle without his gun, and encounter a conspiracy of accidents and treacherous endocrines as one might meet a hungry pack of wolves" (*Frustration*, chap. VI).

Wells's fear and loathing of this infested jungle persisted through his last novel, but in his penultimate novel he intensified his favored constellation of images. The title itself, *Babes in the Darkling Wood* (1940), makes this apparent. The novel has nothing to do with literal forests and, as an account of the maturation of two exceptional young people at a dismal period of human history, resembles the earlier *Joan and Peter*. The cover design of the original edition shows a young man and woman emerging from a tunnel of tall trees to face a dawn rising behind an open hillside. One chapter is entitled "The Guide and Friend in the Deep of the Forest," and a subsection is headed "Possible Path in the Wood?" Beyond these blatant signposts, the metaphorical structure is constantly evident, though not obtrusive. Like Oswald Sydenham, Stella has a dream of wandering in a dark forest becoming darker along a disappearing path. In the midst of her dream she encounters the Unseen Guide, represented in waking life by her uncle, Robert Kentlake, who will lead her out of the shadows. The imagery accompanying Wells's solution to the problems stated in the novel is customary. "I can see a world before me, Stella," says Gemini, having recovered his hope for the future after a crushing mental depression, "as full of peace, order, beauty and variety as a well-kept garden, and as full of life, freedom and energy as—there's nothing with which to compare it." In contrast, he describes "*our* world" as "full of weeds" (*Babes*, bk. IV, chap. III: 5).

If the world of passions and entanglements was represented as a jungle populated by threatening animals, the salvational world was just the opposite—a garden where all pernicious wild life was controlled and beauty and order reigned. As we have seen, this metaphor was both personal and derivative. The world-become-garden of *The Time Machine* (1895) is a bitter variation upon the optimistic theme since the garden is untended and represents the defeat, not the triumph of human control. But Wells overcame this negative sentiment and in most of his writing the image of the garden represents success of the human dream.[11]

The marvelous land that Mr. Cave sees in the crystal egg in the story of that name is a wide and spacious country with a "magnificent garden." And beyond the magical door of "The Door in the Wall" (1906) Wallace discovers an "enchanted garden" with beautiful untended flowers growing in weedless beds, where he can play unafraid with beautiful spotted leopards. Gardens were the antithesis of the disorder men knew. In the changed world of *In the Days of the Comet* (1906), the world abounds with handsome gardens symbolizing the control man has established over life, whereas before the Change wars and other events happened "as weeds happen in abandoned gardens" (*Comet*, bk. I, chap. III: 4).

Wells did not confine his use of the garden metaphor to his fiction. In *New Worlds for Old* (1908), his characterization of socialism, Wells developed the image at length. He describes the socialist's mode of planning thus:

> But he seeks to make a plan as one designs and lays out a garden, so that sweet and seemly things may grow, wide and beautiful vistas open, and weeds and foulness disappear. Always a garden plan develops and renews itself and discovers new possibilities, but, for all that, what makes all its graciousness and beauty possible, is the scheme and the persistent intention, the watching and the waiting, the digging and burning, the weeder clips and the hoe. That is the sort of plan, a living plan for things that live and grow, that the Socialist seeks for social and national life. (*New Worlds*, chap. II)

Wells admits that socialism's task is enormous, but at the end of the struggle, he foresees a world made garden.[12]

Wells developed his garden image most fruitfully in the novels. *The New Machiavelli* (1911) is a good example. Richard Remington's father, who suffers a "natural incompetence" as a gardener, is a sympathetic but ineffective socialist, denouncing property as the curse of life and insisting that one must live by plan, even though he himself is incapable of such control (*Machiavelli*, bk. I, chap. II: 3). Predictably, he is also an incompetent science teacher. From his early years Richard feels a strong desire for order. His search for this order is the main theme of the novel. With his father's example in mind, he reckons that order is an exceptional rather than a common condition in human affairs. Yet he knows that for men to have their way they must establish and maintain a directive scheme. Richard's father stands for the personal and social inability to guide and direct human destiny. Richard represents the human craving to impose a necessary order. The garden metaphor gives depth to this opposition, for it reminds us how constantly and how minutely man must work first to establish and then to preserve the order he seeks.

Though Wells took himself seriously, he could also tease himself by restraining his brighter visions with contradictory arguments. He did this in *Meanwhile* (1927), which takes place mainly in the lovely and elaborate gardens of the Rylandses' Italian estate, Casa Terragena where an odd collection of persons slowly becomes aware of the necessities of their troubled time. Mr. Sempack, a philosopher who decides that he must act and not merely discourse, declares that "some day men will cultivate their happinesses in gardens, a great variety of beautiful happinesses, happinesses grown under glass, happinesses all the year round. Such things are not for us. They will come. Meanwhile—" (*Meanwhile*, bk. I: 3 and 5).

Signor Vinciguerra, a fugitive from Italian fascism given shelter at Casa Terragena, warns that the great civilization toward which progress seemed to be so inevitably moving has been "waylaid and murdered" by Mussolini and his kind because right-thinking men had not labored toward its advance. The great civilization cannot come of itself. "Nothing comes of itself except weeds and confusion," he says (*Meanwhile*, bk. II: 19).[13] Through Vinciguerra, Wells indicates that men of the present must toil in the wilderness until the garden world is possible again. Moved by this and other events, the Rylandses decide that they must abandon their protected existence and join the struggle for a finer world, which means giving up Casa Terragena. The gifted intellectuals will abandon their lovely garden world and return to the unweeded jungle around them, for the garden world is not real until it embraces all of the world and is accessible to all men. This is an elaborate and serious joke Wells makes at the expense of his own beloved metaphor.

But the metaphor is more complicated yet. Mr. Sempack explains that not only is the world threatened by the external jungle of fascism, violence, and social disorder but man's impulses constitute an equally treacherous jungle. Even Sempack is distracted from his high musings by the insistent mutterings of his hormones. Men can no more live in an enchanted garden while their inner natures are untended than they can with fascist madness abroad. Early in the novel Sempack had hinted at this point.

> The whole region of sexual relations for example was still a dark forest, unmapped; we blundered through it by instinct. We followed such tracks as we found and we could not tell if they had been made by men or brutes. We could not tell if they led to the open or roundabout to a lair. We followed them, or we distrusted them and struggled out of them through the thorns.
> "But a glimpse now and then of a star!" said Mr. Plantagenet-Buchan— his best thing, he reflected, that evening.
> "Or a firefly," said Lady Catherine.
> The psychologist, the physiologist, would clear that jungle in time. In time. (*Meanwhile*, bk. I: 5)

Wells tactfully indicates the strength and the weakness of his own metaphor while asserting his faith in its reliability. A figure of speech may be useful in making a point clear, but it is perilously subject to fluctuating interpretations. The gleam that invites seekers of a new world may be no star's fire but some fugitive insect's blink in a swamp. Wells appreciated the vulnerability of his entire vision as much as of his specific metaphor. Nonetheless he hoped that if men had a wide prospect of the historical landscape, they would discover a path through the jungle to a clearing at its end. To gain order, it was first necessary to perceive the disorder enveloping mankind. Wells amused himself with sly references to his own obsessive images; thus in *All Aboard for Ararat* (1940), God explains to his latter-day Noah, "My original idea was of an immense responsive universe, with a delightful garden at the centre, pervaded by a sort of appreciative exaltation called love" (*Ararat*, chap. I: 2). The plan does not work. "I found my Garden was in for procreation before I had time to turn round," God complains (*Ararat*, chap. I: 3). What followed was the passion and craving that man has known since.

The garden is the ideal, but even for God it is not easy of attainment. Wells pursued this subject in *The Happy Turning* (1945), where, like Huxley, he discovers his most satisfactory exercise in old age is tending his backyard garden.[14] Holy Writ tells us man was created a gardener, says Wells, and men yield readily to the suggestion, seeing it as a comfortable retirement activity. But Wells discovers that his tiny garden is a Cosmos and that "there is no real difference except in relative size between my seedling antirrhinums and the Pleiades. They both mock me—in a parallel manner" (*Turning*, chap. VIII). In it he witnesses the incredible fierceness, nastiness, and brutality of the Vegetable Kingdom which man overlooks in his haste. "I doubt," he adds pensively, "if Voltaire ever came face to face with that garden of his without some intervening help; he wrote the end of *Candide* and died before he realized the truth" (*Turning*, chap. VIII).[15] Wells has realized the truth before dying, and it has not enhanced the thought of passing. Throughout his life beasts and jungles had frightened him. He wished to tame the one and transform the other to gardens. Now, at this late date, he is forced to admit that even should one succeed, the same persistent demands continue, though on a different scale. Beyond Utopia and its perfect gardens is the threat of the year 802,701 with its ruined museum and its Eloi living in fear of predatory Morlocks in an untended garden gone rank.

Jungle and beasts are nature external and internal. The garden represents the control of that nature but offers no guarantee of orderly continuity. It requires strict supervision lest it rebel and betray. But man does not consist merely of animal impulses. Benham conquered his tiger by declaring himself man, the thought of the world. Though part of nature and subject to its laws, the human mind somehow rises above its material seat. Only man is capable of conceiving what does not exist, of imagining and then making that imagining real. Wells knew the dangers inherent in man's capacity to think, to reason, to imagine, but he believed that the potential for good surpassed the likelihood of evil. His ambivalence on this point is evident, however, in *The Island of Dr. Moreau*, where Prendick, obliged to maintain his dominion over the partially humanized animals without the aid of weapons, cows them with the tale that their "creator," Dr. Moreau, still exists and watches them. "An animal may be ferocious and cunning enough," Prendick gloats, "but it takes a real man to tell a lie" (*Moreau*, chap. XXII). Once free from the hellish island that represents all that is bestial in man as well as the abuse of what is finest, Prendick settles on a goal for his life in the study of astronomy.

> There is, though I do not know how there is or why there is, a sense of infinite peace and protection in the glittering hosts of heaven. There it must be, I think, in the vast and eternal laws of matter, and not in the daily cares and sins and troubles of men, that whatever is more than animal within us must find its solace and its hope. I hope, or I could not live. And so, in hope and solitude, my story ends. (*Moreau*, chap. XXII)

Just as the mind represents the potential for order and law above the organic possibilities of betrayal, so do the stars in their distance and their regularity. Intelligence too can fail of its high purpose, but it can aspire in a way not available to mere flesh. Once again, although this image of the stars was by no means novel, it had personal significance for Wells.[16] In his early essay "The Sun God and the Holy Stars" (1894), a review of Norman

Lockyer's *Dawn of Astronomy*, Wells acknowledged the identification of stars with human aspiration.[17] Even Ugh-Lomi in "A Story of the Stone Age" (1897) observes a fact that he is not yet prepared to fathom. "No animals look up—they have too much common sense. It was only that fantastic creature, man, could waste his wits skyward" (*Stories*, "A Story of the Stone Age": 3). *The Food of the Gods* (1904) ends with one of the giants declaring that they represent the spirit of growth aspiring to the stars (*Food*, bk. III, chap. V). Like them, Wells's future and Utopian men aspire to the stars in *The World Set Free* (1914) and *Men Like Gods* (1923). William Leadford of *In the Days of the Comet* (1906) asks, in the midst of his agony over betrayed love, "What earthly significance has anyone found in the stars?" (*Comet*, bk. I, chap. III: 3). His answer is implicit throughout the novel, but more particularly in his friend Parload, whose stargazing gives him the power of dispassionate observation. His is the reasonable mood that will later descend upon all of mankind when the comet's gases soothe the earth. It is almost as though his concentration on the comet has lured it with its benevolent ether to earth.

When Wells wrote that "the stars in their courses were pointing our race towards the organized world community," he was not simply running out a tired cliche. He meant it literally. In *The Fate of Homo Sapiens* (1939), he asserted that as a young scientist in 1888, freed from the Judaeo-Christian mythology, "I saw a limitless universe throughout which the stars and nebulae were scattering like dust, and I saw life ascending, as it seemed, from nothingness toward the stars" (*Homo*, Introduction). Wells dramatized this sense of aspiration in *The Undying Fire* (1919), where Job Huss has a dream in which he struggles out of a great forest toward the crystalline region of the stars. As his faith wavers, he asks God if he is right to venture above the stars, and God answers, "On the courage in your heart all things depend. By courage it is that the stars continue in their courses, day by day." If courage fails, all things go out, leaving nothing (*Fire*, chap. VI: 1). All of *Star-Begotten* (1937) depends upon this conceit. Since man has failed to reach upward to the stars, the stars have reached deep into man and made of him *Homosideralis*, star-born. In *Babes in the Darkling Wood* (1940) the leading characters have become stars. "Stella" Kentlake and "Gemini" Twain are young lovers who, after a series of difficulties, decide to help lead mankind toward its high destination. Wells calls attention to the significance of their names, and when the two lovers have settled down to practical work toward the new world, Wells informs us that the "ideas they had shaped floated above their preoccupied minds like the guiding stars of heaven in a night of cloud and storm" (*Babes*, bk. IV, Tailpiece).

If the stars were not yet attainable, by laying out orderly plans men could imitate their regularity. A practical version of such planning was map making. From childhood Wells enjoyed poring over maps. He described his mind as a small-scale map of wide ranges, talked about mapping or charting social and economic programs, and referred to efforts at improving the human condition as "attempts to map a way out for humanity" (*Going*, chap. V; *Frustration*, chap. XIII; *'42*, pt. II: 5).[18] Obviously there is a connection between this image and the more forceful and prevalent image of the jungle; and in *New Worlds for Old* (1908), he made that connection clear by identifying scientists and socialists as map makers and planners in the wilderness. Maps provide a sense of command over vast areas. Wells liked to see things laid out as though from some height. In his stories adventurers often view prospects in this way. It may be ethereal and disembodied as in "The Stolen Body" (1898) or outward from a tower as in "The Crystal Egg" (1897), or it could be a diver's view of a civilization on the sea bottom as in "In the Abyss" (1897). Wells associated his Utopias with high places—such as the mountainous terrain in *A Modern Utopia* (1905), *The World Set Free* (1914), and to some extent *Men Like Gods* (1923), or the tower of the old writer which is the setting for the utopianized world of *In the Days of the Comet* (1906). We have already noted that Wells's characters struggle out of metaphorical swamps, valleys, and jungles toward uplands; accordingly, his powerful figures often find themselves looking out at the world from high places, either metaphorical or real.

Wells considered this spaciousness of vision a feature of his own thinking. "My scientific training and teaching confirmed and equipped all my inherent tendency to get things ruthlessly mapped out and consistent" (*Autobiography*, chap. VIII: 5). The achievement of an elevated, objective position was central to his entire approach and was the basis for his "outline" books, of which *The Outline of History* (1920) was the first and the most successful. It gave mankind the first bird's-eye view of its own life story. He described *The Work, Wealth and Happiness of Mankind* (1932) as "an aerial reconnaissance" of one area of human life (*Work*, chap. II: 7). In a novel more like a course in universal knowledge than fiction, Wells described his attitude about this method. William Clissold admits that he has been attempting a diagram of the whole of human life as he sees it passing before him. After an involved disquisition on social issues, he remarks, "I return from this long flight, this bird's eye view of human affairs in the sluices of change, to the hangar, so to speak, of this room. I clamber out of my framework of generalizations. I come back from map scale to life-size again" (*Clissold*, vol. II, bk. VI: 8).[19]

In this metaphor Wells has suggested one reason for his fascination with flying. Not only did he consider it a certainty well before it was a reality, but he always maintained a conviction of its intellectual and strategic importance.[20] Beyond these practical features, though, it is clear that he was enamored of the very sensations of flight, even before he had actually experienced them, and that the notion of ascent signified release for him, along with all his favorable associations of height, spaciousness, and vista.[21] Wells's fictional flyers are all impressed by the panoramic thrill of the experience. Graham's preliminary fears disappear quickly as he becomes accustomed to aircraft flight, and a fair space of *When the Sleeper Wakes* (1899) is given up to describing his pursuit of this hobby. With greater seriousness, George Ponderevo in *Tono-Bungay* (1909) trains himself rigorously for his experiments in flying; like Graham before him and Trafford after, his broad vision of humanity is associated with his interest in flying. Peter Stublands in *Joan and Peter* (1918) is quicker to grasp the meaning of his wartime experience with flying, which represents for him an escape from the past. "Hitherto Man had been living *down there*, down on those flats—for all the world is flat from the air. Now at last, men were beginning to feel how they might soar over all ancient limitations" (*Joan*, chap. XIII: 23).

Drawing upon his own fears and aspirations, Wells composed a sort of personal cartography for finding Utopia. As a child he feared wild animals of the jungles, and these fears never left him, becoming associated with all the confusion, muddle, brutality, and frustration that he sought to escape in his life. Spacious uplands characterized by freedom, cleanliness, and order signified a sane life of clear thought. Airplanes and air flight became symbols of man's ability to rise above his earthly limitations. Ultimately the stars, representing as they have for so long in man's history hope, guidance, and regularity, were Wells's images of aspiration. What is most interesting in Wells's use of this metaphor-complex is the thoroughly conscious manner in which he exploited personal obsessions by dramatizing them and thereby transforming his personal weaknesses into communal strengths. That he could also view his aspirations with a realistic irony is evident in much of his writing but perhaps more pointedly in the nicknames he chose for himself and his lover, Rebecca West. He was Jaguar and she was Panther.[22] Obviously, there were some things in the jungle that weren't half bad.

# 3

# Flesh and Blood

Nature's way was the way of the jungle for Wells and man's aim was, as we have seen, to escape that jungle. But even when man's mind permitted him to soar above the tangle of natural life, it could not release him from his own rootedness in the earth. Wells viewed man as essentially animal and considered him a species open to improvement or to degeneration like all other species. He had no illusions about the creature. Human history was a brutal chronicle of evolution from the grossest bestiality to a shaky civilization. The title of *Mankind in the Making* (1903) indicates Wells's conjecture that the process was still under way. He scoffed at noble savagery, calling the image of a "large, naked, virtuous, pink, Natural Man, drinking pure spring water, eating the fruits of the earth, and living to ninety in the open" a fantasy. To him the real savage was physically loathsome and morally deplorable. Echoing Huxley, he explained that "the very existence and nature of man is an interference with Nature and Nature's ways." Any return to Nature would be utter degeneration; hence, he felt that to rebel against instinct and conquer the forces that dominate him is the fundamental being of man (*Mankind*, chap. III: 1).

Man, though part of Nature, finds the uncontrolled processes of Nature inimical. His evolution requires a rooting out of a part of his very being. Unmodified human nature is no better than untamed physical nature.[1] Both require cultivation. In *New Worlds for Old* (1908), Wells asserted that control of mankind could be achieved only through communal action, hence through socialism. Admitting that socialism was against human nature, he pointed out that any social system was inevitably so. Moreover, he said, "human nature is against human nature. For human nature is in a perpetual conflict; it is the Ishmael of the Universe, against everything, and with everything against it; and within, no more and no less than a perpetual battleground of passion, desire, cowardice, indolence, and

49

good will" (*New Worlds*, chap. IX: 7). Wells admired and quoted F. W. Sanderson's condensation of this attitude: "The great duty and service of science [is] to change human nature" (*Schoolmaster*, chap. III: 2). It is just this conscious change that Mr. Polly and other Wells characters demonstrate in a spontaneous fashion. This is what it means to climb out of the pit, to discover the path out of the jungle. Man does not really kill the beast; he tames it. He does not escape the jungle; he turns it into a garden. He does not escape the prison; he redesigns it.

There was no lack of human traits for Wells to deplore, but he singled out for fierce criticism one of the most intimate. His most vivid metaphors of jungle and beast were frequently associated with the tangle of emotions surrounding sexual passion, which expressed itself in the need to possess and dominate and in the destructive impulses of jealousy and hatred. In an essay of 1897 "Morals and Civilization" Wells credited the gradual taming of the sexual impulse as an important step toward human improvement. Although Wells did not honor this conventional view for long—either in theory or in practice—he preserved a quasi-scientific belief in the danger of wasting energy in sex and promoted a hypothesis of the conservation of sexual energy. Thus "the monogamic family, with an entire prohibition of wasted energy" becomes "the moral ideal, so far as sex is concerned, of the modern militant state." Wells then asserts that "States and nations that fall away from that ideal will inevitably go down before States that maintain it in its integrity" (*Early Writings*, chap. VI).

Reviewing the history of mankind, Wells frequently warned of the dangers of sexual indulgence. There was a dilemma here that touched Wells at home, for he also believed that forceful men were more inclined to sexual activity. It was a fault in Philip of Macedonia that "like many energetic and imaginative men, he was prone to impatient love impulses" (*Outline*, chap. XXXIII: 2). One can almost hear the whip striking Wells's own shoulder, for his licentiousness was almost legendary. Perhaps he soothed himself with the observation that the numerous love affairs of so great and active a figure as Charlemagne "did not interfere at all with his incessant military and political labours" (*Outline*, chap. XXXII: 6). He seems to have embraced the old athlete's tale that sexual indulgence endangers the game, though he had no taste for cold baths and lonely beds. Nonetheless, from his young manhood onward, Wells identified loss of energy through sexual vice as a characteristic of the final decadent stage of civilizations (*Early Writings*, chap. VI).

These opinions were neither unusual nor new. Various theories asserted the role of ungoverned lubricity in the decadence of whole civilizations.[2] Wells needed no theories to persuade him, for he began his career at a time when sensation, sensuality, and sex in various guises were widely advertised and applauded. It was the time of Oscar Wilde's infamous trial and more infamous offenses. Often in later years Wells adverted to the sexual outrages of the fin de siècle. He was censorious of sexual license in his youth but fastened on this subject because he was not free from the urgings of a sensuality which he dreaded as a lapse back into the condition of the ape in the jungle. It is a dilemma well stated and examined in *Love and Mr. Lewisham* (1900).[3]

Despite claims to the contrary, Wells seems to have felt that sex was unavoidably soiling. "I do not like filth," he wrote bluntly in *The Happy Turning* (1945). At first blush this may sound like hypocrisy from one who was sometimes regarded as the Don Juan of his day. But here, as almost always, I think we can trust Wells's candor. He was not above telling a racy story or making double-entendres, but in regard to sex he seems to have kept an eye fixed on the sacred image while wrestling in a sweaty bed below. Always he dreamed of man's passions tamed to a suitable communality. One expression of this aim was in *In the Days of the Comet* (1906) where he pictured human love "enlarged and glorified" and varied beyond the limits of proprietorship (*Comet*, bk. III, chap. I: 1 and chap. III: 4).[4] Another was in *Star-Begotten* (1937), written long after he had ceased to maintain monogamy as an exclusive ideal. People of the future will not live in a rational desert without passion, Wells explained, but will experience sex with "a lovelier poetry to guide them, a pervasive, penetrating contempt for ugliness, vanity, and mere mean competitiveness and self-assertion. . . . How can we imagine what the sexual life of sane men and women can be like?" (*Star*, chap. IX: 1). As early as *Anticipations* (1901) his main position was clear. "Our current civilization is a sexual lunatic" he wrote and signaled the principal danger of this lunacy when he added that unbridled sensuality was destructive because "it aims not at life, but at itself" (*Anticipations*, chap. IX).

Sex offended some fastidiousness in Wells. He took it personally. His judgment on his age reflected his own initiation. "I took my first lessons in sexual practice with a certain aversion," he said, and it is evident that this aversion remained (*Autobiography*, chap. III: 5). At times it became a rejection not merely of fleshliness, but of the flesh, as in the short story "Under the Knife" (1896), where Wells described escape from the body in exhilarating terms. Wells had been and was again to be extremely unhealthy around the time he wrote the story, and this surely influenced his mood, but the notion of escape from the flesh obviously appealed to him. In *The World Set Free* (1914), the heroic Karenin, himself an invalid, asserts that man's chief aim is to liberate himself from the body, and other Wells characters echo this distrust of the flesh and its sexual functions.

As with so many of Wells's central concerns, there is a deep personal discomfort associated with the theme of sex. But there were broader difficulties with the passion. I have already mentioned Wells's notion that sexual indulgence wasted energy. He seems genuinely to have admired certain qualities in his Martians who "were lifted above all these organic fluctuations of mood and emotion." They are "absolutely without sex" and therefore untroubled by turbulent feelings, having brought the flesh fully under control of the mind (*War*, bk. II, chap. II). They are not, of course, attractive to human beings, upon whom they feed, but their passionlessness gives them a scientific detachment which makes them superior. In "A Story of the Days to Come" (1897), of this same time, a doctor of the future explains to the self-indulgent Bindon, "You see—from one point of view— people with imaginations and passions like yours have to go—they have to go" (*Stories*, "A Story of the Days to Come": 4).[5]

Wells modified this early view, but throughout his life he described sex as a thief of peace and time. William Clissold complains that man lives besieged by sex. It is the driving force of life, but its allurements are as threatening to his freedom as are society's inhibiting traditions. He had hoped to devote himself to the purity of science, but sex caught him unawares one day and "wrenched away the mastery of my life from science. . . . I married for the sake of a kiss, and I made a great entanglement for myself in life" (*Clissold*, vol. II, bk. IV: 2). Sex snares such innocents as Kipps and Polly as well. Some, like Clissold, discover that sexual passion is simply a concentrated form of the life force or will to live, and try to direct their attention to its broader manifestations.

Much as he complained about it, Wells admitted the reality of sexual passion. Unlike some of his characters, he fully recognized its power. In *Mankind in the Making* (1903), he said the flow of sex comes "like a great river athwart the plain of our personal and egoistic schemes," but it is also "the source of all our power in life and the irrigator of all things" (*Mankind*, chap. VIII: 1). Wells understood the problem well even though he could not solve it, for his personal life was filled with affairs and *passades* which pleased yet troubled him.[6] Rachel Bernstein, a promiscuous and unattractive character in *The Bulpington of Blup* (1933), voices some of Wells's opinions on sex in the splendidly appropriate setting of the Monkey House at Kew Gardens. Theodore Bulpington is reluctant to consider sex as the chief moving force in men, but Rachel insists. Sex comes in everywhere, she says, motivating the pursuit of power in all fields—Art, Science, Literature, Statesmanship, Religion. When she argues that all of life can be reduced to this central point revealed by Freud, Theodore objects that she is obsessed with the subject. "All the world is. That's his greater discovery," Rachel retorts. "Why don't you look facts in the face? I tell you we live in a

Monkey's Cage and you sit there and argue. When you get rid of plain sex and accessory sex, sublimated sex and perverted sex, you get rid of human life" (*Blup*, chap. II: 5). That Wells often saw love as antagonism or conquest suggests that his own passions were not free from the infection he described.

Sex is everywhere in Wells's novels, so I need not repeat his opinions unnecessarily. He did that for us, and nowhere more so than in his last two novels.[7] In *Babes in the Darkling Wood* (1940), Wells fabricated a scholarly book entitled *The Expansion of Sex* by one Cottenham C. Bower so that he could quote tracts of his own thoughts as though they were another's. Sex is the central subject of this novel and Wells's views on it are familiar, though brought up to date by recent psychological theory. Gemini and Stella, the two young lovers of the novel, agree that sex must be subordinated, though they appreciate it as a source of energy. For Gemini, it also serves as a cure for his near-catatonic illness resulting from a combination of shell shock and sex guilt. Having effected Gemini's recovery, Stella argues that moralists have been ungrateful to sex, considering that it has spread its energy over the whole mental and physical life of man. Gemini now agrees that "Sex *is* the quintessence of life. The *go* in life" (*Babes*, bk. IV, chap. III: 4). But this admission leads to an important caution. "Sex drives you into action," he says, "but there's no reckoning on the sort of action it may drive you into. We can't get anywhere without that urgent motor, but it's our affair to see that it takes us where our intellectual conscience wants to go" (*Babes*, bk. IV, chap. III: 5).

In his last novel, which we shall return to later, Wells took a more negative approach. Young Edward Albert Tewler of *You Can't Be Too Careful* (1941) is brought up in ignorance of sex because his mother is concerned about his purity. Tewler's ignorance of sex and his inability to deal with his passionate impulses lead him into an unwise marriage and a humiliating first copulation that ruins that marriage. It is a coarser version of George Ponderevo's failure with Marion. *Babes in the Darkling Wood* had shown the power of sex and recommended some means of utilizing that power, but *You Can't Be Too Careful* described the maiming consequences of sexual ignorance. It is indictment from beginning to end—the angry, but amusing, outburst of a man crippled by the sexual customs of his time and struggling to free himself from rooted desires he could never fully master.[8]

In *God, The Invisible King* (1917), Wells declared that among man's primary duties was the supervision of his own passions, a plea for restraint that had been present in his writing from the beginning and that was part of the lesson he had learned from Huxley. The theme of renunciation had been familiar in the literature of the preceding age, thanks partly to

German authors such as Goethe and Schopenhauer who had recommended it. Wells offered many versions of this motif. In *The Sea Lady* (1902), a tale of competing attractions, Chatteris is drawn to the mysterious Thalassia Waters, who represents the world of dreams and of desire. He decides not to succumb to her allurements.[9] But the choice Chatteris believes he is going to make is clearly not easy for him.

> Renunciation! Always—renunciation! That is life for all of us. We have desires, only to deny them, senses that we all must starve. We can live only as a part of ourselves. Why should *I* be exempt. For me she is evil. For me she is death. . . . Only why have I seen her face? Why have I heard her voice? (*Lady*, chap. VII: 5)

He does not renounce the life of desire, but yields himself to the world of moonshine and death.

Chatteris's case suggests that renunciation was an important step for Wells toward the self-discipline required in the task of reordering the world. Mr. Sempack, the Olympian philosopher of *Meanwhile* (1927), is wrenched out of his tranquility by an intense, if temporary, passion for Lady Catherine Fossingdean. Cured of this folly, he resumes the conviction that scientists, philosophers, and all who struggle to gain an objective view of life in order to guide it properly must remain undistracted by physical passion. "'Essentially,' he said, 'they must be celibate'" (*Meanwhile*, bk. II: 9).

Restraint, dispassionateness, and sublimation can channel energy for larger purposes. With Sempack and Karenin, but also with the Time Traveller, William Leadford, and others, these larger purposes are in the best interests of mankind. However, suppression of animal instincts can also lead to more ambiguous results as in the careers of Dr. Moreau, Griffin, or Rud Whitlow. This last is a notable case. Through fear and revulsion, Whitlow does not permit himself the gratifications men normally seek from women. His associate Chiffan, too much given to womanizing, acknowledges, "That's the difference between us—and why I shall never be a leader" (*Terror*, bk. I, ch. III: 4). However, when Whitlow has achieved the purpose for which he channeled his energy, when he has brought about the World Revolution, he begins to go bad because he no longer has an acceptable form of release. Chiffan theorizes that "security and abundance release sex. Gallantry and art break out. Sex lies in wait for every sort of success. It follows success about." He warns that men will have to deal with the surplus energy released by the security and abundance of world peace and speculates that sex may be "the actual line of relief. An efflorescence of sex—and sublimated sex, art, decoration, music, may be the natural and necessary relief" (*Terror*, bk. IV, chap. I: 9). But Whitlow, incapable of art and the finer manifestations of sensibility, degenerates as the targets for his energy disappear. When women are provided for his sexual pleasure, he can enjoy only brutal and perverse acts. Finally, he is quietly murdered because he is the most minatory force in the world peace he has created.

Wells saw the value of controlling sexual impulse, but he also knew that renunciation, self-control, and celibacy were not complete solutions. If he recognized and depicted the crude features of human sexuality, he also understood man's need for a broader aspect of passion—the beauty and sentiment of desire which exist alongside its animal features. At a rudimentary level, the sex drive serves a useful purpose. It may entangle the individual in vulgar details and swamps of natural desire, but it is also one of man's highest impulses. It may tempt man into the slavery of nature's circle, but it may also free him from egotism and thus become a means to greater freedom. In comparing the sexual and religious drives, Wells emphasized the greater freedom of the more refined impulse. Love passion was transient; religious passion, lasting. Love stirs man out of his egotism to serve the ends of the race while religion takes the individual out of his egotism for the service of the community. A reasonable man, he suggested, could learn to transform mere passion into love. It was a notion familiar to Christians.

Though Wells advocated this movement from *eros* to *caritas*, he rooted his argument less in Christian tradition than in biology. He saw man moving by stages from a primitive fascination with his self toward interest in others through the lure of passion and thence to a concern for community and race manifested in what Wells called the religious impulse. The sexual impulse served a genuine purpose in this process. Though men might always yield to a cruder sexual impulse and lapse back into self-gratification and egotism, sex could serve a constructive purpose beyond mere generation. Dr. Martineau in *The Secret Places of the Heart* (1922) isolates this quality. " '*Sex not only a renewal of life in the species*,' noted the doctor's silver pencil; '*sex may be also a renewal of energy in the individual*' " (*Heart*, chap. IV: 6). The idea that sex could be a therapeutic aid to man appealed to Wells, who was more and more obsessed by sexual matters as the years went by. Perhaps it gave him some relief to theorize that his indulgences were so many specifics for the malady they constituted. It was a convenient homeopathy.

Sexual energy is inescapable and vexatious, and thus resembles all powerful sources of energy in Nature. Sexual impulse is intermittent and often fierce, but its intermittence can be channeled to consistent use and its fierceness made a means of liberation from the ego or from conventional restraints. Though physical passion does not aim at liberation, it may inadvertently make freedom possible. Once this liberation is effected, a new liberty becomes possible beyond physical passion. *Ann Veronica* (1909) offers a sketch of this procedure. *Marriage* (1912) chronicles the transformation. After some years of marriage, Trafford and Marjorie realize that their passionate love is over. But Trafford discovers that his love for Marjorie can be renewed and elevated to a higher plane when he learns to view her, not as his intellectual inferior, but as his human partner. Both then feel themselves part of a larger unity—the race, the mind of man. Marjorie shares this desire to participate in the awakening of the race. Though she has understood this impulse more dimly than Trafford, she realizes that woman's true role is to release man and save him from "the instincts and passions that try to waste you altogether on us. . . . We're the responsible sex. And we've forgotten it" (*Marriage*, bk. IV, chap. IV: 12). Through a conscious effort, this couple's potentially destructive love evolves into something nobler—a true partnership in the service of mankind, a mutual selflessness in a higher purpose.[10]

*The Passionate Friends* (1913) repeats this lesson in more melancholy terms, for it is the record of a failure. Stephen Stratton's romance with Mary Christian is secretive and furtive and soon the broad interests they share begin to pass out of their intercourse. Endymion's cave becomes a dungeon as passion forecloses a higher love. When they are forced to separate, Stratton suffers a mental and spiritual collapse from which he recovers by dedicating himself to the idea of a Great State. But Mary warns him that women, more sexual than men, are a threat to that ideal.[11] Stratton himself had already detailed a similar view that summarizes the basic theme of his and Wells's story.

> The servitude of sex and the servitude of labour are the twin conditions upon which human society rests to-day, the two limitations upon its progress towards a greater social order, to that greater community, those uplands of light and happy freedom, towards which that Being who was my father yesterday, who thinks in myself to-day, and who will be you to-morrow and your sons after you, by his very nature urges and must continue to urge the life of mankind. The story of myself and Mary is a mere incident in that gigantic, scarce conscious effort to get clear of toils and confusions and encumbrances, and have our way with life. We are like little figures, dots ascendant upon a vast hillside; I take up our intimacy for an instant and hold it under a lens for you. I become more than myself then, and Mary stands for innumerable women. (*Friends*, chap. VI: 7)

Stratton was not fortunate in his great friendship because he confused it with passion. Once Mary is dead, he realizes that she was a prototype of the woman to come: a self-reliant, independent "sister-lover who must replace the seductive and abject womanhood, owned, mastered and deceiving who waste the world to-day" (*Friends*, chap. XII: 3). Stratton believes that Mary's venturing spirit is spreading in human affairs and will replace the old brutish usages with a new awareness. Wells might have modeled her on Amy Catherine Wells, the wife to whom he remained dedicated but to whom he could not be faithful.

*The Passionate Friends* concentrates upon the problem of sex and states clearly the relationship of woman to the achievement of a finer civilization. While the imagery of the novel associates sexuality with entrapment and a higher love with escape, it also clearly states a very practical consideration, for it asserts the importance of encouraging women to be equal partners with men in the making of a new world. Wells treated this subject frequently, worrying it from one direction or another throughout his long career. Sometimes his novels show men incapable of breaking through their egotism to a genuine love, despite the suppressed or raging physical yearning, as in the first part of *In the Days of the Comet* (1906), *The Bulpington of Blup* (1933), *The Holy Terror* (1939), and *You Can't Be Too Careful* (1941). Sometimes they show the dangers women occasion for the aspiring spirit as in *Love and Mr. Lewisham* (1900), *Tono-Bungay* (1909), *The World of William Clissold* (1926), and *Apropos of Dolores* (1938). Many novels describe a woman's awakening to her position in a masculine society. Jessie Milton in *The Wheels of Chance* (1896) and Ann in *Ann Veronica* (1909) are examples. Others present women capable of understanding and contributing to the Great State of the future, such as the heroines of *The Wife of Sir Isaac Harman* (1914), *Joan and Peter* (1918), *Christina Alberta's Father* (1925), *Meanwhile* (1927), *Brynhild* (1937), and *Babes in the Darkling Wood* (1940).

One of Wells's great achievements, considering the times in which he wrote, was the creation of sympathetic, believable women who confront their own sexuality, its hazards and its pleasures, just as men confront theirs. The woman of independent spirit was not a new figure in English literature; Meredith had offered several variations and so had Hardy; and ever since the sensational novels of the 1860s spirited, self-reliant, if not always ethical, women, figured in English fiction. Ouida and Maria Corelli had rendered similar types more acceptably romantic, bringing English readers as close to Flaubert and George Sand as they could be expected to go. Grant Allen went further, expecting rebuke, but discovered that the depiction of sexual rebellion paid, as long as the rebel suffered for her audacity. But Wells did something more. He showed female sexuality as natural and robust, as a potentially positive or negative force; and more importantly, he encouraged full freedom for women to understand the passional life so powerful in shaping the lives of all beings.

Although he was their champion, Wells's view of women was complicated.[12] He treated their dilemmas sympathetically, but his opinions were often strangely divided concerning their proper role. In *Anticipations* (1901), he observed that "a virile man, though he too is subject to accidents, may upon most points still hope to plan and determine his life; the life of a woman is all accident" (*Anticipations*, chap. IV). Wells argued that this was not a healthy situation for the race since women, much as they may liberate themselves from the duties of wives and mothers, are nonetheless the bearers of children and it is mainly through them that the race continues. In *Mankind in the Making* (1903), he recommended that the State endow mothers, making motherhood a worthwhile and honorable occupation and providing women with personal independence and responsibility.[13]

Just as Wells describes young men finding their roles in a frustrating society, so he often depicts young women coming to terms with their desires and struggling out of hostile circumstances toward some purpose more profound than simple maternity. In some cases, as with Ann Veronica, the first step toward freedom is economic, but more often the first stage of liberation is to escape the enslavement of sex. Christina Alberta's career is an example. Whereas earlier generations of women suppressed sex to achieve emancipation, thereby making it a fiercely negative presence and themselves negative instead of positive women, Christina Alberta escapes the tyranny of sex by making it cheap and thus a thing of mere intermittent moods and impulses. Bobby Roothing, who loves Christina, speculates that in the future there may be many women who achieve this freedom, breaking away to "a real individual life—a third sex. Perhaps in the new world there would cease to be two sexes only; there would be recognized varieties and sub-divisions" (*Christina*, bk. III, chap. IV: 7).

Despite his assertion that there was no special science of women, Wells frequently declared that women were subject to special forms of experience, and his novels provide examples of this belief in the attempted seductions of Jessie Milton and Ann Veronica, or the puzzling love dilemmas of Lady Harman and Mary Christian. Clearly he felt that there were important differences between men and women, and he tried to state these differences. Marjorie Trafford admitted that women were more concerned with feeling than broad intellectual issues, and Nellie Stuart in *In the Days of the Comet* (1906), grappling with the possible new relations between the sexes, admits that "a woman believes nothing by nature. She goes into a mold hiding her secret thoughts almost from herself" (*Comet*, bk. III, chap. I: 4). Thanks to the liberating power of the comet, Nellie can come out of that hiding. Wells wanted women to be like men in their ability to face life and their own impulses honestly, to struggle for some aim transcending egotism, and to achieve a vision of a finer, cleaner existence. But he also realized that, like men, women were confined by physical instincts, psychological fears, and social customs. Women can do what men do in the world, but they are constitutionally more inclined to sex issues and psychologically more reined in by personal reference.

As far as I can judge, Wells never did settle the terms of the treaty of mutual tolerance between the sexes, and his fluctuating sentiments on the issue are reflected in his depictions of women in fiction. His range of feminine characterization was not wide, but he was capable of creating believable variations upon certain basic types to illustrate the important themes he wished to treat.[14] Ann Veronica may resemble Christina Alberta, but she is not much like Dolores Wilbeck. No more is Lady Harman like Stella Kentlake. Wells acquired very early from J. J. Atkinson the idea that woman was the peacemaker and socializer of the race. She protected young men from the old and taught the primary taboos. "Human societies in their beginnings were her work, done against the greater solitariness, the lonely fierceness of the adult male" (*Stories*, "The Grisly Folk"). But it was just her reverence for social custom and her concentration upon feeling that made her hazardous to the adventuring intellect of modern man. Wells created women characters to fit all stages of this complex relationship between the sexes, and he offered varying examples of their liberation from social slavery. He pictured the woman who can strive toward a better life on her own, the woman who can serve as a supportive helpmate to a striving man of power, and the woman who can be a sister-lover, equal in the conquest of a new world. In each case some form of love replaces simple sex passion as a binding or guiding force.[15]

This theme and this pattern are prominent in *Meanwhile* (1927), which offers us a detailed examination of one of these female types. Cynthia Rylands adjusts to her husband's escapade with a tartish young woman and becomes the moral bookkeeper of his libido, helping him to direct his substantial energies more purposefully. Mr. Sempack counsels her to overlook Philip's conjugal lapses. Later, Philip himself tells Cynthia, "A woman is a man's keeper. A wife is a man's conscience. If he can't bring his thoughts to her—she's no good at all" (*Meanwhile*, bk. II: 2).

This was one kind of woman of which Wells could approve. It was his "Picture of a Lady." Cynthia Rylands is far superior to the ladies satirized in *First Men in the Moon* (1901), who are noble looking and richly adorned, but who exhibit, "save for their mouths, almost microscopic heads" (*Moon*, chap. XXIII). Nor does she fit Mr. Stanley's Victorian preconceptions. To him girls and women were creatures "either too bad for a modern vocabulary, and then frequently most undesirably desirable, or too pure and good for life" (*Veronica*, chap. I: 3). But beyond the noble, sustaining type, Wells valued another brand of woman whose image was deeply seated in his mind and heart. This ideal figure does not act merely as man's conscience; she is an amazonian protectress or fellow warrior in the battle of life. In *What Is Coming* (1916), Wells presented his clearest portrait of the type.

> The real "emancipation" to which reason and the trend of things makes is from the yielding to the energetic side of a woman's disposition, from beauty enthroned for love towards the tall, weather-hardened woman with a spear, loving her mate as her mate loves her, and as sexless as a man in all her busy hours. (*Coming*, chap. VIII: 1)

This Amazonian figure recurs throughout Wells's fiction. She is Eudema in "A Story of the Stone Age" (1897) and Elizabeth in "A Story of the Days to Come" (1897); she is Ann Veronica hiking with Capes over the mountains and Marjorie Trafford in the Labrador wilderness. But although her attributes are consistent with Wells's claims upon women, she derives from an image rooted in Wells's own sexual awakening. In his autobiography Wells singled out certain female types that appealed to his youthful eye, such as the illustrated figures in *Punch*: "Tall and lovely feminine figures, Britannia, Erin, Columbia, La France, bare armed, bare necked, showing beautiful bare bosoms, revealing shining thighs, wearing garments that were a revelation in an age of flounces and crinolines. My first consciousness of women, my first stirrings of desire were roused by these heroic divinities. I became woman-conscious from those days onward" (*Autobiography*, chap. II: 5).

Tenniel's Britannia and the statues at the Crystal Palace, which Wells referred to again in *The Secret Places of the Heart* (1922), were not exclusive figures. They were typical. In *The King Who Was a King* (1929), Wells selected the form of "a brooding woman rather like the beautiful Sibyl in the Sistine Chapel in Rome" to symbolize the approach of the Empire of Mankind (*King Who*, chap. VI: 1), a figure he developed more elaborately in *The Bulpington of Blup* (1933). In that novel the dreamy, undisciplined Theodore Bulpington fashions a fantasy self called the Bulpington of Blup, replacing his real mother with a fantasy surrogate who is "rather like Britannia in the Punch cartoons" (*Blup*, chap. I: 3).[16] The Bulpington of Blup moves from the Britannic ideal to a dark, soft, comforting figure, but the Delphic Sibyl takes on its own function, being identified with a specific romantic possibility, for when Theodore first meets Margaret Broxted he identifies her with the sibyl, and the association surfaces periodically thereafter, showing us that Margaret's values are correct values and that when Theodore turns away from her he is turning toward a false world, a world of the past refashioned by lies to suit his fantasies. He is unworthy of the heroic woman who, had he been stronger, might have served him as a noble mate.

Near the end of the novel, Bulpington, now totally submerged in his falsified world, comes accidentally upon a picture of the Delphic Sibyl, identified, for him, with the new race of scientifically disciplined reshapers of the world whom he fears because they make him aware of his own meanness and the bogus character of all his airy sentiments. By smashing the picture, he consigns himself to the company of the lost, while for the reader and Wells the sibyl remains an image of hope, of positive feminine force.

Wells's picture of the modern, emancipated woman untroubled by sex and braced to reshape the future was of a piece with his longing for a life freed from the entanglements of lust, jealousy, and hatred. He pleaded constantly for openness in human intercourse and for sexual honesty. Freedom in love was as desirable to him as political freedom. He made it an important feature of his Utopias (*Utopia*, chap. II: 4).[17] Wishing to spare young people the crude introduction to sex that he had suffered at school, he argued steadily for rational sex education (*Autobiography*, chap. II: 5). In *In the Days of the Comet* (1906), Leadford describes the "conspiracy of stimulating silences" that the world maintained toward the young so that when Nature moved in its courses, the young "were ashamed and full of desire." What should have been natural and comprehensible became a guilty secret (*Comet*, bk. I, chap. II: 2). Wells recommended complete freedom in adult literature and judiciously expurgated literature and art for the young. Severe restriction he considered unwise and unhealthy.

Wells deplored the traditional schoolmaster's moral teaching, which was "to inculcate truth-telling about small matters and evasion about large, and to cultivate a morbid obsession in the necessary dawn of sexual consciousness" (*Forces*, "The Schoolmaster and the Empire": 3). He became more fervid on the subject of sex education as he grew older, until finally, in his last novel, which is a condemnation of all timid retreat into convention, all fear of change and renewal, he concentrated on the nature and consequences of the kind of introduction to sex that men and women of his day had suffered. In *You Can't Be Too Careful* (1941), Edward Albert Tewler is cramped and disfigured in mind and spirit, but Wells dwells largely upon his sexual mutilation. Concerned about her growing son, the widowed Mrs. Tewler seeks help regarding Edward Albert's sex life. She fears sending him to school. Mr. Burlap, her minister, agrees that boarding schools are a bad idea, for they are, "without exception, Sinks of Iniquity. Especially the Preparatory Schools and the so-called Public Schools" (*Careful*, bk. I, chap. III).[18] He recommends Mr. Myame, who maintains the "proper" religious attitude in his school. Myame gives Edward Albert Dr. Scaber's *What a Young Man Should Know*, a guide that is "at latest Victorian." The book tells of the fearsome consequences "of the vicious life in either its social or solitary aspect," but especially the latter.[19] It does not prevent Tewler from yielding to private sin. Later he learns from the conversation of his peers that his sin is common, but he never overcomes his sense of shame regarding it. His negative sex education leads to sexual disasters, an unwanted child, and an unhappy marriage which comes to an early and acrimonious end.

Wells regularly portrayed characters bedeviled by sex and encountering one or another foulness associated with it. His purpose in taking up this theme was not to wallow in its disgusting or lascivious attributes, but to offer a nobler picture of what sex could be.[20] In *The Salvaging of Civilization* (1921), he recommended that men imitate the ancient Hebrews and compose a modern Leviticus setting forth the knowledge necessary for men to preserve their health and to comprehend the facts of sex. He wished to free it from its jungle origins and associate it with grander notions of love. Although he was frank in describing the love affairs of his characters, he was never licentious. Despite his many private escapades, he deplored mere lubricity.

We have seen that Wells demonstrated in his fiction his assertion, stated early in *First and Last Things* (1908), that true love is "that complex of motives, impulses, sentiments, that incline us to find our happiness and satisfactions in the happiness and sympathy of others and to merge ourselves emotionally in a design greater than ourselves," while hate is all that separates and isolates the self (*Things*, bk. III: 5). Of course Wells was always alert to the deceptions Nature practices on man; thus Mr. Britling realizes that his craving for an ideal companionship in love may be nothing more than Nature "pulling, as people say, his leg," but this does not prevent him from periodically joining "the great cruising brotherhood of the Pilgrims of Love" (*Britling*, bk. I, chap. IV: 4).

Throughout his career Wells continued to rage against the cruel entanglements of sex while praising the beauties of genuine love. He was pleased to observe that the old domination of morality by sexual concerns had been mitigated during his lifetime and that sex had become decently private, though the progress from suppression to frankness had been accompanied by what he considered unseemly perversions and avowals reminiscent of the extremes of the nineties. Although he associated sex with animalistic hunger and violence, Wells constructed a far happier picture of what love could be. Like so many of his ideals, that picture of love sprang antithetically from the loathsome sketch that unaltered Nature offered.

Wells's vision of human beauty is equally antithetical. The world of his youth, he said, "was so clothed and covered up, and the rules of decency were so established in me, that any revelation of the body was an exciting thing" (*Autobiography*, chap. II: 5). No doubt it was partly this Victorian urge to conceal the human form that prompted Wells to value nudity so much.[21] He was inclined to openness and candor in all things; he liked bare facts as much as bare bodies. When he described the ideal citizen of the future, he said:

> He will not be a fat or emaciated person. Fat, panting men, and thin, enfeebled ones cannot possibly be considered good citizens any more than dirty or verminous people. He will be just as fine and seemly in his person as he can be, not from vanity and self-assertion, but to be pleasing and agreeable to his fellows. The ugly dress and ugly bearing of the "good man" of to-day will be as incomprehensible to him as the filth of a palaeolithic savage is to us. He will not speak of his "frame," and hang clothes like sacks over it; he will know and feel that he and the people about him have wonderful, delightful and beautiful bodies.

He coupled these physical attributes with comparable mental ones, for the ideal citizen would be "truthful in the manner of the scientific man or the artist, and as scornful of concealment as they" (*Forces*, "The Ideal Citizen").[22]

Wells's admiration for clean, unclothed bodies was intensified by a conviction of his own ugliness. He had frequently been unwell as a young man and felt profound humiliation at his weakness and his appearance. "Until I was over forty," he wrote, "the sense of physical inferiority was a constant acute distress to me which no philosophy could mitigate" (*Autobiography*, chap. VIII: 4). In early manhood he yearned for a beautiful body because he wanted to make love with it; hence the "realization that [his] own body was thin and ugly was almost insupportable" and the frustration mortifying (*Autobiography*, chap. V: 7). As late as *The Happy Turning* (1945) he exclaims that for the first time he realizes, though only in a dream, "what it is to have possession of an entirely healthy and balanced body" (*Turning*, chap. I). This last dream is cousin to the Utopias Wells had written in which all the people are healthy and attractive ideal citizens.

From time to time, Wells exploited the frustration he felt at being trapped in an unhealthy and unattractive body. Stories like "Under the Knife" (1896) and "The Story of the Late Mr. Elvesham" (1896) are instances. In the latter a science student loses his healthy young body and finds himself in an old, infirm one instead. His rage could be Wells's as he contemplated his sickly frame. "I had in some unaccountable manner fallen through my life and come to old age, in some way I had been cheated of all the best of my life, of love, of struggle, of strength and hope." "Elvesham" Wells very likely had some of his own attributes in mind when portraying Rud Whitlow as a physically unpleasant and unattractive person incapable of dealing with women and therefore channeling his energies toward political activity. As we have seen, Wells believed that sexual energy was a powerful generating force behind much of human activity. How this energy might be directed depended to a great degree upon people's attitudes toward the human body.

Wells charged the Victorians with covering up the facts of life both figuratively and literally. He was for undoing the damage. Fittingly, he uses images of clothing and nudity to suggest a range of positive values. There is some teasing of stuffy English propriety in *The Wonderful Visit* (1895) when the Vicar of Siddermorton is flustered by the Angel's scanty costume, which exposes much of his beautiful body. Seeking an appropriate French phrase for the situation—English, by implication, being too proper a language to possess such phrases—he strikes upon *sans culotte*. The error is apt, for the exposed body is as much a threat to the conventionally hidebound world of late nineteenth-century England as revolutionaries had been to the France of the 1780s (*Visit*, chap. X).

For Wells the value of nudity depended upon sound health. An unhealthy body could not be lovely. His Utopias were characterized by hygienic values. Like the Angel of *The Wonderful Visit*, the Utopians are beautiful beings lightly clothed. Their bodies are handsome because they are healthy and they are healthy because they have conquered most diseases through scientific research. Consequently, Utopia is represented chiefly by ripe maturity. Because Wells wished to substitute intellectual sexual partnership for selfish sexual delight, he rejected the heat of human passion for the command of a "more powerful emotion." This emotional security is more certain when the humiliation of physical inferiority has been overcome.

The future inhabitants of the earth described in *The Dream* (1924) are radiantly healthy, and Sarnac's reliving of a Victorian life in a dream illustrates the contrast. "Everybody in those days," he explains to his friends, "wore a frightful lot of clothes. You see, they were all so unhealthy they could not stand the least exposure to wet or cold" (*Dream*, chap. II: 3). That abundance of clothing created an unhealthy curiosity about sex. Masking the body was simply one manifestation of a larger impulse for suppression, for people also "wrapped up and distorted and hid their minds" (*Dream*, chap. VI: 4). The world of the future has overcome the limitations of that earlier time, and Sarnac, recovering from his dream, senses the full delight of the finer time. "You cannot imagine how delightful it is for me to sit here again, naked and simple, talking plainly and nakedly in a clear and beautiful room. The sense of escape, of being cleansed of unnecessary adhesions of any sort, is exquisite" (*Dream*, chap. V: 8).

Mr. Barnstaple, in *Men Like Gods* (1923), is as much struck by the "mental nakedness" of the Utopians as he is by their beautiful bodies. Their conversation is candid and free from concealments and pretensions. Ultimately, Mr. Barnstaple concludes that the whole life of the Utopians is "not only cleanly naked and sweet and lovely but full of personal dignity" (*Gods*, bk. III, chap. II: 6).[23]

Men may be willing to strip away garments that cloak a lovely body, but not all drapery conceals beauty. Nonetheless, the more naked a fact is, the better, for all disguise is pernicious. The wise Utopian Uthred exclaims, "These Earthlings still lack the habit of looking at reality—undraped" (*Gods*, bk. I, chap. VI: 5). The opposition of values is clearly stated in *The New Machiavelli* (1911) when the conservative Margaret tells her husband, Richard Remington:

> There's this difference that has always been between us, that you like naked-ness and wildness, and I, clothing and restraint. It goes through everything. You are always *talking* of order and system, and the splendid dream of the order that might replace the muddled system you hate, but by a sort of instinct you seem to want to break the law. (*Machiavelli*, bk. IV, chap. III: 5)

To appreciate nakedness one must be willing to face reality. When you have done that, you can truly value what is beautiful. Wells's treatment of nudity accords with his constellation of metaphors leading from jungle, to upland, to stars. He used nudity as an actual and metaphorical motif. Ann Veronica argues for the beauty of the body specifically but more generally is outraged by the thought "of all the beauty in the world that is covered up and overlaid" (*Veronica*, chap. V: 6 and chap. VIII: 5 and 8). It is the "wrappered life" of fears, conventions, and hypocrisies from which she struggles to escape, achieving freedom finally in her romance with Capes, who exclaims, "That wrappered life, as you call it—we've burnt the con-founded rags! Danced out of it! We're stark!" (*Veronica*, chap. XVI: 6).

Wells's metaphors for clean, frank communication reveal his basic physical associations of nudity and truth. He is explicit in *The Anatomy of Frustration* (1936). "Even to-day," he says, "candour shares the prejudice against nudism. There is a real resentment in most minds against people who talk or depict too nakedly" (*Frustration*, chap. XXII). Camelford in *The Autocracy of Mr. Parham* (1929) compares the institutions of man-kind to garments that must be let out or replaced (*Parham*, bk. II, chap. I). This Carlylean conceit is repeated in *The Holy Terror* (1939) when Richard Carstall declares that "the world needs some sort of scavenging, a burning-up of the old infected clothes, before it can get on to a new phase" (*Terror*, bk. I, chap. II: 7).

Although it is important for men to strip away the outmoded garments of old creeds, it is essential that they bare themselves to themselves. Imagi-nations as well as bodies may be disguised. Wells often gives his characters such glimpses of a world ungarbed. Mrs. Palace in *Brynhild* (1937) has a waking dream in which the world parades before her "wearing artificial faces, artificial bodies"; even familiar faces reveal themselves as masks. She anticipates a sudden stripping bare when everyone would cease to pose. What sort of things, she wonders, would run out or scuttle snarling for shelter? What, she wonders further, was behind "the fine arras of kindly gentility" of her own husband? "And what if presently she began to turn round and look for her own unmasked self?" (*Brynhild*, chap. II: 3).

The act of stripping away applies not only to the exposure of current conditions, or to the clearing away of useless social or political encumbrances, but to the very center of the self. Without this initial nudity, no other signifies. William Clissold describes what happens when, in the unprotected moments of a sleepless night, this involuntary divestiture occurs. "Then for all our resistances we find ourselves taken and stripped and put upon the rack of these blundering contradictions of standard and desire. Then come writings and cries. The angel and the ape appear" (*Clissold*, vol. II, bk. VI: 8). With morning, the self resumes its disguises and masks, eager to forget the revelations of the night. Clissold's images call up a comparison with medieval torture—some star-chamber device for extorting truth. But they also recall images of the operating table, even perhaps the distant House of Pain of Dr. Moreau, who dreamed of angelic humanity but who succeeded only in bringing pain among the apes. What Moreau imposed upon his man-animals was a system of lies; Wells taught the necessity of abandoning those lies. Prendick is literally stripped bare of civilization and culture on Moreau's island and is thus reduced to the ultimate truths of human nature which he can never after forget when he returns to the world of men, seeing always the hidden animal behind each human-seeming disguise.

Wells's final requirement is *utter* self-knowledge, a gift that he confers upon few of his characters. One of these is Christina Alberta, who when she brings herself before her own judgment does so with "cards on the table, everything in evidence, no etiquette, not a stitch on, X rays if necessary" (*Christina*, bk. I, chap. III: 3). Her salutary example begets amazement and admiration in others, particularly the susceptible Bobby Roothing, who is uneasy about this new directness. "Christina Alberta's thoughts and speech seemed to him to be moving about without a stitch on, like the people in some horrible Utopia by Wells" (*Christina*, bk. III, chap. III: 3).

This playful allusion brings us full circle. Unquestionably Wells wished to associate physical beauty and openness with intellectual beauty and openness. He identified uncloaked physical beauty with intellectual candor. We shall see later that he had a special metaphor for intellectual *clarity*, but for candor, nudity was his appropriate figure. As with all of his main metaphors, nudity was complex, acting at literal and metaphorical levels and representing both external and internal states. Like his other main metaphors, it sprang from a profound private sense of injury, frustration, and yearning. Although Wells used his metaphors consciously—as his teasing self-reference in *Christina Alberta's Father* shows—he was not therefore less obsessed by them. But he recognized the obsession, for, like the characters he applauded, he was relentless in self-examination and quick to yank away the protective shreds from any unattractive secrets in himself. Moreover, he had the wit to turn them to account.

Wells never overcame the anguish occasioned by his under-nourished, unattractive, fragile body. He hated the circumstances that had maimed him and, from an early age, associated nudity with bodily perfection and with honest communication. He yearned to strip away all ugly covering, all disguise, to reach the beauty or truth hidden beneath. Most wrapping up he connected with guilt, egotism, dishonesty, and disease. This entire complex of themes and images appears throughout *The Shape of Things to Come* (1933). Philip Raven, whose dream constitutes the body of the book, tells the narrator that he is not deceived by the complications that occupy politicians. "Complications are their life. *You* try to get all these complications out of the way. You are a stripper, a damned impatient stripper. I would be a stripper too if I hadn't the sort of job I have to do" (*Shape*, Introduction). The narrator—or Wells—observes that old forms of behavior have become "a dissolving and ragged curtain" but believes that a new type of behavior is emerging and draws a "pathological analogy" between the irregularities of growth in the body and in the "social corpus." The insanity of public economy following the world slump is like a disease preventing healthy growth, and the advancement of the European peoples beyond 1920 requires the purging of the chronic mental disease of hate (*Shape*, bk. I: 1, 3; bk. II: 3, 7). This vile infection is gone by the time the World State is established. What intervenes almost symbolically between the diseased world and the healthy World State is a prolonged epidemic of what the historian calls "maculated fever." "This obscure disease, hitherto known only as a disease of captive baboons, seems to have undergone some abrupt adaptation to the kindred habitat of the human body," he notes, thereby introducing a sly joke at mankind's expense, for much earlier, in "The Stolen Bacillus" (1894), Wells had described a bacterium that seemed to cause "the blue patches upon various monkeys" (*Shape*, bk. II: 10). The Anarchist who steals this germ believes it to be the cause of Asiatic cholera and plans to poison London's water supply with it, but the tube containing the liquid breaks accidentally and the Anarchist drinks the remainder, hoping to become a personal carrier of the disease. Actually he will become a spotted spectacle. Anarchism and egotism transform this pitiful creature into an outlandish mottled ape. There is no need, Wells implies, for any drug to make man that. *The Shape of Things to Come* confirms this diagnosis, for we learn there that the real disease afflicting man after his outburst of wars "may have been not the maculated fever at all, but the state of vulnerability to its infection. . . .

The actual pestilence was not the disease but the harvest of a weakness already prepared" (*Shape*, bk. II: 10).

In contrast to the disease-ridden past is the orderly future, which benefits from the services of the Educational Control. A photographic history demonstrates the results.

> As the student turns over the pages he sees man straighten himself again, grow physically, become more alert. The slouching foot-dragging men and women, the aimless faces, the fattish and lumpish figures of improperly nourished people, the wretched clothing and ignoble makeshift gear of the Second Decline and Fall, disappear; after 1990 clothing is fresh and simple, and after 2010 it begins to be austerely beautiful. (*Shape*, bk. IV: 4)

People of the old time wore clothing to indicate social prestige, a practice unnecessary in a society of equals. Corresponding to this simplicity of raiment is a simplicity and honesty of discourse.

Always set against Wells's image of health and simplicity is the contrary notion of disease which he binds to physical degeneracy but easily extends to social conditions. The disease motif runs throughout *Tono-Bungay* (1909).[24] Anything detrimental to man's communal well-being is a threat to the health of society. "The 'expert' quack and the bureaucratic intriguer increase and multiply in a dull-minded, uncritical, strenuous period as disease germs multiply in darkness and heat," Wells said before World War I (*Forces*, "Of the New Reign"). *The New World Order* (1940) constantly describes the diseased state of modern civilization and even the puff on the dust jacket begins, "To the near-mortal disease of human civilization Mr. Wells brings the sharp surgeon's knife of revolution and the health-producing diet of liberal culture and eternal values." I would not be surprised to learn that Wells wrote these words himself. A few years later he concluded in *The Happy Turning* (1945), "These are the unavoidable distresses of a sick world. There is no way out of it. Every human being is a poisoned human being. We are all infected. A thousand contagions are in our blood. There is no health in us" (*Turning*, chap. VII: 1). Sick baboons all with maculate fever. The cure did not take.

Wells was always trying to act as metaphoric surgeon to a sick world and constantly reiterated propositions for the physical improvement of the race. In a later chapter I shall discuss eugenics and birth control. Here it is enough to note that Wells's antiseptic proposals were rooted first in practical physical expedients even though they extended metaphorically to the more abstract conditions of the human race. Man was an animal in constant danger of degeneration; he was also a moral creature ever open to the infections of hatred, jealousy, and war. Undisciplined technological growth, undisciplined political ambition, and undisciplined propagation were all of a piece. If one could guide the race by eugenics, why not also by some organized and rational scheme of political and technical restraint?

Much as Wells praised physical beauty and promoted and yearned for a life of generous love, his own life was troubled throughout by a fierce image of fleshly sexuality. In *First and Last Things* (1908), he warned others against the very human weakness he suffered from—the idealization of crude experience. "Our minds fall very readily under the spell of such unmitigated words as Purity and Chastity," he wrote. "Only death beyond decay, absolute non-existence, can be Pure and Chaste" (*Things*, bk. I: 1). There is an echo here of that Decadent fascination with frustrating ideal purity that makes the real world loathsome, and Wells was surely affected by the Decadent writers so prominent in his formative years.[25] Still, he was more than an idealist. He fought against that subtle lure with a program of realistic investigation of the true nature of life as he had learned to perceive it in his scientific training.

In *The Anatomy of Frustration* (1936), Wells's mouthpiece admits, "My personal relations, and particularly my sexual history, have been in the main a story of puerile and primitive reactions by the way. . . . My character, my personality, has not kept pace with my wits" (*Frustration*, chap. XIX[c]). It takes only the briefest glance into his private relations with women to see how desperately Wells craved love, how unsettled and insecure he was without it. No wonder that he should candidly admit that the second main system of motive in the working out of his personal destiny was the sexual system. It is only fair to note that the first system deals with activities of the brain.

Wells assumed that men were capable of escaping the biological round. He hoped that men would utilize this new freedom to wise ends, and he recommended the system of his own *Modern Utopia* as an ideal. With very little irony he said that "if people were completely free to do anything they pleased in sexual matters, they would do, only more easily and happily, much the same things that we take great pains to insist they shall do and compel them to do now" (*Going*, chap. XVIII). His writings dwell upon sex because mankind does. He enjoined us to admit the obsession.

In numerous ways he urged men to strip life bare and not to swathe it in "feelings and self-projections," and yet that nakedness he so often championed could be terrifying (*Going*, chap. XX). In his early tales, written before he had achieved at least a superficial confidence and during the time his body continually reminded him of his frailty, nakedness was fearful not joyous. The Time Traveller, marooned in the future, says, "I felt naked in a strange world" (*Machine*, chap. III). All of *The Invisible Man* (1897) exploits the common dread of exposure. There is no shame in this nakedness, only endless vulnerability.

Wells fought bitterly against his fears, anxieties, and personal humiliations to create a picture of better circumstances for man. Despite his inability to control his own sexual appetite, he proposed regulations that would

direct and channel such powers profitably. Looking back from a more liberal age to the healthy but restrictive early days of the Modern State, the
dream historian of *The Shape of Things to Come* clearly approves the control of sensuous and emotional energy at that time.

> The new sexual puritanism differed from the old in its toleration of birth con-
> trol, its disregard of formal marriage, and a certain charity towards the first
> excesses of youth, but it insisted with even greater vigour upon public decency
> and upon the desirability of sexual seriousness, enduring connexions, and
> complete loyalty between lovers. As a result the world was far more monog-
> amous, more decorous and decently busy after 2000 C.E. than it had ever
> been before. (*Shape*, bk. V: 4)

This coupling of license with greater seriousness and restraint is not so
absurd as it first appears. As we shall see, apparent contradictions in
Wells's stories or tracts are frequently detailed examinations of one or
another feature of the complex polity of H. G. Wells. Once he had broken
free from conventional modes of thought and behavior and faced the challenge presented by external and internal nature, man had a more subtle
realm to explore—human identity itself.

# 4

## Identity:
## Self and
## Race

There seems never to have been a time when Wells was not conscious of the divisions within man and thus within himself. In "Human Evolution, An Artificial Process" (1896), Wells wrote that civilized man contains an inherited factor, the natural man, and an acquired factor, man as a product of tradition, suggestion, and reasoned thought. There is nothing remarkable about this assertion, but to this conviction of a division within the self, young Wells added the notion of mutability and uniqueness. He liked to toy with possibilities about the material universe and the self. Thus in an early version of *The Time Machine*, his Time Traveller says that psychology cannot help him understand what he has experienced because the mind represents, not conditions of the universe, but only necessities. "From my point of view the human consciousness is an immaterial something falling through this Rigid Universe of four dimensions, from the direction we call 'past' to the direction we call 'future,'" he says (*Early Writings*, chap. III). Before this, in "The Rediscovery of the Unique" (1891), Wells had declared his skepticism of human logic that tries to reduce the universe to a regularity that it does not really exhibit. Mankind, he objects, "is inoculated with the arithmetical virus; he lets a watch and a calendar blind him to the fact that every moment of his life is a miracle and a mystery" (*Early Writings*, chap. II).

Because he believed in the evanescent and mutable character of human identity, he speculated on some of its more extreme possibilities in his stories, exploiting the current taste for spiritualism and psychic research.[1] At the same time that he was writing about a scientific dimension beyond the normal, he was also writing about spiritual dimensions where the soul is freed from the body, as in "The Plattner Story" (1896) and "The Stolen Body" (1898). In "The Story of the Late Mr. Elvesham" (1896), Edward George Eden, whose spirit has been transferred from his youthful, healthy body to the wretched carcass of Egbert Elvesham, the aged student of mental science, rages, "Dreams of the personal identity indeed!" as he realizes that no one believes what has happened to him. "I have been a materialist for all my thinking life," he says, "but here suddenly, is a clear case of man's detachability from matter."

Although Wells seems never to have entertained a serious belief in a spiritual dominion beyond matter, he was always intrigued by the spiritual dominion within it. His speculations on human identity culminated finally with a thesis submitted to London University for the doctoral degree in 1943 entitled "A Thesis on the Quality of Illusion in the Continuity of the Individual Life in the Higher Metazoa, with Particular References to the Species Homo Sapiens." "It is the body that holds the mind together and not the mind the body," he wrote there. Moreover, that mind is various. The many "selves" in a human being are actually "a collection of mutually replaceable individual systems held together in a common habitation" (*'42*, Appendix I: 1). Wells worked his way gradually to this formulation and I shall return to it later in its proper place. Now I simply wish to indicate that Wells remained concerned about the issue of duality, which he approached in many different ways.[2]

In *The Anatomy of Frustration* (1936), Wells rejected the dualism of matter and spirit which, by suggesting a spiritual track parallel to the material one, offers the promise of immortality (*Frustration*, chap. III). But he took very seriously the incompatibility between conscious desires and unconscious impulses. The former, he says, "scarcely penetrate at all into that more primitive and substantial mass which is the true reservoir of motives and impulses" (*Frustration*, chap. VII).[3] If man is to survive, that dualistic approach must end. And it can only end if man honestly examines his conscious aspirations and his unconscious motivations.[4]

I have already mentioned Wells's demand that men face themselves nakedly, stripping themselves of all their protective illusions. Honesty with oneself was the ground base of his creed. Sometimes he treated the theme playfully. In "The Apple" (1896), a stranger gives young Mr. Hinchcliff an apple which he claims is the fruit of the Tree of Knowledge. Tasting it should yield absolute knowledge. This terrifies the stranger, but Mr. Hinchcliff claims not to fear knowledge. The stranger is chiefly troubled by the self-knowledge it might bring "—to know yourself, bare of your most intimate illusions." Hinchcliff is not awed by this prospect, but later, embarrassed to be seen carrying the apple as he approaches the village where he wishes to make a good impression as a new teacher, he throws the fruit away. This easily, Wells suggests, social convention makes cowards of us all.

Wells saw his career as a writer in terms of self-scrutiny. Rejecting

Arnold Bennett's attempt to compare his work to that of other writers, he declared, "For my own part I am a purblind laborious intelligence exploring that cell of Being called Wells and I resent your Balzac."[5] He knew what to expect from this scrutiny too, asserting that "all men are mixed in motive. . . . In all of us the intimations of a new world and a finer duty struggle to veil and control the ancient greeds and lusts of our inherited past" (*Outline*, chap. XI: 6 and chap. XXXVII: 2). He candidly reported the contradictions and inconsistencies he uncovered in himself ('*42*, pt. I: 1 and pt. II: 5).[6] Still, he kept up the investigation.

Wells did not believe in the unity of the self, but the subordination of warring elements within the self was one of his principal aims. That subordination was possible only through a confrontation with one's baser self, but it was equally important to face one's ideal self. Many pages into *A Modern Utopia* (1905), Wells discovers why he is *in* Utopia, that is, why he is writing it into existence—discovering it under his pen. He observes that "the idea of an encounter with my double, which came at first as if it were a witticism, as something verbal and surprising, begins to take substance. The idea grows in my mind that after all this is the 'someone' I am seeking, this Utopian self of mine." His Utopian self will be much different from his ordinary self and so the desire to discover it becomes overwhelming: "That I have come to Utopia is the lesser thing now; the greater is that I have come to meet myself" (*Utopia*, chap. VII: 3). As this work suggests, Wells did much of his self-examination publicly, shielded only by a thin veil of fiction; but he was entirely frank about himself and human personality in his autobiography, where he credits both physiological and environmental influences in the shaping of the self and asserts the malleability of personality. He also recognizes the role of the individual will in constructing his persona, which he defined as "the private conception a man has of himself" (*Autobiography*, chap. I: 2).

When he had been at the task of self-examination for several years, Wells concluded in *First and Last Things* (1908) that there was "a duality in life . . . so that we are at once absurd and full of sublimity, and most absurd when we are most anxious to render the real splendours that pervade us" (*Things*, bk. II: 7). Now and then he rendered the absurdity and the splendour together. In *The Wonderful Visit* (1895), Doctor Crump examines the Angel for mental problems, explaining that there is such a thing as double personality and citing the case of a man who "was sometimes English and right-handed, and sometimes Welsh and left-handed" (*Visit*, chap. XLI). But Crump is a fool whose example simply highlights the larger point of the novel that the true duality in man encompasses a banal daily self and an angelic potential. The only way the angelic ideal can be preserved is by leaving this world.

*The Sea Lady* (1902) makes a similar point in a different way. Chatteris is torn between two women representing two widely different outlooks on life. He is engaged to the worldly and commonplace Adeline Glendower, but attracted to the mermaid, Doris Thalassia Waters. The story describes the same conflict between "wide public interests" and the "swift rush of imaginative passion" evident in *Love and Mr. Lewisham* (1900) and *The New Machiavelli* (1911), yet beneath this conflict is a more immediate and personal one as Chatteris realizes (*Autobiography*, chap. VII: 4). We are human beings, he says; "we are matter with minds growing out of ourselves. We reach downward into the beautiful wonderland of matter and upward to something. . . . Man is a sort of half-way house—he must compromise" (*Lady*, chap. VII: 4). Of course Chatteris does not compromise. He chooses mystery, moonshine, and death.

*The Sea Lady* is a fanciful experiment; *The New Machiavelli* is more serious. At the outset Remington tells us that he will write of "the subtle protesting perplexing play of instinctive passion and desire against too abstract a dream of statesmanship." (*Machiavelli*, bk. I, chap. I: 1). The novel develops this subject but also broaches the allied theme of a divided self. In this case, Wells describes the self as composed of frontage and hinterland, of which the latter is more promising, for it is "a far more essential reality, a self less personal, less individualized, and broader in its reference" (*Machiavelli*, bk. III, chap. I: 1). It is the part of the self in touch with racial drives and yet, as a source of energy, the embryo of the ideal double Wells described in *A Modern Utopia*.

Wells's favored characters acknowledge themselves to be assemblages of motives, fears, impulses, and desires; they discover the separation between the frontage that works in the world and the hinterland that connects them with the flow of life. In *The Secret Places of the Heart* (1922), Sir Richmond Hardy believes that his alarm at the incipient breakup of civilization has generated his mental distress; but after his first visit to Dr. Martineau, he begins to consider the personal origins of his dismay.

> I am astonished to discover what a bundle of discordant motives I am. I do not seem to deserve to be called a personality. I cannot discover even a general direction. Much more am I like a taxi-cab in which all sorts of aims and desires have travelled to their destination and got out. Are we all like that?

Martineau replies that man's personality is held together by "leading ideas, associations, possessions, liabilities" which Hardy describes as "a prison of circumstances that keeps us from complete dispersal." There is also "a consistency, that we call character," which, though it changes, changes consistently with itself (*Heart*, chap. IV: 2).

Arnold Blettsworthy of *Mr. Blettsworthy on Rampole Island* (1928) admits his own self-division at the start of his narrative. Written with a subtitle and chapter headings that hint at early tales of fanciful exploration and adventure such as *Peter Wilkins* or *Candide*, to which the novel is dedicated, *Mr. Blettsworthy* is a modern voyage of discovery into the human psyche whose central adventure begins when the gentle Blettsworthy is betrayed in love. His violent response makes him doubt his own nature and forces him to an examination of his identity. "Was Arnold Blettsworthy no better than the name and shell of a conflicting mass of selves?" he asks (*Blettsworthy*, chap. I: 6). He cannot reconcile the newly emergent Angry and Lustful Egoist with the upright Blettsworthy who knows the standards of honour and goodwill or with the Cynical Observer who impugns his earlier values. Blettsworthy has been shocked out of complacent assurance into a realization that the self is not automatically or permanently fixed and secure. It is a tangle of impulses and dreads organized by relaxation into tradition and habit, submission to dogma, or imposition of the will.

Blettsworthy's lawyer recommends that he travel to forget his misfortune and recover his peace of mind, and so the young man sets out on a voyage that will lead him into parabolic depths of human nature. It is a far more persuasive journey than Sir Richmond Hardy's similarly suggestive tour of England's archeological monuments. Blettsworthy had never questioned his benevolent creed until betrayal revealed horrors within him. Now, amidst an uproar of Nature at sea and en route to a new world, he reviews his situation.

> The broadest fact, the foundation fact so to speak, of the situation, was this, that I had started out in life with the completest confidence in myself, mankind and nature, and all that confidence was gone. I had lost all assurance in my personal character; I had become alien to and afraid of my fellow creatures and now my body was in hideous discord with the entirely inhospitable world into which it had come. (*Blettsworthy*, chap. II: 5)

Much of the novel is an account of Blettsworthy's adventures among the savages of Rampole Island, which account constitutes a vicious, sometimes crude satire upon modern civilization but which also plumbs certain traits of human character. Later, Dr. Minchett explains that for a period of four and a half years Blettsworthy has been living with a divided personality, his practical self going about doing commonplace things, while "all the while it was nothing but a detached part, a hewer of wood and a drawer of water for the main romancing complex of [his] brain," which accepted the hallucination of Rampole Island (*Blettsworthy*, chap. IV: 2). The pattern is normal, says Dr. Minchett; Blettsworthy's case is simply an extreme example.

The result of Blettsworthy's experiences is that he cannot afterward bring himself to trust mankind. The characteristically clever and self-reflexive dialogue that ends the novel projects two important features of

Wells's own personality. The inveterate planner Lyulph Graves argues that better times are coming, that great adventures are ahead for mankind, whereas Blettsworthy, who cannot shake off his memories of Rampole Island any more than Prendick could forget Moreau's Island, doubts that humanity is capable of any advance. He is not persuaded by arguments about an improved educational system and the wonders open to men who have learned self-discipline in the service of their kind. But Wells gives his ebullient, if somewhat undependable, projector Graves/Wells the last word. "You are the doubter—always," he says to Blettsworthy/Wells. "Take my word for it—it is your Rampole Island that will pass away, and I who will come true" (*Blettsworthy*, chap. IV: 14).[7]

There is no resolution, just an expression of hope at the end of *Mr. Blettsworthy*, but the dialogue that concludes that novel did not end there. Wells kept it up without much change until, old and weary, he found himself on Rampole Island again and wrote *Mind at the End of Its Tether* (1945). Some of the later variations on this theme are worth looking at. For example, in *The Bulpington of Blup* (1933) Wells developed the possibility of a Blettsworthian mind choosing to stay in its dream world. Theodore Bulpington's fantasy world, composed of lies and falsifications, finally pervades his daily life, smothering reality. His retreat is an act of cowardice and egoism, not transcendence.

The situation is somewhat different for women, who, according to Wells, cannot hold themselves together with an abstract concept. Brynhild Palace in *Brynhild* (1937) wishes to follow her father's advice. "The one precious thing in life," he told her, "is integrity—an inner integrity." His oath to himself becomes a guidepost to her. "May the Almighty damn and destroy me utterly and for ever, if I compromise in one particle when I am thinking in my own private thoughts" (*Brynhild*, chap. IX: 5). This assertion is the antidote to Bulpingtonism. But Brynhild is a woman who clearly acknowledges that "*the will of a woman is different from a man's*" (*Brynhild*, chap. IX: 7). So she aims at no vast scientific, educational, or political scheme as one of Wells's heroes might. Instead she makes the amazing decision (for a Wells character) to retreat behind a facade and live her real life within herself, but this resolution is because she has determined to bear children and raise them as rebels against the falseness of the society represented by her husband (*Brynhild*, Envoy).

In the same year as *Brynhild* Wells published an odd fantasy entitled *Star-Begotten* (1937) in which he summarized his attitude toward human personality and offered a fresh version of his usual solution. As a boy, Joseph Davis, though instructed in the utter reality of the institutions of his time—church, monarchy, social hierarchy, and so on—perceives a clear dualism between the world-that-is and the world-that-might-be. He is puzzled that the ostensible world that is an accumulation of falsity remains a going concern. He is uncomfortable in this universe because for him the world seems "translucent and a little threadbare, and as though something else quite different lay behind it" (*Star*, chap. I: 2). As an adult, Davis is assailed by a "mental duplicity," a doubt of himself which prevents him from writing his *Grand Parade of Humanity* (*Star*, chap. I: 3), and he develops a theory that Martians are creating a new kind of being among humans.

The benign invasion of humanity by superior Martians is just another way of distinguishing the animal and the angel or, more correctly, the mundane and the ideal elements in man's composition. But Wells goes on to clarify a point implicit in his earlier suggestions for self-unification. In order to bring the warring parts of the self together in harmony, one must believe that there is a similar unity in Nature. Keppel explains that one hindrance to the full development of the human mind is the insidious belief in a secondary—spirit or ghost—world, a belief that has lodged itself in language and in everyday assumptions. Thus for every man we assume a spirit and for the universe a Great Spirit. But this assumption of a spirit world is a dangerous trap.

> Whenever the mental going is a bit hard, whenever our intellectual eyes feel the glare of truth, we lose focus and slither off into Ghostland. Ghostland is half-way to dreamland, where *all* rational checks are lost. In Ghostland, that world of the spirit, you can find unlimited justifications for your impulses; unlimited from rational obligation. That's my main charge against the human mind; this persistent confusing dualism. The last achievement of the human mind is to see life simply and see it whole." (*Star*, chap. VIII: 5)

This is a stylized and simplified resolution to the problem of the divided self, but perhaps more helpful to critics as a result. Man's inner division begins with a rudimentary sense of the unreality of all those social factors that constitute his "world," combined with a confusion about traits in himself which he can identify as related to the world of matter and those that seem divorced from material operations. Wells stated the case unequivocally in *The Work, Wealth and Happiness of Mankind* (1932).

> From his very dawn into the world *Homo sapiens* is a creature at war within himself; he has a moral conflict; he controls his impulses, he does things that he dislikes, and in particular he toils to escape other possibilities that he fears will be even less agreeable. This internal conflict is essential to the nature of man. He can never escape from it; never return to the simple internal unanimity; the "state of innocence," the direct unencumbered reactions, of lower animal types. (*Work*, chap. VIII: 1)

This is what *The Island of Dr. Moreau* has to say in parabolic form. In a discarded version of the story, the message is more explicit than in the finished narrative, for Montgomery says to Prendick that his presence on the island has reminded him what a horrible thing he and Moreau have done in transforming happily balanced brutes into caricatures of God's image at war with themselves. The beast people have a notion of morality that is their worst acquisition.[8] To mediate this inevitable conflict, two things are necessary—to perceive the essential unity of all life and to act positively on that perception. In a later chapter I shall discuss some forms of action that Wells recommended.

*Star-Begotten* is too diagrammatic to be a genuine solution to anything. It is more blueprint than narrative. But in other late novels, some of them unfairly neglected, Wells could be subtler and more expansive. *Apropos of Dolores* (1938) is not about personal identity, but the subject comes up frequently and underlies the larger themes of the novel. The optimistic Stephen Wilbeck believes that "there is a magnificent bias for truth in the heart of man," and thus old images of the cosmos and of the self gradually pass away and new ones form (*Dolores*, chap. II: 3). More than his philosophical friend Foxfield, Wilbeck believes that man can adapt to the rapidly changing circumstances of his life and has faith in the speed with which education can wean a generation from old feelings. He expounds his views in a monologue addressed to a pony. The animal has powerful senses and reactions but cannot think "I am" or "I ought to be." "But," Wilbeck continues, "I am one of these thinking beasts who have been afflicting the world and ourselves for the last few hundred thousand years or so. We have got a new thinking and co-operating apparatus called language and in some ways it has proved remarkably efficient," for it has provided man with a freedom and power to shape events and material circumstances unknown to any other creature. It also brings dismay and sleepless nights. "You may be man-rid," Wilbeck says to the pony, "but I am brain-rid. And as uncertain of the journey ahead." Nonetheless, there is great hope, for it is obvious to Wilbeck that the brain itself is adapting and evolving. "First the evolution of the conscious brain gathered *Homo* up into an individual egotism like a clenched fist, and then it (Nature or the Life Force or what you will) seemed to realize it had gone too far and turned upon itself. And so we have our moral conflict" (*Dolores*, chap. V: 6).

Through most of the novel Wilbeck has before him an example of the rudimentary level of brain evolution—the furious egotism of his wife, Dolores, whose personality is powerful but disorderly. Hers is an undigested, accumulated self governed by egotism alone. Wilbeck believes that there is something in him which goes beyond her crude egotism and makes him better.[9] To get beyond the self, to see life simply and whole is the answer. But men are still evolving and are caught in a quandary between brain, egotism, and heart. The best compromise with life, Wilbeck reflects, "must be to obey our reason as far as we can, play our rôle that is to say, sublimate or restrain our deep-seated instinct for malicious mischief, and gratify what we can of our heart's desire, so far as and in such manner as, our consciences approve" (*Dolores*, chap. VII: 3).

*Apropos of Dolores* is not primarily about human personality, but *Babes in the Darkling Wood* (1940) is. Its main action is the return of a troubled mind to health, its main intent a focusing of human energy toward the creation of a World State where race-purpose replaces ego-purpose. And underlying this action and this intent is a conception of the self more thoroughly set forth than elsewhere in Wells's fiction. If men can accept this vision of the human self, he suggests, they will be more suited to accomplish the great ends he proposes. The fictitious theorist, Cottenham C. Bower, dismisses notions such as "soul, spirit, mind" as begging the question and asserts that man is not a simple unified mind or psyche at all, but a "neuro-sensitive apparatus" that extends all over the body. The multiple reaction systems in the individual "have a common core in his belief that he is really one person, because they are not only all aboard the same body, but also built round a similar conception of himself, his 'persona,' as Jung has it. But really, says the Behaviourist, they are *a collection of mutually replaceable individual systems held together in a common habitation*" (*Babes*, bk. II, chap. II: 4).

When Gemini requires psychological help, Stella's Uncle Robert, whose views about human personality resemble Cottenham C. Bower's, undertakes the cure. He rejects the notion of a unified self, yet his cure involves returning Gemini to the personality he had before his war experiences and his sexual infidelity made him pessimistic and impotent. Uncle Robert begins the cure by reasoning with Gemini about the world situation, and Stella completes the job by taking Gemini back to the setting of their early love tryst and arousing sexual desire in him. After his recovery, Gemini concludes that "the one and sole *reality* in human life is mental. . . . Our selves are the mental assemblage of our activities." Actions are the realizations of ideas, and man's mastery over life depends upon knowledge and clear thought. Each individual, by improving his mind, is like the individual polyp contributing to the huge mental reef that will harbor the Hope and Will of man.

Though Wells's notion of the self became more complex, it remained basically consistent. It is healthy to remember that the discipline of psychology was growing up concurrently with Wells himself. Necessarily, later articulations of his ideas are more sophisticated. His reading of William James and then of Freud, Jung, and Adler, and then of Pavlov and Watson, helped him to expand and refine his views. He admits his debt to these psychological experimenters in his doctoral thesis and in *The Conquest of Time* (1942). In these two works Wells reemphasized in a more pedantic manner the notions aired in his fiction. The self he called "a *serviceable synthetic illusion of continuity* that holds the individual behaviour together" (*Conquest*, chap. III). The illusion of a detached ego worked well enough "to stampede the dawning human intelligence" (*Conquest*, chap. VII). Now, however, the individual ego must subordinate itself to the common creative task "which is the conquest and animation of the universe by life" (*Conquest*, chap. X). The self is an illusion pieced together from moment to moment; it is a self-conscious part of a larger life.

Wells believed that the inner self was divided or multiple, but he also insisted that there was a division between inner and outer self. In *First and Last Things* (1908), he announced his belief that the external and the internal and himself made one universe in which every part was ultimately important. Conceding that this was an arbitrary and essentially indefensible belief, he nonetheless asserted, "I dismiss the idea that life is chaotic because it leaves my life ineffectual, and I cannot contemplate an ineffectual life patiently" (*Things*, bk. II: 1).

Although Wells's working hypothesis assumed the oneness of the universe, his habit of mind was toward polarities, and the polarities he perceived were rooted in essential attributes of mind. In *Experiment in Autobiography* (1934), for example, he compared his mind to his friend Lord Northcliffe's. "Mine was a system of digested and assimilated ideas; it was an assembled mind; his was a vast jumble into which fresh experiences were for ever tumbling" (*Autobiography*, chap. VI: 4). Add a strong dose of egotism to Northcliffe and one has the contrast that Wilbeck draws between himself and Dolores.

Time and again Wells described similar oppositions of temperament. Very often the contrasts are sexual.[10] In *The Research Magnificent* (1915), "Amanda loved wild and picturesque things, and Benham strong and clear things; the vines and brushwood amidst the ruins of Salona that had delighted her had filled him with a sense of tragic retrogression" (*Research*, chap. IV: 1). But it would be a mistake to assume that Wells endorsed one outlook over another automatically. In *The New Machiavelli* (1911), Margaret, who inclines to obey laws, might appear to be a favored character, whereas our sympathies are actually solicited for Remington, who *talks* about order and system but who inclines to lawlessness. Remington is both maker and destroyer, with a strong emphasis on destruction first.[11] Trafford explains this apparent inconsistency in *Marriage* (1912): "Organization and genius are antipathetic. The vivid and creative mind, by virtue of its qualities, is a spasmodic and adventurous mind; it resents blinkers, and the mere implication that it can be driven in harness to the unexpected. It demands freedom" (*Marriage*, bk. I, chap. V: 2).

Wells knew his own mind to be both orderly and impulsive, capable of logical thought, yet given to imaginative flights, determined to compose constructive plans, but delighting in the demolition of the hateful and hurtful. His mind contained multitudes. He vacillated and was aware of his vacillations. For the most part, however, he resolved these alterations in terms of basic polarities. He did not draw absolute distinctions but presented opposites, opposites that changed from one depiction to the next. Thus in *Boon* (1915), Reginald Bliss contrasts Boon's nature with his own. "His was indeed essentially one of those suspended minds that float above the will and action; when at last reality could be evaded no longer it killed him; he never really believed nor felt the urgent need that goads my more accurate nature to believe and do" (*Boon*, chap. I: 2). This seems to be no more than the traditional philosophical distinction between the competing merits of a life of contemplation or one of action, but Wells does not have that philosophical chestnut in mind, for both Boon and Bliss are Wells. The polarity Wells describes is both internal and external. Much later, in *Babes in the Darkling Wood* (1940), he cloaks the idea in psychological terminology when he has Gemini declare "that every impulse to act in a human being and maybe in every animal with a cerebrum, carries with it a countervailing disinclination, just as every visible body casts a shadow" (*Babes*, bk. IV, chap. I: 3).

In his very early work Wells drew this distinction more simply. "Every poor mortal is torn by the conflicting dreads of being 'commonplace,' and of being 'eccentric.' He, and more particularly she, is continually imitating and avoiding imitation, trying to be singular and yet like other people," he wrote in "Of Conversation and the Anatomy of Fashion" (1895) (*Uncle*). This rather commonplace social observation became more complicated as Wells pursued it from book to book. Many of his major characters manifest such vacillations of spirit. The trait is a rudimentary attribute of Remington's being, finally tearing him from the world of action and offering him instead the seclusion of love. Other characters, such as Benham, Trafford, George Ponderevo, and William Clissold, feel conflicting calls to an active life amidst the crowd and to contemplative retirement. In *A Modern Utopia* (1905), Wells explained that the soul of man is in perpetual vacillation between the desire to assert individual difference and the terror of isolation (*Utopia*, chap. X: 1).

Wells's declared belief was in the unity of existence, but he did not entirely escape the conventional outlook of his day that divided things into dualities, beginning with assumptions of good and evil, man and beast, matter and spirit. He attributed the divisions that he discovered in individual nature to the community at large. In *New Worlds for Old* (1907), he described the collective mind as "afflicted with a division within itself that is strictly analogous to that strange mental disorder, which is known to psychologists as multiple personality." Socialism, Wells explained, was one attempt of this divided mind "to pull itself together, to develop and establish a governing idea of itself" (*New Worlds*, chap. XIII: 3).[12] As we have already seen, this is precisely what socialism and later his schemes for a New Republic, a Utopia, and a World State were for Wells. He had characters like William Clissold say it for him, but he admitted it directly in nonfictional books from *First and Last Things* to *The Conquest of Time*.

When he wished to be simple and direct, Wells carried his perception of human duality to extreme degrees, even to abstraction, as he did in *The King Who Was a King* (1929), which employs an allegory of the conflict between Man the Maker and Man the Destroyer. Wells had already gone further than this in *God, the Invisible King* (1917) where he established a similar opposition between conceptions of God as Creator or Redeemer. The one was identifiable with Nature, aloofness, and awe, and Wells rejected him; the other was the absolute God of the human heart whom Wells embraced. This duality is yet another version of the basic antagonism Wells had learned to recognize from Huxley—the conflict of man with Nature. God the Creator is Nature, but God the Redeemer is the power that turns individuals away from their selves to serve the developing purpose of the race.

I have said that Wells used his characters as representatives of opposing human types, but there is a variation on this method, for often the antagonists share a bond that hints at their occult union. This device is most obvious in *The King Who Was a King*, to which I have just alluded. Paul Zelinka represents the disciplined, constructive power of man. He is simple and direct, and represents Man the Maker. His cousin and nemesis, Prince Michael, is not an exact opposite, not anarchic and wild. Instead he and his followers are like fascists, employing an external discipline to gratify a feral ego. He represents Man the Destroyer. Ultimately Paul exorcises Michael with a bullet.

*The Brothers* (1938) has the same Ruritanian setting and the same theme, though it is more complicated. Richard Bolaris seeks to become Master Citizen of his nation by overthrowing the government. By chance his antagonist, Robert Ratzel, falls into Bolaris's hands, and they soon discover that they are twin brothers. Brought up in a working-class home, Ratzel has proletarian sympathies that make him the authoritarian Bolaris's apparent opposite. But as they exchange histories and convictions, the two men discover their resemblances. Both broke a leg at age fifteen, thereby giving them a time of enforced leisure during which they read hungrily and developed their views of the universe. The same thing happened to Wells. Both men conceived a strong indignation about the existing social and political structure, feeling, as young Wells did, that it prevented the emergence of a truly free world. Rapidly it becomes clear that both seek power in order to discipline men in the service of a new world. The two brothers join forces to work for the new world, but the story does not end happily, for both die at the hands of Handon, Bolaris's militaristic and reactionary second-in-command.

*The Brothers* is a particularly obvious example of Wells's projection of an internal conflict to an external opposition of characters, but he had been doing this for some time. I have already referred to the playful manner in which the Voice of *A Modern Utopia* (1905) realizes that he is seeking a Utopian double in his excursions through that wonderful world. But there is another joke in the characters of this tale, for while the Voice addressing us may be taken as Wells the idealist, his odd companion, called the botanist, a man of exactly Wells's age, represents human types whose scientific attitudes are flawed by a tendency "to conceal and shape their sensuous cravings beneath egregious sentimentalities, they get into mighty tangles and troubles with women" (*Utopia*, "The Owner of the Voice"). In short, just as the Voice is an exaggeration of the idealistic side of Wells, the botanist caricatures his worldly self. Moreover, it is the emotional weakness of the botanist which destroys the Utopian illusion and whisks both men back to the ordinary world. Wells explained that he offered this conversing pair in the setting of Utopia to overcome the difficulty of rendering a utopia that must include general ideas as well as individualities. The pair, who are opposed just as the elements of the narrative are opposed—ideal and real— embody the conflict of the mind itself.

Wells was not always this obvious about the linked couples he used to display his ideas. I have already noted the oppositions that are not compatible and do not represent clear projections of Wells's own sense of division—as with Remington and Margaret in *The New Machiavelli* and Wilbeck and Dolores in *Apropos of Dolores*—and I have mentioned the brief and humorous opposition of Reginald Bliss and Boon in *Boon*, which imitates the technique of *A Modern Utopia* distantly, a technique repeated in *The Shape of Things to Come* (1933), where Philip Raven, the creator of the dream history, is the differing double of the editor who presents it to us. But it is in pairs, from the narrator and Time Traveller of *The Time Machine*, Graham and Ostrog, Teddy Broxted and Theodore Bulpington, Benham and Prothero, William and Dickon Clissold, or Wilbeck and Foxfield, that we see Wells working out in dual characterization the divergent impulses in his own nature. Graham and Ostrog represent two contending political sentiments that tempted Wells—rule by the common man or leadership by an elite. Wells later tried to resolve this issue in *The Brothers*. Teddy Broxted is levelheaded science and Theodore Bulpington esthetic dreaming. Benham and Prothero are also two aspects of Wells, with Benham the idealist who "looked to Prothero to keep him real."

Wells's ideas, modern as they seemed to himself and his contemporaries, had their roots in attitudes developed in the thought and literature of the nineteenth century, which Wells was so eager to put behind him. His plea that men learn "to see life simply and see it whole" echoes Arnold, and his division of society into opposing dualities owes something to Arnold's Hebraism and Hellenism, just as his view of man's divided self owes something to Arnold's claim that man has an ordinary and a buried or better self. His structure of that self as a contending triad of "brain, egotism, and heart" resembles Meredith's ascending pattern of blood, brain, and spirit. And Wells's conviction that language, the symbolization of thought, was the only reality, was akin to Tennyson's belief that language was the authentic connection between an illusory material world and a true spiritual realm.

I offer these fairly obvious connections from literature because I do not have the time to develop here the many strands of political, social, scientific, and metaphysical thought that contributed to Wells's views. What I wish to emphasize is the wholeness of Wells's vision, not its originality. If we turn to Wells's theories of human personality, we see that in fiction he had been forestalled by Robert Louis Stevenson and other writers who had perceived the dual nature of the self and theoretically by early psychologists and even by an amateur like Frederic W. H. Myers, who wrote in *The Human Personality and its Survival of Bodily Death* (1903) that "our psychical unity is federative and unstable; it has arisen from irregular accretions in the remote past; it consists even now only in the limited collaboration of multiple groups."[13]

The ideas that Wells assembled into a consistent perception of existence were abroad, then, and I do not intend to give him credit for formulating any new philosophical notions. He was an assimilator. But the virtue of such assimilating and synthesizing is that it can create a clear, yet complex, view. Wells was always conscious of the writer's power to shape human consciousness. He stated more than once—and I have quoted him—that fixed forms, from material features of the world to human personality, were illusions. What Wells despised above everything was what we might call the domesticated imagination—the human mind closed to speculation. In *The Croquet Player* (1936), he made his narrator an idling sort of fellow who has converted his imagination into a pet that he likes to play with. "I do not think it will ever claw me seriously," he says; "it's a pussy now which knows where to stop." Even this emasculation of the imagination is courageous, however, compared to the normal human attitude as represented by Frobisher's aunt, who "flies into a regular passion at the suggestion that anything irregular or unusual can ever occur" (*Croquet*, "The Skull in the Museum").

Wells understood very early in his career that human perception was heavily dependent upon convention and that to see something new was a great achievement. Discussing astronomers' anticipations of some change on the surface of the moon, he wrote in "The Visibility of Change in the Moon" (1895), "Yet it may be that already such change has happened in the field of some watching telescope, and only escaped observation because the eye that watched was set against the expectation of change" (*Early Writings*, chap. IV). Much of Wells's writing dealt directly with this inability of the conditioned eye, the conditioned mind, to perceive the reality of change. But there was another hindrance to human understanding more rudimentary than the blinkers of convention. Wells expressed it many times in many ways, but he expressed it most vividly in *The Brothers*. Bolaris wonders near the end of this tale if the world is really reasonable, as the man of science supposes, "or are the ruling patterns of life something quite different? Running right across all that we think rational—some perversity?" Suppose, he asks his lover and companion, that what we call words and reasoning have only a chance fit upon reality, that the real world, though systematic "has an irrational but elaborate order that diverges more and more from the order in our minds." If that is so, Bolaris concludes, "then all the views of life and its courses that we conceive, are no more than echoes made by the patterns in our eyes and brains." Bolaris decides that men cannot endure that version of reality and foresees instead a time when "the scale of our lives and the starry intervals, will cease to be a disharmony" (*Brothers*, chap. VI: 3).

The vision of flux, of the inescapable elusiveness of reality could be terrifying or inspiriting. For if man could not, by his very nature, perceive the scheme of all of Nature that did not think, he could nonetheless give that external Nature any form he chose. In a later chapter I shall take up this subject in detail, for it is at the very root of Wells's achievement; but for the time being it is enough to say that he perceived Nature and human personality as atomized matter capable of reconstitution, just as Gestalt psychologists describe the form-creating power of the human mind.

If we keep this fundamental belief in mind, it is easier to reconcile Wells's uniform view of the universe with his habitually dualistic representation of it. You will recall that Wells had Stephen Wilbeck describe the evolution of human consciousness as Nature or the Life Force gathering the conscious brain into an individual egotism and then realizing that it had gone too far and turning upon itself. Within the greater unity of all Being, a conflict is in progress between Will and Consciousness. Drawn from Schopenhauer and filtered through Nietzsche, Hartmann, and Shaw, this dualistic view replaced the old perception of good and evil, beast and man, body and spirit, though the old terms could still be used to gain effects with an audience unprepared for new terminology and new perceptions at the same time. Of course Wells came to the full import of his ideas only with the passage of time, and his late works are more precise than most early statements. Nonetheless, the underlying assumptions remain the same.

Wells's social experiences and the lessons he learned as a science student taught him that life was a struggle. Calvinism and Huxley both instructed him that suffering and pain were necessary in shaping character.[14] The new evolutionary ideas had appropriated a basic Victorian moral value to their own ends. But Wells soon discovered that external conflicts were not always the most important ones, that often the serious conflicts were internal. His earliest conception of these internal struggles was dualistic—ape and angel, impulse and idea, body and mind. Later, though they retained this essential division, his perceptions of the self became more complex. Always, however, they called for the same solution. Rather than allow plastic human personality to receive its shape from chance and circumstance, man should seize control of his own nature and shape it to his desires through the action of his disciplined will. Unity in the self, as in the race, would have to be man's own invention.

In his life and in his craft Wells exploited this sense of embattlement and struggle. What better way to train the will than to set it in opposition to some undesirable power? Wells was a polemicist perhaps by nature, but certainly by choice. Contention was his meat and drink. It was a device to give his own warring impulses shape and direction.[15] When the ineffectual Trumber in *The Camford Visitation* (1937) tells Vicar Bream that he has heard a Voice challenging his views on education, Bream replies that this Voice is "the projection of a long-standing conflict in your subconscious between the aesthetic pretentions of your criticism and your suppressed sense of its lack of spiritual value." Although Bream is not a character Wells would endorse completely, he does express a Wellsian opinion when he goes on to say that "in everyone, in everyone, even in God's holy saints, there is an undercurrent of adverse self-criticism in the subconscious. There is an interrogation—an opposition to whatever direction you have given your life." Unsureness, he adds, "is integral to human life. The mind would have no play without it" (*Camford*, chap. II).

Wells was more willing than most men to live with and even exploit that unsureness, which is merely another way of stating his conviction that all things are provisional. Time and again he tried to show men that liberating their minds from settled assumptions might be helpful. In 1927, he expressed his concern about a revival of spiritualism because spiritualism assumed the complete and incurable integrity of the eternal human person from the rest of the universe, whereas he wished to persuade men that "we may be but parts of a larger whole, as the quivering cells in our living bodies are parts of us" (*Going*, chap. XXVII).

This clinging to individuality and the concrete ego was a version for Wells of the "still raw humanity" that held the race back from stupendous achievements (*Outline*, chap. XXIII: 3). Adventuring—not entirely fearlessly, but bravely—into his own self, he faced the chaos of impulses and ideas that hindered him personally from accomplishing all that he desired. Once again, the individual is a small model of the race, and Wells is the test case. He put this matter rather charmingly in a late fable *All Aboard for Ararat* (1940) where God explains to his modern Noah that from the moment he created the universe, he had a shadow. " 'That,' said God, 'is what your philosopher Hegel is fumbling about when he says that nothing can exist without its contradiction' " (*Ararat*, chap. I: 2).[16] This applies to man as well; as he grows clearer and firmer, he too casts a shadow. The contraries cannot be abolished, but they can be subordinated. Man, for example, will remain a complex assemblage of discrete response systems, but he might be able to govern them. Mr. Lammock, the new Noah, has read his Behaviorists and accepts their theory that repudiates the idea "of any primary unity in man, and wrenches the mind round to the conception of an assembling mentality struggling to impose order upon an indifferent chaos, without and within." Going beyond the Behaviorists, Lammock adds, "It *is* not, it strives to *be*. Unity, co-operation, harmony, the strong peace of mankind, the real creation of the world, lies ahead of us if we can win it" (*Ararat*, chap. II: 5).[17]

Because Wells recognized this contention within himself and assumed it in all men, he made virtue of the ordeal by converting his fictions into laboratories where he could test possibilities of himself. What if I had turned another way? he seems to have asked himself in creating those antithetical "brothers" to his chosen role in life—the Parhams, Bulpingtons, or Whitlows. Wells found these figures—their aspirations, fears, weaknesses, and strengths—in himself. He let them out like circus animals to perform in the safe cages of his fiction. Like that other trainer of circus animals, W. B. Yeats, he comprehended fully the worth of that Mask which reveals the self to the self, and like Jung, whose theories he preferred to Freud's, he understood the meaning of the anima and the persona. Unlike Yeats, Wells did not believe that the scheme of man's nature or his destiny was predictable. Today he is seen as a materialistic champion of science; we call him a realist in literature and in social thought. But he was never thus deceived about himself. For him, the self was a misty dream mysteriously encompassing a tempest of fear and desire. It was a dream that could freeze into a dangerous rigor or congeal momentarily to a shape worthwhile for temporary ends but pretending to no permanence. And because he believed that the individual self was such a shapeless but shapable force, he believed as well that all of mankind was similarly unshaped but shapable. He saw his destiny as that atom of the whole, who, by making a version of the dream seem vividly real, created a finer destiny for mankind.

In *The Conquest of Time* (1942), Wells set out more concisely and conclusively than in any other place I can think of his picture of the universe, emphasizing the creative effort necessary to man's improvement in the face of mystery.

> It may be well for greater clearness and emphasis to repeat what has been said here. The past and future *exist permanently* in this universe, and our consciousness is a series of delusively unified conditioned reflexes. That illusion of a unified personality joins up a series of traces which constitute our conscious life, and this conscious life *takes the form* of a fall or flight, along the spatial dimension we call time. It is a rigid form. From the standpoint of the space-time-continuum there is no movement; the whole system is rigid. It is simply from the subjective and illusory point of view that there seems to be free movement. The four-dimensional universe is rigid, Calvinistic, predestinate; the personal life is not a freedom, though it seems to us to be a freedom; it is a small subjective pattern of freedom in an unchanging all. There is no conflict between fate and free will; they are major and minor aspects of existence. The major aspect of life is Destiny; the minor is that we do not know our destiny. We struggle because we must; and that struggle *is* life; but the parts of the drama we enact belong to a system that has neither beginning nor end. (*Conquest*, Appendix II)

Wells was not preoccupied with the tribulations and opportunities of the individual. Always he saw the individual as a functioning unit in a larger organism. Man meant men but also Mankind, which was, like the individual, a unity composed of millions of independent cells. Just as the individual had to create the drama it enacted through time, so Mankind, through the Mind of the Race, had also to fashion its own drama to fulfill. We shall return to this idea in a later chapter, but for the time being, it is worthwhile to note how important it was for Wells to see men as units contributing to a whole, not as random particles.

Wells cited Schopenhauer as a pioneer who pictured individual wills as temporary manifestations of an ampler will, but modified that philosopher's pessimism with the great truths revealed by Darwin, by which he meant the possibility of conscious evolution. Each individual is a contributing part of that larger life, and it is in that larger life that he discovers purpose, for by admitting his relationship to a larger Being, man's warring motives are reconciled, he achieves both concentration of himself and self-escape. The merging of the self with a greater reality paradoxically intensifies its consciousness of itself. Wells explains by way of an image: "The race flows through us, the race is the drama and we are the incidents." Then he is more direct: "In so far as we realize ourselves as experiments of the species for the species, just in so far do we escape from the accidental and the chaotic. We are episodes in an experience greater than ourselves" (*Things*, bk. II: 9).[18]

Herbert Spencer had established the metaphor of the Social Organism as one of several nineteenth-century schemes directed toward seeing mankind as unified in its aims.[19] Wells did not appreciate Spencer's conclusions, but he appropriated the organic concept, tempered by Huxley's picture of man in *Man's Place in Nature*. Wells took the organic image seriously. "It is not a metaphor," he asserted, "it is a statement of material fact that mankind is growing up, and that we are passing towards a more distinctly adult life as the main stretch of existence, in comparison with the feverishly youthful and transitory life of the past" (*Going*, chap. I). Spencer's organism was one of objective law. Wells reintroduced the notion of mind governing that organic growth.[20]

As the years went by, Wells's doubts of man's ability to control his own evolution increased, but he continued to plead against racial folly. "As our eyes have opened," Mr. Lammock says in *All Aboard for Ararat* (1940), "it becomes clearer and clearer that the individual life is doomed to frustration and death, unless it can escape into the synthesis of mankind." All self-centered individuality must perish forever. The individual life is worth nothing at all. "Live for all life or do not dream you are living" (*Ararat*, chap. II: 5).[21]

Much of what I have said in earlier chapters implies this Wellsian equation between individual and race; much that I shall say later assumes it. It is integral to Wells's philosophy. Essentially, he believed that individual men are to the species—otherwise called Man, Mankind, Racial Man, God, and so forth—as cells are to an organism; and just as individual men recapitulate the evolution of the race in their biological development, so Racial Man recapitulates the life of the individual sample, advancing from infancy to maturity. Only in the subordination of his self to the higher purpose of the race can a man find salvation. Wells does not mention Samuel Butler's *Life and Habit* (1877) or "God the Known and God the Unknown" (1879), but these works, like Wells's, present man as part of a "huge, compound creature, LIFE," identifiable with God, who himself might be part of a yet larger being.[22] Butler also praised Giordano Bruno's much earlier perception that material existence, including man, was a single creature of which God was the soul.

In *The Outline of History* (1920), Wells made a monumental effort to provide a detailed account of man's gradual movement out of the darkness of fragmentary egotism toward the light of unified communal service. If the *Outline* did not make Wells's religious view of the unity of mankind sufficiently evident, *The Conquest of Time* (1942) settled the issue, for there Wells described his faith in a chapter clearly entitled "The Religion of The New Man." The old Bible of Judaism and Christianity was largely backward looking and fabular, and Wells wished to replace it with one that was forward looking and factual. Because every religion requires a record of its origin, Wells provided a history to show man where his new religion began and how it came to be what it was. Assumed in all of this advancement and improvement was a sticky conception that often troubled Wells and yet which he found essential to his creed—the belief in what is known as progress.

# 5

# Progress

Accompanying Wells's conviction of an evolving racial unity was a belief in the necessity of progress, definable as the successful adaptation to changing circumstances. And change was one of Wells's presiding themes. He reported that a vast change of scale had taken place, encompassing the rate and dimension of change itself. He persistently warned that unless mankind adapted to the rapidly shifting conditions, it faced decay and extinction. He pleaded for a change in man's mode of perception to approximate the change in the scale of things around him. *The Food of the Gods* (1904) illustrates this need by fable. *The Salvaging of Civilization* (1921) is prosier, explaining that the cessation of the great uprush of modern civilization resulted from the same forces that led to that uprush. The expansion of knowledge enlarging the physical range of human activities has been accompanied by no corresponding adjustment in man's political ideas. Thus although an innate force impels man almost mathematically toward a future of communal assistance and harmony, it cannot guarantee the necessary human adaptation. A halt or stoppage might occur that would prove fatal. To avoid such a stoppage, mankind as a species must become aware of its own potential and solidify its purpose.[1]

In his autobiography Wells maintained, "We are, as a species, caught in an irreversible process" (*Autobiography*, chap. V: 5). Man's own development has begotten the process he must now continue. He cannot choose but go forward with the reconstruction of social and economic organizations. A planned world state is not merely desirable, but necessary.[2] So far men had failed to achieve satisfactory political and social agreements because they had failed to make plans. Certain assumptions widely held in the nineteenth century made such anticipatory planning seem unnecessary. "Providentialism was in the spirit of the age. Belief in the necessity of progress anyhow, was almost universal. Even Atheists believed in a sort of

Providence" (*Autobiography*, chap. V: 5).[3] Wells admitted that his youth-ful awareness of the wonderful possibilities open to mankind was based upon this widespread faith in the inevitable march of progress. For him, it was particularly the result of Science.

Although he indicted himself along with his contemporaries for taking human progress for granted, Wells's early writings indicate that he was not such a dupe as he imagined. The early science articles on evolution, espe-cially human evolution, and such tales as *The Time Machine* and *The War of the Worlds*, indicate how far Wells was from a complacent confidence in progress. Loudly as he proclaimed his faith in human progress, Wells never assumed that it was inevitable. He learned from Huxley how perilous man's situation was and fully believed that man's fate was in his own hands, which meant that man could cancel his own future as well as transform it to Utopia.[4]

From the beginning Wells was willing to face the implications of evo-lution regarding the theory of progress. In *The Time Machine* (1895), the Time Traveller is shocked by his discovery in 802,701 A.D. that his facile assumptions about human progress may be faulty. In the long perspective of natural law, the outlook is not good, for the very sun and its dependent earth will eventually fail. But even at the closer range of a few centuries, the prospect may be unattractive. *The Island of Dr. Moreau* (1896) suggests that men are beasts and will remain so. Only the faintest hope for im-provement is offered by Prendick's vaguely putting his faith in "the vast and eternal laws of matter" where "whatever is more than animal within us must find its solace" (*Moreau*, chap. XXII).

Wells shows in "The Star" (1897), *The War of the Worlds* (1898), and other narratives that human progress might be interrupted by forces beyond man's control. His frustration and anger, however, were prompted by sources of resistance within society and within the individual. He real-ized that men were maddeningly capable of accepting the idea of progress while rejecting the insistent reality of change. *The Food of the Gods* is his earliest elaborated treatment of this theme. Largeness comes upon the world, not entirely by accident, but indiscriminately. This largeness is the change of scale that Wells insisted had overtaken man. The common people react to the giants produced by Herakleophobia by talking of "the bank-ruptcy of science, of the dying of Progress." It is true that the tiny revolu-tions of the past—the throwing out of one monarch or another—are over, "but Change had not died out. It was only Change that had changed" (*Food*, bk. II, chap. I). The frightened multitudes of small people represent "the little things of the vanished nineteenth century still holding out against Immensity" (*Food*, bk. III, chap. I). Wells did not endorse all the forces making for change, newness, and largeness, but he did not deny that they were at work and had to be recognized. However, in this novel, his giants, who represent the increasingly conscious control of change, fight against the smallness of the past, not for themselves, but for "the life of the World." They see themselves as transmitting this spirit—what Wells would later call the undying fire—from the "little folk" of the past to "still greater lives" to come.

Men, Wells noted, were willing to accept the comforts and conveniences provided by Science but were unwilling to accommodate themselves to the vast changes accompanying scientific discovery. It became a commonplace among Wells's critics that he put an absolute and foolish trust in science to redeem the world.[5] But a glance at his early writings shows how sensitive he was to the uncontrolled nature of scientific discovery and the fallibility of scientific investigators. Bensington and Redwood in *Food of the Gods* are good examples, especially the former. They are intellectually curious and capable of the necessary objective endurance to produce results, but they are not capable of controlling the results of those results. "One does not know which is the most amazing," Wells exclaims, "the greatness or littleness of these scientific and philosophical men" (*Food*, bk. I, chap. V). Filmer, in the story of that name, is another example of a weak nature succeeding in a monumental project. He creates a machine that can fly, but he lacks the courage to test it. Cavor in *First Men in the Moon* (1901) is comically impractical about most things, even the results of his stupendous discovery. Bedford, in his avariciously practical way, expresses contempt for Cavor's objective curiosity. "Really," he says to Cavor, "you conducted researches because you had to. It's your twist" (*Moon*, chap. XV). Much as he placed his faith in men who valued the scientific cast of mind, Wells never forgot that most scientists were simple, even severely limited, men outside their work.[6]

If Wells knew that scientists were the same as other men except for their method and their curiosity, he knew as well that they could turn their discoveries to good or ill, or leave them to be so utilized by others. In *Love and Mr. Lewisham* (1900) and "A Slip Under the Microscope" (1893), the main characters look forward to lives of dedication to scientific research beneficial to man. In a less specific way, Parload in *In the Days of the Comet* (1906) and Ann Veronica consider science as a sure hope for man, and George Ponderevo makes it his religion. Increasingly thereafter the scientist appears as one of the most likely candidates for leadership in human improvement, though in stories such as *The World Set Free* (1914), *The Autocracy of Mr. Parham* (1930), and *The Holy Terror* (1938) the average scientist is as much exploited as any one else by men craving power. Already, however, Wells had warned about the possible abuse of science by men like Moreau and Griffin. Ivor Brown was too lively when he said that "one leaves the first phase of Wells with the mental vision of a runaway horse called Science, striding in a mad gallop of destruction none knows whither."[7] But he at least saw that Wells was not a slavish worshipper of science. Wells never placed a false trust in scientists; he simply asserted his faith in scientific method, which he insisted was little more than honest, untrammeled, and disciplined observation and common sense. Augustin Filon understood this when he wrote of Wells, "He never loses sight of the reciprocal evolution of Science and Humanity. Men create science, and science in its turn remakes mankind."[8]

Science could be beneficial to man if he anticipated and controlled the consequences of its discoveries.[9] In *The Work, Wealth and Happiness of Mankind* (1932), Wells stated that progress was not inevitable, and neither were the evils that accompanied it. Men had to realize that all institutions are provisional, that men were now completing the intellectual release that Athens had begun and were passing from a civilization based upon tradition to one taking its shape from deliberate planning. The main hindrance to this important advance was the sluggish resistance to all change so much a part of the human makeup.

As early as 1903 a reviewer offered Wells a warning. "In assuming . . . that the moral changes of the next hundred years" he wrote, discussing *Anticipations* and *Mankind in the Making*, "will be on the same scale as the mechanical changes of the last hundred years, he seems to us greatly to underrate the conservatism of human nature."[10] Wells must have been astonished to read this, since he certainly had a healthy respect for the depth of that conservatism and challenged it constantly. About 1937, for example, he gave three variations on the theme in three short fictions. The gloomiest version is in *The Croquet Player* (1936), a story narrated by one George Frobisher, who describes himself as having "led a life largely of negatives and avoidances" and possessing "soft hands and an ineffective will" (*Croquet*, "The Croquet Player Introduces Himself"). To this representative of average humanity, Dr. Finchatton confides a terrifying account of the return of primitive savagery amidst mankind; Dr. Norbert confirms the symbolic import of the story. Man, he says, is still a beast that has been marking time and dreaming of a progress it has failed to make. "There has been no real change, no real escape. Civilization, progress, all *that*, we are discovering, was a delusion."[11] Norbert urges Frobisher to face the facts. "Do as I have done and shape your mind to a new scale. Only giants can save the world from complete relapse—and so we—we who care for civilization—have to become giants." He calls for the Mind of Man to arise, but Frobisher is unwilling to have to think about the future. This may be the sunset of civilization, he says, but "I am going to play croquet with my aunt at half-past twelve today" (*Croquet*, "The Intolerable Psychiatrist"). And so the tale ends.

The *Camford Visitation* (1937) is more positive. Wells's principal representative of retardation in this story is Mr. Trumber, a university lecturer in English who "was all against what he called this 'so-called progress'. Progress that was not 'so-called' did not exist for him. He lived for revivals and restorations" (*Camford*, chap. II). The Voice that challenges Trumber's attitudes explains that mankind's accomplishments so far have been disorderly. Now its creative force seems to be flagging. Camford's intellectual community resembles the croquet lawn because the habitués of both are enamored of familiar conditions and therefore fear and dislike change. In *Star-Begotten* (1937), a character states the dilemma pungently: "But bringing a human mind up against the living idea of progress is like bringing a badly trained dog into a house; its first impulse is to defile the furniture" (*Star*, chap. IX: 3). The Visitant of *The Camford Visitation* opposes all final doctrines and all recourse to definitiveness. "He was progress articulate. He was the spirit of the provisional. His message was an intellectual drive without a glimmer of surcease" (*Camford*, chap. V). After a term of perplexity, Joseph Davis in *Star-Begotten* finally accepts the likelihood that man will continue to improve though the change in him might be strange and unsettling. So does his wife, who brings the novel toward its close with these words: "Why should one be afraid of change? All life is change. Why should we fear it?" (*Star*, chap. X: 3).

This was the question that Wells asked time and time again; still, though he welcomed change as an escape from an unsatisfactory past, he recognized its ambiguous character. Wells began *The Outline of History* (1920) with a description of the evolutionary process and then fixed the reader with the simple fact that "in a world that changed, life *must* change in this way, modification and differentiation *must* occur, old species *must* disappear, and new ones appear" (*Outline*, chap. III). It wasn't a question of good or evil, but of necessity. Man cannot choose whether he will change or not, no matter what may result from those changing conditions. Wells encouraged his reader to believe that life was not limited, but open to growth beyond what is currently conceivable. Throughout the *Outline* he shows how dangerous resistance to change is for man.

Wells spoke more forcefully in *The Fate of Homo Sapiens* (1939). Noting the important contributions of Darwin and Freud to man's self-knowledge, he observes that this enlargement of man's outlook created a wave of optimistic assurance. However, while people accepted the advances of science, progress, which seemed automatic, remained independent of the daily lives of everyday people. "We are only beginning to realize," Wells warns, "that the cornucopia of innovation may perhaps prove far more dangerous than benevolent" (*Homo*, Introduction). Man must keep up with his own innovations. He must change himself as fast as he changes his environment. He has the knowledge to do this if he has the will. "We know that the everlasting hills are not everlasting, that all our working conceptions of behaviour and destiny are provisional and that human nature and everything about it is being carried along upon an irreversible process of change" (*Homo*: 2).

That is the key. All human conceptions are *provisional*. Man's picture of history changes as it unfolds; his image of the future must be re-created as he grows toward it. Nothing remains fixed, and man is subject to the same laws of nature that bind all other living species.[12] At the end of *You Can't Be Too Careful* (1941), Wells has his representative of cautious conservatism ask what the good is, what *finality* there will be, in bringing about a new world of abundance and equality. "None whatever is the answer," says Wells. "Why should there be? Yet a vista of innumerable happy generations, an abundance of life at present inconceivable, and at the end, not extinction necessarily, not immortality, but complete uncertainty, is surely sufficient prospect for the present" (*Careful*, bk. VI, chap. V).

In his various fictions Wells acknowledged the unpredictable quality of change by extrapolating current circumstances according to different coefficients, thereby arriving at differing results. Two roughly similar narratives illustrate this point. *The War in the Air* (1908) is a fantasy describing one consequence of international warfare. The opening sentence of the novel states the theme. " 'This here Progress,' said Mr. Tom Smallways, 'it keeps on' " (*Air*, chap. I: 1). As his name suggests, Smallways represents the ordinary man of his day who is unequipped to deal with a world of rapid change that is disconcerting for most people, though not for Tom's son Bert, the "progressive Smallways." It is appropriate that the most modern Smallways should be literally "caught up" in the most monstrous outcome of progress—an air war involving the advanced nations of the world, a war that becomes increasingly destructive, dissolving the normal economic and social structures. Bert soon realizes that a "swift and unexpected systole" has replaced the long diastole of European civilization (*Air*, chap. X: 3). For three hundred years the movement of the world seemed wholly beneficial to mankind, and no one attended to warnings that moral organization was not keeping pace with physical progress since constructive forces balanced for a time destructive powers in nature and in man. Complacent mankind assumed a necessary progress toward which it had no moral responsibility, but all the while the opportunity to guide this progress was passing. Soon civilization collapses and men are reduced to primitive conditions, living in small communities like those described in Jefferies's *After*

*London; or, Wild England* (1885) or in the early stages of Morris's Utopia in *News from Nowhere* (1890). Some order is gradually restored under the guidance of a transformed Bert Smallways and others like him, but Wells's judgment concerning the war and the failure of civilization is condensed in old Tom Smallways's sentiment that ends the novel. " 'You can say what you like' he said, 'it didn't ought ever to 'ave begun' " (*Air*, Epilogue).

The World Set Free: A Story of Mankind* (1914) offers an alternate scenario. In this version of the future men prove capable of taking advantage of dramatic changes. Holsten, the discoverer of radioactive power, knows that most men are not adventurers but incline to domestication and stolidity. By himself he cannot seriously alter the course of history, but he is eager to make his contribution. "I am a part, not a whole," he reflects; "I am a little instrument in the armoury of Change" (*Free*, chap. I: 2). Holsten's contribution brings about monumental results, for the radioactive power that he makes possible undermines the old order by providing cheap power. Though world economic structures are altered, political structures remain pathetically unfit to guide the collective intelligence of men. The consequence is war. But fortunately King Egbert and others like him seize this opportunity to fuse the common will in the establishment of a World State, which ushers in a finer time for mankind.

These are two examples. I could go on. In *Men Like Gods* (1923), Uthred the Utopian recounts a similar outbreak of world war that disrupts the financial and economic machinery and looses greedy adventurers who speed the disorganization of society. But on the threshold of a new Dark Ages, mankind fortunately realizes that "creative service" must replace social competition. What follows is the birth of Utopia. The process is much slower in *The Shape of Things to Come* (1933), but it is worked out in greater detail. Other tales of the future, from *When the Sleeper Wakes* (1899) to *The Holy Terror* (1939), offer further variations, showing how flexible Wells's attitude toward the future was. Everything, including his scheme for a World State, was provisional.

If Wells was always willing to describe the future of progress, he did not therefore shirk an examination close at hand. *The Wife of Sir Isaac Harman* (1914) is about a great deal more than progress, but in this novel Ellen Harman's liberation begins when she discovers that her husband's profitable bakery business is not the undiluted benefit to mankind that it seems to be. Gradually she realizes that her husband's successful company obliterates smaller independent bakery shops; and when she raises this matter, Sir Isaac's response is: "Progress is Progress, Elly." Like the more volatile Edward Ponderevo, he equates progress with the success of his business and, in praising largeness, almost parodies Wells's own defenses of multinational, organized concerns. Reflecting upon this puzzling new problem, Ellen reasons that "there had to be progress and the survival of the fittest." In her imagination she pictures the endangered small business-man as a "kindly, furry, bunnyish, little man," in contrast to "the ferrety face and stooping shoulders and scheming whistle of Sir Isaac" (*Harman*, chap. V: 8). Beneath the apparent advance of civilization, the jungle con-flict endures. Sir Isaac's version of progress is the ancient game of predator and prey. It is Spencer's Social Darwinism, not what Wells understood as progress.

Sir Isaac's schemes of organization, consolidation, and simplification are compatible with Wells's own design for progress toward a unified World State. What converts Sir Isaac's scheme from paradigm to parody is the element of human greed. Sir Isaac thinks only of profit and power. His totalitarian system offers no consideration for his employees; it is not a selfless communal venture. Moreover, when Ellen attempts to modify her husband's system by introducing neat, orderly, inexpensive living quarters for the young women employed in his plants, Sir Isaac promptly attempts to reduce this benevolent scheme to the harshly disciplined pattern of his other profit-making schemes. To her dismay, Ellen realizes that this idealis-tic plan creates hardship for London landlords who, like the small bakers Sir Isaac has put out of business, will lose their custom to her hostels. Clearly Wells was willing to face the many disturbing consequences of prog-ress and change, but he was no mere slave to all growth. Although he admired men like Northcliffe and Harmsworth for their brilliant business successes and their mastery of large concerns, he called for a new spirit still lacking in selfish men's ambitions for growth and progress. In *Tono-Bungay* (1909), he offered Edward Ponderevo's elaborate unfinished house, Crest Hill, as a symbol "of all that passes for Progress, of all the advertisement-inflated spending, the aimless building up and pulling down, the enterprise and promise" of the age (*Tono*, bk. IV, chap. I: 2). It is all that selfish striving can lead to—pretentious, but incomplete, expan-sion.

In *Tono-Bungay* Wells faced the immediate ramifications of change mainly in realistic terms.[13] But he also engaged the subject at a more exalted level. Upon occasion he argued that man's virtues, especially his intellect, resulted from the constant pressure of necessity. In *The Time Machine*, the Time Traveller asserts that "intellectual versatility is the compensation for change, danger, and trouble. . . . Only those animals partake of intelli-gence that have to meet a huge variety of needs and dangers" (*Machine*, chap. X). But although Wells accepted this principle of nature, he did not stop with it. He tried to show men that there would always be great endea-vors to test them and that mere struggle did not necessarily sharpen man's intellect more than it barbarized his nature.

In *The Undying Fire* (1919), Dr. Elihu Barrack declares himself a spokesman for those who credit practical evidence. He believes in a Process by which man gradually improves. "*I* think we struggle against one another by nature and necessity," he says, "that we polish one another in the struggle and sharpen our edges. I think that out of this struggle for existence come better things and better" (*Fire*, chap. V: 3). Barrack contradicts Job Huss's mystical faith in an "undying fire" that prompts man to finer and finer achievements. But Huss says that Barrack's Process is indifferent, begetting both good and evil. He cites modern war as a product of the Process by which men "improve" themselves through mutual struggle and urges that "unless we do now ourselves seize hold upon life and the Process while we are in it, the Process, becoming uncontrollable again, will presently sweep us altogether away. . . . Your Process is just Chaos; man is the opportunity, the passing opportunity for order in the waste" (*Fire*, chap. V: 4). This is the authentic Wellsian note.

Wells believed that his own time was the crucial period in the destiny of mankind. In the pivotal term of his lifetime the die would be cast. He encouraged men to believe that the Process of Nature was governable, that in a world of chance human will could direct the course of events. He demonstrated this in various ways in his many novels. At the personal level, there is Mr. Polly's discovery that if one doesn't like his life, he can change it. At the general level Wells declared his faith in the human ability to direct progress, beginning at least as early as *The Time Machine* where the narrator sets his hopeful view of man's future against the Time Traveller's larger scepticism.

Wells identified progress with the enlarged scale of human circumstances. *The Food of the Gods* is an early parable of the dangers and the promise involved, but much later William Clissold likens the growing spirit of modern liberalism to "the spirit of a young giant striving against almost intolerable bonds, bonds in which he was born and which cripple and threaten his growth and existence." For Clissold, liberalism is a releasing force capable of sweeping away the barriers that separate men and smoothing out the dark places that breed unhealthy passions of greed and suspicion. It is a purifying of life, what Clissold calls a "progressive simplification." He needs this image of clear purpose for his peace of mind. "Without the idea of progress life is a corrupting marsh. If this present age is not an assembly for great beginnings, confused and crowded still but getting into order, then it is a fool's fair, noisy, tawdry, unsafe, dishonest, infectious" (*Clissold*, vol. II, bk. V: 16).

Clissold claims that his life is serene; Wells never did. We have seen that Wells was keenly alive to the dualities of human character and of human destiny. Man had the capacity to control the forces of Nature and achieve a splendid future, but he was equally capable of succumbing to destructive animal instincts and passions. Because he believed that he was living at the point of crisis for mankind, Wells's moods veered strongly from hope to dismay, though he never gave himself entirely to either. He debated the issues in his books, remembering that all existing conditions were provisional and open to the influences of tradition and reasoned reform, and to chance and accident as well.

Clissold and Wells candidly avow that life would seem vapid, even horrible, without a faith in man's capacity for progress. His *Outline of History* was Wells's attempt to persuade men—and perhaps himself—that the sweep of history proved the case for human progress. But Wells conceded other motives than the lure of a beautiful future for accepting change and hoping that the control of that change would lead to a finer world for men. The stifling and shadowy past was as powerful an impulse toward the future as the shining mirage of the future itself.

In *Meanwhile* (1927), Mr. Sempack makes the revealing statement that "Progress has always been a battle of the bored against the contented and the hopeless" (*Meanwhile*, bk. I: 4). Although Sempack argues constantly for change and the human direction of that change toward an ideal future, he begins with the highly charged word "bored." One seeks change because one is bored, discontented, and frustrated with the present. It is a visceral response. Feeling unable to live fully and completely, man whips himself into a furor of effort toward something new and different. Sempack's plan for Utopia eventuates more from physical discontent than from intellectual design.

While Sempack is arguing the need for change, Mrs. Rylands, sounding like a tentative Job Huss, replies that change may be directionless and uncontrolled. Then she launches into an illustration.

> We may 'meanwhile' for ever. People may be driven this way and that. Some may go down and some up. Old types may vanish and new ones come. Some of that may be progress but some of that may be loss. Nature gives no real guarantee. Change may go on until men are blue things three feet high and rats hunt them as we hunt rats and your great civilization may never arrive— never arrive at all. It may have loomed up and receded and loomed up again and been talked about again as you talk about it, and then things may have slipped back and slipped back more and gone on slipping back. And the rats may have got bolder and the disease germs more dwarfing and crippling, and energy may have ebbed. (*Meanwhile*, bk. II: 9)

Sempack agrees that Mrs. Rylands has raised an important problem and concludes that the thinkers—those who have gone apart to construct a plan for the guiding of man's future—must step back into the market place and promote their ideas, make men realize that change can be directed toward some desirable end. But Mrs. Rylands's demurrer has not been fully answered. It is the ever-threatening alternative future of *The Time Machine*, *When the Sleeper Wakes*, and other tales which can never be fully expelled. The need to recognize these alternatives is an important part of *Meanwhile*, which is based on the premise that our current existence is a "meanwhile" between the unsatisfactory past and the world yet to be. "In the measure in which one saw life plainly the world ceased to be a home and became a mere site of a home. On which we camped. Unable as yet to live fully and completely" (*Meanwhile*, bk. I: 5). This is simply one more way for Wells to emphasize the provisional nature of all things and man's ability to shape that malleable present to his own ends.

The idea of progress was central to Wells's thinking. The examples I have given demonstrate this, but one can turn to his novels almost at random and find one or another treatment of it. Sometimes, as in the boldly Utopian tales, he pictures what progress could become; elsewhere, as in *The Shape of Things to Come*, he provides plans for its consolidation; and in yet other stories, such as *The War in the Air*, he shows man's inability to realize what progress really represents. In *Mr. Blettsworthy on Rampole Island* (1928), Wells imitates the flavor of *The Island of Dr. Moreau* to portray mankind's primitive reluctance to shed its outworn habits, beliefs, and institutions, even comparing conservative mankind to cannibals who eat all those who try to teach them their lives can be improved. Blettsworthy has a dream of this kind on "the night when Sacco and Vanzetti died" (*Blettsworthy*, chap. IV: 13).[14]

Some novels explore in detail the maneuvers of the conservative mind in resisting the opportunities offered by the vision of constructive change. *You Can't Be Too Careful* denounces stupidity and *The Autocracy of Mr. Parham*, blind reaction. *The Bulpington of Blup* scrutinizes a more ambivalent type. In this elaborate study of progressive self-deception Wells gives his main character every chance to take advantage of the spirit of change abroad in his time, but unlike the positive types contrasted with him, he is unable to seize any. The Broxted family—father and children—are dedicated to the idea that men can command their destinies through a knowledge of history and science. Theodore Bulpington, more inclined to subjective and aesthetic experience, both admires and fears them as a new race of "Inheritors" who see life with a "cold inhuman clearness" (*Blup*, chap. II: 5). Like too many liberals, Wells would have said, Bulpington is willing to accept improvement, but he has not conceived a plan for bringing it about.

The onset of the Great War alters Teddy's and Theodore's views of progress. Teddy is amazed to discover that the rulers of the world have not shared his confidence in the necessary progress of mankind toward an organized world. Theodore lapses into a conservative fear of change. Both

Teddy and Theodore took progress for granted. World war called that faith in doubt. Theodore turned in disappointment to the past, Teddy more radically to the future. Theodore's unreasoned faith in progress collapses; Teddy's is transformed. By establishing this brash contrast, Wells indicates more clearly than before what the failures of the past have been as well as what the mistakes and requirements of the future may be.

Edwin E. Slosson summarized Wells's favorite theme as "*the reaction of society against a disturbing force.*"[15] It is a good way of presenting his overwhelming interest in promoting change, for it balances reaction against disruption. Wells saw the dangers of both but believed that disturbance of things as they are was the way of natural forces. Anything fixed was wrong. From an early age he was engaged in attacking established shams of all sorts.[16] Geoffrey West described Wells's code for human improvement in these terms.

> Change, intelligently planned and directed towards the greatest possible freedom and happiness, was his aim. The means was clear to him: for the individual, education (his own Jacob's ladder); for society, again education, pointing to some form of communal organisation and control. "Individualism in ethics, socialism in economy" he expressed his creed. For the rest, the determination and the courage to overcome the inertia and cowardice of tradition.[17]

Arnold Bennett caught Wells's purpose very quickly. "*I had taken it as a matter of course,*" he writes, repeating another's words, not his own. "That is precisely the attitude of which Mr. Wells's attitude is the antipodes."[18] Many friends and critics assumed and continue to assume that Wells believed that progress was inevitable.[19] He believed that *change* was inevitable, not *progress*. That had to be earned. Some critics have gone too far in the other direction. Jack Williamson exhibits the problem. His summary of Wells's attitude is sound.

> Progress, for Wells, was never the universal law of Comte's Positivism, nor the historic logic of Marx's dialectical materialism, nor even the benign force of Spencer's evolution. His most splendid dreams of better possible worlds were always curbed by the stubborn respect for fact that he had learned from Huxley, and by the realistic awareness of human imperfections that he had gained from his own unsheltered life.[20]

But later he declares that Wells "preached progress not out of confident hope, but out of cold desperation."[21]

I like C. P. Snow's conclusion in this matter. "His own sense of life," he writes, "was, in essence, dark. . . . Wells was often more sanguine than most men; he was sanguine because he revelled in the joys of life: but in the end he had no illusions."[22] Sanguine, but no illusions. That phrase crystallizes Wells's position. After all, as John Middleton Murry wrote when

Wells was dead, "To say that Wells ignored human limitations may be true. But if it is intended as a criticism of his work and aims it badly misses the mark. What conceivable advantage would have accrued to him or the world if he had not continued to rebel against human stupidity?"[23] Mencken accused Wells of messianic delusions, but Dreiser, equally unconvinced by Wells's propaganda for an improved mankind, said, "He seems to suspect an ultimate chaos out of which anything can take its rise, even a pleasant, orderly, kindly and fairly stable society of humans."[24] These words put it rather well. But perhaps Wells stated his position best, stripped of all dogmatic language, even all idealism, when he put his sentiments in God's mouth in *All Aboard for Ararat* (1940). "Let us set ourselves honestly to the only brave thing in life, which is beginning again" (*Ararat*, chap. I: 6).

Wells knew the difference between progress and mere change. Progress was shaped change. Mainly it was change instigated and governed by science in the broadest sense of that word. In *The Outline of History* Wells referred repeatedly to the new dimensions that science had created— greater factories, larger ships, and so on. "There are people," he pauses to observe, "who sneer at this kind of progress as being a progress of 'mere size,' but that sort of sneering merely marks the intellectual limitations of those who indulge it," for, in the old structures "matter was dominant—the material and its needs had to be slavishly obeyed; in the new, matter has been captured, changed, coerced." Man's advance is manifest in "this great and growing mastery over substances" (*Outline*, chap. XXXVIII: 1). In *The Work, Wealth and Happiness of Mankind* (1932), Wells examined material progress, the subjection of matter, in detail.

Wells's progress was not confined to technological change. He knew the many theories of progress either stated or implied in social and historical treatises of his time and before.[25] He knew that along with theories of material progress went convictions about the perfectibility of man. And he knew how fragile all of these formulations were. The narrator of *The War of the Worlds* learns that progress is not guaranteed, but at the same time he comprehends that mankind can benefit even from such a catastrophe as the Martian attack. The Martians succumbed to bacteria incapable of harming man, whose billion deaths have "bought his birthright of the earth," and this fact convinces the narrator that "neither do men live nor die in vain" (*War*, bk. II, chap. VIII). The attack from beyond the earth instructs mankind that it is not safe and secure, that it must consciously work for its future welfare.

"Continual progress," Wells warned in 1927, "can only be assured by an incessant acutely critical vigilance" (*Going*, chap. XVII). Wells was frequently criticized for wanting to turn the future over to scientists and technocrats, and there is no doubt he preferred them to politicians; but he was no slave of scientists whom he described as being more like bees than guiding angels, and he indicated frequently enough in his novels, stories, and other writings that scientists were capable of abusing their accomplishments like anyone else (*Conspiracy*, chap. XIII). He used them as types of the progressive mind because they exhibited that devotion to knowledge which he felt was essential to progress. The scientist keeps an open mind or he fails. It was this willingness to accept change and to recognize its potential for control that he sought in any person, though he felt it was more likely in scientists.

If Wells saw progress intimately tied to technological advance though not certain of success, he also believed in an urge toward a higher progress that transcended implements and structures, an evolutionary aspiration in the race itself. Only in *Mind at the End of its Tether* (1945) did Wells abandon this conviction. That cry of despair may have been Wells's last published utterance, but it was not his last word. I prefer to think that other statements more truly represent his testament. After a full life arguing the same case in different ways, Wells returned to the theme of progress in *Babes in the Darkling Wood* (1940), where Gemini Twain argues for change and a reconstruction of human affairs against his father's vigorous defense of the existing social order. Ultimately Gemini learns what other Wells characters learned—that if we desire life to have a shape, we must shape it. An unsculpted block of alabaster symbolizes to Gemini and Stella the duty that awaits them. "I used to think these things would really come of themselves and that we should be carried along by the stream, cheering things on and pretending we were steering them," Gemini confesses. Now he realizes that "belief in inevitable progress is the end of progress. . . . There is no automatic progress in things. None at all. Progress is here for the taking, but it's not a free gift. I know now that this world of our desire will never come about unless men—no, *we*—make it come about" (*Babes*, bk. IV, chap. III: 5). For Wells, the Natural Process was simply one of chance. If man was to escape that process, he must employ his intellect, shape his ideas into acts, and take command of that chance. Natural Process, stripped of randomness and shaped to a purpose was what Wells meant by progress.

And yet randomness, too, could be exploited. Wells had good personal reasons for trusting to chance, for he viewed his life as a succession of fortunate accidents.[26] Accidents are not necessarily evil, and even those that appear so might be turned to advantage. Man himself was an accident from Wells's point of view.[27] Accidents are helpful because they remind men that routine, habit, and tradition are neither permanent nor secure.

They disclose strange new patterns in life and call the familiar patterns in question. Many of the early science-fiction adventures exploit some chance discovery or accidental event, but Wells utilized the same device in the circumstances of his other fiction. As early as *The Wheels of Chance* (1895), he was calling attention to his use of coincidence and fortunate accident.

In a chaotic, unplanned world, accident is the only true opportunity. Men like Kipps and Polly and Bunter take advantage of chance occurrences to alter their lives for the better. Chance and accident constitute a prevailing theme in *Tono-Bungay* (1909). Even death could prove a beneficial chance event where an unexpected inheritance is involved, as the story "A Catastrophe" (1895) shows. War could prove a similar lucky accident for humanity, upsetting entrenched order and providing opportunities to reconceive institutions and social mores. *The World Set Free* (1914), *Mr. Britling Sees It Through* (1916), *Joan and Peter* (1918), *The Shape of Things to Come* (1933), and other novels illustrate this point.

Progress is the seizing of accidental opportunities and bending events to the service of a presiding scheme. Wells frequently solved the problem of transition from an unfavorable to a favorable state, from an unperceiving to an illuminated condition, by introducing some form of accident. The benevolent cloud of gas in *In The Days of the Comet* (1906) is a notorious example. But even the Utopian society of *Men Like Gods* (1923) came into being because "a fortunate conspiracy of accidents rather than any set design had opened for them some centuries of opportunity and expansion" (*Gods*, bk. I, chap. V: 3).

Apparent accidents, whether personal or racial, may prove favorable in the long run. Wells insisted that accidents were part of the evolutionary advance of mankind. Human development was a history of happy accidents helped on by man's cunning and adaptability. When Wells used the literary convention of accident and surprising chance events, he did so with conviction, for he believed that accidents had cosmic significance and challenged man to continue a progress painfully begun. Beyond the influence of chance on human affairs and evoked by it was a potentially greater power—the power of human will. But to put that will into effect, man had to see clearly what was to be done. Vision precedes act as plan should deed.

# 6

# Organization, Order, and Education

We have seen that Wells expected man to escape from conventional modes of thought by honestly facing the reality of Nature and human nature before he could establish command over his destiny. He aimed at a lucidity that existed only through human intellect. Despite his evident delight in the pleasures of the senses, Wells always yearned for a purity and clarity not easily attainable in ordinary experience. He frequently identified purity with open, upland terrain. When he coupled the desire for purity with a desire for order, the open terrain became a garden. Beyond the upland garden was heaven and stars, which were emblems of an enduring ideal. But along the way, related to this design, but also germane to Wells's assumption that human progress was a combination of accident and rule, another image appears. For Wells intense clarity and intense order combine in the crystal. The crystal forms with relative suddenness, creating splendor out of common elements. Abruptly, chaos achieves order and brings a new mode of perceiving. Although not precisely the same as accident, the crystallizing process represents the same gift of illumination inherent in the operation of chance events. But whereas accident releases through disorder and disassembling, crystallization releases through a sudden fixing into form.

Wells uses the image of crystallization to signify beauty and favorable processes in man and mankind. The crystal is a splendid outcome of an unseen rigorous process. The human analogy is the sudden consolidation of mind or will. Wells suggests the molecular character of this activity in Artie Kipps. "The ripening mind seeks something upon which its will may crystallise, upon which its discursive emotions, growing more abundant with each year of life, may concentrate" (*Kipps*, bk. I, chap. III: 1).[1]

This passage implies that the crystallization of the will is natural and desirable, for if the necessary concentration does not occur and the emotions are not forced into some orderly design, they might overwhelm the individual. At the least he will be left with disconnected impressions and an unformed identity. This situation resembles the conflict of jungle and garden. A fundamental fear of unruly emotions and impulses begets a yearning for some organizing force. But just as man does not plan, but can exploit accident, so he cannot predict, but can benefit from the sudden fixing of his thoughts and emotions upon some central purpose.

Wells admired the crystallizing process but was aware of the dangers and problems involved. In *World Brain* (1938), he noted that it might prove disastrous to have the project of a World Encyclopedia crystallize out prematurely and produce "a rigid obstructive *reality*, just *like enough* to our actual requirements to cripple every effort to replace it later by a more efficient organization" (*Brain*, chap. II). Much earlier Wells had examined the hazards of this process in *Marriage* (1912), where the crystallographer Trafford learns from his wife that human experience cannot be organized entirely along the lines of physical science. It was good altogether, Marjorie concludes, "to be turned from the study of crystals to the study of men and women" (*Marriage*, bk. III, chap. IV: 15). Although the crystal is a form of perfection and completeness, it is an ambiguous figure for Wells because it suggests the end of a process.

The apparent conflict in the yearning at the same time for the fixed beauty of the crystal and for fluid freedom beyond it can be resolved at a cosmic level. In *The Dream* (1924), Starlight explains that "life and death alike are within the crystal sphere that limits us forever. Life cannot penetrate and death will not penetrate that limitation." But some day, Starlight says, we may be able to recover all of human memory, "until the whole past is restored to us and life becomes one. Then perhaps the crystal sphere will break" (*Dream*, chap. VIII: 1).

This is a strange image indeed, for while the crystal sphere represents a form of order and control, it also appears as a restraint, not a release. True unification of all life will shatter the crystal, transcend the apparent order. At first it appears to be a contradictory or confused utilization of the crystal image, but I think that it is actually quite consistent. Crystal is the stage of organization that supersedes an elemental chaos or disorder. It represents that moment when obscure matter assumes a clearly discernible and beautiful form. Psychologically it is the moment when vague perceptions solidify according to a single coherent design. But this design, though useful, must itself give way to a yet higher, perhaps more complicated, perception. The atoms must be rearranged. The crystal, lovely as its arrangements have been, must break and permit a grander, more spacious possibility. Wells believed in a rigid universe that appears fluid through the operation of time. Man conceives of the universe as rigid because he sees the absolute operation of certain laws. One of these laws is the inevitability of temporal movement. But if man could succeed in transcending that law, of recovering all of human memory, his picture of the universe would change. That perfect crystal would be broken and a new vision would begin to form out of renewed chaos.

This is a broad picture of what the image of the crystal meant to Wells. But the image took on its own special significance within different contexts. Wells signals the superior quality of the Utopian world of *Men Like Gods* (1923) by naming Mr. Barnstaple's youthful cicerone, the ideal boy of the future, Crystal. This identification of crystal with clarity, excellence, and order is evident in an early story that forcefully establishes Wells's main associations. In "The Crystal Egg" (1897), the crystal egg that has come into Mr. Cave's possession gratifies his early scientific yearnings, for, by gazing into it, he can see "a wide and spacious and strange country," which turns out to be Mars. The Martians presumably have a similar power to examine earth. Crystal is literally a medium for outlandish visions. In *The Bulpington of Blup* (1933), the outmoded ideas to which Theodore adheres are characterized as an entrapping crystal sphere, while the new scientific order of things represented by the Broxted family is described as crystallizing slowly out of the confusions of the day. In this novel Wells seems almost to be teasing himself about his familiar image. Surely he shows more than one trait of the crystal as it operates in different minds.

Although he might present the image fantastically in "The Crystal Egg" and ambiguously in *The Bulpington of Blup*, Wells also developed it fully and seriously. William Clissold explains that during his student days he "was drawn by an overwhelming fascination to the lovely facts of crystalline structure," and asks, "Did I, in those days, in some faintly anthropomorphic way regard the glittering planes and beams and passages and patterning in those translucent depths into which I pried, as being accessible, as being physically accessible? Did I somehow conceive of myself as presently walking out of the ordinary paths of everyday into those magic palaces?" The wonder he felt for crystals resembled his awe in contemplating the stars. Now, he says, both experiences have disappeared, and he has become prosaically reasonable (*Clissold*, vol. I, bk. I: 8). But an important element of that wonder survives, for Clissold begins the account of his life and thought with a crystal image that alludes to both of his youthful fascinations. There were times, he says, when the everyday world "was less the sphere that enclosed me and made my all, than a sort of magic crystal into which I peered and saw myself living." In these moments he felt that it would "be possible to turn away and look at something else quite different from this common-sense world—another world. The individual in that crystal globe of time and space has a hundred thousand traits by which I know him for myself. How, then, can I be the onlooker also, of whom I know nothing at all except that he sees?" Clissold speculates that these sensations may be nothing more than tricks of the body's chemistry; but whatever the cause, he has sensed this strange detachment and now, he says, "it is the world in the crystal I want to write about, this crystal into which I seem to have been looking now and living for nine-and-fifty years" (*Clissold*, vol. I, bk. I: 2).

Clissold's image of a crystal sphere that encloses his life but into which he is also the viewer is a variation upon Wells's familiar separation of the ordinary self from a detached intelligence that observes it as though from a great height. And just as that intelligence must order the multiple traits of the personality, the crystal becomes an ordering device that contains Clissold's multiple selves and gives him a traceable identity. The crystallizing process offers a fixed scheme, but that scheme is not the final product. It is a pattern that should prompt action. It is a model, not an end.

We have seen that Wells used his crystal image to describe mental processes: sudden illumination, followed by resolution leading to action. Almost invariably he associated crystal with a mental condition leading on to some high purpose. In *God, The Invisible King* (1917), he pictured the revelation of his new religion as a process of crystallization. "Out of the most mixed and impure solutions a growing crystal is infallibly able to select its substance. The diamond arises bright, definite, and pure out of a dark matrix of structureless confusion" (*Inv. King*, Envoy). The old order is broken up and a new order forms; but implicit in the crystallization of this more enlightened form is the probability that it, too, will eventually yield to a yet newer organizing principle. In both individual and society such moments of crystallization are welcome. They are necessary precursors of realignments within self and society.

Wells's fascination with the crystallizing process is explicable, since, like his faith in the utility of accident, it reveals an impatient desire to reach in a sudden bound a desired end that might otherwise require tedious and sustained endeavors. Himself gifted with great powers of intuition and insight, Wells perhaps overrated his fellow men while underrating the value of patient labor. He believed that transformation could come suddenly, like religious conversion or molecular precipitation. In "Democracy Under Revision" (1927), he praised the serious minorities who worked for a better world. "I see them ready to crystallize about any constructive idea powerful enough to grip their minds" (*Going*, chap. V). About the same time, Wells said of the mounting political discontent, "It needs but a crystallizing touch to give that impatience a form and a direction" (*Going*, chap. VI).

Wells found evidence of this crystallizing process in the past. "The mind of the Jew," for example, "had crystallized about the idea of the Promise of the One True God and the coming of a Saviour or Messiah" (*Outline*, chap. XXVIII: 2). Such crystallizations were not permanent. Periodically there were social recrystallizations that reshaped human existence. Whereas the Jews crystallized around an idea, Western Europeans in the sixth, seventh, and eighth centuries crystallized around individual men. "The analogy of the aggregation of feudal groupings with crystallization is a very close one," Wells asserts with his finger in our buttonhole (*Outline*, chap. XXXII: 2).

To Wells the crystal was an apt analogue for the precipitating of intelligence out of animal impulse. In *Star-Begotten* (1937), Keppel says of the supposed new race of superior beings that one part of them is human and fallible, "while the other side is like a crystal growing in mud"; it is, in effect, intelligence rising out of matter (*Star*, chap. VIII: 3). Just as man struggled from swamp toward stars, just as bird's-eye or aerial views stood for detached, organized intellect, crystal represented the beauty of order suddenly rescued from the muddy chaos of undisciplined existence. Wells's utilization of the crystal as a metaphor had this equation at its base—the orderly intellect is a crystal. It is this conjunction that exposes the most interesting facet of the analogy. Intellect arises out of instinct and is made manifest in language. Language is the refinement of thought. Thoughts crystallize into expression just as emotions crystallize into thoughts. For Wells the highest form of crystallized thought was written communication. Therefore transcribed thoughts most resemble the beauty of the crystal.

In *Apropos of Dolores* (1938), because he finds it difficult to tell himself precisely what he means, Stephen Wilbeck writes his thoughts down to clarify them. He feels that his mind is "encumbered like a crystal trying to form in a magma loaded with irrelevant matter." Although he considers himself "muddy-minded," he believes that if many people combine their thoughts, a general clearing up is possible.

> When a substance which has been loaded and opaque, crystallizes and becomes clear and definite in its form, thrusting the alien stuff aside, it is because its particles have fallen into place one with another. Nothing new has come, nothing that was not already there, but only a better arrangement has been made. (*Dolores*, chap. VII: 4)

As a publisher, Wilbeck hopes to promote such a crystallization by bringing ideas together. Meanwhile, Wells is attempting to achieve a crysallization in himself through the act of writing his novel and, moreover, hopes to precipitate a similar crystallization in his readers.

But writing must be more than simple crystallization, for it must awaken feeling as well as thought. Rowland Palace's writing is exquisite but lacks the fire of the innovative Mr. Bunter. Palace has cold craft, but Bunter has something more, as his account of his discovery of his writing talent reveals.

> I began to like the steady deliberation of setting things down, correcting them, choosing a better phrase and a better word, more and more. After one has heard words coming in a whirling rush like a spout of muddy water bursting a dam, it was marvelous to find they could also be still things, shining in their depths like crystals in a setting. (*Brynhild*, chap. X: 5)

Earlier Brynhild Palace, in attempting to change the course of her conversation with Bunter, refers to the fine afternoon weather as being "like a crystal—only with warmth in it," a description she thinks resembles a passage from a novel (*Brynhild*, chap. X: 2). This phrase is our clue. The finest writing is not merely crystal, but crystal with warmth in it—thought enlivened by feeling, a magical crystal like the crystal egg in which visions are possible.

Writing is the consummate organizing power, for it brings together ideas that are, by themselves, powerless to cause effective change but can, when ordered by an artist of language, create an illuminating pattern that symbolizes attainable ideals and provokes men to strive for them. The finest writing offers the clarity of crystal with the warmth of humanity. Ideas cloaked with human forms aptly describes Wells's own fiction.

Images of crystals, crystal balls, and crystal spheres were common in the literature and art of Wells's early years. John Dixon Hunt notes the popularity of the crystal ball in paintings of the late nineteenth century.[2] Walter Pater, writing of Rossetti's talents, said that "if the spiritual attains the definite visibility of a crystal, what is material loses its earthiness and impurity," and Swinburne referred to "the spirit that watches in the depth of its crystal sphere the mutable reflections of the world."[3] "Crystal" was a familiar adjective in one of Wells's favorite tales, La Motte Fouqué's *Undine* (1811); and W. H. Hudson's Utopian novel, which Wells admired, was entitled *A Crystal Age* (1887). Either the basic image was very common or his close friends had picked up a mannerism from Wells and perhaps even teased him with it. Rebecca West, for example, while living with Wells as his lover, described a vision in which a character must choose between two worlds, each represented as a crystal ball.[4]

The crystal image is by no means unique, but Wells combined a novel scientific meaning with its familiar aesthetic use, thereby creating a highly charged figure with profound meaning for himself. Throughout his life he aspired to clarity tempered by sympathy. Although emotion in its cruder manifestations was the enemy of disciplined thought, it could render that thought noble when subdued. Wells's crystal embodies that yearning for clarity and purity. It is the resolution of the dilemma posed by beast and jungle, for it is as detached and dispassionate and predictable as the beast and jungle are engaged, passionate, and random. It has permanence, the jungle transience. Like the jungle and its inhabitants, it obeys immutable laws, but it holds them suspended for a moment in time so that man may gaze upon it and recognize that these laws have an order and beauty to be admired and imitated. Like the stars, the crystal signals to man the desirability of the reign of order. For Wells that reign of order was incarnated in the written word, where human emotions were fixed in a clarifying form— such was the ultimate enactment of his cherished image.

Wells knew that "art, poesy, philosophy, literature, are not permanent things. They change in their methods, their function, their essential nature. . . . They are living processes like ourselves who breed and pass, and not dead things like crystals and cut gems" (*Going*, chap. V). He knew that the clarity he wished to describe was living and essentially different from the process he used to convey it. Nonetheless, his affection for the crystal image emphasizes the conflict he felt between generative, turbulent creative force and calm, ordered reason. He saw his own autobiography planning "itself as the crystallization of a system of creative realizations in one particular mind" (*Autobiography*, chap. I: 2). A book could be the crystal into which a reader gazes, glimpses a vision of beauty and hope, and then turns to the world to make that vision real. Later I shall show how important Wells considered the actual practice of writing, but first we must realize that all of this writing was in the service of one great calling. Above all else the crystal maker wished to educate.

Wells felt that mankind's survival depended upon a growing awareness of the interrelationship of all men through constantly improving means of communication. His highest priority in the shaping of the future was education.[5] Man's capacity for extending his continuity of experience in this world set him apart from all other forms of life, even fellow mammals, who were educable, but not to his degree.[6] Very early in his career Wells stressed this fact. Monogamic marriage, he wrote in "Morals and Civilization" (1897), "is not the marriage service and a joint honeymoon, as the modern Young Lady has been foolishly taught, but the birth and education of children." He believed that man had attained an intellectual level where he could reach a common sense of the aims of education.

Education had matured slowly. "It is only nowadays," Wells wrote in 1920, "that men are beginning to understand fully the political significance of the maxim that 'knowledge is power' " (*Outline*, chap. XXVI: 9). The pursuit of knowledge has been prompted mainly by dedicated individuals, many of whom sought power through knowledge, but "it is only when knowledge is sought for her own sake that she gives rich and unexpected gifts in any abundance to her servants" (*Outline*, chap. XXXIV: 6). Yet while knowledge may derive from the isolated discoveries of individuals, true education must be a collective function. Education is the preparation of the individual for the community with religious training usually at its core. As we have seen, Wells preferred a secular faith; he called for "*a new telling and interpretation, a common interpretation of history*" (*Outline*, chap. XL: 1).[7]

Correct education was to be the foundation of the new World State. But when Wells looked around him, he found an educational system totally incapable of achieving this high purpose. The need for *more* education had been recognized in the nineteenth century but not the need for a new *kind* of education. The schools as they existed in England represented a system of conservation and actually fostered a distaste for work while providing no genuine education, Wells argued in *Mankind in the Making* (1903). It is no accident that most of Wells's central characters are serious self-educators, both those who have passed through the national or private schools and those who have not. Their distinctiveness is the result of open and inquiring minds. Wells appreciated the movement toward popular education and William Briggs's standardization of school examination boards; still, whereas he recommended a common body of shared knowledge, he disapproved of all processes of standardization in education. The satirical conclusion of *The First Men in the Moon* (1901) shows how little he favored education as a means of producing specialized types. He wanted a common body of information supplied to students, but he did not wish to produce robots. He was willing to utilize education ruthlessly as a means of healthy propaganda.[8] Nonetheless, he foresaw the dangerous trends of politically controlled education and pointed to them in *When the Sleeper Wakes* (1899) and *The Food of the Gods* (1904).

Ironically, while the English were standardizing their school product, the English process of education remained a mess. "I do not see," Wells moaned, "how we can hope to arrest and control the disastrous sprawling of world affairs until we have first pulled the philosophical and educational sprawl together" (*Autobiography*, chap. V: 3). More often than not he was so enraged by what he saw in educational institutions that he would rather have pulled them apart than together. He had been attentive to education and its institutions from an early age. He was a superb student, gaining one award after another and finally achieving a scholarship to the Normal School of Science. He had been an assistant teacher before this; and after he left the Normal School, he taught once more at private schools and for a university extension service. He knew what he thought education should be, and he saw it nowhere in existence in England and only adumbrated elsewhere. Although defending Bromley Academy, he nonetheless declared his education there inadequate. More broadly, he dismissed the national schools altogether as a genuine remedy. Holt Academy, where Wells had been a teacher for a time, though it looked good on paper, was a decaying fraud. And Henley House, which was far better, still fell short of fulfilling its proper function, as did all schools as far as Wells was concerned.

*Love and Mr. Lewisham* (1900) offers a vivid picture of the circumstances and substance of education as Wells knew it. Mr. Lewisham fights through this stultified disorder to a coherent picture of man's purpose, but few could imitate him. Mrs. Whitlow in *The Holy Terror* (1939) is described as a woman of intelligence who "had had a good modern education, which had confused her mind considerably" (*Terror*, bk. I, chap. I: 3). Hooplady House in the same novel is one of those private schools Wells understood so well. It "never gave a thought to character and the finer shades of conduct—except on Speech Day" but was solely concerned with preparing students for board exams. "Beyond the lines laid down by these examining bodies it did not adventure" (*Terror*, bk. I, chap. I: 5). Mr. Polly went to a national school where an untrained staff subjected him to information it could not explain; later he was finished off at "a private school of dingy aspect and still dingier pretensions." As a result, he had lost his natural capacity for learning and his perception of the world had been reduced from wonder to boredom (*Polly*, chap. I: 2). Mr. Polly is one of Wells's better examples of a youth maimed by education who nonetheless manages to find some middle ground of contentment in later life. There are many others, from Artie Kipps and Hoopdriver to Mr. Lewisham or Ann Veronica, but there are also those who do not break free, and Edward Albert Tewler is one sample of that.

Although Wells fluctuated somewhat in his views about American schools, in *Mankind in the Making* (1903) he felt safe in contrasting their efficiency with "those wretched dens of disorderly imposture," the English middle-class schools (*Mankind*, chap. V). He had no more respect for the prestigious public schools than for the private or national schools. Denigrating references to them appear throughout his works. Wells's objections to the schools were those of his contemporaries.[9] Later William Clissold blames England's "gradual lapses from a subtle and very real greatness and generosity, to imitative imperialism and solemn puerility" on "the mental and moral qualities of the men who staff [England's] public schools" (*Clissold*, vol. II, bk. V: 14).

Still, if Wells had little that was good to say about the public schools, he admitted from time to time that they could provide some of the best education available in England. His respectful treatment of Sanderson of Oundle in *The Story of a Great Schoolmaster* (1924) shows that he appreciated serious attempts at innovative education. In *Star-Begotten* (1937), he commented that there was much unreasonable criticism of the public schools and that it was "indisputable that they do give a sort of education to an elect percentage of their boys" (*Star*, chap. I: 2). That elect was itself selected from a mere fraction of the population since the public schools, like the universities, were and had remained "part of the recognized machinery of aristocracy" (*Outline*, chap. XXXV: 12).[10]

If Wells was occasionally lenient toward the public schools, he seldom relented with the universities. The Utopian Sarnac, recounting his experiences from the nineteenth century in *The Dream* (1924), elaborates on the failure of university education.

> The rank-and-file of the men they sent out labelled M.A. and so forth from Oxford and Cambridge were exactly like those gilt-lettered jars in Mr. Humberg's shop, that had nothing in them but stale water. The pseudo-educated man of the older order couldn't teach, couldn't write, couldn't explain. (*Dream*, chap. V: 8)

Even the learned are not necessarily well educated. Mr. Parham, in *The Autocracy of Mr. Parham* (1930), maintains an unhealthy veneration for the past and all established things while rejecting what is new and therefore unsettling. His convictions are challenged by the forceful and progressive Sir Bussy Woodcock who sees no reason for going on with "the schools and universities that served the ends of our great-grandfathers." He accuses Parham of fearing change because it will require him to learn something new, and Parham is troubled by flickerings of doubt. "Oxford educated for quality," Parham thinks, "but did it educate for power?" (*Parham*, bk. II, chap. II). *The Autocracy of Mr. Parham* provides a close study of a type and condemns it implicitly by identifying it with the excesses of fascism. But scattered through Wells's canon are numerous less elaborate indictments of the traditional universities.

In a chapter division of *Babes in the Darkling Wood* (1940) entitled "Uncle Robert Tells the Real Truth about University Education," Wells has his sage assert that university education does not initiate its graduates into a mastery of life. He recounts the universities' failures to keep up with developing thought and explains that this has happened because teachers have been less concerned with students than with their own research. Uncle Robert concludes that he would comfortably let the old universities go in favor of a "world where one never graduates. Where one goes on and learns and learns to the end" (*Babes*, bk. II, chap. III: 3).

At the end of this novel, Gemini dedicates himself to a career in education and urges Stella to do the same because he has decided that "the one and sole *reality* in human life is mental" (*Babes*, bk. IV, chap. III: 6). It was because Wells believed that mental life was the true reality that he placed such emphasis on education. Mind could adapt most swiftly to change, and education could facilitate that adaptation. Necessarily, he argued, the institutions of learning must be in the forefront of thought, not bogged down in the past. And education itself could not end in a classroom but must become a lifelong endeavor.

Wells always recommended change in the educational system, but his constructive opinions on education matured over a long period. In *Anticipations* (1901), he presented a sustained argument against the existing system of education, singling out the public schools and their schoolmasters as inappropriate and outmoded. England required an accessible and varied educational program, perhaps assisted by endowments from men like Andrew Carnegie. In the spacious opportunity offered by the New Republic there would be no term to one's education, for the whole world would constantly be thinking and learning. In a chapter of *Mankind in the Making* (1903) entitled "Schooling," he surveyed the contemporary educational process while advancing his own sketch of what education should be. He stipulated that students should have ample free time for their own interests and recommended some specific texts for their reading.[11] In another chapter, "The Organization of the Higher Education," he offered a comparable plan for advanced levels of learning.

Some of Wells's arguments were perennial complaints. In *The War in the Air* (1908), for example, he protested the waste of riches upon weaponry, wealth which might better have been spent on learning and exercise for the young. But mainly he sought to promote conceptual changes. In *Social Forces in England and America* (1914), he alleged that education experts were making a bad situation even worse as they stagnated, and he appealed to the schools to do their part in enlivening public consciousness "because there more than anywhere else is the permanent quickening of our national imagination to be achieved" (*Forces*, "Of the New Reign" and "The Labour Unrest"). Much later he stated clearly how to accomplish this enlivening. "Vitalising education is only possible," he wrote in *The New World Order* (1940), "when it is under the influence of people who are themselves learning" (*Order*: 8). That is, modern education depends upon research, which implies continued openness to change and a corresponding aversion to dogmatism. Wells urged his contemporaries to reconceive the established educational institutions. Finally he concluded that men of revolutionary spirit would have to bypass or even eliminate the old system to create a rational scheme.

Education had to focus on the young. This was the basic biological pattern. But Wells stressed the permanent character of education. In an era of rapid change, men could never complete their education. It must be a lifelong effort. He realized that most adults were not amenable to the expansion and alteration of their thoughts. New ideas must therefore be offered in assimilable, recognizable form. The shift to new conceptions cannot be radically sharp. While he offered many detailed plans for improving education, mainly he called for a quickening of the imagination. Marcus Karenin in *The World Set Free* (1914) explains that universal education is the paramount concern for shapers of a new world. The premise of socialism for Wells was equality of opportunity, which he believed was achievable only through equal education. "Ultimately," he said, "the Socialist movement *is* teaching, and the most important people in the world from the Socialist's point of view are those who teach" (*New Worlds*, chap. XIII: 1). Only through revision of the species can the species survive. More than once Wells warned that "human destiny is a race between ordered thought made effective by education on the one side, and catastrophe on the other. So far catastrophe seems to be leading" (*New America*, chap. III). He never had occasion to alter that sentiment.

Gradually it became apparent to Wells that the traditional educational institutions by themselves could not achieve true education. In *New Worlds for Old* (1908), he set forth a broad plan, declaring the three fundamental principles of the socialist creed as freedom of speech, freedom of writing, and universality of information. He pictured a world in which all forms of communication serve to educate the whole people. "The post office," he declares, "must become bookseller and news agent." The State itself will become a distributor of information. "Everywhere balanced against the town hall or the Parliament house will be the great university buildings and art museums; the lecture halls open to all comers, the great noiseless libraries, the book exhibitions, and book and pamphlet stores, keenly criticised, keenly used, will teem with unhurrying, incessant, creative activities" (*New Worlds*, chap. XIII: 4).

Wells's presiding ideal was to have the State participate in the universal education of its citizens. But by the time he wrote *The World of William Clissold* (1926), he no longer believed that the existing social and political system could be cajoled or forced to make the necessary changes. Clissold warned, "People are too apt to identify schools and education. Never was there a more mischievous error. Schools may merely fix and intensify those adolescent qualities it is the business of education to correct" (*Clissold*, vol. II, bk. V: 14). Allowing for some formal schooling, Clissold recommended contact with the real world for boys over fifteen and encouraged parallel activities for girls. The schools and universities were now dangerous bulwarks protecting prejudice and outworn institutions. Like many other institutions they must be bypassed or subverted. Clissold and his brother plan to effect the necessary changes along the lines of private enterprise. "The world university must be a great literature," William says. Through a worldwide publication scheme, the Clissolds hope to make that literature available to mankind (*Clissold*, vol. II, bk. V: 15).

It was only with *The Work, Wealth and Happiness of Mankind* (1932) and *The Shape of Things to Come* (1933) that Wells felt he recognized "that public education and social construction are welded by the very nature of things into one indivisible process" (*Autobiography*, chap. V: 5). In the first of these works Wells asserted that "educational revolutions must accompany economic and political revolutions" (*Work*, chap. VII: 2). He therefore devoted an important part of the book to the role of education in human society, defining education as modification of instinct. Education in the past had been the preserver and transmitter of tradition, he explained, but the education of the future should replace subjugation with the training of "self-disciplined individuality" (*Work*, chap. VIII: 4 and 10). He repeated that formal education was more a withdrawal than an enlargement and declared that much education was now taking place outside the classroom. This broader concept of education, Wells said, was "our sole reason for hope" in a better racial future (*Work*, chap. XV: 6).

*The Work, Wealth and Happiness of Mankind* sought to describe conditions as they were. In *The Shape of Things to Come* Wells presented a future scenario of how things might go. To begin with, the world required a complete revolution in education. One solution was to have nuclei replace family schools as educational forces, providing intensive study circles and associations for moral and physical training.[12] The new education would not preserve tradition but keep steadily ahead of contemporary social fact.

As early as *Mankind in the Making*, Wells had begun to put his main educational emphasis on literature. Through the best thought of man preserved in literature, not through the stultified institutions of school and college, the main business of education will go forward. Wells describes this transformation in *The Holy Terror* (1938), beginning with an account of the state of education before Rud Whitlow and his associates have assumed direction of the first world government. It is worth quoting as an example of what Wells felt he was fighting against.

> Education still for a large majority of human beings meant little more than teaching them in a primitive fashion to read and count a little. It was only in the most advanced communities that the need of continuous education throughout the whole life was recognised. For the multitude, such world-pictures as they had, had been supplied in a haphazard fashion by the talk of the people about them, by the unscrupulous statements of the advertisement newspapers, concerned chiefly with the sale of worthless drugs, adulterated foodstuffs and plausible commodities, by political propagandists and the appeals of religious organisations. A few hundred so-called universities, of unequal merit, a flimsy network of impecunious scientific societies, a loosely organised trade of book publishing and distribution, were all that there was to

guide the general mental operations of the entire world community. The common man at large had remained mainly ignorant even of what was known, and had floundered through life in a muddle of prejudices, misconceptions and downright delusions.

In place of this disorder, Norvel promotes the worldwide distribution of cheap books while exploring the educational potential of the many new devices for mental stimulation, such as cinema, radio, and microphotography. He extends the old structure of thought, research, and instruction, training armies of teachers and establishing community centers to replace schools and home instruction. Despite his swift successes, Norvel realizes that "the mental reconditioning of mankind would be a task that would demand the sustained devotion of hundreds of thousands of workers through some scores of years" (*Terror*, bk. III, chap. I: 1).

The educational schemes in *The Shape of Things to Come* and *The Holy Terror* reintroduce the supervisory role of the State but not according to the simple socialist design of Wells's earlier writings, for the role of authority is greatly increased. Nonetheless, despite Wells's distrust of the governmental machinery of his own day, his hope had long been to make government the main authority for organized education, as a glance at two widely separated Utopias indicates. In the world of *A Modern Utopia* (1905), education is carefully controlled through the fourteenth year, after which all but the mentally incapable go on to college. They leave college at eighteen by taking an examination, which may be repeated if they are unsuccessful. Citizens who wish to become "Samurai" must pass such an examination and demonstrate command of some technical aspect of life. Similarly, in the Utopia of *Men Like Gods* (1923), education is closely supervised during the early years so that "by eight or nine the foundations of a Utopian character were surely laid, habits of cleanliness, truth, candour and helpfulness, confidence in the world, fearlessness and a sense of belonging to the great purpose of the race" (*Gods*, bk. III, chap. II: 3). Only after these formative years do children develop close ties with their families, which are stronger because parents do not exert any unjust power over their offspring. The Utopian child grows under healthy conditions; it learns forms of communication and civility, the history of its world and race; its desires are refined, and sexual passions are turned against its selfishness; its curiosity flowers into scientific zest and it grows toward honorable participation in the common achievements of the race. This educational pattern is contrasted with what Mr. Barnstaple remembers of his own and his friends' poverty and neglect.

What Wells expected from education was indoctrination for a free, healthy, progressive life, a training for communal living. Because he recognized the primary importance of early conditioning, he rated very highly the role of the teacher. No social contribution could be greater than that of the authentic educator. Wells viewed himself as an educator. He began by appreciating the simple pleasures of teaching, but when he became a successful writer, he began to consider himself a teacher of another order; and even though he often expressed contempt or pity for the outmoded teachers of his time, he always felt a lively respect for those who had, against overwhelming obstacles, managed to introduce new ideas into the educational process—hence his respect for F. W. Sanderson.

By 1924, Wells had known many important persons, yet in the first paragraph of *The Story of a Great Schoolmaster* he wrote of Sanderson, "I think him beyond question the greatest man I have ever known with any degree of intimacy." Part of Sanderson's greatness lay in his vision of his profession. "He saw the modern teacher in university and school plainly for what he has to be, the anticipator, the planner, and the foundation-maker of the new and greater order of human life that arises now visibly amidst the decaying structures of the old" (*Schoolmaster*, chap. I: 1). Sanderson recognized the importance of science in the school curriculum, and he realized that it was more important to stimulate interest in some actual work than to concentrate upon classics and competition. More importantly, he invited the participation of all boys in the collective function of the school. Sanderson always stressed the positive features of education. He encouraged natural aptitudes and did not pit students against one another in futile competition. He showed that science, while practical, was an art.

Sanderson believed that the school should be a working model of a world in which men progress through communal work rather than competition, where the constructive, rather than the aggressive, aspects of man's nature predominate. That world resembles the Utopia that Wells himself frequently described. Perhaps Wells so keenly admired Sanderson because his views were so like his own. But there was more. Whereas Wells was constantly frustrated in his attempts to change men by argument, Sanderson got practical results. "He filled me—a mere writer," Wells confesses, "with envious admiration when I saw how he could control and shape things to his will, how he could experiment and learn and how he could use his boys, his governors, his staff, to try out and shape his creative dreams" (*Schoolmaster*, chap. VIII: 4). How Wells would have loved this command over actual events, this prompt conversion of ideas into practice! One worked on a small scale at Oundle while the other chose the world as his laboratory, but both men agreed on what the final aim of their experiments was. Both believed in the latent greatness of mankind.

Sanderson was the model for Job Huss in *The Undying Fire* (1919), a parable about the testing of an idealistic educator's faith. Huss has to struggle against the antiquated and commercial values of the governors of the school who cannot appreciate his interest in logic, philosophy, and history since they want children to be trained for work. "A modern school ought to be a modern school," one Gradgrinderish governor says, "—business first and business last and business all the time" (*Fire*, chap. III: 1). Huss's notion of the teacher's task is entirely different. "It is the greatest of all human tasks. It is to ensure that Man, Man the Divine, grows in the souls of men." The teacher can save man from his beastlike egotism.

> An untaught man is but himself alone, as lonely in his ends and destiny as any beast; a man instructed is a man enlarged from that narrow prison of self into participation in an undying life, that began we know not when, that grows above and beyond the greatness of the stars. (*Fire*, chap. III: 4)

This was Wells's position from the beginning. It is a position consistent with his broader desire to transform animal man into intellectual man. Beyond technical learning and sophisticated techniques for conveying that learning—all of which deeply interested Wells—was the more profound purpose of putting down the ape and tiger in man and fostering a spirit of selfless service. For him, education was precisely what proper writing was. It did not merely transmit and repeat the knowledge of the past but created a model for the future and, by doing so, made that future possible.

After this brief encyclopedia of Wells's treatment of education as a general subject, I think that it is important to examine in greater detail the way he integrated his theme into his fiction. Two examples should be sufficient, one where the theme of education is secondary and one where it is central. In *The New Machiavelli* (1911), Richard Remington's father is a teacher—and a bad one. Public education is new in his day, and the pattern of educating students to become grant-earners rather than informed citizens determines the teacher's function. Remington's father is typical. "First he posed his pupils with questions and then dictated model replies" (*Machiavelli*, bk. I, chap. II: 2). As an unqualified science teacher, he rarely conducts actual experiments; when he does, they fail. His inability to command or convey his subject matter is reflected in his incompetence in cultivating a simple garden. He urges his son to make a plan for his life and stick to it, but the father can do neither himself, nor can he help his son to follow his advice.

The muddle and inefficiency of Mr. Remington's school world reappears not only in his tiny garden but also in the world at large, for it is simply one nucleus of the general theme of disorder and order which spreads through the novel. Richard comprehends his father's failure and makes it his purpose to escape all that his education represents. Being a sharp lad, he rescues something from his formal education at a small local preparatory school and City Merchants School in London, but he cannot help feeling how "infinitely more effectually" the public schools might have gone about their task of educating young men. Though placed near the center of one of the world's greatest cities, his school remains locked in its traditions and concentrates its efforts upon Greek and Latin, which the teachers themselves cannot fully master but which they assume provide a strengthening and orderly discipline for the mind. In fact, cricket is more interesting to some masters than their classes. Remington's real education comes from his private reading, which he later supplements through conversation with intelligent peers who share his interest in promoting ideas through literature.[13]

When he enters politics, Remington sees his educational scheme as the starting point for his projected reorganization of political life. Convinced that the public schools and universities are too rooted in useless tradition, he wishes to replace them with a consolidated system of practical service schools and a new college system emphasizing modern philosophy, history, and literature as well as the sciences, education, and sociology. "I should have aimed at making a hard-trained, capable, intellectually active, proud type of man. Everything else would have been made subservient to that," he reflects (*Machiavelli*, bk. I, chap. IV: 3). Remington's finer and broader education will educate an elite group first. This echo of the Fabian spirit differs somewhat from Wells's earlier socialist views, though the idea of a well-trained elite is by no means new. Wells afterward broadened his concept of education greatly, as we have seen.

Education is the principal theme of *Joan and Peter: The Story of an Education* (1918). Remington survived his schooling and concluded that proper education was the essential foundation for all human improvement. Oscar Sydenham has little of Remington's analytical skill, but he has a similar conviction that England and the world are desperately in need of a new form of education. He too believes that an elite should be educated for leadership. Throughout the novel he reasserts his belief that a more scientifically planned and operated educational system must replace the chaos of the existing schools. "Give me the schools of the world and I would make a Millenium in half a century," he says (*Joan*, chap. II: 4). At the end of the novel, Oswald urges Joan and Peter to work toward the shaping of a new world after the war, which he describes as "an educational breakdown" (*Joan*, chap. XIV: 3). His own education, he says, is ended, but Joan and Peter are just beginning theirs.

The history of Joan and Peter's education details Wells's views on the subject. After Peter's parents die in an accident, he and Joan, the bastard child of Peter's maternal uncle, are sent to an experimental school called St. George and the Venerable Bede run by two dilettantish women who have little knowledge and less skill to transmit it. In spite of the hazards Peter and Joan emerge basically undamaged from their early schooling. But Lady Charlotte Sydenham, their toryish trustee, removes them from this "fad school," sending Peter to "a *real* school" with no nonsense about it and Joan to a private home. Mr. Mainwearing, the proprietor of High Cross preparatory school, has come into education in a careless fashion; he "had no special training as a teacher. He had no ideas about education at all. He had no social philosophy" (*Joan*, chap. VIII: 9). Like so many schools of the time, his is largely a sham. It is more a hindrance than an aid to mental growth, being designed less to educate than to prepare for a formal set of examinations. Peter's experiences here are unpleasant, for not only is the teaching poor but the conditions are emotionally and morally unhealthy. Wells hints at the dangers of crowding boys of all ages together. Bullying is common and altogether the experience is damaging, but once more Peter emerges whole.

Wells compares private schools of this type to eddies in the flow of life which caught impressionable young minds "with a grip of iron and spun them round and round for six or seven precious years and at last flung them out" (*Joan*, chap. VIII: 10). Oswald intensifies this image later. Searching for a public school for Peter, he concludes that they are "whirlpools into which the living curiosity and happy energy of the nation's youth were drawn and caught, and fatigued, thwarted, and wasted" (*Joan*, chap. X: 3). The maelstrom increases as the educational process goes on. Presumably one is utterly drowned at university. Oswald finds no clear philosophy or social purpose in the schools, only habit. Even their best products are too predictable. Wells gives an amusing description of the type in young Troop, who, in asserting his liberalism, reveals a deep strain of traditional bigotry.

University education is no better, history being taught in a fragmentary manner and all subjects lacking an ordering principle. Nonetheless, Peter glimpses the "fascinating uplands of wisdom" available to him through scientific research, though his fusty superiors consider that "going out on those uplands was straying from the proper work." Ultimately, Peter and Joan feel that their education has not "linked them up to any great human solidarity" or offered them any appropriate direction.

Other of Wells's characters venture opinions of English education. One young soldier, writing from the trenches of the First World War, castigates British ineptitude. England has failed to produce leaders, he says, because "education in England is a loafer education; it does not point to an end; it does not drive through; it does not produce *minds that can hold out* through a long effort" (*Joan*, chap. XIII: 5). He hopes to correct this failing by becoming a schoolmaster himself after the war. He never does. A German shell blows him to bits.

*Joan and Peter* is a sustained complaint about the state of England with specific reference to its careless training of the young. It ends with Oswald's advice to his wards—one of whom wishes to be a medical doctor or researcher, the other an architect—to throw out the old men now running things and initiate a new order. But there is something even more elemental at the bottom of Wells's plea. What Joan and Peter discover for themselves at the end of the novel is the great love they share. The discovery of this powerful generative force within them gives them confidence to hope for the future; "making love is still at the heart of us humans," Peter exclaims optimistically (*Joan*, chap. XIV: 9). This exclamation and what it represents might be read as a romantic cliché or an upbeat turn of the plot; but it is something far more significant in Wells's scheme of thought, for education has failed the young here as it has in every other realm of experience, and it has failed at every level—from home, to school, to university, to the wider education of British culture generally. At the most elementary and intimate level of his experience, modern man lives in appalling ignorance.

> Right up to full age, we still fail to provide the clear elemental facts. Our young men do not know for certain whether continence is healthy or unhealthy, possible or impossible; the sex is still assured with all our power of assurance, that the only pure and proper life for it is a sexless one. Until at last the brightest of the young have been obliged to get down to the bare facts in themselves and begin again at the beginning. (*Joan*, chap. XIII: 12)

Getting down to bare facts and beginning again is what Wells's plans for education were about. Get down to the bare facts of human history and the history of the earth on which man lives. Get down to the bare facts about the laws according to which the material world moves. Get down to the bare facts about the relationships of men in communities. Get down to these basics, and one will find that all of them, like the facts each individual discovers in himself, have an organic continuity and interconnectedness. What Wells hoped to see was an educational process which illuminated that interconnectedness by revealing as much of the truth as was possible to as much of the human race as was possible. Once that was done and unity was forged out of disorder, men would discover their true interests and grow beyond the self-indulgent egotism and stultifying habit of the present circumstances and fashion a richer and more rewarding community.

In 1939 Wells wrote, "By the early thirties I was one of those who were becoming fully aware that the systematic reconditioning of our mental life was not a secondary but a primary need for all mankind. It has beyond all question become now the most urgent and important thing in the world" (*Homo*: 9). I hope that I have shown that this awareness was implicit at an early stage of Wells's career as a spokesman for change. A true teacher, he saw, would always be one in the forefront of thought, an adventurer of the mind, a leader out of the jungle to that upland garden where the stars in their crystalline brightness promise wonders. Just as he saw mankind biologically recapitulating the individual man, so he saw education as a live thing equally subject to biological principles, thus "the under-development of universities and educational machinery is like some under-development of the brain and nerves, which hampers the whole growth of the social body" (*Outline*, chap. XXXVI: 6). Because education was an integral part of the whole development of individual and society, it could not be confined to specific institutions. All of life was learning. It remained to give that learning form and direction, to crystallize the desire for knowledge around some few cardinal beliefs. This could best be done, not in the stifling enclosures of the schools, but in the world out of doors.

Wells considered himself a teacher.[14] He had known one of the great teachers of his time, T. H. Huxley, and to some extent he emulated him. He poked double-edged fun at men with "a weakness for writing edifying literature," who aspire to teach Nations, yet he felt the Carlylean call himself from an early age.[15] His Time Traveller, pondering the fate of man, "tried a Carlyle-like scorn of this wretched aristocracy in decay" but couldn't maintain the role (*Machine*, chap. VII). Wells could. Late in his life he was still insisting that "the supreme task before our awakening minds is the re-education of the world" ('*42*, pt. II: 10). In the guise of William Burroughs Steele, he complained that "colleges are to this day conducted mainly to put back the new generation where its parents began." But education should look forward and offer objectives. Steele offers one of Wells's most concise general statements of what genuine education is.

> The purpose of education is to anticipate insurgences from below the conscious level and so escape self-frustration. Education has a social and an individual side; it can be considered from the point of view either of the whole or of the unit, but its objective in each case is the same, the control of dividing, contradictory and dissipating impulses. No religion, no philosophy, is of any value unless it implies a complete ethic and educational purpose, and no ethics or education can have the slightest value without a clearly-defined foundation in general philosophy. (*Frustration*, chap. VIII)

Wells possessed a complete ethic and philosophy, and he felt it was his duty to educate mankind to its fundamentals.

Sometimes, like an irascible schoolmaster, Wells chided his pupils. In *You Can't Be Too Careful* (1941), he says that "no dissertations, no arguments, above all no projects nor incitements nor propaganda, shall break the flow of our narrative; no more of these damned 'ideers' shall there be" (*Careful*, Introduction).[16] It isn't long, however, before he finds himself having to explain the nature of metamorphosis in man, and he breaks out waspishly at the reader. "I have fought the academic classical tradition tooth and nail. If the idea of a metamorphosis is a new one to you, you have only those wretched impostors who pretended to educate you to blame. If you find anything perplexing and unusual in what is written here, here and in the first Chapter of Book the Third, ahead of you, it is due to their default" (*Careful*, bk. II, chap. III). He ends the harangue by advising them to buy his *Science of Life*, newly available in an updated one-volume format. In giving an account of Tewler's education, Wells details its many shams and failures then concludes menacingly, "The world knows little as yet of what it owes to its teachers. But it is beginning to suspect" (*Careful*, bk. II, chap. XIV).

By the time he wrote *You Can't Be Too Careful*, Wells had been after his fellow men to improve for some sixty years, and he had grown impatient. But almost to the very end, and perhaps even then, Wells did believe that man could teach himself to live in the world he had made—if only he would take hold of himself, break free from the prisons and jungles, strip himself clean and free, and climb toward the stars. He could, by exploiting accident, benefiting from luck, and applying the designs conveyed with crystallike clarity by thoughtful writers, guide his own progress. It was so obvious. All that he had to do was consolidate his will, master the story of his life, and write it down. In the subsequent chapters of this book we shall see how Wells suggested that this be done.

# 7

# The Will

It is commonplace in Wells criticism to turn sooner or later to that important passage in *The History of Mr. Polly* (1910) which states concisely one of Wells's central convictions. "But when a man has once broken through the paper walls of everyday circumstance, those unsubstantial walls that hold so many of us securely prisoned from the cradle to the grave, he has made a discovery. If the world does not please you *you can change it*" (*Polly*, chap. IX: 1). And yet few scholars have troubled to follow up the sources for this stunning assertion.[1] Wells tells us that he had discovered the two guiding principles of his life while still an adolescent. "'If you want something sufficiently, take it and damn the consequences,' was the first and the second was: 'If life is not good enough for you, change it'" (*Autobiography*, chap. IV: 1). He was not such a fool as to believe that man, influenced by heredity and environment, could, in an instant, thoroughly alter his circumstances. But, if he changed his attitude and began to deal with life as a malleable thing, he could bring a new life into being.[2] Wells's optimism often seems little more than a flight from his pessimistic moods, but he grounded his positive opinions in a consistent view of the universe. At the root of this view was his belief in free will. There are complications, subtleties, and sophisms involved in his explanation of this belief, but ultimately he operated according to it.

There is a chapter in *First and Last Things* (1908) called "Free Will and Predestination." In it Wells says, "If you ask me, I think I should say I incline to believe in predestination and do quite completely believe in free will. The important working belief is free will." In a note he identifies free will with self-determinism and sees predestination as "equivalent to the conception of a universe rigid in time and space" (*Things*, bk. II: 3). His reconciliation of the two resembles Henri Bergson's.[3] Each human is a circle of thought between an internal and an external world and "each self

137

among us, for all its fluctuations and vagueness of boundary, is . . . invincibly persuaded of Free Will. That is to say, it has a persuasion of responsible control over the impulses that teem from the internal world and tend to express themselves in act. The problem of that control and its solution is the reality of life" (*Things*, bk. II: 5).[4] The last sentence sums up the chief struggle Wells perceived in himself and in others. There could be no such struggle without free will. To bring order to the self and then to the species was possible. There were analogies in Nature. But consolidation of the will preceded everything. What all men desire is "more oneness, some steadying thing that will afford an escape from fluctuations" (*Things*, bk. II: 7). If man is free, he can effect this consolidation himself. Strength of will, for Wells, assumes freedom of will.

Wells greatly admired Plato and patterned his vision of a New Republic on Plato's. This man was important to human development because he was the first to tell men that they could take hold of their lives. Wells gives a homely version of Plato's position in "This Misery of Boots" (1907) when he explains that the person who has been obliged to wear poor boots that pinch his feet feels sympathy for the downtrodden when he witnesses their suffering; "he no longer recognises the Pinch of Destiny. His rage is lit by the thought that there are fools in this world who ought to have foreseen and prevented this. He no longer curses fate, but the dulness of statesmen" and others who have not remedied conditions ("Boots," 2). This rage with a concrete object is valuable, for "it is passion, it is enthusiasm, and indignation that mould the world to their will" ("Boots," 4).

The conflict between free will and fate is a temporary one occasioned by an imperfect way of life. In *Anticipations* (1901), Wells assures us that the New Republicans will know that will is free, and this conviction will make them feel a personal moral responsibility urging them to serve a higher purpose, such as the establishment of a World State, and thereby contributing to the strengthening of the universal will of mankind (*Anticipations*, chap. IX). Thus far Wells's view resembles the traditional Christian notion that man has free will to choose good or evil, even though his acts are part of a foreknown providence—an issue that exercised theologians for centuries. Wells's elucidation is no more conclusive than theirs. "It is in the nature of Man, it is in the present purpose of things," he says, "that the real world of our experience and will should appear to us not only as a progressive existence in space and time, but as a scheme of good and evil." Good and evil constitute no more than a limiting condition of human beings. God, says Wells, is no moralist. "He comprehends and cannot be comprehended, and our business is only with so much of His purpose as centres in our individual wills" (*Anticipations*, chap. IX).

Although Wells sometimes identified the larger Will with divinity, usually he stated the relationship between free will and determinism in scientific terms. In "The Rediscovery of the Unique" (1891) and "Scepticism of the Instrument" (1903), he argued that the universe, though apparently bound by certain laws, nonetheless permits minute variations. Nothing is ever repeated exactly. The human mind, in attempting to order and classify experience, overlooks this fact. By insisting upon its own abstractions, it creates problems that do not exist. It is a faulty instrument.

> Take life at the level of common sensation and common experience and there is no more indisputable fact than man's freedom of will, unless it is his complete moral responsibility. But make only the least penetrating of analyses and you perceive a world of inevitable consequences, a rigid succession of cause and effect. Insist upon a flat agreement between the two, and there you are! The Instrument fails. ("Scepticism of the Instrument")

More than a quarter of a century later, Wells maintained the same basic position. As in *First and Last Things*, he draws a distinction in *The Science of Life* (1930) between the outer and the inner realms of experience. Predestination and fate are elements of what we call objective experience because that experience can be measured and predicted. Free will is a characteristic of subjective experience, where there is no such causal certainty. Wells makes no absolute claim for free will here. He is playing the dispassionate scientist. But again he questions the precision of man's reasoning faculty and concludes:

> Quite conceivably minds are very complex weighing-machines and this freedom of choice may be a delusion, but it is a delusion woven into the very stuff of the weighing-machine. The mental weighing-machine can never realize it is a machine. A theologian might put it that predestination is the universal law, but free-will the law of the individual moral life within the frame of that universal law. Or, returning to the language of eighteenth-century philosophy, predestination is objectively true and free-will subjectively true. Each is true in its own sphere and there is no way of synthesizing these two into one. (*Life*, bk. VIII, chap. IV: 1)

Going over this same ground in 1934, Wells asserted that causation had not been proven, that there was still an element of indeterminacy in the operations of the universe, and that some modern physicists had even discussed the possibility of "objective free-will" (*Autobiography*, chap. V: 2).[5] A couple of years later, his William Burroughs Steele wrote:

> My last words about this self I have been ransacking, are this, that this creature *has had, has and transmits free will.* Not much free will, not much courage, or assertion, but some. More than the fly on the flypaper has. An increasing amount. And free will *is* individuality, and individuality is nothing else. Individuality is intrinsic uniqueness and spontaneous initiative. Spontaneous initiative is creation and creation is divinity. (*Frustration*, chap. XXIII)

After a lifetime speculating on the subject and living as though he was free, Wells restated his belief in much the same terms as those with which he began. In a passage from *The Conquest of Time* (1942) which I have already cited in another context, Wells describes a four-dimensional universe that is rigid, Calvinistic, and predestinate, in which free will is not true freedom, "but a small subjective pattern of freedom in an unchanging all." There is no conflict between fate and free will, which are merely the major and minor aspects of existence. "The major aspect of life is Destiny; the minor is that we do not know our destiny" (*Conquest*, Appendix II). In *The Science of Life* Wells had phrased the same idea differently. "We are each of us a part of Fate, and the sense of free will is one of the methods through which our destiny is achieved" (*Life*, bk. VIII, chap. IV: 4).[6] Obviously it is a slippery thought. But Wells believed in free will by necessity. He balanced his conviction of objective determinism against a faith in subjective freedom. He could accept no other scheme. Without this much, he could not have acted. At least he could not rationally have defended action.

This may not be a satisfactory philosophical position for many persons, but it was the basis of most of Wells's thinking. He was candid, too, about the problem, always admitting the provisional nature of human circumstances and human perceptions. In *First and Last Things* he says that he calls his "unfounded and arbitrary declaration of the ultimate rightness of things" the Act of Faith (*Things*, bk. I: 1). He cannot prove it; he merely believes it. No more can he prove free will.

Wells regularly speaks of fate and destiny, terms not normally regarded as compatible with the idea of free will. In fact, except where he or his characters use these terms loosely (the "destiny" of the British Empire, and so forth), Wells is mainly consistent. Destiny and fate are names for the pattern that we believe in without understanding, but that pattern does not deny the operation of free will. In his autobiography Wells thanked his Fate and called attention to his guiding Destiny several times, explaining at one point, "the real commander of my destinies was a singularly facetious Destiny, which seemed to delight in bowling me over in order to roll me through, kicking and struggling to some new and quite unsuspected opportunity" (*Autobiography*, chap. VI: 1). Destiny is a pattern, but not an absolute one; it is more like a drift or tendency; it is simply what happens. Mr. Polly's drift toward marriage is described as fate and destiny, and the small shopmen at Fishbourne caught up in the commercial "gale of fate" see a great door opening in the "fabric of destiny" when Polly burns their buildings down (*Polly*, chap. VI: 3; chap. VII: 6; chap. VII: 5).

Destiny and fate are patterns perceived after the fact, directions recognized after the journey is under way. For those who are alert to events, destiny itself can be governed. In *The Shape of Things to Come* (1933),

Wells writes that the maimed lives of the modern world call to mind the myth of Tantalus who "was put within apparent reach of the unattainable by the inexorable decrees of the gods. Mankind was under no such pitiless destiny" (*Shape*, bk. I: 2). Wells designed his tale precisely to show that man can make his own destiny.

Wells's belief in free will is essential to his hope for continued human progress. It is to this faith what indeterminacy is to physics.[7] That is why accident and chance are so important in Wells's scheme of progress. But free will is a potential. Man can be free, yet fail to direct his life. Beyond the recognition of the ability to transform conditions—which is freedom of the will—is the need for the intention to do so. That is will. This will is a feature of personality, a strength of character. Will is free will conscious of itself in action. Such is the positive view. But a stoic strength of will is as likely to appear in fatalists as a hopeful strength of will is in optimists.

Wells abhorred fatalism because it denied men free will and robbed him of all purpose, all reason to struggle against Nature. As early as "The Limits of Individual Plasticity" (1895), Wells complained that careless generalizations about heredity had created a "fanatic fatalism" that confused a scientific theory "with theological predestination" (*Early Writings*, chap. II). He rejected this limiting notion. He objected to Marxism too because "it carries the conception of a necessary economic development to the pitch of fatalism" (*New Worlds*, chap. XI: 2). The evil here is that men are less likely to struggle for the triumph of socialism if they feel that it is inevitable. "Socialism," Wells counters, "is to be attained, not by fate, but by will" (*New Worlds*, chap. XI: 4).[8] In *The Undying Fire* (1919), Job Huss tells Dr. Barrack that his belief in a Process working through Nature to some designed end is dangerous. This "modern fatalism" is pernicious because it encourages men to "be themselves," which really means ceasing to struggle against the animal in them. It means relinquishing faith in man's ability to take command (*Fire*, chap. V: 2). In *Apropos of Dolores* Foxfield recites Wells's usual warning that man must consciously adapt himself to his rapidly changing environment or "suffer some complex biological dégringolade," or extinction. "He made human destiny," says Wilbeck with admiration, "look like a madly plunging horse—with an amateur in the saddle" (*Dolores*, chap. II: 3). The amateur, nonetheless, would have to learn to ride. It was the indolence of that amateur which excited Wells's dismay and prodded him to harangue his fellow man. The greatest danger to the race was a faulty will.[9]

Many conditions of existence are beyond the control of the will, but Wells believed that steady application, such as he had exerted upon his own destiny, could bring about a desired change (*Autobiography*, chap. VII: 2). In his autobiography he summarized this message.[10] He claimed that he had made the outlines of the human prospect clear for himself and for others and had demonstrated that human life as it is, is simply raw material for what it might be. Mankind can pull itself together and seize a finer future. But the necessary changes demand courage and integrity. "They demand a force and concentration of will and a power of adaptation in habits and usages which may or may not be within the compass of mankind. This is the exciting and moving prospect displayed by the crystal I have brought out of solution" (*Autobiography*, chap. I: 2).

We have already seen how fervently Wells toiled to wrench men from the acceptance of social habits and usages merely because they were the habits and usages that prevailed. The individual had first to become conscious of his ability to escape these forces. That, in itself, was a major achievement. Men were free, Wells insisted, but he did not deny that great effort was required for most men to realize this. When Mr. Brumley in *The Wife of Sir Isaac Harman* (1914) slips into egotistical dreams immediately after imagining that he has transcended selfishness, Wells compassionately observes that "you must not sneer too readily at him, for so God has made the soul of Mr. Brumley and otherwise it could not do" (*Harman*, chap. IX: 10). This sentiment sounds deterministic, but it is essentially Wells's way of indicating human fallibility. Characters regularly suffer epilepsies and breakdowns of the will. Sir Richmond Hardy's crisis in *The Secret Places of the Heart* (1922) is brought on by a failure of will (*Heart*, chap. VII: 7). He says that his will had "come untwisted and was ravelling out into separate strands" (*Heart*, chap. I: 2). William Clissold's will is temporarily crippled by his desire for a woman; he dreams of a "little white house where I can think things out and recover my will" (*Clissold*, vol. II, bk. IV: 13 and 14).

The problem with men is failure of will, but recognizing this fact does not necessarily provide the requisite strength. Men fantasize. In his fantasies, Hoopdriver is a resolute and clever hero. "Invariably this person possessed an iron will" (*Wheels*, chap. X). Theodore Bulpington becomes a virtuoso of self-deception. Having retreated into an extreme and illusory conservatism, he bellows in a drunken harangue against the universe that he is what he chooses to be. "He was about to declare that his Will had triumphed over Reality, that there he was at last, the Captain of his Soul, the Master of his Fate, and then abruptly he became aware that he was talking to nothing, to nothing whatever" (*Blup*, chap. IX: 7).

Some men do manage to put their wills in order. George Ponderevo, looking back on his youthful naivety, remarks, "It is the constant error of youth to over-estimate the Will in things" (*Tono*, bk. I, chap. III: 7). The failure of his marriage seems "like a thing fated" and beyond his and Marion's control. "Our own resolve carried us on our predestined way," he says, revealing a curious contradiction illuminated to some extent by George's sense that, after this disaster, he is without an object to hold his will together. He fastens on science, which gives his life order and saves him from despair, though, in his case, it brings no final solution, as he admits (*Tono*, bk. II, chap. IV: 9-10).

As I suggested earlier, focusing of the will is not of itself a good thing, for misdirected strength of will is also an evil. Rud Whitlow succeeds in so fortifying his will that he leads mankind to a new organized society but is blind to the limits of individual will. There is "nothing whatever to override Will in human affairs," he tells his henchman, Chiffan. "And like it or not . . . I am the Will." But Chiffan is not silenced. "What has come over you?" he admonishes. "Will is all about us, the collective will, guided by the free wisdom of thousands of brains. Will can never be concentrated in one individual. Power you can grab but will escapes you. You of all people understood that so well—once." (*Terror*, bk. IV, chap. II: 6).

The individual man can discover his role as a part of a larger purpose without seeking to bring about a world revolution. When Wells preached socialism, he meant individual wills coalescing in a larger, more powerful will capable of effecting its great purpose. *The Food of the Gods* (1904) allegorizes this subject. Bensington, who lacks the courage to pursue the consequences of his discovery, plunges into "obscure speculations about the Will" but ends by fleeing responsibility (*Food*, bk. I, chap. III). Meanwhile, the giant children represent what Bensington cannot face. "They did not know themselves for what they were. They were children, slow-growing children of a new race. The giant strength grew day by day—the giant will had still to grow into purpose and an aim" (*Food*, bk. II, chap. I). This was a fable of developing will, but Wells was explicit elsewhere. In *New Worlds for Old* (1908), he says there is food, shelter, and wealth enough for all men in the world if they but know it and will it (*New Worlds*, chap. I: 4). They have not so willed because they do not realize the importance of collective action. Wells goes back to fundamentals in his definition of socialism. "It is the denial that chance impulse and individual will and happening constitute the only possible methods by which things may be done in the world. It is an assertion that things are in their nature orderly; that things may be computed, may be calculated upon and foreseen" (*New Worlds*, chap. II). Although present social mechanisms make the focusing of collective will difficult, socialism seeks to enlighten man by preaching collective ownership and control, which imply a collective will. If socialism is to prevail, it must bring its scattered utterances together into "an ordered system of thought, art, literature, and will" (*New Worlds*, chap. XIII: 3).[11]

Though he was opposed to nationalism, Wells sometimes championed the formation of a national will. This is not surprising from an avowed pacifist who cheered men to war. In *Mr. Britling Sees It Through* (1916), he argued that the leaders of the country had "no idea of the Will that surges up in England" to fight against the Germans, who are already united and organized (*Britling*, bk. II, chap. II: 3). The Germans have discipline and science on their side, but Mr. Britling does not believe that the German nation is moved by one will as the allies are.[12] England has been a confused nation, Mr. Britling writes near the end of the novel, but "there is a great people here even as there is a great people in Russia, a people with a soul and character of its own, a people of unconquerable kindliness and with a peculiar genius, which still struggle towards will and expression" (*Britling*, bk. III, chap. II: 5).[13] Later, in *Joan and Peter* (1918), Wells glimpsed in the organization forced upon England by the war "a great and growing understanding and criticism and will, of a rediscovered unity, which was England—awakening" (*Joan*, chap. XIII: 4).

Even as he used these immediate signs of a developing national will, however, he was urging men to something beyond that paltry beginning. The story of Joan and Peter is the story of the species at that time in history. Their education has left these young people with "wills as spontaneous, indefinite and unsocial as the will of a criminal." Although their ideas are not confused, they now face a world of impending disaster "with no clear will in them about it or themselves" (*Joan*, chap. XII: 1).[14] On a visit to Moscow, Oswald tries to convince a disillusioned Peter that the big idea of human reconstruction is not beyond men. Life is real, life is earnest, says Oswald, and Peter retorts, "No. . . . but it ought to be." Oswald is convinced that science brings light. "We shall see the Will plainer and plainer." Peter seems to balk at the capitalization. " 'Our own will then,' said Oswald. 'Yours, mine, and every right sort of man's.' " And Peter replies, "It won't be a national will, anyhow" (*Joan*, chap. XII: 2). Oswald examines the problem privately, realizing that this notion of will is something fairly recent with him, too. Herbert Spencer's pernicious contribution to English social thought was the belief that unrestrained human impulses were not chaos, but direction, in the name of evolution. Oswald has broken free from this kind of thinking. Once he thought of nations and empires as things in themselves, now he realizes that "they are will forms; they present a purpose that claims the subordination of individual aims" (*Joan*, chap. XII: 3).

In *The World Set Free* (1914), Wells had declared that this common will had to transcend national boundaries. If he boasted of a developing national will during wartime, he did so as an expedient. Already King Egbert had declared to the assembled European powers after the Great War that Science was to be the new king of the world, not his royal family or the emancipated peoples of the democracies. The new sovereign "is that common, impersonal will and sense of necessity of which Science is the best understood and most typical aspect. It is the mind of the race" (*Free*, chap. III: 3). At the end of the novel, Marcus Karenin expands this image. Man came into life bringing "mind and memory that dies not when men die, but lives and increases for ever, an overmind, a dominating will, a question and aspiration that reaches to the stars" (*Free*, chap. V: 7).[15] We return here to Wells's persistent analogy between the individual and the species. If one man can so govern his will as to shape his own destiny, then eventually all mankind can do the same.

Just as Wells urged national unity as a model for world unity, so he recommended individual men as examples of leaders who might crystallize the larger will. Sanderson was such a man who set out to draft like spirits to his cause—the creation of a more orderly, unified world. Perhaps, Wells muses, Sanderson's efforts will germinate in a crop of new, creative men of energy. We have seen that Wells was hostile to the great-man theory of history, believing that most human achievement came about through the efforts of innumerable small men; but he recognized the role of leadership and fostered the notion of a highly disciplined elite corps trained to guide the general population. Any leader must first have conviction and strength of will. Theodore Roosevelt was a leader Wells admired. Though he had no "effectual disproof of a pessimistic interpretation of the future" and could not say that mankind would not culminate and pass, Roosevelt "chose to live as if this were not so." Even should the outcome pictured in *The Time Machine* come to pass, Roosevelt said to Wells, "*That doesn't matter now. The effort's real. It's worth going on with.*" This was a spirit clearly akin to Wells's. He remembered the American president "as a symbol of the creative will in man, in its limitations, its doubtful adequacy, its valiant persistence, amidst perplexities and confusions" (*Autobiography*, chap. IX: 9).

Wells praised great leaders whose power of will gave them their positions of leadership, but he saw the dangers of misguided willpower as well. He mocked and besmeared world leaders such as Mussolini and Hitler for their frenzied egotism and for their betrayal of principles he felt were inherently sound. Both dictators had built up corps of disciplined and highly motivated young people to carry out the idealistic schemes of a small elite. So far, so good. But the schemes were reactionary, national, and grossly tainted with egotism. *The Autocracy of Mr. Parham* (1930) was an early examination of this type with Sir Oswald Mosley as an obvious model.

Mr. Parham is a highly educated Oxford don, but faced with the energy and power of Sir Bussy Woodcock, he doubts his own force of will and yearns to increase it. At a seance, he gets his wish. Incorporated into a being called the Master Spirit, he discovers that "an immense power of will had taken possession of him, that he lived in a new vigour, that he was still himself and yet something enormously more powerful, that his mind was full and clear and certain as it had never been before (*Parham*, bk. II: chap. V). He immediately attracts a following, overthrows the ineffective democracy in power, and sets up a new, ordered, and aggressive regime. The trouble is that Parham's ideas are all traditionalist and radically unsuitable for the new world. His force of will and virtue of persuasion are applied to improper ends. Scientists and technicians, the spokesmen of the future, finally halt Parham's insane program, which has been appropriated by military zealots. The whole adventure turns out to be no more than Parham's dream. *The Holy Terror* (1938) was an updated version of this dilemma of misguided will in a strong leader, with Hitler as the model and the story not a dream, but a fantasy.

Wells was a careful teacher. Although he argued his case forcefully, he took the trouble to illustrate its negative potential. He was equally generous in his methods of persuasion. He would cajole, frighten, or seduce to make his point. While enumerating the failings of his time, he heartened his readers with the promise of human progress. The achievements of science and the humanities "express the thought and embody the will—the growing changing thought, the developing will—of mankind," he wrote in *The Way the World is Going* (1929) (*Going*, chap. V). Such assurances recur throughout Wells's writings. They serve as friendly compliments, the kind of encouragements a coach might use to coax a team to greater effort in a game where the outcome remains in doubt. Sometimes he took a heartier tone. In *The Open Conspiracy* (1928), for example, he says that mankind is capable of taking a great stride into a new life but that this advance will not come about inadvertently; it requires "an organization of will and energy to take it as this world has never seen before" (*Conspiracy*, chap. IV). Once man has made that great stride, the game will not be over. Wells offers no final victory, rather constant challenge and a succession of victories. After it has controlled population, warfare, and monopolization of wealth, mankind will face the universe with a great and increasing surplus of will and energy, and life will become an adventure of discovery, not a routine of endurance and mischance. He ends this rousing volume with the words, "the ultimate decision of the fate of life upon this planet lies now in the will of man" (*Conspiracy*, "Marginal Note").

Wells tried to scare mankind into changing its ways in his early works. *The Time Machine* (1895) and *When the Sleeper Wakes* (1899) are examples. He modified, but never relinquished, this weapon. "Could mankind have prevented this disaster of the War in the Air?" he asks in his futurist novel of that name. That, he answers himself, is an idle question. "They could not, because they did not, they had not the will to arrest it." Then he adds, almost maliciously, "What mankind could achieve with a different will is a speculation as idle as it is magnificent" (*Air*, chap. II: 1). This note remains to the end, becoming querulous in *The Croquet Player* or *You Can't Be Too Careful* and definitive in *Mind at the End of its Tether*.

Wells preferred to lure his readers to a better world by offering them one or another realization of it. This was the purpose of the Utopias. The world of *A Modern Utopia* (1905), for example, "is just our own vast mysterious welter, with some of the blackest shadows gone, with a clearer illumination, and a more conscious and intelligent will" (*Utopia*, chap. IV: 2). Conditions in Utopia imply a common purpose and steadfast movement of will essential to the conquest of human egotism. Order and justice are the result of will, not nature. And health itself depends upon the "constant exercise of will that makes life good" (*Utopia*, chap. IX: 6). Thus Utopians allow much liberty to their children "so that their wills may grow freely" (*Utopia*, chap. IX: 8).

Having presented his picture of a superior, if not entirely ideal, community, fundamentally based upon a firm, active, and common will, Wells admits that, though there is little to prevent man from attaining such a community, that effort is too much for the contemporary mind. His summary of the importance of that effort amounts to Wells's creed.

> The new things will be indeed of the substance of the thing that is, but differing just in the measure of the will and imagination that goes to make them. They will be strong and fair as the will is sturdy and organised and the imagination comprehensive and bold; they will be ugly and smeared with wretchedness as the will is fluctuating and the imagination timid and mean.
>
> Indeed Will is stronger than Fact, it can mould and overcome Fact. But this world has still to discover its will, it is a world that slumbers inertly, and all this roar and pulsation of life is no more than its heavy breathing. . . . My mind runs on to the thought of an awakening. (*Utopia*, chap. XI: 5)

Everywhere in the Utopia of *Men Like Gods* (1923) this creed is in operation. These remade men long ago shed the old fatalism that went by the names of God or Evolution or any presumed Power beyond the self which excuses men from their duties. Urthred tells the Earthlings, "With Man came Logos, the Word and the Will into our universe, to watch it and fear it, to learn it and cease to fear it, to know it and comprehend it and master it" (*Gods*, bk. I, chap. VI: 5). This understanding and mastery the Utopians have accomplished, and their clean and spacious life is free from disease and strife. Mr. Barnstaple admires how boldly the human mind has taken hold of the life and destiny of the race. When he reluctantly returns from Utopia, he thinks, "The Sons of the Earth also, purified from disease, sweet-minded and strong and beautiful, would go proudly about their conquered planet and lift their daring to the stars." This is a tantalizing picture, but Wells informs his enchanted readers that there is a price. " 'Given the will,' said Mr. Barnstaple. 'Given only the will' " (*Gods*, bk. III, chap. IV: 3).

   *The Shape of Things to Come* (1933) is not so much a Utopian novel as a continuation of the *Outline of History* into the future. It carries the world of the 1930s ahead some centuries along probable lines. Here Wells projects in greater detail than anywhere else in his fiction the manner in which the human will might achieve the necessary consolidation to plan and bring into being an ordered world. Wells doubted the capacity of democracy to achieve this end.[16] Nonetheless, in *The Shape of Things to Come*, he asserts that whereas revolution must begin with an elite group, it had to spread to and saturate the minds of the many. "Then, and then only, could the necessary will-power be marshalled and directed to the effective reorganization of earthly affairs" (*Shape*, bk. I: 13).[17] And that is what happens. The new world government does not come into being easily. War, pestilence, and dispute precede it, but gradually power focuses. It focuses at times with great severity, for the new government intends to control moral teaching, and such an intention involves the extermination of certain religious forces. Ultimately the constantly developing World State not only rules the will, it becomes the will. The offices of government are a form of being. The Department of General Psychology (including all aspects of education) has become "the thought, as the World Council had become the will, of mankind acting as a whole" (*Shape*, bk. IV: 5).

   Wells hoped that by depicting a future or another dimension in which the failings of the world were corrected, he would teach men to desire it. He told them that it was relatively easy to achieve, if they had the will to strive for it. The small, but utterly crucial, detail in this scheme was that the cleaning up of the will came first. Men don't just start willing a desired object with all the concentration and energy of their being unless they have trained that will. Wells could point to few places in the world where this training of the will was accomplished by educational or other means. The great religions of the past had been approximations of what he wanted. But the days of Buddha, Mohammed, and Aristotle (a secular candidate) are past, Philip Rylands says near the end of *Meanwhile* (1927). The new movement requires countless men and women working for the cause without a single figurehead. This new world cult must be held together "by a common confession and common repudiations. Its common basis must be firstly the history of all life as one being that grew in wisdom and power, and secondly the completest confidence in the possibility of the informed will to comprehend and control" (*Meanwhile*, bk. II: 21).

The secret is to inspire a sufficient number of persons to work for such a new revolution. Passion and objectivity, fire and discipline must unite. William Clissold's image of this possibility was the process of crystallization. He believed that material life acquired its shape from the creative mind. He sought to teach men unity of self so that they might learn racial unity. His own source of strength is simple. "I have this strange conception of world revolution, of the great creative work of setting up a World Republic, to which I give myself. By that I unify my aims and my life" (*Clissold*, vol. II, bk. VI: 10).

Richard Remington likened mankind's emerging communal mind to the upward-tending coral colonies, an image that suitably describes Clissold's aim as well. As the individual man stretches upward, he constrains himself to a design. As others do the same, and their ideals come together, a massive communal pattern develops. The pattern of the past grows clearer and man continues to yearn upward, still creating. But man differs from the coral, for he can control the shape of the future by looking back and by looking within. Moreover, the larger life for mankind will resemble the desired life of the individual. "I see the nearness of an order in the world," Clissold says, "like the order of a garden, of a workroom, of a laboratory, a clean life and a direct life and a powerful life for men; the jungle and all its sufferings gone at last for ever" (*Clissold*, vol. I, bk. I: 15).

The scheme so far runs this way. Wells asserted the freedom of man's will insofar as man can perceive it in a four-dimensional world. Since he is, in this sense, free, he can change himself and the world around him though partially confined by heredity and environment. This transformation is self-conscious and begins as a subjective act. It requires a power of self-discipline identifiable with the human quality called will. This organizing power gives unity and purpose first to the self and ultimately to a community of selves that create for themselves a larger Will, through which unimaginable things can be achieved. All of this begins, however, with a manifestation of the consciousness of freedom in action.

Mr. Polly learned that if he didn't like his life, he could change it. For Wells, that generally meant escape from a restricting condition in order to create a liberating one. I have already shown how ingrained this need for escape is in Wells's books. It is difficult to say if the need for escape required a belief in free will or if a conviction of free will demanded the initial capacity for escape, but the two are intimately linked. Almost all of Wells's central characters seek to take charge of their lives. Many actually do; some perish in the attempt; others delude themselves about their relationship to fate. Motives for escape vary. If Ann Veronica and Ellen Harman seek to free themselves from roles thrust upon them by a male-dominated tradition, Arthur Kipps and Alfred Polly long for emancipation from economic entanglement, William Leadford from class confinement, and Wells himself from the imprisonment of what he considered a dead and decaying culture.

We have already seen that Wells presented accident and chance as opportunities for change and liberty. In *Kipps* and *The History of Mr. Polly* inheritances are the agents for freeing characters from entrapment.[18] In *The Time Machine* and *The Invisible Man*, on the other hand, extraordinary scientific discoveries provide promises of freedom which end ambiguously or worse. In *The World Set Free* world war is the abrupt means for liberating mankind and starting it on the road to self-realization. Most incredible of all is the transformation of mankind in *In the Days of the Comet* when a comet passing near the earth purifies the atmosphere with its gases, leaving men purged of their grosser natures and capable of working toward salvation.

The nature of salvation also varies. Hoopdriver in *The Wheels of Chance* accidentally encounters a young woman who provides him with a promising jolt out of his narrow life. He is barely started on the road to salvation, but he is aimed in the direction of greater awareness. Kipps and Polly are further along the way—the one establishing himself as a book-dealer in circumstances comfortable enough to permit him to read and think at leisure, the other achieving a quiet, simple life as general factotum of the Potwell Inn. George Ponderevo in *Tono-Bungay* glimpses a broader vision of salvation that extends beyond his personal circumstances.

Freedom of will, once recognized, calls forth strength of will. Whether it comes by chance or by concerted effort, individual disenthrallment must be pursued through strength of will. Only in this way does one achieve genuine freedom. Beyond this, as Ponderevo recognizes, man learns to submit his private will to a larger purpose. Some of Wells's characters do not see this; some see it, but cannot achieve it; others do both. Ann Veronica, in demanding her own modest liberty, senses that greater purpose. She sees herself as part of a "Bios" encompassing all people and things, and this view enables her to discard what she calls the "wrappered" life and to open herself to new experiences. By contrast, Ramage means to be "master of his fate" by seducing Ann, and Manning egotistically imagines that Fate makes Ann love another man just so that he may prove his devotion by rescuing her from him. It is Ramage who observes of Ann Veronica, "There's something about you, a little flavour of Will, I suppose, that makes one feel—good luck about you and success" (*Veronica*, chap. III: 7). And as she learns to exert her will, she does succeed, though not without setbacks, ultimately seeing herself and Capes as part of a younger generation that must struggle against the limited perceptions of its predecessors, exerting a will sufficient to overcome the inertia of things as they are and participating in the onward movement or progress of the race. Ann's and

Capes's achievement is a modest one—they succeed in running off together, eventually marrying, and being accepted socially.[19] In any common
romance this might have seemed a routine incident; but because Wells
makes his characters representative of broader ideas, the achievement is
more consequential than it appears.

Richard Remington has a more elaborate view of how personal liberation forms a part of the larger process of unification in the species. Early in
his life he saw that the dominant force in existence was chaotic impulse, and
man's principal endeavor was to overrule that chaos, bringing ethical order
into being after the manner recommended by Huxley in "Evolution and
Ethics." Remington is acutely aware of how slender that control can be. A
childhood incident in which he struggled with young bullies for the possession of a knife was his awakening. "It was the first time I glimpsed the
simple brute violence that lurks and peeps beneath our civilization" (*Machiavelli*, bk. I, chap. III: 3). But although he labors for order and human
reconstruction through political means, Remington is himself a disruptive
force. Finally, he chooses private gratification over social sacrifice. His
powerful will is canceled in the larger realm. Later characters would more
successfully subordinate their personal wills to the larger purpose of the
World State. William Clissold is one of the better examples outside the
futuristic tales.

For a writer often charged with stultifying didacticism, Wells fills his
novels with an astonishing amount of real and figurative movement. But
physical movement is necessary to depict will operating in a world of
change and progress. In this, his narratives, especially the fantasies and
romances, strongly resemble the adventure tales popular at the turn of the
century. In the sensational tales of Kipling, Haggard, Correlli, Stoker, and
a wide assortment of other writers, the will of a central figure is tested
through a series of vivid incidents. Exertion of will in these stories is often a
passionate resistance against the threat of nothingness. It is restless rather
than constructive. In his life and in his writing Wells combined restlessness
and construction. This is his description of his yearning for an appropriate
setting for his work: "I have built two houses and practically rebuilt a third
to make that Great Good Place to work in," he explains, almost as though
he were providing credentials, and then adds, "I have shifted from town to
country and from country to town, from England to abroad and from
friend to friend, I have preyed upon people more generous than myself who
loved me and gave life to me" (*Autobiography*, chap. I: 1).

In this revealing passage Wells evokes a sense of himself as a restless
creature thrashing about in a trap. Clearly movement is a release. The last
sentence repeats in its form a pattern that is manifest in most of Wells's

writings. It begins with what appears to be an attempt at location. What could be more stabilizing than the building of a house? But when one builds two, and then three, it is obvious that another, more powerful impulse than stabilization is at work. It is the movement that is important, not the construction and localization. Admitting this commanding impulse, Wells moves to an admittedly locomotive account, first describing a shift from one region to another, and then from one nation to another. Finally, as the nature of the locomotion becomes clearer, the journey or quest becomes a hunt and Wells a beast feeding on the human beings that he overtakes and consumes. From the very first, the pursuit for the Great Good Place has, in reality, been prompted by an all-consuming hunger. The very energy that drives him from a world confused and disordered by human passions and irrationalities spurs him toward an equally irrational and passionate ideal.[20]

Locomotion was an essential detail in Wells's scheme of ideas. His first thoughtful presentation of an ordered view of the future, in *Anticipations* (1901), began with his perception of the enormous changes that improvements in transportation and communication were bringing about.[21] Most of his early stories are based upon radical movements. There is movement through time in *The Time Machine* and *When the Sleeper Wakes*, and movement to distant, exotic locations in *The Island of Dr. Moreau* and *The First Men in the Moon*. Later there is movement to another space/time dimension in *A Modern Utopia* and *Men Like Gods*. More traditionally, tales such as *The Invisible Man, The Wheels of Chance, The War of the Worlds, Tono-Bungay*, and *The History of Mr. Polly*, to go no further, are posited upon frequent, sometimes extremely agitated, movement.

Some of this movement is nothing more sophisticated than flight and chase. "A Story of the Stone Age" (1897), for example, is largely a record of a Pleistocene *Homo sapiens*'s peregrinations and accompanying encounters with beasts and men. Nonetheless, it is a sort of voyage of discovery, whereas "My First Aeroplane" and "Little Mother Up the Mörderburg" (1910) are almost entirely slapstick. Increasingly, Wells guides the turbulent movement of his tales in specific directions. It becomes journey, even quest. We have seen in Wells's topographical image-constellations how geographical and spatial his concept of liberation was. It should not be surprising that this relationship appears in the very structure of his narratives.

Time and again characters set forth with an objective in mind only to be interrupted, redirected, and to some extent, reeducated. Hoopdriver on his bicycling tour is a simple, realistic example. Bert Smallways's planned tour becomes an international journey in *The War in the Air (1908)*. Núñez's climb into the Andes turns into an adventure with a lost people in "The

Country of the Blind" (1904), whereas William Leadford's murderous pursuit in *In the Days of the Comet* (1906) ends in a renovated world. *A Modern Utopia* (1905) begins as a walking tour in the mountains and divagates into Utopia. Wells was an early cycling enthusiast, but he also loved cars, so he sometimes uses an automobile excursion as the structural basis for a narrative. *The Secret Places of the Heart* (1922) is a good example, since it is an overt psycho-quest. The device appears fancifully in *Men Like Gods* (1923), where Mr. Barnstaple sets out on a therapeutic tour something like Sir Richmond Hardy's, but ends up in Utopia, not in love. A driving vacation is the underlying structure in *Apropos of Dolores* (1938), where it mirrors a pursuit of ideal beauty. Sometimes, even when it is a minor element, it can serve the same function; thus Mr. Britling plans to drive out to visit his mistress but wanders instead over the moonlit roads of England where he decides upon a new direction for his life.

There are far-ranging quests of varying merit in *Tono-Bungay* (1909), *Marriage* (1912), *The Research Magnificent* (1915), and *Mr. Blettsworthy on Rampole Island* (1928), all of which exhibit this same feature of an unexpected shift in course. The important thing is the starting out, the charging of the will to action. No one can say for sure where the journey will end. This is just what Wells was saying about human progress and human destiny. In a few instances, he showed that men might sometimes bypass their destinations without knowing or even purposely. "The Door in the Wall" (1906) is a moving example of the second possibility, just as *The Happy Turning* (1945) is a fanciful resolution of it. In this late tale Wells describes the route he takes in a recurrent dream that leads him to a place where his repressed fancies are fulfilled and where he can examine— sometimes with the help of a down-to-earth Jesus Christ—the problems facing mankind.

Wells's topographical foundation for his ideas was not confined to jungles, uplands, and so forth. Often he commandeered the traditional image of the road, path, or way to his purposes. If a tangled forest path was Wells's image for the state of mankind, his image of the hoped-for corrective was a clear road; but just as science might help man to correct many material difficulties without leading him toward some ultimate purpose, so Wells's roads might lead nowhere. Also, although loitering on the open road is obviously reprehensible in Wells's grander schemes, sometimes it may be desirable, as in *The History of Mr. Polly*. In writing his autobiography, Wells said that he was making a pause to consolidate his powers; he compares his mood to the wayside halt from fatigue "of a belated tramp on a road where there is no rest-house before the goal" (*Autobiography*, chap. I: 1). Here Wells conceives of a goal for the journey; elsewhere the journey itself must determine the goal. In *The Undying Fire* (1919), men are urged to avoid the "blind alleys" of selfishness and follow instead the "high road of salvation," but that high road does not exist until man exerts himself (*Fire*, chap. V: 4-5; chap. VI: 2-3). Man creates out of his own will the truth and the way he follows. Seen differently, it is as though man is constructing a highway through difficult terrain and can be certain of his progress only by examining the road itself as it grows.

Sometimes even those who have glimpsed the upland are denied the goal. William Clissold and Clementina have dedicated themselves to Clissold's great scheme of world education. Their way looks clear, but the unpredictable world of fact intervenes. Driving out of a gorge on a narrow road, Clissold swerves to avoid a child who carelessly darts in front of the car. The car runs off the road and plunges into a ravine. It is a highly symbolic scene. No man can be sure, Wells suggests, that he will follow the road all the way to the end, but he can set out, and he can plan the route so that others may follow.

Here too force of will was essential. In order to map out the way ahead, one had to muster one's knowledge and subordinate it to a general course of behavior. Capriciousness is not a map maker's trait. Wells was thorough and much given to broad planning and strategy even in small things, as *Floor Games* (1911) and *Little Wars* (1913) show. We have seen that he favored a broad perspective, a view of the landscape from an imagined height, that made planning a route more practicable. For this detachment, an achievement of the will was necessary. It began at home. He said, "In my own behaviour just as in my apprehension of things the outline is better than the detail. The more closely I scrutinize my reactions, the more I find detailed inconsistencies, changes of front and goings to and fro. The more I stand off from the immediate thing and regard my behavior as a whole the more it holds together" (*Autobiography*, chap. I: 3). This fluctuation in his perception of the world between clear broad outline and complicated detail reflects the difference between high road and jungle path. It explains his literary movement between broad, sweeping general projects for human advancement and novels concerned with ambiguous individual human dilemmas. Wells sought the high road but calculated that a good deal of local terrain would have to be cleared before the paving could be laid down. No matter how clear the map, local complications will arise. One needs a plan for life, but unexpected accidents will alter that scheme for good or ill.

Perhaps the most memorable plan for life in Wells's fiction is young Mr. Lewisham's Schema—a plan that sets out the ambitious student's detailed timetable for acquiring knowledge and disciplining life. But Lewisham disregards his own warm blood, and before long the Schema is abandoned in favor of a certain Ethel Henderson. This romance passes and Lewisham returns to his demanding plan of education. But when Lewisham meets Ethel again some years later, the Schema falls once more. Finally, Lewisham looks back upon his Schema as mere play compared to the real life he now pursues in accordance with Natural Selection.

Like the journeys that do not end at their destinations, plans, says Wells, have a way of going amiss. George McWhirter Fotheringay of "The Man Who Could Work Miracles" (1898) discovers his ability to work a miracle, which he himself defines as "something contrariwise to the course of nature done by power of Will, something what couldn't happen without being specially willed." The story instructs us that willpower is nothing without a coherent and reasoned plan. Fotheringay consistently fails to foresee the consequences of his miracles. In the end he is driven to will the power away.

Even in the admired realm of science plans could be insufficient. Thus, while the experiments in *The Food of the Gods* have the appearance of being charted and designed, in fact the charters are surprised by the consequences of their research. Only when the giant Cossar brothers, with wills and minds of a new dimension, decide to act is a new scheme for the improvement of England proposed. It is promptly resisted. The superior intelligence of the Martians in *The War of the Worlds* seems to have projected a flawless scheme for the domination of the earth until an unforeseen microbe destroys the invaders.

Will comes first, followed by a plan, but neither guarantees success. One must be able to exploit chance and accident, to adapt to sudden alterations of circumstance. As Wells saw it, this was the history of the species. His successful planners, good and bad, the Rud Whitlows and the Utopians, adjust their plans to fit their needs. Wells enjoyed games of various descriptions but was impatient of rules that prevented him from winning. His favorite games seemed to have a good measure of free-for-all in them. In effect, Wells believed that projecting plans and mapping out a route were necessary steps in focusing the individual and communal will, but he was conscious that no maps were flawless guides in the terra incognita that mankind had to traverse. Nonetheless, faulty as they were, these maps were helpful.

The broader the schemes, the better. Begin with man's will to subjugate Nature and one has a start. Even there, however, Wells could project some surprising consequences in *The Time Machine*. As we have seen, Wells placed a great deal of faith in scientific research while remaining fully aware of its limitations. He inherited the general trend of nineteenth-century science away from historicism and toward experimental observation. Scientists were less inclined to confuse history and causation, more interested in searching out practical forces. Wells, too, rejected history as causation and was interested in discovering guiding principles or laws by which to construct theories that would remain provisional, but useful, guides.[22]

Much as Wells believed in the objectivity of the scientific method, he placed it in a larger purposive design. He was not unaffected by the aspiring thought of the previous century. Comte's positivist scheme describing a progressive history of the human mind from a theological, to a metaphysical, to a positive or scientific phase was still alive in works that Wells admired, such as William Winwood Reade's *Martyrdom of Man* (1872), which divided the universal history of man into four progressive stages, the first characterized by War, the second dominated by Religion, the third representing Liberty, and the last expressed as the triumph of Intellect by which he meant Science. "It is Science alone," he declared, "which can ameliorate the condition of the human race."[23] Wells shared this faith and proffered evidence to convince his readers that science could solve men's troubles. It is impossible to examine in detail Wells's many ideas on how science could be utilized in constructing large-scale plans for man's development. He mentions many of these in *The Work, Wealth and Happiness of Mankind* and elsewhere. At present we can glance at one practical example.

Malthusian thought survived into the twentieth century largely by way of Herbert Spencer and Social Darwinism, but near the end of the nineteenth century scientific experiments began to demand modifications of accepted attitudes. For example, if the human population could be not only controlled but remolded, the prospects for the future were intriguing. During the Edwardian years, many people voiced fears that the English were in danger of degeneration and decay. Some argued that this degeneration was an evolutionary adaptation to the new industrial conditions. The mood of pessimism was widespread. Samuel Hynes remarks that Wells might have borrowed his picture in *The War in the Air* of civilization's decline through a failure of will from Kipling.[24]

If Wells shared the fear of racial degradation, he was also aware of proposed remedies. The career of the noted American scientist Thomas Hunt Morgan reveals the trend of thought on this subject during these years. Beginning as an antagonist of Darwinism in *Evolution and Adaptation* (1903), Morgan gradually accepted its main assumptions, and then, beginning again with serious scepticism of Mendelian genetics, he ended by confirming the method of genetic study in *The Mechanism of Mendelian Heredity* (1915). Wells's acceptance was swifter. Darwinism he accepted from the start, and Mendel seems to have given him no trouble.[25] But there were other proposals abroad that confused the issue.

Darwin's cousin Francis Galton offered a concrete application of

Darwin's theories through a "science" of eugenics designed to improve the human stock. Darwin had his doubts about this, but after a time the idea caught on.[26] The notion was current in Wells's youth and entered into his thinking. And he remained interested in eugenics, even joining the Eugenics Education Society, founded in 1907.[27] Wells valued Malthus's calling attention to the fact that the main business of human life centers on reproduction. But he rejected Galton's oversimplified remedies for the problems arising from indiscriminate breeding.[28] He ended his section on "The Problem of the Birth Supply" in *Mankind in the Making* (1903) by saying that "our main attack in this enterprise of improving the birth supply must lie . . . through research." Perhaps our children will discover a method hidden to us (*Mankind*, chap. II). Characteristically, Wells did not leave it to the children. He signed a letter defending Margaret Sanger against federal indictments for her work with birth control.[29] He became vice-president of Marie Stopes's Society for Constructive Birth Control and Racial Progress formed in 1921. Its motto was "Babies in the right places."[30] Wells and Bennett were both vice-presidents of the Malthusian League in that year, and in 1930 Wells became a member of the National Birth Control Council, established to coordinate the work of existing birth control societies and promote scientific contraception.[31]

Despite his reputation for utopianism, Wells was a soundly practical thinker. On this topic he wished to foster plans for nurturing children who came in the usual way. He did not recommend tampering with genes. He applied his broad scientific principles to society but defended the privacy of the individual family. And, as usual, he spoke out boldly. At a birth control conference in 1922, he announced:

> The choice before us is not a choice between innocence and knowledge. It is a choice between whispering, leering, red-eared and furtive-eyed knowledge on the one hand, and candid, straightforward knowledge on the other. We stand in this movement for the open way, for the scientific method and for light.[32]

A few years later, he was a member of a deputation to the Ministry of Health, encouraging the dissemination of information about birth control. He commented afterward, "I think that a married woman who knows nothing about birth control is little better than a serf, a mere helpless breeding animal, and when I find an obscurantist Roman Catholic sitting in the light at the Ministry of Health, I think myself entitled to make a noise about it."[33]

Although he rejected Galton and the kind of eugenics developed by Alfred Ploetz in Germany as a racial hygiene for the human species, Wells did believe in a control of reproduction and supervision of child rearing. He was more concerned about individual willpower than scientific control. In

*A Modern Utopia* (1905), he proposed state control of child nurture but did not support enforced selective breeding.[34] Job Huss has a vision of the world organized by a collective will when "there will be no blind thrusting into life and no blind battle to keep in life, like the battle of a crowd crushed into a cul-de-sac." (*Fire*, chap. V: 5). Because he believed in this kind of control, he defended Margaret Sanger, Marie Stopes, and others who championed birth control. In *The World of William Clissold* (1926), he has Clissold say, "Birth control embodies in the most intimate and vivid form, the essential differentiation of the newer conception of life from the old. The old was based upon the idea of a meticulous Providence." It childishly abandoned its own will to "the way of Nature and the Will of God. But the new idea of life admits no limit to man's attempt to control his destinies. It plans as largely as it can; it would plan more largely if it could; it gathers together every available force to free man from accident and necessity and make him master of the universe in which he finds himself" (*Clissold*, vol. II, bk. V: 12).[35]

Wells laid out his basic views on these subjects most extensively in *The Work, Wealth and Happiness of Mankind* (1932). By this time, overpopulation of the earth seemed to be less likely since men and women were learning to be selective in their reproduction of their young thanks to the widespread practice of birth control. Wells openly declared that it was biologically bad for the race that persons inherently feeble of mind or body should survive and reproduce. No doubt he considered his position charitable. "Our world is wealthy enough for them to live out their lives as pleasantly as they are capable of living them," he said, "but the persuasion spreads steadily that by birth control in some form, by humane sterilization —now a proven possibility—such strains should be brought to an end" (*Work*, chap. X: 7). On the other hand, he still maintained that "eugenics is not yet to be regarded as a practical proposition" and gave reasons why (*Work*, chap. XIII: 2-3).

Wells was concerned with the detailed, even intimate control of humanity's future, but he realized that any specific scientific or political advances depended upon an important first step—an elementary act of the will, the perception of design. What does not yet exist cannot have a form. The map for the future is a figment since it describes a landscape that has not come into being. The great act of the will is to create the shape of the future, to give it a form for men to live into. "We have to create a vision" of the World State, Wells wrote in *The Salvaging of Civilization* (1921), "to make it seem first a possibility and then an approaching reality" (*Salvaging*, chap. III). And once that configuration of the future has been imagined, all mankind need do is grasp the shape and believe. Wells presents an absurd, but not foolish, version of this process when Mr. Preemby tries to persuade the patrons of a restaurant that he is Sargon, bringing the new world. "You may cease to be things of habit and servitude, and you may become masters of a world reborn. Now! This moment. *Will* the change with me and the change is upon you!" (*Christina*, bk. II, chap. II: 5).

This may sound like Mr. Polly's discovery again, but behind it is a concept both old and very modern. The epigraph to *The World of William Clissold* is Heraclitus' maxim, "all things change." Wells associated the idea of continual flux with a perception of existence reduced to its atomic constituents. For example, he warns that Mr. Barnstaple's sense of security and stability while admiring a lovely sunset is mistaken, for "that effect of immense tranquillity was a delusion; that still evening peace was woven of incredible billions of hurrying and clashing atoms" (*Gods*, bk. III, chap. I: 3). Upon this atomized world any gestalt may be imposed by man, the form-making creature. Clissold admits that he has "never encountered even a stain on a wall or a glowing cavity in a fire upon which my mind could not impose a design" (*Clissold*, vol. I, bk. I: 12). Man imagines a shape for his life so that he may believe that it has purpose; he shapes the world of matter, giving it new forms and new directions; in the same way he can fashion his own future. "There is nothing beyond man," Job Huss warns, "unless men will that something shall be" (*Fire*, chap. V: 4). In *When the Sleeper Wakes* (1899), Graham finds it difficult to believe that he has awakened after more than two hundred years to the position of King of the World. Helen Wotton urges him to accept the responsibilities of his role.

> "I know how great this kingship of mine is," he said haltingly. "I know how great it seems. But is it real? It is incredible—dreamlike. Is it real, or is it only a great delusion?"
> "It is real," she said; "if you dare."
> "After all, like all kingship, my kingship is Belief. It is an illusion in the minds of men."
> "If you dare!" she said. (*Sleeper*, chap. XVIII)

Daring and dreaming are intimately connected in Wells's thinking, and the ambivalence is evident in Graham's case. Wells describes two processes in one when Graham, waking into a new world, grapples with his own identity.

> What a wonderfully complex thing! this simple seeming unity—the self! Who can trace its reintegration as morning after morning after morning we awaken, the flux and confluence of its countless factors interweaving, rebuilding, the dim first stirrings of the soul, the growth and synthesis of the unconscious to the sub-conscious, the sub-conscious to dawning consciousness, until at last we recognize ourselves again. (*Sleeper*, chap. III)

When he becomes conscious of the amazing qualities of the new world,

Graham wants to believe that it is real and tells himself it is no dream. His happiest dream in the past was that of flight and now he can indulge that desire as he learns to fly. But there is a tiny, suggestive pattern in the novel hinting that Graham *is* dreaming. Graham meets Isbister near the seashore and lapses into his trance in a room at the seaside village of Boscastle. When he regains consciousness, he hears a sound, a "rise and fall, like the murmur of breakers on pebbles" (*Sleeper*, chap. III). Later, that same sound, the voices of the people, was "as the soughing of the sea upon a pebble beach," and later again "like the sound of waves upon a pebbly beach," and still later Graham tells Ostrog that the noise of the people is "a sound like the sea. Not voices—but a Voice" (*Sleeper*, chap. XIII, XVI, and XXII). Before falling asleep, Graham had considered suicide by jumping from a cliff. At the end of his story he is plummeting toward earth in his aircraft, thinking, "In such a fall as this countless dreams have ended. But in a moment he would wake" (*Sleeper*, chap. XXIV). He keeps hoping this to the end, but we see him neither wake nor smash.[36]

It was "low water" in the bad old days when Graham fell asleep. Waking two centuries later, he finds conditions for the common people unimproved, but through his leadership the tide rises and washes Ostrog and his oppressive tyranny away. The hint is subtler than we normally expect from Wells, but in the next chapter I shall show that he was entirely capable of this subtlety. The motif of rising from sleep to action is the basic foundation of this novel's plot, but Wells makes its significance clear. "My age was an age of dreams—of beginnings, an age of noble hopes," Graham says. Now, Helen Wotton exclaims, "the people have awakened" (*Sleeper*, chap. XXIII). Noble hopes, the projected shapes of the future, are the products of eager wills; but just as the human imagination may conduct plans impossible to put into immediate effect, so mankind might foresee an orderly world but be unable to make it real. Dreams could be sound models for the future or mere delusions. Wells himself wavered in his attitudes about the metaphor, but he used it repeatedly to illustrate the transformation that a disciplined will could bring.[37]

William Leadford in *In the Days of the Comet* (1906) repeats Graham's sentiment about the bad old days, which were "a dream from which no one on earth expected an awakening" (*Comet*, bk. I, chap. II: 1). But if the past is a bad dream, the future is a good one. In the bad time, "it was the dream of any better state of things that was scouted as lunacy" (*Comet*, bk. I, chap. III: 7).[38] But with the passing of the comet, mankind awakens clean-eyed before life. The new world is not perfect, but, Leadford says, "we have found our poor reasonable minds, our wills to live well, ourselves, adrift on a wash of instincts, passions, instinctive prejudices, half animal stupidities. . . . Here we are like people clinging to something—like people awakening—upon a raft" (*Comet*, bk. III, chap. I: 4).

Wells based this metaphor, like several others, upon a physical reality. In his doctoral thesis, he described the process of awakening.

> Forthwith a rush of exterior stimulations, which arouse memories and establish reactions, pours in upon—not you altogether, *but into that arena of the neurosensitive apparatus which for the time being you imagine you are.* There is a rapid expansion of activities.
>
> Before that occurred the activity of the awakening moment dominated everything else. It was a dream, yes; but the dream was for the moment *you.* It was the ruling sequence. Then, as the expanding system of outside reactions became dominant, the dream-self receded into insignificance, over-powered by the new ascendant system. Usually in a few moments the neurosensitive apparatus (you) can recall hardly anything but a few vivid aspects of the dream that ruled it so recently, but even that much it is busy rationalizing. ('*42*, Appendix I: 1)

Wells described Graham reassembling his personality after centuries. In *Men Like Gods* (1923), Mr. Barnstaple goes through a similar procedure his first morning in Utopia. Sometimes Wells's characters awake from the dream of their own lives to new possibilities, not the limits of the old self. "Most of my time I've been half dreaming," Mr. Polly says. "I married like a dream almost. I've never really planned my life or set out to live. I happened; things happened to me" (*Polly*, chap. X: 3). And just as Barnstaple and Graham reassemble their selves in amazing new circumstances, Sir Richmond Hardy and Miss Grammont in *The Secret Places of the Heart* (1922) make a larger attempt to "remember" the incidents of mankind's youth, as though, finally awake themselves, they can establish a necessary unity.

One does not always awaken gradually. Mankind, Wells suggested, probably requires some jolt to bring it to consciousness. In *First and Last Things* he says, "It seems to me that the whole living creation may be regarded as walking in its sleep, as walking in the sleep of instinct and individualised illusion, and that now out of it all rises the Spirit of Man, beginning to perceive his larger self, his collective synthetic purpose to increase Power and realise Beauty" (*Things*, bk. II: 11).[39] Throughout his writings Wells refers to the dreamlike quality of life. It is not only men who have had extraordinary adventures who doubt sometimes if they wake or dream.

In one sense all mankind is dreaming because it has not yet wakened to its full consciousness, but in another it is dreaming in anticipation of that consciousness. Wells warned in *First and Last Things* that men have a tendency to reason between terms on incompatible planes and therefore arrive only at confusion, an idea he had already expressed in "The Rediscovery of the Unique" and "Scepticism of the Instrument." The level of common experience is one plane while that of scientific analysis is another. Hence terms applying to molecular physics or the question of free will and determinism are inapplicable in the daily life of common sensation. Similarly, anticipations and schemes for the future operate at one level of human thought, but the terms used to describe the future do not translate directly to immediate problems of existence.

Positive dreams are ideals—necessary formulations of the future, pictures of what is not yet but may be. The conception of a Great State, Wells notes in *Social Forces in England and America* (1914), "is still altogether unsubstantial. It is a project as dreamlike to-day as electric lighting, electric traction, or aviation would have been in the year 1850" (*Forces*, "The Great State": 4). Those dreams became real, Wells implies, and therefore the Great State might too.

Dreaming is prelude to waking. Dreams may be nightmares or they may be visions. "A Dream of Armageddon" (1901) offers an unpleasant picture of the world to come. Wells preferred favorable dreams. He had imitated the dream-vision technique of William Morris and others in his early writing and he employed dream narratives throughout his career, but he also saw dreams as practical speculations on the future.[40] Luxuriating in the upwelling flood of scientific information, Wells exults in "The Possible Individuality of Atoms" (1896), "This is indeed a time for dreaming." (*Early Writings*, chap. IV). Dreams can be useful. Even for a Pleistocene man like Ugh-Lomi dreams reveal important truths. In "The Discovery of the Future," Wells delights in the very unpredictability of mankind's dream of a finer future. It is a spur to effort, not a deterrent.

All human conceiving is an artificial assembling of material data into arbitrary form. The life we live today is a dream, an imagined scheme that confines us. Wells made this point in *The Autocracy of Mr. Parham* (1930), one of his cleverer dream narrations.

> All life has something dreamlike in it. No percipient creature has ever yet lived in stark reality. Nature has equipped us with such conceptions and delusions as survival necessitated, and our experiences are at best but working interpretations. Nevertheless, as they diverge more and more from practical truth and we begin to stumble against danger, our dearest dreams are at last invaded by remonstrances and warning shadows. And now this dream that was the life of the Lord Paramount was changing; more and more was it discoloured by doubt and adverse intimations. (*Parham*, bk. IV, chap. II)

If all life is shifting and dreamlike, why not make that dream as fine as possible by extending it into a splendid future? It is through dreams, for example, that Joe Davis pictures the finer world of Martians that he anticipates in *Star-Begotten* (1937). Many who have had dreams of brotherhood and human unity doubt them, as Bolaris does in *The Brothers* (1938). "Am I," he anguishes, "after all, just a wilful dreamer of a world that can never arrive?" (*Brothers*, chap. VI: 3). Clissold, too, has his moments of doubt.

Men, he says, so far from achieving a better world, do not even desire it. "The republic of mankind is a dream." This assertion would seem to end the matter, but Wells continues immediately with a moving passage in which the dream returns, gradually becoming the true fact while the world shrinks to insubstantiality.

> But here in this secluded peaceful place and especially at night when every-thing is still, one can take a larger view, see things upon the scale of history, see the wide-sweeping radius of destiny tracing its onward path across the skies. Then change has a countenance of purpose, the World Republic like the stars seems close at hand, and it is the fashions of pose and occupation and the multifarious ends and conflicts of the hurrying eddying crowds that dissolve like the mists in the morning and take on the quality of a dream. (*Clissold*, vol. II, bk. V: 16)

Wells cherished the abstract vision of the mind. He knew how difficult it was to reduce that dream to act. Richard Remington speaks for him. He writes of his inner conflict between a "subtle protesting perplexing play of instinctive passion and desire against too abstract a dream of statesman-ship," of "a world of men better ordered, happier, finer, securer," of "an ideal state, an organized state as confident and powerful as modern science" (*Machiavelli*, bk. I, chap. I: 1; chap. IV: 10). Before Remington can translate his dream into fact, the uncontrollable world of passion upsets his scheme. He has tried to live on two planes at once—the ideal and the real. His misreading of his wife mirrors his misconstruing of life at large. He saw her as the ideal caught in a substantial form, but she was no more than a typical woman. The lesson is clear. Ideals do not abide in this world to be caught by men. Men must put them here.

Lady Harman is similarly deluded when trying to reduce her ideals to reality in *The Wife of Sir Isaac Harman* (1914). She dreams of constructing hostels to provide economical comfort for working women, but serious alterations occur in the execution of her plans, for Sir Isaac transforms the hostels into repellant, rule-bound institutions. "It was a dream subjugated to reality," Wells comments. Lady Harman fears that all dreams are thus subjugated to reality and sees her whole life reflected in the example of the hostels. " 'Caught and spoilt,' that seemed to be the very essential of her life; just as it was of these Hostels, all the hopes, the imaginings, the sweet large anticipations, the generosities, and stirring warm desires" (*Harman*, chap. XI: 7).

Wells understood how difficult it is to embody a dream in action with-out grave mutations occurring in the process. But this did not prevent him from urging men to an attempt. Without the will to improve, mankind would degenerate. In his Utopias and future histories Wells offered, not answers, but inducements. Mr. Barnstaple, in *Men Like Gods*, feels that "all his life he had been a citizen of Utopia exiled upon Earth" (*Gods*, bk. II, chap. III: 1). As an Earthling, he cannot remain in Utopia but must serve Utopian ideals on Earth. Men may visit Utopia as they may daydream, but they must always return to practical reality. This is the basic premise of *A Modern Utopia*, which is simply a daydream being composed as its characters go along and is constantly vulnerable to the chill blast of scepticism and doubt. Finally, the botanist's outraged challenge to the narrator—"We are the scars of the past! These *dreams*, these childish dreams!"—snaps them back to their original world (*Utopia*, chap. XI: 1). The passionate, sensual self overwhelms the dreamer and the dream ends. Even back on Earth the speaker is reluctant to accept the actual world as real, and when the botanist points to a drunken mother with her filthy child, exclaiming "Isn't *that* reality?" he denounces this grim image as a nightmare. " 'The world dreams things like that,' I say, 'because it suffers from an indigestion of such people as you' " (*Utopia*, chap. XI: 4).[41]

Man's mind may dwell in Utopia or, as in *A Modern Utopia*, play there, consciously fabricating, but ultimately the ideals represented by Utopia must be applied in the material, daily life. In *The Work, Wealth and Happiness of Mankind* (1932), Wells acknowledged that most human beings were playing only a passive part in the drama of the race. "They are living as it were in a dream" (*Work*, chap. XIII: 1). By contrast he points to the aspirations of forward-looking scientists and men of business, men who cannot be dismissed as "dreamy Utopians or impractical propagandists," who are recommending projects similar to his own. He, of course, was the one so often charged with dreaming and propaganda (*Work*, chap. X: 7). But Wells wanted dreams made real. Mankind itself has moved in this direction. "We can trace our escape from dreams to ordered thinking" (*Work*, chap. IX: 10). As man grows up, "he begins to reason things out instead of dreaming them out" (*Work*, chap. II: 1). Wells felt that he was in the transition. He still dreamed vast dreams, but he worked to make them real through ordered thinking. He made no secret of the fact that he preferred action to speculation. He urged men as fervidly as Carlyle did in his day to find the work that suited them and to dedicate themselves to it. In his mind the map seemed clear, the roads straight. Utopian visions seemed accessible by a brief effort of will. In actuality, those dreams had to struggle into being in a world bedeviled by evasive uniqueness and constant flux. Though all detailed patterns or designs for the future were provisional, the grand scheme was worth pursuing. One had to see the broad outline and then contribute one's share. Wells's share was as a writer who shaped the ideal for other men to see, and in so doing converted his own idea into act.

In the next chapter of this book I shall discuss Wells as a writer—his ideas about his craft, his techniques, his accomplishments and failures. But one aspect of his role as a writer is intimately related to the matter of free will and strength of will. Whether consciously or not, a writer must at some time conclude that what he does is either free or guided by some law outside himself. In some ages this problem may be openly stated or the guiding power—providence, for example—taken for granted. The late nineteenth century was a confusing period in which many accepted notions were losing their hold upon men's minds. Writers were naturally highly conscious of this change.

During the nineteenth century, the novelist's role as creator had often been equated with that of a deity, controlling and shaping a world of matter and the beings in it. The novelist's will determined the course of events in the novel as absolutely as God was supposed to determine the events of the universe.[42] But, when the idea of a divine being presiding over an existence that it has created lost power, the analogy for the artist was also called in doubt. The novelist did not therefore become less conscious of his shaping role; on the contrary, he became more intrigued since he was no longer imitating some greater ordering force but was now the only being capable of composing a world according to its own will. The only other shaping force was a vaguely conceived Natural Law operating through such subordinate forms as Evolution or Progress or Will. Some felt that man was a slave of this law; others did not. The consequences of either alternative could be monumental.[43]

Describing intellectual conditions at the end of the nineteenth century, Alan Sandison lists the possible ways of viewing existence open to a writer.

> These were firstly that there *was* a principle of order in the universe and that it was dictated by God; secondly, that there *was* a principle of order in the universe, but its determination was purely mechanical with accident as its first cause; thirdly, that there was *no* order inherent in the universe and chance dominated all. There is, occasionally, the merest hint of an interesting fourth possibility—that what order there is in nature has been put there by man.[44]

Sandison argues that writers like Haggard and Kipling were unable to achieve a convincing resolution to the dilemma and created heroes who, though they doubted the benevolence and purpose of Nature's processes, refused to yield to despair. Against the massive doubts occasioned by the new ideas of his time, Haggard offered stoic determination. His characters are sensitive men of action who act as though they can control fate yet occasionally admit that they do not really believe in this power. For unblinking faith they substitute "firmness of character, strength of will, sense of duty, reserves of fortitude."[45] Down-to-earth political and social misgivings increased the burden of these metaphysical doubts. Alan Sandison sees the imperial idea in late nineteenth-century literature as "a medium through which to express the fearfulness and pessimism which underlay political and artistic expression alike, a pessimism which more accurately represents the real character of late Victorian empire-building."[46]

Despite prevailing beliefs in progress and the beneficial drive of evolution, many of the more forceful writers of the age viewed Nature as a hostile or indifferent power. Bernard Bergonzi and John A. Lester, Jr., have shown that a mood of depression was widespread enough to warrant labeling late nineteenth-century culture fin de siècle.[47] This mood of defeat and weariness was variously interpreted, but implied in it was a suggestion that man was not in control of the material world from which providence had disappeared, but that the world of matter controlled man and it was mindless. Science, which had once sought to discover the secrets of a Nature under God's restraining control, was now a weaker scrutinizing a stronger antagonist. Scientific observation was no longer the hobby, avocation, or obsession of isolated investigators, but a necessary defense against the forces of circumstance. If God did not govern Nature, then man must achieve that dominion. In doing so, man must also discover the sources and limits of his own being. He was forced like the victim of some horrible antique torture to witness his own dismemberment. This witnessing was not confined to scientists, for the literature of the nineteenth century is characterized by a fascination for observation and recording, from Balzac and Dickens through Zola and Gissing. Wells came at the end of this tradition of external observation; and although it would be possible to give a long list of his contemporaries for whom observation was the basic posture, I shall select just a few to compare with Wells. All of them were at one time closely acquainted with Wells and exchanged opinions with him.[48]

For George Gissing, Joseph Conrad, Henry James, Arnold Bennett, and H. G. Wells, the universe presented a vast spectacle, probably ungoverned, though interesting and sometimes terrifying to observe. Each of these writers dealt differently with that spectacle. Underlying conceptions of existence affected the nature of their creative work. All of them asserted the importance of precise observation. All felt pleasure in recording what they observed. But while some reconciled themselves to a determined existence, others retained a conviction that man could, to some degree, alter his circumstances. Gissing once declared, " 'My attitude henceforth is that of the artist pure and simple. The world is for me a collection of phenomena which are to be studied and reproduced artistically.' On another occasion he asserted, 'Human life has little interest to me, on the whole—save as material for artistic presentation.' "[49] Gissing's pose as indifferent observer was sometimes extreme, as in a letter to Wells in 1897: "I have a conviction that all I love and believe in is going to the devil; at the same time, I try to watch with interest this process of destruction, admiring any bit of sapperwork that is well done."[50] In a later letter, Gissing agreed with Wells that there must be a coherency and purpose in things. "On the other hand," he continued, "I do doubt whether *we*—in any sense of the pronoun—shall ever be granted an understanding of that purpose."[51]

Jacob Korg writes that for Gissing "the social order, with all the evils it produced, seemed to be the expression of a cosmic necessity too powerful for human resources to resist."[52] Certainly the characters in a novel such as *The Nether World* (1889) have little opportunity to resist circumstances. They themselves acknowledge the force of an inescapable determinism. Clara Hewett follows the line of least resistance and then blames her experiences on fate.

> Fate was busy in all that had happened during the last two days. Why had she quitted her situation at a moment's notice? Why on this occasion rather than fifty times previously? It was not her own doing; something impelled her, and the same force—call it chance or destiny—would direct the issue once more. All she could foresee was the keeping of her appointment with Scawthorne to-morrow morning; what use to try and look further, when assuredly a succession of circumstances impossible to calculate would in the end constrain her?[53]

Clara later revolts against the dominion of circumstance and is defeated. The milder Jane Snowdon is incapable of such a revolt against the "tyranny of circumstances"; and even the sturdy Kirkwood admits that there seems to be a "vice inherent in the nature of things."[54] It is not surprising that Gissing's characters should feel so governed by forces beyond their control, since the author himself, in describing a character's fateful decision, intrudes with a sigh: "So do we play our tragi-comedies in the eye of fate."[55] An unknowable fate oversees the blind courses of men.

In *The Emancipated* (1890), Reuben Elgar, a man given up to his own impulses and incapable of bringing his life under control, is a spokesman for the determinist view. "A man is what he is, and will be ever the same," he asserts to Ross Mallard, whose character seems to belie the charge. "Have you no tincture of philosophy?" Elgar adds. "You talk as though one could govern fate."[56] He expresses a similar feeling to his wife. "Does it depend on myself how I act, or what I think? Do you believe still that we are free agents, and responsible for our acts and thoughts?"[57] After describing one of Elgar's outbursts on the same theme to Mallard, Gissing steps in as author to explain his character.

> This repeated expression of fatalism was genuine enough. It manifested a habit of his thought. One of the characteristics of our time is that it produces men who are determinists by instinct; who, anything but profound students or subtle reasoners, catch at the floating phrases of philosophy and recognize them as the index of their being, adopt them thenceforth as clarifiers of their vague self-consciousness. In certain moods Elgar could not change from one seat to another without its being brought to his mind that he had moved by necessity.[58]

Mallard is unimpressed by Elgar's fatalistic sentiments. "What if that be true?" he asks. "In practice we live as though our will were free. Otherwise, why discuss anything?" Elgar's response is characteristically sophistic. "True. This very discussion is a part of the scheme of things, the necessary antecedent of something or other in your life and mine."[59]

Here and there Gissing suggests a modest possibility that men might have "the strength of character which will subdue all circumstances," but in fact most of his tales describe one or another "noble nature overcome by sordid circumstances."[60] Everywhere he refers to the fates of his characters, and coincidence and chance almost invariably make them pawns in a sequence of accidents beyond their control. He considered men destined by heredity and environment, and his metaphysic, such as it was, left no room for genuine freedom.[61] He rarely addressed himself to the philosophic question of free will but was aware of the pessimism arising from a belief in absolute causation. He did not deal often with cosmic determinism, but social determinism is the wellspring of pain for his characters, who are incapable of altering the courses of their lives. Many of his characters are trapped and ground down. A few, who are carried along by currents they have the cunning to exploit but who are unable to govern their lives beyond some simple maneuvers, have the illusion of freedom. Most do not even have that.

If Gissing doggedly traced the fates of his doomed characters, Conrad explored them with loving fascination, but with a similar tone of weary observation. Though they occasionally become aware of their condition, his characters rarely have the power to change their fates. In a letter to Cunninghame Graham, Conrad described his view of existence.

> There is a,—let us say,—a machine. It evolved itself (I am severely scientific) out of a chaos of scraps of iron and behold!—it knits. I am horrified at the horrible work and stand appalled. I feel it ought to embroider,—but it goes on knitting. . . . And the most withering thought is that the infamous thing has made itself: made itself without thought, without conscience, without foresight, without eyes, without heart. It is tragic accident,—and it has happened. You can't interfere with it. The last drop of bitterness is in the suspicion that you can't even smash it. In virtue of that truth one and immortal which lurks in the force that made it spring into existence it is what it is,—and it is indestructible!
>
> It knits us in and it knits us out. It has knitted time, space, pain, death, corruption, despair and all the illusions,—and nothing matters. I'll admit however that to look at the remorseless process is sometimes amusing.[62]

Conrad did not believe that men could alter the operations of the machine of inexorable natural law, but that disbelief did not prevent him from wishing to record its fascinating operations. Ineluctably the destinies of such insignificant characters as Verloc or the two misfits of "An Outpost of

Progress" or the more energetic Razumov of *Under Western Eyes* and Willems of *An Outcast of the Islands* work toward their resistless conclusions. Men may try to escape their destinies, but they can do so in prospect only, not in fact. Circumstances doom them. Lord Jim believes that he has overcome the failure of will that caused his early shame, but the substance of the event returns to haunt him.[63] Heyst achieves a new vision of existence, but it cannot save him. The mechanical piano and Stevie's circles in *The Secret Agent* are better indications of Conrad's views on human freedom than most others, though the relentlessness of a larger fate is evident in all of his major works—to my mind most notably in *Nostromo*. In that desperate history the strong-willed Charles Gould comes to see that his idealistic scheme of progress only temporarily masks "the cruel futility of things." Like others, he recognizes that the whole attempt to "improve" Costaguana is a "tragic farce."[64] And the sophisticated Martin Decoud, when faced with the physical symbol of cosmic emptiness, concludes, "No intelligence could penetrate the darkness of the placid gulf."[65] Costaguana itself, and there may be a foul jest in the name, is little more than a thread of civilization beween the turmoil of the jungle and the abyss of the sea. More overtly in *Chance*, a novel that assumes and plays upon the ironic capriciousness of circumstances as men perceive them and which caught the mood of its day, Conrad has his mouthpiece Marlow declare as he relates the unraveling of events, "I conceive that the Book of Destiny has been written up from the beginning to the last page."[66]

Henry James also viewed life as a spectacle worthy of elaborate investigation, though he was less concerned with the meaninglessness of that spectacle than with the manner in which art could confer a design upon it. Arnold Goldsmith has shown that while James agreed with the naturalists' belief in the importance of heredity and environment in determining character, he allowed for some play of chance in life and emphasized the power of the stoical will to overcome the capriciousness of fate. James reconciles free will and fatalism through the medium of refined consciousness. "Only by withdrawing into their consciousness that contains the finite world in microcosm can James' heroes and heroines be superior to their destinies."[67]

Stephen Donadio has shown, by comparing James's implied views with Nietzsche's explicit assertions, that like the German philosopher, the American novelist believed in a universe open to the operations of the will. This is not to say that man has a clearly defined free will, but that, through art, man can reconstitute his picture of existence. Art is the triumphant illusion that protects men from the real world. But this victory, such as it is, is exclusive to the great artist. "The individual 'cases' (to use one of his favorite and most revealing words) which James observed so scrupulously and imagined in such meticulous detail served to confirm his general and somewhat gloomy view of the way of the world and the pitifully small chance for freedom it afforded."[68] As the brother of William James, Henry James could not be indifferent to the question of the will, but he did not favor it as a subject for discussion.[69] Nonetheless, it is possible to conclude, as Donadio has, that he allowed a minimal freedom of choice to ordinary men who were basically confined by circumstance.

Arnold Bennett, despite his reputation as a popular philosopher, was the least certain about the spectacle he delighted in rendering. He urged control of the will and mental discipline but rarely asserted any conviction about such overriding subjects as free will and determinism.[70] Stuart P. Sherman, writing in 1917, felt that Bennett was interested in extending the dominion of the human over the natural power in himself and beyond.[71] He observed that Bennett's characters did manage somehow to come to terms with their circumstances. "The secret of this 'somehow' is that Mr. Bennett implicitly recognizes as an artist what he explicitly declares as a popular philosopher, namely, the existence in the individual of something deeper than the body, deeper than the mind—an ultimately responsible, independent, spiritual, self with the power to control, in some measure, its circumstances."[72] The "somehow" is also a sign of how unresolved Bennett was on the subject. Walter F. Wright concludes that Bennett remained uncertain about the nature of the universe and his place in it and that the impression his philosophizing gives is "a sense that Bennett himself was bewildered by life's magnitude and multiplicity."[73] In his fiction there are few clear expressions of philosophy, though Bennett now and then in his serious novels suggests his own outlook. Edwin Clayhanger, watching at his father's sickbed, is appalled by the man's suffering. But he adjusts as the hours pass. "Edwin became hardened to the spectacle. . . . There was nothing to be done. They who were destined to suffer had to suffer, must suffer; and no more could be said. . . . Fortitude alone could meet the situation. Nevertheless, the night seemed eternal, and at intervals fortitude lacked."[74]

Bennett's fictional world is not one of purpose and successful assertion of human control, but more akin to Gissing's, with accident, chance, and coincidence more instrumental than plan or design, and resignation more common than rebellion. Throughout the Clayhanger trilogy, for example, Bennett emphasizes the unpredictability of life. At one point Bennett notes of Clayhanger, "Accident—that is to say, a chance somewhat more fortuitous than the common hazards which we group together and call existence—pushed Edwin into the next stage of his career."[75] What Bennett calls their destinies or fates do not arise from what his characters attempt, but from what happens to them.

Bennett wished to report the oddities of the cosmic spectacle faithfully and in detail.[76] Wells sought to change that spectacle. He stands apart from his colleagues in his clear assertion that men are free and can shape their own destinies. More amazingly, he attributes this power not only to individuals but to the species as a whole as well. Of course Wells was not alone in his defense of free will. Galsworthy treated the theme thoughtfully in *Jocelyn* (1898) and Chesterton admitted that he required a religious faith that allowed for free will.[77] He took pleasure in arguing the question of free will and determinism with Robert Blatchford.[78] The topic is vast, worthy of a book in its own right. Obviously, I cannot pursue it in further detail here. What I do wish to examine is the way that Wells's philosophy affected his craft. His belief in free will made a difference in the way he conceived of character, and we can compare his approach to those of his friends I have mentioned.

Few of Wells's creations are passive. Even when they fail, they have had a taste of struggle and have seen the possibility of victory or escape. Some achieve this escape or victory in the material world, not merely in the mind. The difference between Wells and the contemporaries I have named was nicely summarized by Theodore Dreiser in his introduction to the Sandgate Edition of *Tono-Bungay* where he declared that he disagreed with Wells's picture of man. "Constructively, as I see him," Dreiser wrote, "man is much more led or pushed than he is leading or pushing."[79]

Characterization is the most obvious area in which a novelist's assumptions about free will and fate might find expression, but choices of narrative form reveal these assumptions as well. Simply put, it is likely that writers convinced of a determinist world will construct fictional schemes having causal intensity. The narratives of those who believe in a capricious world of accident will follow a detailed, complex, but rapidly shifting, line. In both cases as long as the author is essentially passive, the plot will be either relentless or intricate. Once past his early romances, Wells depended little upon plot or design. Believing that existence was formless and merely took the shape imposed upon it by human perception, Wells made perceiving the organizing principle of his novels. From one point of view, his novels after *Love and Mr. Lewisham* (1900) are recorded assertions of human will against chaos.[80] Because he was concerned with such exertions more than with plot or internal development of characters, Wells brought several innovations to English fiction, some of which I shall discuss in the next chapter.[81]

Wells discussed his beliefs freely and detailed their relationship to his craft as a writer, but most novelists do not often comment upon the philosophical bases for their artistic choices. Now and then, however, a revealing clue escapes them. In his account of Conrad's theory of fiction, Ford Madox Ford quoted, under the heading of "Structure," Conrad's demand that a story convey a sense of inevitability. "The problem of the author is to make [the character's] then action the only action that character could have taken. It must be inevitable, because of his character, because of his ancestry, because of past illness or an account of the gradual coming together of the thousand small circumstances by which Destiny, who is inscrutable and august, will push us into one certain predicament."[82]

With all of the writers I have examined here, except Wells, this inevitability is a principle of composition. It accords with their notions of form. Gissing was never a whole-hearted determinist, though he allowed very little room for human freedom. Of *Demos, Thyrza,* and *The Nether World,* Michael Collie says, "Gissing so shapes these three stories that a conscious resignation to the circumstances of existence constitutes the full measure of a character's freedom."[83] Collie also identifies a conflict in Gissing's use of fictional form. The relative insignificance of plot, he says, "was inevitable for a writer who did not observe plots in contemporary life and who felt sure that meaningful sequences of events were unlikely."[84] At the same time his novels depended heavily upon coincidence, chance, and other contrivances incompatible with a view of life as unreasoned frustration.[85] Gissing saw the same spectacle that Wells did when he looked at life, but he lacked Wells's faith in the power of the will to bring shape to that chaos.[86] Thus, for him, as John Goode observes, "the only structure possible, towards which his fiction evolves, is a vagueness of conclusion, a destructuring of the rounded conception of life."[87] His fictional structure demands "a plotless network of circumstance in which the possibilities of liberation are confined to mental states."[88]

Henry James also confined the liberation of his characters mainly to mental states, but these liberations are positive where Gissing's are almost entirely negative. For James, fiction is an improvement upon life and therefore an illustrative model. Beyond the actual case that the novelist takes from reality, "his germ, his vital particle, his grain of gold, life persistently blunders and deviates, loses herself in the sand."[89] The artist can do better than that, though his product remains an imaginative illusion. James's style is involved and incessant, like the hands of a sculptor constantly patting and gently gouging his clay until it assumes the anticipated form.

Gissing had to create contortions of plot in order that perverse destinies worked themselves out to grimly ironic ends. The involutions of Conrad's and James's styles reveal in the one case a bewildered attempt to trace out the inscrutable pattern of destiny, in the other a luxurious appreciation of the intricate way in which the inevitable can be imagined to impose a design possessing the orderliness of art. With Bennett, manner and narrative are more obvious. In "The Author's Craft" his basic counsel to potential writers concerned the importance of observation. Bennett is a novelist who sees and tells. He does this well, but there is little beyond that achieve-

ment. He remarks how important it is "to realise that all physical phenomena are inter-related, that there is nothing which does not bear on everything else."[90] Although his characters do not discern this interrelatedness,
Bennett guides his readers to that superior awareness. Bennett's plots move
on directly and causally just as events occur. He maintains interest in his
plots by disguising the outcomes of events yet makes them appear credible
after they have occurred. This sense of credibility or inevitability he often
refers to as destiny. In the Clayhanger novels we have the interesting opportunity to see destiny shaping up along two converging lines of so-called
accident. First we follow Edwin's sequence of "accidents" and then Hilda's,
and then we witness the consequence in their married life where "bitterness
and melancholy" seem unavoidable and only Edwin's final sense of adventure and romance in his marriage is surprising.

For Gissing, Conrad, James, and Bennett, accidents and coincidences
are primarily plot contrivances that gradually hem characters in. For Wells
they are not steps toward a finality, but doorways opening into freedom
and mystery. His plots demonstrate this quality of liberation. The early
fantasies are by their nature escapes from the ordinary. But even in more
traditional narratives sudden shifts reflect psychological changes as in *Mr.
Blettsworthy on Rampole Island* and *The Autocracy of Mr. Parham*, or
movements from personal to social concerns as in *Tono-Bungay* and *Brynhild*, or from a closed to an open view of existence as in *The History of Mr.
Polly* and *Ann Veronica*. Wells cheerfully calls attention to the novelty of
his work.[91] He gloried in his departures from convention. While his stylist
friends excluded more and more from their fictions, Wells became omni-
vorous. He wanted to break the frame of fiction; they wanted to put the
work of art behind glass. His directness is reflected in the clarity and
straightforward dash of his style. It is uneven, sometimes downright bad,
but always filled with surprising expressions and vigorous drive. Meanwhile, his friendly antagonists relentlessly chastened their styles, sometimes, with James and Conrad, into near impenetrability. I am not here
passing judgment on the relative merits of these writers. I read them all with
great pleasure, even Gissing. I simply wish to show by this brief comparison
with some of his contemporaries that Wells's notions about the universe at
large were not only remarkably consistent but also consistently evident in
his theory and practice of fiction.[92]

Wells wrote at a time when the notion of will in its many forms was
much on men's pens. He himself commented on its appearance in the writings of Schopenhauer, Shaw, and others. His own attitudes reflect the basic
notions expressed by Schopenhauer, Nietzsche, and Hartmann. "I have
seen life clambering out of drifting slime towards consciousness and will,"
says the Voice in *The Camford Visitation* (1937). "I have watched the as-

cent of your species to the dawn of understanding and the beginnings of power. I care for you, and now I am impatient with you" (*Camford*, chap. VI). Unlike Schopenhauer and Hartmann, Wells believed in will as a positive force, not a movement toward renunciation or oblivion. For him individual will was the channeling of impulses—of sex and power—toward personal integrity, and racial will was the channeling of cosmic forces toward integrity of species. To believe all of this, he had to believe that man was free.

Of course Wells had his moments of doubt which he faithfully recorded in the thoughts of his characters. In *The World Set Free* (1914), Frederick Barnet speculates:

> I saw how little and feeble is the life of man, a thing of chances, preposterously unable to find the will to realise even the most timid of dreams. And I wondered if always it would be so, if man was a doomed animal who would never to the last days of his time take hold of fate and change it to his will. Always, it may be, he will remain kindly but jealous, desirous but discursive, able and unwisely impulsive, until Saturn who begot him shall devour him in his turn. (*Free*, chap. II: 8)

And Mr. Britling wonders, "Was Huxley right, and was all humanity, even as Mr. Britling, a careless, fitful thing, playing a tragically hopeless game, thinking too slightly, moving too quickly against a relentless antagonist?" The whole universe, he considers, might be witless, will-less, and cruel (*Britling*, bk. I, chap. IV: 7). These are night thoughts, and Mr. Britling throws them off as he does his bedclothes to find comfort in tea and his writing desk. The constant question before men was what Sir Richmond Hardy, recovering from anemia of the will, asks—"Can our wills prevail?" (*Heart*, chap. VI: 5).

Until the end, Wells, despite misgivings, did believe that our wills can prevail. Like Benham in *The Research Magnificent* (1915), he believed that this is a world of choice, that before each human, "planless indeterminate lives" opened out, providing choices between "salvation and damnation." But will can prevail. "We have to clench ourselves upon a chosen end," says Benham. "We have to gather ourselves together out of the swill of this brimming world" (*Research*, chap. I: 15). Later he reasserts his faith in both the freedom and the power of the will. "In this world one may wake in the night and one may resolve to be a king, and directly one has resolved one is a king" (*Research*, chap. V: 7). Peter Stubland, in a voice-to-voice confrontation with God, learns that he has what used to be called free will, that is, the ability to work out his own salvation. What's more, God tells him, "there isn't a thing in the whole of this concern of mine that Man can't control if only he chooses to control it" (*Joan*, chap. XIII: 15).

To focus the will, as Wells said again and again, man has to clench himself upon a chosen end. William Clissold believes in progress. He must. "Without the idea of progress," he says, "life is a corrupting marsh." Without it, "I should be glad to get out of the glare and turbulence of so unmeaning a spectacle, and I should not be particular what way I took back to nothingness and peace" (*Clissold*, vol. II, bk. V: 16). Wells confessed to the normal lapses and inconsistencies of men but added, "I find nevertheless that this faith and service of constructive world revolution does hold together my mind and will in a prevailing unity, that it makes life continually worth living, transcends and minimizes all momentary and incidental frustrations and takes the sting out of the thought of death" (*Autobiography*, chap. IX: 10).

Wells's moods fluctuated widely all of his life but apparently more often in his later years when frustrations mounted maddeningly. In a mood of levity in *All Aboard for Ararat* (1940), he gives God's account of his discussions with Satan about ending the experiment of the universe. "It might be, Satan suggested, that even if we, both God and Satan, decided to conclude, man, if he was aware of it, might be able to go on of his own free will. Not merely that. He might even *have* to go on—anyhow" (*Ararat*, chap. I: 6). The next year he was glowering in *You Can't Be Too Careful*, "Can Edward Albert, in view of the fact that he is a creature, have such a thing as free will?" (*Careful*, Introduction). While stating that the answer no has never convinced mankind, he refuses an opinion of his own. Later in the novel he grudgingly allows that *Homo sapiens* might be able to wrest his destiny from Nature, but no such species yet exists. By the end of the novel, he has withheld any clear assertion. The most he can say for any of his characters is that the rebellious Evangeline "is less of a resultant and more of a will than anyone else in this story" (*Careful*, bk. VI, chap. IV). Still the novel ends with an expectation that in some future time a true *Homo sapiens* will emerge to shape its own destiny.

In his autobiography Wells said that one powerful function of his concept of a World Revolution was that it gave shape and purpose to his life. We have seen how important this shaping impulse was to him. His own vocation called for precisely such a shaping ability, and although he renounced the title of artist, he often used the image of art as a way of conceiving the shaping process he had in mind for mankind.[93] In *Mankind in the Making*, for example, he says that the New Republicans "will in their own time take this world as a sculptor takes his marble, and shape it better than all our dreams," a figure that recurs in the symbol of the block of alabaster in *Babes in the Darkling Wood* (*Mankind*, chap. XI). For the writer, the function of the will is to create a vision that will persuade men of its reality. Of the great revolutionary writer De Windt, the historian of *The Shape of Things to Come* says, "He put all the main structural factors in the establishment of the Modern State so plainly and convincingly before his fellow-men that soon thousands and presently millions were living for that vision, were bringing it out of thought into reality. He made it seem so like destiny that it became destiny" (*Shape*, bk. III, chap. I). Wishful thinking! Yet much can be understood and appreciated about Wells's world view and his view of his craft if we comprehend how necessary the operation of an active free will was to both. One of the most revealing passages along these lines is one from *God, The Invisible King*, which does not mention will. "Now the turning round of the modern mind from a conception of the universe as something derived deductively from the past to a conception of it as something gathering itself adventurously towards the future, involves a release from the supposed necessity to tell a story and explain why. Instead comes the inquiry, 'To what end?' " (*Inv. King*, chap. VI: 2). Ironically, in a few years Wells was to go back and tell the story of mankind, but he did this in order to show that humanity was gathering itself adventurously toward the future. From his earliest tales and essays almost to the last novels and articles, this was his chief purpose. It was an attitude and purpose that could not but affect his opinions about his craft.

# 8

# Writing

"With speech humanity begins," Wells wrote in *Mankind in the Making* (1903). It was a central tenet of his belief and the justification of his life's effort. Language was what set man off from all other forms of life and made his development toward consciousness and freedom possible. It was his most valuable tool and treasure. Throughout his life, Wells urged men to keep that tool sharp. "The prevailing ignorance of English in the English-speaking communities enormously hampers the development of the racial consciousness," he admonished in 1903 (*Mankind*, chap. IV: 2). In 1932 he was still reproving. "Language is far less important as a means of talking about things than as a means of thinking about things, but we use it now almost entirely as a means of talking about things" (*Work*, chap. XV: 6). Always he called for training in language, since clear expression was essential to clear thought, and clear thought to human improvement. With the increasing swiftness of communication around the world, men could rapidly aid one another to greater cooperation. Wells even proposed a universal lingua franca. English seemed most appropriate to him.[1] The barrier of language was just one more frontier Wells hoped to abolish.

In *The Outline of History* (1920), Wells emphasized the unique part language played in the development of the race. Without it "there could have been little thinking beyond the range of actual experience, for language is the instrument of thought as bookkeeping is the instrument of business" (*Outline*, chap. XI: 1). By a natural series of steps, writing grew out of the life of man; and once he could record his thoughts, man established a new, permanent kind of tradition. "Life, through mankind, grew thereafter more and more distinctly conscious of itself and its world" (*Outline*, chap. XVI: 4). The great bards of antiquity fostered a sense of man's history. They were "living books, man-histories," guardians of a new tradition. With the appearance of printed books, what had been a trickle became a flood. Knowledge was more widely and more easily disseminated (*Outline*, chap. XXXIV: 4).

A few years earlier, Wells had attributed the bustling achievements of modern man to "the quickening and increase of man's intelligence and its reinforcement through speech and writing" (*Forces*, "The Human Adventure"). Everything rested on the premise that the proper use of language was man's paramount concern. It became Wells's main reason for writing. It is why he stressed the growing need for improved communications, for a World Brain or universal library, and for a common world language. More importantly, language was the principal agency that "created" the world. Men *learned* to perceive the world in one form or another, and that form could be changed through persuasion.[2] Wells sought to create a new picture of the world. His utensil was language.

Wells repeatedly advised men that great events begin in language. The great revolutions of the world, he said, were attempts to reeducate man, an accomplishment achieved through language and the words of a great teacher, prophet, or disciples. The leader of such a revolution might be successful without being good. The world revolution in *The Holy Terror* (1939) "was begotten of a sentence, it was fostered in talk. In the beginning was the Word. There is no strong, silent man in the history of the world renascence" (*Terror*, bk. III, chap. I: 13). Looking back upon man's confused past, the fictional historian of *The Shape of Things to Come* (1933) says that in old times the men who mattered most seemed always "to have something to say that was at once profoundly important and yet not quite true or not quite truly said." Followers tried to understand and often merely rephrased and misapplied the original teachings. But there was a common quality in "these madmen, prophets, teachers and disturbers of the mental peace. The species was learning to talk and use language. The race was, as it were, trying to think something out; was attempting to say something new and enlarging itself. It was doing this against great resistance. Its intellectual enterprise was playing against its instinctive fear of novelty" (*Shape*, bk. III, chap. IV). Many of these early prophets died for their efforts, but eventually inquiry and expression grew and developed. In the world of the twenty-second century, language has achieved its proper place. Man has finally learned to state his case, to shape his argument convincingly. Wells summed up his conviction about the power of language in *The Autocracy of Mr. Parham* (1930). "In the long run," he wrote, "man will be lost or saved by argument, for collective human acts are little more than arguments in partial realization" (*Parham*, bk. IV, chap. V).

Wells's characters often recognize the role that language plays in human events. Some are conscious of the need for apt phrases to consolidate their own thoughts or to persuade others. Remington strikes upon a phrase that condenses his purpose and promises to attract others—"love and fine thinking" (*Machiavelli*, bk. III, chap. I: 9). Rud Whitlow learns to write "a good, nervous prose" and develops "a certain gift for effective phrases"; both skills aid him in his rise to power (*Terror*, bk. I, chap. I: 5; bk. II, chap. I: 2).[3] Other characters exploit language for less exalted ends. Edward Ponderevo aims at commercial success and Rowland Palace at self-aggrandizement. Wells himself was an adept phrase maker and seemed to believe that the ability was innate. Conrad and Hueffer, he said, labored the question of precise words and perfection in writing, whereas he felt that "the happy word is the gift, the momentary capricious gift of the gods a flash of mother wit. You cannot *train* for it; you cannot write well and forcibly without at times writing flatly, and the real quality of a writer is, like divinity, inalienable" (*Autobiography*, chap. VIII: 5). It is a view consistent with Wells's trust in the lucky chance of progress and the fortunate accident of human development.

Language, though a means of seeking truth, was equally capable of disguising it. Prendick gives a bleak version of man's gift for speech when he declares in *The Island of Dr. Moreau* (1896), "An animal may be ferocious and cunning enough, but it takes a real man to tell a lie" (*Moreau*, chap. XXI). Sometimes man lied to save his skin, as Prendick did. But more than physical dangers have haunted men from the time they could be called such. Wells repeats the dark vision of man's power of language in Theodore Bulpington's admission that it is not always possible to face the truth. "One gift that poor ape had to help it in its hideous battle with fact. It could lie. Man is the one animal that can make a fire and keep off the beasts of the night. He is the one animal that can make a falsehood and keep off the beasts of despair" (*Blup*, chap. IX: 7). William Burroughs Steele in *The Anatomy of Frustration* (1936) is obsessed with the failures of language which beget confusions of thought; "needless personifications, dramatizations, false classifications, tautologies, and mixed metaphors" waste mental energies (*Frustration*, chap. II). Language subtly implies erroneous perceptions of existence as with the false distinction between matter and spirit. Steele reflects that "every effort at extreme definition is apt by its sheer intensity to thrust through exaggeration towards absolute and therefore contentless statements. Language is all too apt to *oversay*" (*Frustration*, chap. VII). In short, language is a risky instrument. Even thought may not be capable of grasping one's vision truly. The skill remains imperfect (*Frustration*, chap. XXIV).[4] In *Babes in the Darkling Wood* (1940), Stella's Uncle Robert tries to impress her with the untrustworthy nature of language. "Everybody alive suffers from an impediment in his speech," he says. "Intelligent statement is still merely an ideal, and life is full of unspeakable things" (*Babes*, bk. III, chap. I: 3). Earlier in the novel, Uncle Robert had praised young men like Ogden, Richards, and Chase who were laboring to clear up the meaning of words (*Babes*, bk. II, chap. III: 3). Without that initial clarity, man's progress would constantly be undermined.

Though he realized how shifty an instrument language was and how easy it was for men to obscure the truth from themselves and others, he sought the truth above all things and valued few things more than honesty and candor.[5] In *First and Last Things* (1908), he urged his fellow men to attend to the truth-seeking virtue of language, even while admitting its imprecisions. Later, in *The Work, Wealth and Happiness of Mankind* (1932), he praised that strain in *Homo sapiens* that maintained pride. "His tradition is all against suppressions and smothered whispers. Tell the truth though the heavens fall, is the heroic phrasing of it" (*Work*, chap. XV: 9). It was dedication to truth that made him value the scientist's approach to life (*Work*, chap. XII: 11).[6]

The most dangerous lies are not necessarily those told to others. Theodore Bulpington is a model self-deceiver, adept at concocting personal false histories which he persuades himself to accept. Before he falls away entirely from the truth, he receives a posthumous letter from his mother in which she tells him what she has discovered herself and what until now she has failed to impart to him. The world would be far different, she says, if people "got down to simplicity and frankness—the ultimate achievement of the mind." Instead, men abide in self-deception (*Blup*, chap. VIII: 8).

Wells deplored lying and was quick to outlaw it in his *Modern Utopia* (1905). Even cosmetic lies were unacceptable. He sketched a humorous indictment in "The Truth About Pyecraft" (1903) where Pyecraft's many troubles follow from what Formalyn calls his "sin of euphemism." Instead of admitting that he wishes to lose *fat*, he says he wishes to lose *weight*. As a result, he becomes weightless without diminishing in bulk. The story is a playful examination of a trick of language but is serious in its condemnation of even the most trivial forms of evasion or disguise.

Many of Wells's characters willfully deceive themselves, but there are others who fall into error because they cannot fashion in language the ideas that tantalize their minds. In pondering Benham's confusion at one stage of his career, his old friend White reflects upon "how dependent human beings are upon statement. Man is the animal that states a case. He lives not in things but in expressed ideas" (*Research*, chap. III: 11). Those ideas are elusive. Language reduces obscure impulses and desires to precise thoughts; it offers the gift of detachment by placing these thoughts at a distance where they may be viewed objectively. Ideas become the equivalents of things and have a real existence and through that real existence affect men's lives. Richard Remington discovers that the true work before

mankind is "the enlargement of human expression, the release and intensi-
fication of human thought, the vivider utilization of experience and the
investigation of research" (*Machiavelli*, bk. III, chap. I: 9). These were also
Wells's high aims and noble reasons for committing words to print, but
there were other more personal, but equally significant, objectives and gratifications that led him to write.

Wells admitted in his autobiography that in the novels he wrote
around the time of *The New Machiavelli* (1911), he was releasing "a long
accumulation of suppression" (*Autobiography*, chap. VII: 4). He began the
autobiography to reassure himself during a phase of fatigue, restlessness,
and vexation, and it achieved its purpose. Beyond these simple consolations, writing represented the broader, more encompassing drive toward
liberation.[7] Originative intellectual workers are like early amphibians,
Wells explained, revealing in his metaphor the biological range of his parallel. We are, he continued, "struggling out of the waters that have hitherto
covered our kind, into the air, seeking to breathe in a new fashion and
emancipate ourselves from long accepted and long unquestioned necessities" (*Autobiography*, chap. I: 1). This emancipation follows the reshaping
of thought through writing, which organizes vague impressions into sharp
expressions. In an introductory note to *A Modern Utopia*, Wells explained
that he wrote *Anticipations* "in order to clear up the muddle in my own
mind about innumerable social and political questions" (*Utopia*, "A Note
to the Reader"). The fable that follows this explanation is a similar, but far
more tentative, experiment.

Many of Wells's characters share his pleasure in setting their ideas
down on paper. William Leadford, in recording the astonishing events of
the days when a comet transformed the earth, admits a literary hankering
but gives a different reason for writing. "I find some such recapitulation of
my past as this will involve, is becoming necessary to my own secure mental
continuity" (*Comet*, bk. I, chap. I: 1). For Alfred Bunter writing resembles
the process of crystallization, but even so dull a figure as Wells's croquet
player says he will feel surer about the fantastic things he has been told if he
sets them down in writing. Figures like William Leadford, George Ponderevo, and Richard Remington stress the importance of making a record
of experience in order to confer form and meaning upon it. William Clissold is particularly insistent on this point. Like Ponderevo, Clissold claims
that he is not a professional man of letters but writes his thoughts out to get
them plain (*Clissold*, vol. II, bk. V: 1; bk. IV: 13). Clissold is trying to
sharpen the outline of the future as Britling and Wilbeck try to focus on the
events of the present at their writing desks. Many of Wells's protagonists
are themselves writers not merely because he wished to use the most eco-

nomical method to talk about himself but because he believed the act of writing was itself a mode of discovery and consolidation of ideas appropriate to the themes he chose to treat.

The urge to compose may be spontaneous, but continued exposition is an act of will. Writing may begin as an almost visceral gratification or escape, but it rapidly becomes a tool for the will to give form not only to the past but to the future as well. The will shapes and is reinforced by the act of writing. Something comparable happens more grandly with the story of mankind, as we shall see later in this chapter. Out of unconsciousness man strives to escape necessity; as he becomes aware of this need, he finds means to express it. That capacity in turn strengthens his dawning self-consciousness. Man's will is supported by the forms and organizations growing up around him even while it gains greater and greater power over those forms and organizations. Ultimately the act of composition is comparable to living, for it is simply one more way—the highest way—by which man bends untrammeled Nature to his desires and makes chaos assume a form of his choosing.

For Wells the true writer was essentially a creative researcher, resembling the scientist in his dedication to a pursuit of truth. Just as his purpose resembled a scientist's, so did his conditions of work. Both secluded themselves to accomplish their aims. Wells demanded some form of temporary withdrawal from life of all persons presuming to lead and instruct. The Samurai of *A Modern Utopia* for seven days out of every year must "go right out of all the life of man into some wild and solitary place" away from inhabited houses "into the bare, quiet places of the globe." This requirement trains them physically, "but partly, also, it is to draw their minds for a space from the insistent details of life, from the intricate arguments and the fretting effort to work, from personal quarrels and personal affections, and the things of the heated room" (*Utopia*, chap. IX: 7).

Wells explained in *World Brain* (1938) that he recommended a world governed by the scientific spirit, which was not confined to scientists. He had given many instances in his writing of the blunderings and misconceptions of individual scientists. The science to which George Ponderevo and William Clissold dedicate themselves is something far grander than mere probings and measurements. "But scientific work is a world apart, a magic island cut off from futility," Clissold says. "There is a protective isolation about most of the arts. But Science has most of this precious detachment. And yet it is profoundly real." Clissold was once among the happy laborers on that magic island and so speaks knowledgeably (*Clissold*, vol. I, bk. III: 18). So Wells might have spoken in his own voice. His lifelong yearning for recognition from the scientific community was less mere egotism than a desire to be numbered among those whose contributions could be weighed and calculated as a scientist's are. Wells admired scientists for following the discipline of science, not as individuals. They made their contributions, but so did writers. In an article comparing Ivan Pavlov and G. B. Shaw, Wells admitted that "scientific inquiry takes its workers into remote and lonely places where they do a little lose the faculty of ordinary speech" (*Going*, chap. XXV). In his seclusion the scientist discovers ways to alter or control material things; the writer, in his, hones his gift of apt articulation and may be harder to forget. The scientist may convince by fact; the writer can persuade memorably.

Neither scientist nor writer can be a leader. Wells felt that the very nature of their contributions puts them at odds with their aim—a greater community among men through greater understanding. From the point of view of general living, Wells writes in *World Brain* (1938), "men of science, artists, philosophers, specialized intelligences of any sort, do not constitute an *élite* that can be mobilized for collective action. They are an extraordinarily miscellaneous assembly, and their most remarkable common quality is the quality of concentration in comparative retirement—each along his own line" (*Brain*, chap. I). Wells saw an inevitable conflict in the intellectual man who, in leaving ordinary life to seclude himself and intensify his thoughts, paradoxically individualizes himself while seeking to resolve the very problem of egoism and individual isolation. The dilemma was not insuperable, as we shall see.

Not all lonely experimentation leads to measurable results. In *The Research Magnificent* (1915), William Benham devoted himself to a form of investigation far more elusive than the labors of a scientist. He tried to apply principles of detachment to qualities of the human spirit. Though he was to some extent misguided, his was a noble experiment. Unfortunately, he never arranged his thoughts in any final form. His friend and executor, the journalist and novelist White, said, "When Benham thought he was gathering together a book he was dreaming" (*Research*, Prelude: 1). He left merely "an indigestible aggregation" of written observations. Nonetheless, he saw himself as one of that heroic company of which Wells himself dreamed.

> Let men stew in their cities if they will. It is in the lonely places, in jungles and mountains, in snows and fires, in the still observatories and the silent laboratories, in those secret and dangerous places where life probes into life, it is there that the masters of the world, the lords of the beast, the rebel sons of Fate come to their own. (*Research*, Prelude: 11)

Trafford in *Marriage* (1912) is a sustained example of the scientist who craves solitude for his work. Returning to his laboratory and his proper work is like an escape, like shutting a door upon "a dirty and undisciplined market-place crowded with mental defectives" (*Marriage*, bk. II, chap. II: 1).[8] But retreat into the security of research must be more than escape; it must have a positive purpose. For a time Trafford loses that purpose and is compelled finally to recover his whole vision of existence by a literal withdrawal into wilderness. Like the Samurai he leaves civilization so that he may test his mind and body and bring them to a new resolve. And the withdrawal achieves its aim. He recovers a clear ambition. "I want research, and the spirit of research that has died in me," he cries, "and that still, silent room of mine again, that room, as quiet as a cell, and the toil that led to light" (*Marriage*, bk. III, chap. IV: 10). Marjorie, his wife, has also benefited from their adventure. She too sees their future dedication typified by a room, though in her imagination it is no simple cell, but a "tall, fine room, a study, a study in sombre tones, with high, narrow, tall, dignified bookshelves and rich deep green curtains veiling its windows" (*Marriage*, bk. III, chap. IV: 14). It is a "very high room indeed, with a man writing before a fine, long-curtained window" (*Marriage*, bk. III, chap. IV: 16). Trafford the scientist passes into Trafford the writer. The impulse is the same, the effort different, but the same kind of retired setting appeals to both.

Wells began very early to remark the value of seclusion to a writer. It stands to reason that a writer would need peace and quiet to write. But for Wells this seclusion was something more than the necessary freedom from distraction; it bordered on a spiritual condition. It might be waking in the night to think and then reduce those thoughts to pages of manuscript—in order to distract oneself from present troubles, as with Mr. Rowland Palace in *Brynhild* (1937). It might be taking up large, disturbing issues as Mr. Britling does.[9] Most often, though, the solitude required for writing is identified with actual spatial conditions. It is an emblematic place.

*In the Days of the Comet* (1906) opens with a writer at work in his room at the top of a tower furnished in a manner recalling Tennyson's "Lady of Shalott." This is the ideal setting to which other Wells characters aspire. William Clissold's yearning for a place suitable for his labors is typical and explicit. "I have thought of a little white house in the sun, very quiet and simple. A little white house where I can think things out and recover my will" (*Clissold*, vol. II, bk. IV: 14). Unlike many of Wells's other seekers, Clissold finds his ideal cottage. The clean simplicity of the house is emblematic of the ordering process of composition. Its neat environment mirrors the tidying up of his mind. Self and circumstance come together. With one half of his nature Clissold craves the orderliness to be found in crystallography, with the other half he desires more biological things. Consequently, for this orderly house to be complete, for abstract ideas to gain flesh, a necessary fellowship is supplied by pets and a loving woman.

Throughout his adulthood Clissold has recognized the conflict "between sensuous eroticism and creative passion" which has complicated his life, but in his little white house in Provence, Clementina near at hand but excluded from the neat room in which he works, these conflicting forces reach a point of fruitful balance (*Clissold*, vol. II, bk. IV: 13).

Now and then it may happen that active men do not seek retreat but are forced out of the world of obvious deeds into a seclusion that provides an opportunity for them to write. "Just as we owe Marco Polo's book of travels to his imprisonment, so we owe Machiavelli's *Prince*, his *Florentine History*, and *The Art of War* to his downfall and the boredom of San Casciano," Wells observes in *The Outline of History* (1920) (*Outline*, chap. XXXIV: 9). A decade earlier, he had drawn upon Machiavelli's career, identified it with his own defeat at the time, and created *The New Machiavelli* (1911). In this novel Richard Remington compares himself to the great Italian theorist, for just as Machiavelli was forced to retire to his property at San Casciano after the fall of the Florentine Republic, so Remington has been driven into retirement—in Italy, as it chances—after the collapse of his scheme for a New Republic. Remington imagines Machiavelli returning home from his daily intercourse, stripping off his peasant clothes, washing himself, and assuming his court dress, then closing his study door on all the disorder of private emotions and needs and turning to "wider dreams." "I like to think of him so," Remington continues, "with brown books before him lit by the light of candles in silver candlesticks, or heading some new chapter of 'The Prince,' with a grey quill in his clean fine hand." He prefers Machiavelli to Plato as his symbol because he "is still all human and earthly, a fallen brother—and at the same time that nobly dressed and nobly dreaming writer at the desk" (*Machiavelli*, bk. I, chap. I: 1). Remington begins his own book with similar high aspirations. Like Clissold, he has within call the woman he loves, for whom he has abandoned political life.

One way or another the writer seeks out or is compelled to a seclusion resembling the scientist's solitary laboratory insofar as it provides freedom from day-to-day trivialities. "Every book, every *real* book, maybe, is a confession of solitude," says the earnest young novelist Alfred Bunter in *Brynhild*. "It's an appeal." Bunter has been trying to say something plainly about life. His books, he declares, have been his life. "At times I've had a tremendous sense that I was getting something said, putting a shape upon the muddle of existence, finding something out as I wrote. . . . I felt as I suppose the early anatomists or the early microscope and telescope men felt. Laying bare things long hidden" (*Brynhild*, chap. X: 3).[10]

The solitude arising from the desire to get things said, to lay things bare, need not include separation from one's fellow men. By a benign irony it can achieve just the opposite effect, as Stephen Wilbeck concludes in

*Apropos of Dolores* (1938). "A man who sits in a quiet room reading or writing, listening or thinking," he muses, "may seem to be solitary and isolated. But in fact he is in contact with myriads of intimates," for he is communicating with the thought of mankind, the "pervading common brain," of which he is a contributing part (*Dolores*, chap. VII: 5). The solitary writer in his room increases unity among men. The fictional future historian of *The Shape of Things to Come* (1933) quotes the equally fictional Maxwell Brown on the writer's dilemma in the bad old days— Wells's days, in fact.

> In the security and serenity of the study, these men and women could see plainly. In those hours of withdrawal, the fragile delicate brain matter could escape from immediacy, apprehend causation in four dimensions, reach forward to the permanent values of social events in the space-time framework. But even to the study there penetrated the rumble of the outer disorder. And directly the door was opened, forthwith the uproar of contemporary existence, the carnival, the riot, the war and the market, beat in triumphantly. The raging question of what had to be done that day scattered the fine thought of our common destiny to the four winds of heaven. (*Shape*, bk. I, chap. II and bk. III, chap. IV)

Out of these silent havens of study, men work and will work to remedy the disorder of life that tumbles madly outside the door until it is finally possible—as it is with Leadford—to transcribe calmly in the ideal solitude of an ideal room the accomplished harmony of mankind.

Wells had definite views on what literature should do. Many critics have discussed his opinions on fiction, and I shall not wrangle with any of them.[11] I wish rather to enlarge the issue. When Wells spoke of literature, he meant something much vaster than the novel. He had in mind all crafted writing that dealt with the nature and destiny of mankind. It was all, to one degree or another, as provisional as his own. Strip a novel "of its sly nudges and allusions and what would remain of it?" he asks in *'42 to '44* (1944). "No literature is permanent, because no language is permanent; all literature is journalism and will pass away in this changing world. Language will change, ideas will change, there are no immortal works, and I count all 'classics' dead and bores" (*'42*, pt. II: 17).

In "The Lost Inheritance," a short story of 1897, Wells pokes fun at a man who aspires to a Carlylean role as a teacher of Nations, but from the beginning he himself was inclined to pronounce on large issues and admired writers who did likewise, such as Shelley, Carlyle, and Huxley.[12] Above all else, literature, for Wells, was a means of altering existence. His early successes were largely entertainments, but such was the economic necessity of the profession. They were never *merely* entertainments.[13] When he became a successful novelist, he did not limit his notion of literature to fictional forms. That is one reason that his fictional forms were not bound by dogmatic rules. If language was the fundamental tool of human advancement, its use, first in speech and then in writing, had to be central to the welfare of the race. Neolithic man was thinking, but confusedly. "In speech he had woven a net to bind his race together, but also it was a net about his feet. Man was binding himself into new and larger and more efficient combinations indeed, but at a price" (*Outline*, chap. XI: 5). First in speech and then in books men began to tell stories about themselves, the tribe, and its mores, and "the why for the world." Gradually these stories formed a tradition and then a larger sense of community. In *The Fate of Homo Sapiens* (1939), Wells asserted that the cultural life of Europe and the Europeanized world was based upon two Sacred Books. "Spreading over the old sacrificial paganism, there presently appeared what one may distinguish as Book religions." The first of these was the Old Testament, the second was the New. He recounts their ascendancy and mentions the later development of another Book religion, Islam, but mainly he wishes to emphasize that Western culture, until as late as the Russian Revolution of 1917, "was based upon an inter-related system of Bible-centered Book religions which had either obliterated or assimilated the more ancient blood-sacrifice cults" (*Homo*: 11).

The new world required a new Sacred Book. Wells's plan for a World Brain or World Library was one version of his perception that a uniform, organized body of ideas common to all men was necessary to revive a sense of racial hope and commitment. It is clear from what Wells said in *The Work, Wealth and Happiness of Mankind* that he came to see his work as serving that function. If the Sacred Books of the past could give man the faith and fortitude to struggle for common ideals, the same could be true once again, only the new Bible would have to be based upon science and known fact and dispense with supernatural cajolings.

Literature is double-edged. It is powerful for good, but dangerous as well. It is powerful not only because it can persuade and indoctrinate by fixing ideas into expressions that become habits of thought but because it endures. Disputes and dissensions pass, Wells said, speaking of the conflicts of classical Greece, but what does not shrink into insignificance is the literature that Greece produced at this time. Yet in that permanence itself there lay a danger. Ideas lose their aptness. Men require new perceptions in their struggle to adapt to changing circumstances. Old expressions, old books, old faiths may no longer serve but, like all powerful writing, persist nonetheless.

Wells admired the Athenian writers and called them "the first modern men" (*Outline*, chap. XXII: 6). The true value of this group of writers and thinkers was not in the result it achieved, but the attempt it made. "It is not that they answered questions, but that they dared to ask them. Never before had man challenged his world and the way of life to which he found his birth had brought him. Never had he said before that he could alter his conditions" (*Outline*, chap. XXII: 6). As adventurers in thoughts and writing, the Athenians were highly unusual, for most writing reinforces accepted notions. In *The Dream* (1924), Sarnac recalls the situation in turn-of-the-century England. "In all ages," he says, "people have wanted stories about life" to supplement their experiences and widen their judgments. There has been storytelling and literature since there has been language. "And always literature has told people what their minds were prepared to receive, searching for what it should tell rather in the mind and expectation of the hearer or reader—who was the person who paid—than in the unendowed wildernesses of reality" (*Dream*, chap. V: 8).

As a young man, Wells envisioned a future in which the decayed libraries of the world had come to represent just so much waste labor of the mind. (*Machine*, chap. VIII). But fundamentally he believed in the responsible mission of the writer.[14] Through his character Hallery, Boon argues for a definition of literature that makes it "a kind of over-mind of the race," including the Bible, the Koran, the Talmud and other similar books. "Of course," says the conservative Reginald Bliss, "one knows that real literature is something that has to do with leisure and cultivated people and books and shaded lamps and all that sort of thing." But Hallery wants literature to embrace whatever influences the mind of the race. Boon asserts what Wells considered the real significance of literature and the writer. To him "every man who writes to express or change or criticize an idea, every man who observes and records a fact in the making of a research, every man who hazards or tests a theory, every artist of any sort who really expresses, does thereby, in that very act, participate, share in, become for just that instant when he is novel and authentically *true*, the Mind of the Race, the thinking divinity" (*Boon*, chap. V: 5).

What I have shown so far of Wells's concept of literature should explain why he could not accept definitions of the novel promoted by Henry James and others. In his lecture of 1911 entitled "The Scope of the Novel," reprinted as "The Contemporary Novel," Wells stated his case. Essentially, he argued for an open and exhaustive mode of fiction that dealt with the realities of life in an experimental fashion. He dismissed the idea that the novel was merely a "harmless opiate" and argued that it had "inseparable moral consequences." It was "not simply a fictitious record of conduct but also a study and judgment of conduct" and was therefore "a powerful instrument of moral suggestion." He saw the novel as part of the conflict between abstractionism and the importance of the individual instance. All questions were being approached in a new inquiring and experimental spirit, he said, and claimed the whole of human life for novelists embued with this spirit. Here is his expectation for the novel:

> It is to be the social mediator, the vehicle of understanding, the instrument of self-examination, the parade of morals and the exchange of manners, the factory of customs, the criticism of laws and institutions and of social dogmas and ideas. It is to be the home confessional, the initiator of knowledge, the seed of fruitful self-questioning. (*Forces*, "The Contemporary Novel")

Wells held to these opinions about literature. In "Democracy Under Revision" he declared, "The novel should no longer be merely a picture of a spectacle relying for its interest upon adventures and the extraordinary traits of individual characters, in no way responsible for the whole. It should be turning decisively towards responsibility, to what I might call creative propaganda." He maintained, using the state of Democracy as his example, that most literature merely reflects the order or disorder, the thinking or habitual responses of its time (*Going*, chap. V). But because literature was an expression of human will, it struck Wells as a shame and humiliation that it did not direct instead of merely record human destiny. The Voice in *The Camford Visitation* (1937) is unequivocal. " 'Literature,' said he, 'should be a part of man's attempt to take hold of life. You make it a little fiddling with the aesthetic incidents of life,' " he complains to the Oxford don Trumber. "It should rise in masses to transcendent efforts. It should be the solvent glory of reality, the flux of life" (*Camford*, chap. VII)

In order to take hold of life, writers had to deal with immediate things. All of life is change; art, poesy, philosophy, literature are impermanent. That effort has power and meaning which deals with immediate circumstances. "The picture, the music, the book, the research that does not arise out of actual current things—and does not bear upon what we are doing or what we intend to do—does not in reality exist. It is a phantom. It is a pretension. It is Nothing. Science, art, literature, philosophy, all alike record Humanity's impression of the present and its attempt to adjust itself for a future. They express the thought and embody the will—the growing changing thought, the developing will—of mankind" (*Going*, chap. V). A lot of European literature is overrated, Ratzel says in *The Brothers* (1938). Most of it has been aristocratic and bourgeois, "written mainly for people who wanted to feel secure, to please and reassure them." But the literature of the present must deal with realities. It must *create* realities.

Wells frequently denounced literature that withdrew from serious engagement with ideas and events.[15] Like the historian of *The Shape of Things to Come*, he believed that aesthetic life "is conditioned by the times; science conditions the times." Literature and art are time-servers which merely reflect moods or speculate upon them. (*Shape*, bk. III: 7). Like

Ratzel, Wells wanted to make literature as much a conditioner of the times as science was. In *Christina Alberta's Father* (1925), Paul Lambone, in preaching his new religion of communal service, perceives that new forms of narrative reveal a movement in that direction. "History now becomes more important than biography." What in the egotistical past had been the whole of life—the love story, the treasure story, the career, the personal deed and victory—has given way to more selfless aims. (*Christina*, bk. III, chap. IV: 4). William Clissold, promoting a scheme very like Wells's World Brain, states that the workers for a new world order must "evoke a literature and an education that will record and continue and spread their awakening creative spirit" (*Clissold*, vol. II, bk. V: 7). In the next phase of development toward this human community, literature will be a form of social intercourse, not a professional literature that keeps a class of philosophers and men of letters working only toward dead ends of pettiness and pedantry. "It will be a literature of activity," helping men to form their own views (*Clissold*, vol. II, bk. V: 10). Doctor Carstall in *The Holy Terror* (1939), foreseeing the collapse of a world familiar to him, complains that in his day life had some dignity. "Art was subservient and not subversive, its mission was to please and evoke a feeling of complacent approval, and literature, as free as it is to-day, had infinitely better manners" (*Terror*, bk. II, chap. I: 1). But Wells did not want a cropped literature with good manners. He wanted a virile voice crying in the wilderness "Behold ye the way of the World State." He wanted a Word that was the equivalent of the Deed.

Wells's judgments upon literature are reflected in his wider assessment of art. He insisted that the real purpose of art was bound up with social realities and did not sympathize with attitudes that placed it above all other concerns. Even before the controversy with Henry James developed, he teased those who took such a stand. Wells matured his skills in the penumbra of W. E. Henley, whose dislike for aesthetes was loud and direct, and some of his early pieces reveal a basic opposition to aesthetic doctrine. "A Misunderstood Artist" (1894) is an example. The essay opens with a gentleman on a train saying to his companion, "This art for art's sake—I don't believe in it, I tell you. Art should have an aim. If it don't do you good, if it ain't moral, I'd as soon not have it. What good is it? I believe Ruskin." Wells does not take sides in the dispute that develops, making nearly as much fun of the pompous moralist as of the two artists who fall into friendly conversation. One is a young poet who feels misunderstood; his champion is also a misunderstood artist He is a cook enraged by the fact that people expect his meals to be edible as well as beautiful. The story scores off a distorted principle of the art-for-art's sake school. It is no more than *Punch* humor.[16]

Wells gets in similar digs in other early writings. In "House-Hunting as an Outdoor Amusement" (1894), he observes that the true artist of house-hunting does it for its own sake and without a purpose; and in "Thoughts on Cheapness and My Aunt Charlotte" (1895), he writes, "I like my art unadorned: thought and skill and the other strange quality that is added thereto to make things beautiful—and nothing more." He mocks the insincerity and insubstantiality of actors and other theatre people in "The Sad Story of a Dramatic Critic" (1895) and teases the poetaster type for his triviality in "In the Modern Vein" (1894). "The Temptation of Harringay" (1895) is a good-natured spoofing of Oscar Wilde and the aesthete's tendency to deliberate about art instead of creating it. Harringay is an artist who can never make his art come alive. He wonders if his imagination is wrong. The narrator affirms that it is. In a clear allusion to Wilde's *Dorian Gray*, one of Harringay's paintings comes alive as he is painting it and accuses him of not knowing what he is trying to paint. He offers him this advice. " 'The true artist,' said the picture, 'is always an ignorant man. An artist who theorises about his work is no longer artist, but critic.' "

All of this teasing is for fun, and Wells does not confine his objections to aesthetes. Nonetheless, his opinion of art which has as its highest end the perfection of its own technique is manifestly negative.[17] This negativism did not prevent him from appreciating achievements of technique as he surely did with James and Conrad.[18] Just as in the science-fiction romances Wells could excoriate scientists while believing firmly in the principles of science, so he could satirize artists while adhering to certain clear aesthetic principles. He does both in "Filmer" (1901), where a conceited and insignificant poet comments on the career of a scientist who has the intellectual courage and determination to create a flying machine, but not the physical courage and determination to fly it.

Wells was severe on aestheticism because he was not immune to its attraction. He half-inclined to follow the sea lady back to the sea and let moonshine be triumphant. In the early Sandgate days, he said, referring to the years around 1899 to 1905, he was being strongly attracted toward a conception of life dedicated to constructive public ends, but was also "being tugged, though with less force, in a quite opposite direction, towards the artistic attitude. I have never been able to find the artistic attitude fundamentally justifiable but I understand and sympathize with the case for it" (*Autobiography*, chap. VIII: 5). In a letter to Rebecca West in 1934 contrasting his approach to literature with hers, Wells wrote, "I am simplicity. That is why I came off artistically from the beginning and got slovenly later."[19] This remark is not a confession of failure, but rather reflects an ambivalent feeling about his craft. Wells was entirely capable of making claims for his novels as art when it suited his purposes. Thus, when *In the*

*Days of the Comet* (1906) was attacked on moral grounds, he replied that it was beyond such criticism as a work of art.[20] In this instance Wells was not playing fair since his objective was to make his novels into agents of social change. As he progressed, he moved further from aesthetic influences and his attitudes became less equivocal, but remained ambivalent to the end.

As he clarified his own objectives, Wells became more critical of the artistic spirit. Partly this was because those who called themselves artists were critical of his writing. As early as "In the Modern Vein: An Unsympathetic Love Story" (1894), Wells criticised not merely the faulty aesthetics and limited intelligence of the aesthetic type but his emotional sincerity as well. The target is a sort of Richard Le Gallienne—though no specific model is necessary. Wells lampooned the egotistical artist in *The First Men in the Moon* (1901) and sketched the type comically in the Widgetts of *Ann Veronica* (1909). Introduced to Society in the world of the future in *When the Sleeper Wakes* (1899), Graham asks if any great artists or authors are there. His companion replies, "No authors. They are mostly such queer people—and so preoccupied about themselves. And they quarrel so dreadfully!" (*Sleeper*, chap. XIV). This attitude is both playful and serious, and Wells repeated the jest over the years. In *The Wife of Sir Isaac Harman* (1914), he spoke of "the flimsy literary people who mar the solid worth of so many great clubs," with his tongue only partly in his cheek (*Harman*, chap. VI: 7). Later in that novel, Edgar Wilkins, Wells's self-portrait, attacks his own breed.[21] "We people who write and paint and all that sort of thing are a breed of insatiable egotists," he declares, adding that artists like himself are generally plain Rotters. "Nobody can have a greater contempt for artists and writers and poets and philosophers than I, oh! a squalid crew they are, mean, jealous, pugnacious, disgraceful in love, *disgraceful*—but out of it all comes the greatest serenest thing, the mind of the world, Literature. Nasty little midges, yes,—but fireflies—carrying light for the darkness" (*Harman*, chap. X: 4).

By 1915 Wells had pretty well made up his mind about art and he lets Benham state his view in *The Research Magnificent*. Benham is seeking an activity that is noble and worthy of the truly aristocratic or superior man. Science he considers in that category. Then he comes to Art. "Art is nothing aristocratic except when it is a means of scientific or philosophical expression. Art that does not argue nor demonstrate nor discover is merely the craftsman's impudence." Benham wants his world to be real, but to him pure Art is simply "a more splendid, more permanent, transmissible reverie." He concludes decisively, "The very essence of what I am after is *not* to be an artist" (*Research*, chap. II: 13).

Obviously there is some ambiguity still in Wells's use of the terms *art* and *artistic*, but perhaps the confusion is only apparent. A true artist, in

Wells's view, was one who mastered his craft and dedicated it to a higher purpose such as the World State. His work thus became true art. Artists who labored to perfect their craft for the craft's sake or for mere egotism or self-indulgence would produce only pure art, which failed to meet Wells's standard. *The Autocracy of Mr. Parham* (1930) examines this matter through the conflict between the sophisticated Mr. Parham and the crude and practical Sir Bussy Woodcock. Sir Bussy, impressed by Parham's intelligence, seeks his help in trying to comprehend the nature of art which Parham describes as "a kind of getting the concentrated quality of loveliness, of beauty, out of common experience." Sir Bussy approves of this, but Parham's claim that Art makes this beauty permanent does not fully persuade Sir Bussy, who finds the pretentions of art and artists annoying.

Wells is perhaps unfair in not providing Parham with adequate responses to Sir Bussy, but this dispute between the aesthetically refined Parham and the go-getting Sir Bussy is revealing because it objectifies a tension in Wells himself. He knew himself to be a fine craftsman and had been called a fine artist in his day. He was sensitive in a manner superior to his puppets Bulpington and Parham, and he was forceful in a manner superior to Sir Bussy or Rud Whitlow. He was both Alfred Bunter, the eager, moralizing novelist, and Rowland Palace, the masterful success concerned with his position. He was, as he said, a journalist, but not that alone. He was capable, as we have seen, of declaring writers irreplaceable contributors to the Mind of Man and, in other moments of serious reflection, of declaring, like Mr. Britling, that "he was a writer, a footnote to reality; he had no trick of command over men, his rôle was observation rather than organization" (*Britling*, bk. II, chap. II: 1).

Wells was sympathetic to the case for art but did not appreciate it. He explained his ignoring of art in *The Outline of History* by saying that "artistic productions, unlike philosophical thought and scientific discovery, are the ornaments and expression rather than the creative substance of history" (*Outline*, chap. XXXIV: 8). In his own career he sometimes had to draw some sharp distinctions. In *The Salvaging of Civilization* (1921), he acknowledged that his material was a little overdone since it had been designed first for lecture presentation. This simplification, he said, occasioned "a loss of grace rather than of clearness. And since I am stating a case and not offering the reader anything professing to be a literary work, I shall not apologize for summing up and underlining the chief points of this book" (*Salvaging*, chap. VIII). This remark implies that a literary work consists mainly of the addition of grace to statement, but it is clear that Wells valued artistic work more than that. Earlier in this same book, while urging champions of the World State to spread its message, he told them "to create a vision of it, to make it seem first a possibility and then an approaching reality" (*Salvaging*, chap. III). As we have already seen, when he wished to describe the makers of the new world giving shape and substance to their ideals, he likened them to artists.

Clearly Wells had a small and a large meaning for art. In some instances the reader can follow the progression of his thought from one to the other. In *The Work, Wealth and Happiness of Mankind* (1932). Wells described artists of all sorts as "an efflorescence, a lovely and purifying efflorescence on life" (*Work*, chap. XV: 8). From a biological point of view, he remarks, art is a form of constructive play. The artist himself has glimpses of vision and the great artist long periods of confidence, "but for the rest, the artist is an unsure, straining creature, miserably in need of reassurance and failing in courage." Nonetheless, it is through art that life "explores the realms of human possibility beyond the limits of material necessity" (*Work*, chap. XIV: 5).

Wells renders a similar progression of evaluation in *The Anatomy of Frustration* (1936), treating it as William Burroughs Steele's. Steele also says there are no immortal works of art, no "classics." He surveys literature "as if it were no more than a vast pile of old letters and documents." Tradition is the artist's enemy, and "the true artist is innocent of the past." He concludes, "The business of the artist in any field is the enlargement of appreciation. He is a mutation. He is the growing-point of the species. He is perpetually expanding the field for the play of the human imagination." He ends his manuscript with the words "Art—the undying explorer," which to the narrator eliminates the distinction between art and science (*Frustration*, chap. XXI). It is with the elimination of this distinction that Wells's estimate becomes clear. All art is a superfluity from the turmoil of human existence. But that superfluity can be an agency for advance. Most art is nothing more than play, but some is play of such monumental dimensions that it creates new possibilities for mankind. When it has this shaping and directing capacity, it is transformed from art to Art. Freed from tradition, it can create a vision that is truly new and fitting for its time. Like science it becomes another form of the search for truth. For Wells' that search was the justification for Art and for Science.

In his autobiography Wells sought to review his opinions candidly. Because he was a novelist, he spoke candidly about the novel, admitting that it was a difficult subject for him. He had consciously determined to begin writing novels instead of pseudo-scientific stories that dwelt upon imaginative experience rather than personal conduct.[22] Henry James saw the novel as an exalted achievement but had no idea of its possible use as a help to conduct, whereas Wells "was disposed to regard a novel as about as much an art form as a market place or a boulevard. It had not even necessarily to get anywhere." What Wells says of *Marriage* could apply to much of his writing: "I had very many things to say and . . . if I could say one of them in such a way as to get my point over to the reader I did not worry much about finish" (*Autobiography*, chap. VII: 5).

Wells did have a great deal to say. He may have had few genuinely original ideas, but he was fertile in finding new ways to convey them, as I shall show later. Wells believed that writing could change things as long as it did not confine itself to illustrations of common assumptions or retreat from objective meaning and purpose entirely. He believed that literature was intimately interwoven with the many forces operating in society. In his autobiography he described how this involvement worked and how it led to his kind of fiction.

> Throughout the broad smooth flow of nineteenth-century life in Great Britain, the art of fiction floated on this same assumption of social fixity. The Novel in English was produced in an atmosphere of security for the entertainment of secure people who liked to feel established and safe for good. Its standards were established within that apparently permanent frame and the criticism of it began to be irritated and perplexed when, through a new instability, the splintering frame began to get into the picture.
>
> I suppose for a time I was the outstanding instance among writers of fiction in English of the frame getting into the picture. (*Autobiography*, chap. VII: 5)[23]

Wells was so convinced of the interinvolvement of literature and social reality that he considered it impossible to remove art from life. To pretend to do so had to be a pose. He disapproved of poses and thus of art for art's sake. Despite his hostility he was a conscious artist himself in the sense that he knew his craft and how to gain effects with it. In the next few pages I shall demonstrate this fact briefly, though it is a subject worth extensive treatment since too many commentators have taken Wells at his word and supposed him uninterested in, or incapable of, the finer dimensions of the writer's, and especially the novelist's, trade.

Wells always admired the primary fact of good writing. When posing the question "What is the good of Shaw?" he replies, "To begin with the elements so to speak, Shaw writes English extraordinarily well. I feel a sort of benefit of clergy attaches to that alone. . . . Sometimes I try to write English, and I am always keenly interested in the writing of English, and I am even interested in the writing of stuff about the writing of English, and I know enough of the business to know how beautifully it is done by Shaw" (*Going*, chap. XXV).[24] Although some critics and reviewers noted that Wells was not always grammatical or punctilious in his diction, most critics and reviewers admitted that he was a master of style, easily capable of creating a vivid fictional situation or conveying an idea clearly. In explaining his decision to class himself among journalists rather than artists, he says, "I write as I walk because I want to get somewhere and I write as straight as I can, just as I walk as straight as I can, because that is the best way to get there" (*Autobiography*, chap. VIII: 5).[25]

I think Wells can be forgiven a certain exaggeration in this passage. He was, after all, taking a stand, and sometimes when he did this, he had a weakness for clarity at the expense of complete accuracy. Bennett charged Wells with being no artist, but of using art to achieve his ends. I believe Bennett understood Wells and comprehended his weaknesses and his strengths. When he said that Wells could not *endure* art, he did not say that he could not *fathom* it.[26] Wells's own writing shows a fine awareness of artistic technique and his parodies verify that sensitivity. He said that he awakened to the wonders of literary art during the recuperative months of 1887-1888 at Up Park, when he read widely in imaginative literature with serious attention to language and style. He became fully conscious of how vacuous his own attempts at creative writing were. Later he destroyed almost all of it, spurred by "a quickened sense of what writing could be and do" (*Autobiography*, chap. VI: 2).

Wells was always conscious of style. Although he was justly accused of hasty and even careless composition, he certainly rewrote some of his early tales—among them *The Time Machine* and *The Island of Dr. Moreau*—with care.[27] He showed his consciousness of style by alluding to it. At the end of "The Plattner Story" (1896), he declares that he has resisted "the natural disposition of a writer of fiction to dress up incidents of this sort. I have told the thing as far as possible in the order in which Plattner told it to me. I have carefully avoided any attempts at style, effect, or construction." He proceeds to list some devices he refrained from using. In "Mr. Skelmersdale in Fairyland" (1901), the narrator complains that "it is hard, it is impossible, to give in print the effect of [the Fairy Lady's] radiant sweetness shining through the jungle of poor Skelmersdale's rough and broken sentences," just after he has succeeded in conveying this sweetness to the reader. This brand of self-consciousness was familiar in the literature of the time. Writers prided themselves on their stylistic achievements and frequently ran to excesses. The jokes in Wells's "Inexperienced Ghost" (1901), for example, are not very successful. He lingers over Clayton's miserable pun about the ghost who has an honest face and, being *transparent*, can't help telling the truth.[28]

Wells could suit his style to his subject. In "A Story of the Stone Age" (1897), he wrote with a measured simplicity almost as though he wished to give the impression of using a language in its unadorned youth. The style changes in the companion tale, "A Story of the Days to Come" (1897). It is more burdened with subordinations, modifications, complex and compound sentences. This style is appropriate to the description of a time when social values are complicated, life is no longer simple and direct, and objectives must be approached through difficult, roundabout means. Something similar happens within *The Dream* (1924), which begins in a simple and direct manner to describe the purified world of the future but becomes more complicated and involved as it narrates the frustrating conditions of the past. In the epilogue to the tale the style is a modified version of the opening, suggesting that the purified minds of the Utopian characters have been to some degree altered by their knowledge of the past.

As a writer Wells naturally delighted in language, but more than most he liked to prompt it to little adventures of its own, as his letters and the numerous nicknames he created reveal. There was a good bit of Wells in Mr. Polly. "Words attracted him curiously, words rich in suggestion, and he loved a novel and striking phrase" (*Polly*, chap. I: 4). Polly is an incipient Wells, treasuring the "queer incommunicable joy . . . of the vivid phrase that turns the statement of the horridest fact to beauty," without being able to create such phrases (*Polly*, chap. VII: 2).

It is beyond my purpose to range through Wells's canon selecting examples of his skill, but some are necessary to demonstrate that Wells kept the "art" of his craft in the forefront of his mind as he wrote. Take this rather blatant, but skillful, passage about metaphor from *Boon* (1915): "It was extraordinary what a power metaphors and fancies had upon Boon. . . . He would touch a metaphor and then return and sip it, and then sip and drink and swill until it had intoxicated him hopelessly" (*Boon*, chap. V: 2). Wells playfully elaborates a metaphor about the appreciation of metaphor. This is technical display. It is showing off. If he ever objected to James's skill at developing a metaphor, he had no right, since he persisted in the trick himself, though usually with less finesse than James. In *Apropos of Dolores* (1938), Wilbeck mentions a "train of ideas" running through his mind. "This train of thought which began to assemble in Rennes has been picking up passengers ever since." He amplifies and calls attention to the metaphor, then concludes by declaring that "since it is about my journey in this train, wherever it takes me, that I am going to write and not my tour in Brittany," he will suspend any further topographical description (*Dolores*, chap. I: 3). James would have blushed. Mr. Stanley of *Ann Veronica*, wanting to warn his daughter about the dangers of life, writes, "*The life of a young girl is set about with prowling pitfalls.*" He identifies the unsatisfactoriness of the sentence in the mixture of metaphors but is as incapable of creating clear prose as he is of all other mental clarity (*Veronica*, chap. I: 4). Later Ann Veronica herself notes that a metaphor she is developing in her mind is going astray. She is able to correct it (*Veronica*, chap. II: 3).[29] In *Christina Alberta's Father* (1925), Wells calls attention to the implications of metaphor. "The moral of a proverb depends entirely upon the image chosen, and though a rolling stone gathers no moss, a rolling snowball grows by what it rolls upon" (*Christina*, bk. II, chap. II: 2). He goes on to describe Mr. Preemby's progress through the London streets in terms of this figure.

Now and then Wells felt obliged to apologize for his metaphors. In *'42 to '44* (1944), he admits the vitiating anthropomorphism of his image of the universe as a self-expressive creature but blames the limitations of human mind and language (*'42*, pt. I: 5). As we have already seen, Wells was quick to note the traps that others fell into by tricks of language. He wrote in *The Anatomy of Frustration* (1936), "If Socialism was frustrated by an incomplete proposition; the League of Nations . . . was brought to futility by bad analogies" (*Frustration*, chap. XII). In his own discussion of psychoanalysis in *The Science of Life* (1930), he was careful to remind his readers of the "dangers of misconception that accompany metaphor" (*Life*, chap. VIII: 2).

Sometimes Wells became crapulous about his style. " 'Peculiar,' like every other word in this conscientious narrative, is written with deliberation," he says in *You Can't Be Too Careful* (1941) and proceeds to defend his choice (*Careful*, bk. II: 3). He never forgot the importance of diction. Frank Swinnerton testified that Wells's skill with language was not studied, for it was manifest in his speech. "He mimics with extraordinary sense of burlesque character. And every tale he tells, every sentence he speaks, bears witness to his genius in the use of language. I do not know if Wells's vocabulary is really twice the size of the vocabulary of any other man; all I know is that its felicity in every matter of droll epithet is so effortless as to be irresistible."[30] R. Thurston Hopkins, writing in Wells's midcareer, pronounced him "a barbarian in regard to literary usage" but praised his diction and his art that was so close to common language and actual life.[31]

In *Star-Begotten* (1937), Wells wrote, "A literary man carries about with him in his head a collection of edged tools known as his Vocabulary. And sometimes he cuts himself" (*Star*, chap. I: 3). He gives an instance in the same novel, describing how a writer's faltering conviction about his subject reveals itself in his style. Joseph Davis is a good writer of historical romances, who has become infected by doubt. "He wrote with a diminishing ease and confidence and let qualifying shadows creep into his heroic portraits. He would sometimes admit quite damaging things, and then apologize. He found this enhanced the solidity of some of his figures, but it cast a shadow on his forthright style" (*Star*, chap. I: 2).

Wells considered his own style forthright, though he never pretended it was flawless. Bennett constantly pointed out solecisms in his writing and accused him genially of practicing a "higher literary carelessness," but

Wells replied, "The stile of my general design, the stile of my thought—C'est moi!"[32] Maugham acutely noted Wells's tendency to restate an idea in new words immediately after its first statement, a curious trait that Wells recognized and called his "besetting sin of verbal repetition" (*Autobiography*, chap. VII: 3).[33] He trusted a great deal to the spontaneous phrase. As a journalist he had learned the knack of generating effective phrases and learned to count on them, but he saw the dangers of that knack to which he often succumbed. In "The Land Ironclads" (1903), he said, "Journalism curdles all one's mind to phrases," illustrating the success of the method while condemning the fault.

Although he deplored politicians' use of catchwords, Wells felt that, despite their dangers, gripping phrases or slogans might achieve in little what he hoped grand programs of revolution might achieve on a larger scale. In *The Happy Turning* (1945), he wrote:

> Certain phrases—parroted phrases empty of belief—are already to be found in the newspapers and speeches—the abolition of war, the abolition of distance, the abolition of competition and social inequality. But after people have repeated a phrase a great number of times, they begin to realise it has meaning and may even be true. And then it comes true. (*Turning*, chap. I)

He knew that no one man could achieve this transformation and confessed in *The Fate of Homo Sapiens* (1939) that his own thoughts had become so bound to his early experiences and subsequent complex associations that it was difficult for him to reconceive what he wished to say (*Homo*: 10). The difficulty did not prevent him from trying.

Wells's concern for good writing applied to all writing, including fiction, but fiction makes its own peculiar demands. Despite many charges to the contrary, Wells understood those demands.[34] In his early writings he demonstrated a command of the romance tradition and he remained interested in the fable throughout his career, and he considered his novels consistent with the development of English fiction.[35] For example, he maintained the privilege of intruding himself into his narratives. People complained about this, but Wells insisted upon the freedom for several reasons, not the least of which was that he could thereby call his reader's attention to the fact that they were reading a fiction. His purpose was the opposite of James's and Joyce's. He liked the opportunity to be blunt and obvious. In describing Eudena's movements after a difficult night in "A Story of the Stone Age," Wells remarks, "She was stiff, but not so stiff as you would have been, dear young lady (by virtue of your upbringing), and as she had not been trained to eat at least once in three hours, but instead had often fasted three days, she did not feel uncomfortably hungry" (*Stories*, "A Story of the Stone Age": 1).

This gratuitous frontal attack is uncommon. More often Wells toys with his craft rather than his reader. In *The Wonderful Visit* (1895), he begins chapter twenty-one this way: "And thus in the little bedroom over the gable we reach a first resting place in this story. And as we have been hard at it, getting our story spread out before you, it may be perhaps well to recapitulate a little" (*Visit*, chap. XXI). He then summarizes the progress of the story to that point. Later he pauses for an apology. "I am painfully aware of the objectionable nature of my story here," he says, having introduced a servant-girl as a heroine. "I have even thought of wilfully perverting the truth to propitiate the Lady Reader. But I could not. The story has been too much for me. I do the thing with my eyes open" (*Visit*, chap. XL). The narrator of *The Sea Lady* (1902) addresses us apologetically because, although he suspects that when Chatteris and Adeline went into the drawing room and closed the door behind them there was something in the nature of a caress, he is unable to describe it. "I must confess," he laments, "I envy the freedom of the novelist who can take you behind such a locked door as this and give you all that such persons say and do. But with the strongest will in the world to blend the little scraps of fact I have into a continuous sequence of events, I falter at this occasion" (*Lady*, chap. V: 3).

This is a joke upon the practice of some novelists, the reader who accepts certain conventions, and himself. Obviously, while he is criticizing novelists who recount events that could not be known, much as Conrad might criticize them, he is destroying the illusion of his own tale by using the direct address to his audience, thereby assuming an amused pose entirely at odds with Conrad's dicta. Of course, especially in the romances, he sometimes used the Conradian device of the second-hand recounter of a tale confined by his sources, as in "The Empire of the Ants" (1905), but generally he felt quite free to overstep the bounds set down by aestheticians of the novel.[36] *Kipps* (1905) is a good example. The narrator feels free to step in whenever he pleases. Reminding himself that he "should thank my Maker that He did not appoint me Censor of the world of men," he sets off on a digression that leads to a benign suspension of judgment upon Kipps (*Kipps*, bk. II, chap. VI: 3). Sometimes he becomes angry. "The stupid little tragedies of these clipped and limited lives!" he exclaims, and then begins a tirade.

> What is the good of keeping up the idyllic sham and pretending that ill-educated, misdirected people "get along very well," and that all this is harmlessly funny and nothing more? You think I'm going to write fat, silly, grinning novels about half-educated undertrained people and keep it up all the time, that the whole thing's nothing but funny! (Kipps, bk. III, chap. II: 4)

Another time he pretends that he is a customer of Kipps's and in parenthesis pleads with the reader not to reveal to Kipps that he has written a book about him (*Kipps*, bk. III, chap. III: 7).

Those who complained about Wells's use of this device seemed to sup-

pose that he did it inadvertently out of clumsiness. Far from being unde-
signed, it was slyly intentional. In "The Contemporary Novel" he defended
the practice. "Nearly all the novels that have, by the lapse of time, reached
an assured position of recognized greatness, are not only saturated in the
personality of the author, but have in addition quite unaffected personal
outbreaks" (*Forces*, "The Contemporary Novel"). Moreover, he claimed
that "in some cases the whole art and delight of a novel may lie in the
author's personal interventions," and he cited the then popular novels by
Elizabeth, Lady Russell. Not only did Wells value the right of authorial
intrusion as a means of stating opinions, he often used the convention as a
source of humor, setting his reader off balance with casual or bold tres-
passes. At the outset of *Star-Begotten* (1937) he says, "Whether there was
any reality behind [the idea of which he is writing] it is not the business of
the storyteller to say" (*Star*, chap. I: 1). The storyteller does not obtrude his
views, but the very decision to tell the story from Joseph Davis's point of
view is a commitment more important than any outright assertion by the
narrator. Wells is similarly playful at the opening of the second chapter of
*Christina Alberta's Father* (1925). "This story," he announces, "it was
clearly explained in the first paragraph of the first section of the first chapter, is a story about Mr. Preemby in the later years, the widower years, of
his life." He promises not to wander far from Mr. Preemby but explains
that Christina Alberta's life being so interwoven with her father's, he must
say a great deal about her before the real story properly begins. "And even
up to the end, Christina Alberta will continue to intrude." With an outrageous transition, Wells then begins his account of Christina Alberta by
stating, "Intrusion was in her nature" (*Christina*, bk. I, chap. II: 1).

This is simply great fun. The author, in the process of intruding into
his narrative, justifies the intrusion of one character upon another's time
and then equivocates to illustrate that Christina stands for the principle of
intrusion. This resistance to subordination is exactly what Wells's intru-
sions into his narratives represent—an unwillingness to be left out of the
action of his own stories. If anyone doubts Wells's intention in this teasing
passage, he need only consult the title of the novel, which reveals the true
focus of the narrative. Mr. Preemby is not even named but exists there as a
modification, so to speak, of Christina Alberta's existence. The intrusion is
more important than the narrative.

Wells was not always diverting himself with little jokes of this sort. In
novels such as *Marriage* or *The Wife of Sir Isaac Harman* he is just the
chatty first-person narrator who never identifies himself as anyone separate from Wells and who comments briefly or at length about what is occurring in his story while occasionally confiding some of his narrative difficulties to the reader. Oddly enough, it was not this unidentified intruding
author who annoyed Wells's critics, but those claiming identities of their

own, such as Richard Remington, George Ponderevo, William Clissold, and Stephen Wilbeck. These narrators certainly resemble Wells in their thinking and are usually outright exponents of his views, but Wells also employed first-person narrators who were not so clearly mouthpieces for him. Prendick is ambiguous, though close perhaps. The narrator of *The War of the Worlds* may or may not be. Bedford in *The First Men in the Moon* clearly is not. Nor is Frobisher, the Croquet Player.

In any case, Wells did not think it mattered much. To a great extent *Boon* is an enormous spoof of the whole issue. Boon, who is a caricature of Wells himself, explains his purpose in creating a fictional persona to convey his thoughts.

> I invented Hallery to get rid of myself, but, after all, Hallery is really no more than the shadow of myself, and if I were impersonal and well bred, and if I spoke behind a black screen, it would still be as much my voice as ever. I do not see how it is possible to prevent the impersonal things coming by and through persons; but at any rate we can begin to recognize that the person who brings the message is only in his way like the messenger-boy who brings the telegrams. (*Boon*, chap. VI: 2)

Boon makes Wells's point, but he is just Wells's spokesman as Hallery is Boon's. To complicate matters even further, Boon does not speak to us directly, for the book *Boon* is presented to us through the medium of Reginald Bliss, a slack-minded, nearly incompetent editor who records more or less faithfully without understanding. Bliss offers us Boon, who offers us Hallery and the whole shebang is introduced by Wells in an "ambiguous introduction," the main purpose of which is to declare Bliss's book ill-advised and to state that it *is* Bliss's book. "Bliss is Bliss and Wells is Wells. And Bliss can write all sorts of things that Wells could not do" (*Boon*, Introduction).

*Boon* is comedy. *The Research Magnificent* is not, and yet Wells played a similar game with that book. William Benham was so devoted to his great project that he never pulled his notes together into a book, so after his death, his friend White goes through his papers to bring them into some kind of order. It is possible for a reader to miss the point that White never produces the expected book either but is simply a character in a tale told by yet another narrator. Wells used this general device—which has a long history and can be found in such works as Hogg's *Confessions of a Justified Sinner*, Hawthorne's *Scarlet Letter*, and many other famous stories—not only in novels but in such uncategorizable fictions as *The Shape of Things to Come* and *The Anatomy of Frustration*, where the account we read is rendered by Wells from the documents of a second party such as Philip Raven or William Burroughs Steele. *The Shape of Things to Come* is further complicated by Wells's uncertainty whether the document is truly Raven's unbidden dream or a conscious polemic.

It is no wonder that Wells became furious with critics who continued to object to narrators sounding like him. He was driven to protest in "A Note Before the Title Page"—a place designed to get your attention—that William Clissold, despite resemblances, was not H. G. Wells. Critics had missed the point that Boon was supposed to have settled. Wells wanted to convey certain ideas in his fiction. He had to do this through narration concerning characters. What difference did it make if the characters resembled Wells as long as the ideas got across? Later, critics objected to characters conveying Wells's ideas at such great length, and he wrote a defense of the Novel of Ideas as an introduction to *Babes in the Darkling Wood*. Later still, Wells learned that critics didn't want ideas at all, and he became nasty in *You Can't Be Too Careful*, a novel he claimed would be free from "ideers," in which he openly insulted his readers with remarks upon their limitations. Even that role was probably misread, though it makes this last novel a refreshing delight.

Wells's use of his narrators reveals the progress of his philosophy, making manifest his growing confidence in human will and demonstrating the increasing complexity of his thought. In telling his early stories, Wells alternated between first- and third-person narration. The first-person narrators are not initiators of action, even when they become involved in the events they describe. They are, instead, chroniclers.[37]. The Time Traveller in *The Time Machine* (1895) and Moreau in *The Island of Dr. Moreau* (1896) are active agents, viewed by narrators who are obliged to react to the chains of events that these scientists set going. The narrators provide a frame within which the central action occurs. Although the frame is gone and the action is therefore more immediate in *The War of the Worlds* (1898) and *The First Men in the Moon* (1901), the first-person narrators are still observers, not initiators of the central actions. These perceiving and recording agents do not exert their wills to command experience but merely react to forces they do not fully comprehend. The far more imaginative and creative figures—the Time Traveller, Dr. Moreau, the Martians, Cavor— are swept away and the narrators' only way of organizing and verifying their own remarkable experiences is to record them. This recording is a secondary, but significant, act, for the narrators themselves have been educated and altered, and they now transmit the lessons of their adventures to their readers.

The energetic protagonists of these stories exhibit, not disciplined plans for action, but necessary or unexamined urges toward a largely undefined end. Indeed, they seem to represent sheer impulse as it manifests itself in curiosity or aggression, for they seek principally to gain command over some new region of experience. They do so, however, without a completed plan. It lies with the recorders of these events to discover a pattern in them, a pattern that may reveal disillusionment or some modified hope for change. The narrator of *The Time Machine*, though he still believes in progress, has added a qualification to his belief, just as the narrator of *The War of the Worlds* has discovered that a shock to mankind's vanity may be beneficial. Prendick, returned from Moreau's island, has awakened to the bestial element in man and has turned all of his hopes toward the illuminations of science. Bedford, too, in *The First Men in the Moon*, though not so noticeably as these others, discovers that man can escape the confines of his limited and selfish personality.

What is happening in these early first-person narratives is that a powerful, disruptive, and largely unplanned force initiates a series of events which rapidly leads to disorder, meanwhile involving an observer who is permanently altered by the experience that he records, thereby making of it an artifact, a source of instruction for others. In just this manner Wells saw man's increasing intelligence, disciplined by scientific method, observing the elementary impulses in men and gradually controlling and then directing them through observation and understanding. From this point of view, these stories are paradigms of the basic human experience—mind achieving domination over impulse through self-awareness.

At the same time that Wells was writing these first-person narratives, he was also composing stories with third-person narrators. In these stories the narrator seems more a scientist examining specimens than a sympathetic creator. The narrator of *The Wheels of Chance* (1896), sounding like an anatomist, says of his central characters, "And when we open the heads of these two young people, we find, not a straightforward motive on the surface anywhere; we find, indeed, not a soul so much as an oversoul, a zeitgeist, a congestion of acquired ideas, a highway's feast of fine, confused thinking" (*Wheels*, chap. XVI)[38] The events in these stories are largely accidental and uncontrolled, while the characters live confused lives, mainly reacting to circumstances and not governing them. The central characters make plans, sometimes elaborate plans, which do not work out as they should. Hoopdriver's holiday excursion in *The Wheels of Chance* is utterly transformed, and Lewisham's schema in *Love and Mr. Lewisham* (1900) proves unworkable. Even those characters who seem to have control do not. Griffin, for example, in *The Invisible Man* (1897), though he has the power of invisibility, is more the victim of his discovery than its master.[39] He begins his adventure with a crime and performs a hasty experiment on himself which leaves him vulnerable in his invisibility, a condition signified by his nakedness. Moreover, he is dependent upon untrustworthy agents like Thomas Marvel. Similarly, Graham, the hero of *When the Sleeper Wakes* (1899), though he inherits control over the entire world, is actually powerless. He struggles, not to gain command, but merely to understand the conditions which determine his actions. Indeed, despite his aggressive adventures at the end of the novel, he doubts the reality of his experience to the end.

These novels are in the nature of scientific reports on the elementary condition of man. He is, we discover, essentially blind to the forces that shape his destiny and is at all times vulnerable to chance and accident. Even when given an opportunity to command some feature of his environment, his human failings make that command impossible. Only the vision of the objective narrator is clear, and in these novels he offers little in the way of advice or summary. There are only partial hints for the correction of this disorder, as in Hoopdriver's dream of personal intellectual growth or Lewisham's desire to devote himself to a larger cause or Graham's vision of a unified mankind. As in the first-person stories of these same years, the emphasis is upon the disorder and uncontrolled nature of existence. Hope for design and direction in human affairs is there but muted. It is, let us say, an aspiration, not a reality.

Wells's novels before 1901 were chiefly concerned with energetic figures initiating forces over which they lost control, observed by largely passive characters. With the beginning of the new century, Wells underwent a change of attitude toward life and literature. A growing sense of purpose became evident in his writing as he began to express his views in expository works where no fictional apparatus intervened between himself and his audience. His was now the first-person voice speaking for itself. *Anticipations* (1901), "The Discovery of the Future" (1902), and *Mankind in the Making* (1903) represented more than programs for the correction of material and moral conditions; they represented as well the consolidation of Wells's own personality. Accordingly, the novels of this period depict ambivalent characters who become freed, or free themselves, from one or another form of constraint, and in taking command of their own lives, secure their freedoms or initiate controlled actions in their own interests.[40]

From this point on, Wells knew what he believed in. He had formulated what he sometimes called his religion. Hereafter his fiction has a greater or lesser flavor of propaganda, but it is always lecturing. Various critics cite various terminal dates for Wells the novelist; but even though his stories became laden with instruction and took intellectual problems as their themes, Wells did not abandon the novelist's art, he merely subordinated it to his message, sometimes with leaden consequences, as in *The Secret Places of the Heart* (1922) or *Babes in the Darkling Wood* (1940), and sometimes with surprising success, as in *The World of William Clissold* (1926) and *Apropos of Dolores* (1938).[41] Wells's early tales had exploited events; his later novels emphasized ideas. Between the two concentrations, many people felt Wells's characters were lost.

Virginia Woolf was not the first to charge Wells with failing to create real characters, but the final version of her "Mr. Bennett and Mrs. Brown" has become the principal text summarizing objections to his kind of character creation, essentially the building up of an identity by means of details of personal history and environment.[42] Wells's characterization was largely superficial, and this superficiality was perceived as a fault. He has been accused of treating his characters as subjects for scientific examination, and surely there is that quality in his work, but he was not incapable of feeling compassion for his characters. Sometimes he teases the reader with this mixture of sentiments. Refusing to tell precisely what happened on the night of Mr. Polly's encounter with Uncle Jim, he writes, "A novelist should present characters, not vivisect them publicly" (*Polly*, chap. IX: 10). When his blood was up, though, he was quite willing to engage in that anatomical exercise. "I will tell you everything I know about Tewler," he says in *You Can't Be Too Careful*; "I will dissect and demonstrate on the creature" (*Careful*, bk. II, chap. IV).

Wells knew he could create characters, but he no more chose to create them for their own living quality than he sought to fashion a novel for its own sake. One principal objection to Wells's characters was that they were merely mouthpieces for him or were lifeless puppets acting out his theories. In *Boon*, Reginald Bliss, who distrusts fiction as a vehicle of discussion, describes Boon's notion of a new kind of conversational novel. "We would, he insisted, invent a personality who would embody our Idea, who should be fanatically obsessed by this idea of the Mind of the Race, who should preach it on all occasions and be brought into illuminating contact with all the existing mental apparatus and organization of the world" (*Boon*, chap. II: 3). This is precisely Wells's approach after 1901. In his later novels he chose characters who were concerned with ideas and shaped their lives around them. How could he exclude ideas from these novels when ideas were at the core of his characters, who naturally discussed them? Not to allow them to do so would be the real falsification (*Going*, chap. XXVI).

Wells had the same brigand's spirit about character as he did about subject matter. He picked up ideas and themes here and there and fit them into his narratives.[43] He did the same with characters. "Every 'living' character in a novel is drawn, frankly or furtively," he asserted, "from life—is filched from biography whole or in scraps, a portrait or a patch-up, and its actions are a reflection upon moral conduct" (*Autobiography*, chap. VII: 5). As he proceeded, Wells not only continued to draw his characters from life, he began to throw in the live characters whole. In "The Future of the Novel" he defended this practice against Lord Birkenhead's complaints.

The common sense of the reading and critical public has long ago accepted the necessity of putting "real places" into fiction under their proper names and of admitting comment on and discussion of them. Why should there be any objection to the same thing being done with the cardinal figures in the contemporary social landscape? (*Going*, chap. XXVI)[44]

In an early essay "In a Literary Household" (1894), Wells described how a writer learns to exploit his own experiences and to use his friends by turning them into characters in stories. He never yielded that rich source of material but decided along the way that a novel is not real enough unless it describes its characters' times as they are, with the real people in them.[45] Many novelists had drawn portraits of prominent contemporaries in their novels—Benjamin Disraeli is a good example. But Wells reckoned that if he was going to talk about real people regarding their public roles, cloaking them with false names would distort, not improve, his stories. He lamented not having used real names in *The New Machiavelli* because he might have thereby prevented nasty speculations by the meanly curious. Many writers following Wells took eagerly to the depiction of friends and famous persons in their novels. But Aldous Huxley, D. H. Lawrence, C. P. Snow, and Anthony Powell preferred masks to candor. Wells seems to have taken it well when others used him—either masked or openly in their fictions.[46] Dorothy Richardson did a Byzantine turn on this practice in *The Trap* (1925) by presenting Wells in three guises at once—as Wells, Hypo Wilson, and Wilkins (Wells's character to represent himself in his own novels).[47]

Wells believed that he was opening fiction up to new possibilities. He was. Few dared to follow him along some of his courses, but he knew better than they what he was about. Unlike Henry James but like Bennett, Wells believed that fiction was inevitably autobiographical since it was built up out of the experiences of the author.[48] Unlike both of his friends, Wells did not want to disguise this autobiographical element, but exploited it. Yet even as he pressed that form to its limits, he managed to create an illusion often as successful as the objectivity of James or Bennett. In *Apropos of Dolores* Wells begins with this disclaimer: "Every character and every event in this novel is fictitious, and any coincidence with the name or conduct or circumstance of any living person is unintentional." Then he adds slyly, "In this repudiation the author must include himself. The story is told in the first person but the voice is the voice of an invented personality—however life-like and self-conscious it may seem. Never will the author proceed against his publisher for libel" (*Dolores*, Prefatory Note). Wells makes an important point here. The first-person narrators *are* lifelike. He *does* succeed in creating real characters—so much so that he is accused of writing autobiography. His very success is held against him. In his earlier response to Lord Birkenhead's complaints Wells had written, "For years I could not write a book without having half the characters identified each with a dozen different 'originals.' And any figures left over at last, bless their hearts! were me" (*Going*, chap. XXVI).

Wells was not a careful artist. He admitted as much but noted that many of the great figures of English fiction resembled him in that regard. Nonetheless, he knew the craft of fiction and tried to urge it in directions he considered fruitful. It was not his direction that the next generation followed. Essentially, he wanted fiction to serve a purpose. To him the act of writing was important because it called order out of chaos. Fiction was a special version of this activity. In the prefatory note to *Apropos of Dolores* Wells explains how a novel conveys the effect of real life. It should not, he says, "be anything but experience, observation, good hearsay and original thought, disarticulated and rearranged. You take bits from this person and bits from that, from a friend you have known for a lifetime or from someone you overheard upon a railway platform while waiting for a train or from some odd phrase or thing reported in a newspaper. That is the way fiction is made and there is no other way" (*Dolores*, Prefatory Note). In *All Aboard for Ararat* (1940), he put it more simply: "Every great author annexes and plagiarises, so why argue?" (*Ararat*, chap. II: 3).

Wells had a consistent view of what literature was and what it could and should accomplish. This view developed—one might say hardened— as he grew older, but he remained essentially faithful to it. Refusing to limit the novel to the rules composed by James or Conrad or Ford, he took liberties. He was always taking liberties. But in the process he *was* enlarging the scope of the novel. It was his fate that those who came immediately after did not necessarily want it enlarged in that manner. At present few readers seem to be aware of the character of Wells's fiction, aside from the inventive verve of the early romances. There is one trait that shows Wells's intimate responsiveness to ideas and to his profession as a literary craftsman. Since it involves details of the times in which Wells wrote and therefore may have become obscured, I shall examine this Wellsian inclination at some length. In his prefatory note to *Apropos of Dolores* Wells declared that the novel "must present real life and real incidents and not life and incidents taken from other books." In saying this, he was not entirely candid, for his own books draw abundantly upon those of others. It is, in fact, a regular practice. He was a shrewd and amusing jackdaw.

Insofar as he alluded to and borrowed from other writers, Wells was not unusual, for creative writers have always drawn freely upon the facts of history and the creations of literature. But Wells was extraordinary for the peculiar and consistent way in which he exploited the events and writings of his own time. Although he employed traditional literary sources, he is more interesting in his use of contemporary works of literature, which often serve as armatures for his own fictions.[49] In what follows I shall demonstrate that Wells used this technique differently in his early and late novels. The former are powerful largely because they are responsive, whereas the latter lose their force when they become hortatory and autobiographical.

Ingvald Raknem has shown that many of Wells's early stories are probably drawn from the work of such various figures as Kipling, Maupassant, Poe, Corelli, Gourmont, and Flammarion.[50] This sort of influence is commonplace with beginning writers. What interests me is something rather different. It is surprising, for example, how many of Wells's early novels are fashioned as answers rather than as assertions. Without offering a thorough list of his allusions and borrowings, I would like to suggest Wells's method. *The Island of Dr. Moreau* (1896) can be read at least in part as a serious parody of Kipling's sentimental *Jungle Book* (1894) and *Second Jungle Book* (1895).[51] Geoffrey West noted that *The Wonderful Visit* (1895) was based on Ruskin's remark that if an angel were to arrive on earth, someone would shoot it.[52] Bernard Bergonzi indicates that the book is, in some measure, an answer to Max Nordau's *Degeneration* (1895). The obsessed doctor who cannot accept the fact that the Angel is a higher being perceives him instead as a maimed human and cites Nordau as an authority for his way of thinking (*Visit*, chap. VII and chap. XXI). Wells turns Nordau's notion of degenerate genius around, suggesting that the unusual is more often superior than decadent.

Evidence suggests that *The Wheels of Chance* (1896), while an amusing and instructive tale in is own right, is also a reply to Grant Allen's *Woman Who Did* (1895) and to the novels of "advanced" women writers such as Olive Schreiner and George Egerton. In Allen's novel a liberated mother discovers that her illegitimate daughter—the symbol of that liberation—desperately desires the most conventional mode of life. The mother sacrifices herself to her child's desire. In Wells's novel an ostensibly liberated woman who writes successful novels about liberated women is seriously dismayed when her adventurous daughter seems to adopt the code she promulgates. Once again Wells is turning the tables on his "source," using similar conditions to prove an opposite point. Similarly, it is likely that Wells's *In the Days of the Comet* (1906) derives its device of a worldwide gaseous cloud from M. P. Shiel's novel *The Purple Cloud* (1901), which Wells praised. But Wells made the cloud beneficial, whereas for Shiel it was poisonous.

Wells did not mention Shiel's story in his novel, but he did drop a clue to another stimulus. Henry James's phrase and story of "The Great Good Place" twinkles across the opening narrator's mind but passes and leaves no light; for those familiar with that story some light is forthcoming.[53] In

James's story, which first appeared in *Scribner's* in 1900 and then in *The Better Sort* (1903), a successful writer, overburdened with work, accepts help from a young writer. As George Dane watches the young man working at his desk, he feels liberated and finds himself in The Great Good Place—a sort of retreat for the mind where he can recover his soul. Eventually he must return to his own room, waking, as it seems, from a dream, where he feels much better and even contented with his lot. Wells borrowed the initial situation of his story—one person watching another write in a protected retreat—but his tale describes a purification of the soul of mankind, not merely of one weary writer. The contrast is a summary of the differing outlooks of Wells and James.

One point that Wells was making with *The History of Mr. Polly* (1910) was that the ordinary common Englishman had little poetry, beauty, or romance in his life. Much of what he took for beauty and happiness was illusion. Mr. Polly breaks free to a romance of the commonplace after all, but he must do this by facing ordeals and dangers of a vulgar and trivial kind. Wells felt that it was necessary to make this point because much fashionable writing of his day pretended that romance was more easily accessible. The chapter entitled "Mr. Polly Takes a Vacation" is a direct parody and contradiction of that kind of romancing. The specific target was Richard Le Gallienne's *Quest of the Golden Girl* (1896), which was a great success. For various reasons, Wells did not care for Le Gallienne and what he represented, but in this novel he attacked the man's ideas, not the man.[54]

When Mr. Polly starts out on his vacation, he plans to journey along the English roads just in the spirit of Le Gallienne's romantic bachelor. Polly "had dreamt of casual encounters with delightfully interesting people by the wayside—even romantic encounters. Such things happened in Chaucer and 'Bocashiew,' they happened with extreme facility in Mr. Richard Le Gallienne's very detrimental book, *The Quest of the Golden Girl*, which he had read at Canterbury, but he had no confidence they would happen in England—to him" (*Polly*, chap. V: 1).[55] But just such an encounter does occur to Mr. Polly in England. Wells prepares for the onset of this experience in language that mocks Le Gallienne's ornate prose. "And then it happened to Mr. Polly that real Romance came out of dreamland into life, and intoxicated and gladdened him with sweetly beautiful suggestions—and left him. She came and left him as that dear lady leaves so many of us, alas! not sparing him one jot or one tittle of the hollowness of her retreating aspect" (*Polly*, chap. V: 5).

Unlike the encounters of Le Gallienne's character with lovely young women of various descriptions (encounters that resemble a severely bowdlerized pinching from *Mademoiselle du Maupin*), Polly's encounter is a fraud. His lady is a red-haired young girl who speaks to him over a wall while he stands in the road. After their first meeting, at which she comes to call him her Knight, they meet again during the next ten days, but the romance is shattered when Polly finally discovers that his lady love is a schoolgirl who is amusing her companions gathered on the other side of the wall. Polly's judgment on himself implies a judgment of Le Gallienne's pernicious example. " 'Fool,' he said at last; 'you Blithering Fool!' " (*Polly*, chap. V: 7).

Kenneth B. Newell objects to this sequence in Wells's novel because he considers it unreal.[56] But that was Wells's point. Obviously he could not expect future generations to comprehend the object of his satire easily, and clearly ignorance of it hinders a reader's appreciation of what Wells was doing. But Wells did not write for posterity. To me the sequence is a clever means of trashing an entire genre of literature. It is apt for Wells's purpose. If we do not get the joke, it is our ignorance that is to blame. After all, in this instance, Wells named his target.

A few more summary examples will perhaps make my point before I take up two novels in detail. It seems inescapable that both the sensational plane crash at a country house to introduce potential lovers and the amplification of the matrimonial theme in Wells's *Marriage* (1912) owe much to Shaw's *Misalliance*, which opened in London in February of 1910. By naming the popular *Elizabeth and Her German Garden* (1898), Wells singled out a source for one feature of *The Wife of Sir Isaac Harman* (1914). Likewise, the similarity of subjects and titles implies more than a coincidental relationship between *The Soul of a Bishop* (1917) and John Strange Winter's best seller of 1893, *The Soul of the Bishop*. In all of these works Wells employed contemporary works as occasions for contradictory responses, a habitual technique with him. I am not referring to the outright parody made notorious in *Boon* (1915), but to a practice subtler and more profitable which is clearly evident in two works, both minor achievements, one an example of Wells's early fiction and the other of his late fiction.[57]

Wells admitted one starting point for *The Sea Lady* (1902) when he explained that two of his main characters were based upon the conventional stereotypes to be found in the novels of Mrs. Humphry Ward, his conventional heroine being "quite deliberately and confessedly lifted, gestures, little speeches and all, from that lady's *Marcella*," a novel that had appeared in 1894 (*Autobiography*, chap. VII: 4). The numerous references to *Marcella* in the body of Wells's novel show that he meant the parody and the accompanying indictment to be obvious.

Wells was not so candid about a more eligible source for this novel that "stressed the harsh incompatibility of wide public interests with the high, swift rush of imaginative passion" (*Autobiography*, chap. VII: 4). I am not thinking of La Motte Fouqué's classic tale, *Undine*, which Wells does mention pointedly and which had appeared in a handsome new edition in 1896, but of Henrik Ibsen's play *The Lady from the Sea* (1888), which was translated into English as early as 1891 and was performed in England in that same year. It was presented in a better production in May of 1902, when it received reviews in such notable journals as the *Athenaeum* (10 May 1902) and the *Westminster Review* (July 1902).[58]

In Ibsen's play Ellida Wangel is haunted by memories of a love she once felt for a mysterious sailor. For her, the sea represents romance and a "craving for the unattainable. . . . for the limitless, for the infinite."[59] The sea both awes and attracts her, and the men who love her recognize that she is herself like the sea. Early in the play Ellida says, "I think if only man had learnt to live on the sea from the very first. . . . Perhaps even in the sea. . . . We might have developed better than we have, and differently. Better and happier" (act 3). She is, however, reconciled to the fact that "we've taken the wrong track and become people of the land instead of the sea," with no way of putting things right again (act 3). Ellida fears the return of her sailor lover, who, when he reappears, demands that she join him on his new sea voyage. When her husband yields to Ellida's request that she be permitted to make her choice in complete freedom, she decides to banish the romantic Stranger and remain with her dependable husband. Although she is associated with heathen, dangerous, and mysterious qualities of the sea, she decides to become a land creature, turning from the wildness of the imagination to the calmer certainty of reason.

Ellida's case is framed by a pair of references that establish metaphorical dimensions for her behavior. At the opening of the play, Ballested, an amateur artist, explains that at Ellida's suggestion he is adding a dying mermaid to the seascape that he is painting. "She has strayed in from the sea and can't find her way out again. So here she lies dying in the brackish water, you see" (act 1). At the end of the play, Ellida remarks that "once a creature has settled on dry land, there's no going back to the sea"; and Ballested exclaims, "Why, that's just like the case of my mermaid!" but adds that the mermaid dies, whereas men and women can acclimatize themselves. Yes, says Ellida, if they are free (act 5).

Wells was apparently not happy with this resolution to Ellida's or the mermaid's dilemma, and in *The Sea Lady* he arranged a different outcome. His lady from the sea, Miss Doris Thalassia Waters, not only is beautiful and mysterious like Ellida Wangel but also is a genuine mermaid. Moreover, although she has apparently come to land by accident—she is found in a condition strongly resembling that of Ballested's mermaid—we soon learn that she has a determined plan to win the love of Chatteris, a promising young journalist and aspiring politician. Before long, the stuffy society of Folkestone recognizes the threat that the mermaid represents. Melville, a sort of intermediary between the sea lady and the conventional world of which he is a part, explains that she is attractive to Chatteris because she represents openness and naturalness as opposed to duty; she stands for what he is constantly seeking but never understands (*Lady*, chap. VII: 3). The sea lady informs Melville that she comes from the elements, which are nothing more than the imagination. The limited conventional life with all of its trivial cares, its extraordinary little duties and hypnotic limitations, is, she says, "a fancy that has taken hold of you too strongly for you to shake off." She tells Melville, "You are in a dream, a fantastic, unwholesome little dream," and promises "there are better dreams" (*Lady*, chap. VI: 2). Although he did not alter the essential opposition in Ibsen's play, Wells did reverse the conclusion, for Chatteris rejects his Marcella-like fiancée and, in a chapter entitled "Moonshine Triumphant," returns with Miss Waters to the sea and its mystery and romance.[60]

Wells later declared that he had "considerable sympathy for the passion," beauty, and imagination that Chatteris elected in favor of a life of order, duty, and service, but he did not imitate his character (*Autobiography*, chap. VII: 4). As we have seen, Wells rejected the artistic-aesthetic position in favor of a role governed by the principle that all of his "art" should serve the larger purpose of promoting human welfare and bringing about a new world order. At the same time he rejected the codification of rules that put limits upon what the novel could do and how it could do it. Wells's avowed aim was to create a fiction in which "the ostensible writer becomes a sort of enveloping character, himself in discussion with the reader."[61] Viewing this reader as a man occupied with the issues of his own day, Wells mainly eschewed allusions to literary "classics" and drew freely upon contemporary events, persons, and literary works. By focusing attention upon the present—his stories are invariably about the present or the future—Wells forced his reader to consider his ideas in their proper context. This approach made his novels seem ungainly, though we perhaps can see them as a transitional mode between the loose and baggy Victorian model and the nonfiction novel of our own day. Nonetheless, it is not surprising that the artists of the novel, represented principally by Henry James, should have failed to appreciate what Wells was up to. Leon Edel and Gordon N. Ray summarized the difference between the two writers by saying that James looked reality in the face and then refashioned it to art, whereas Wells looked reality in the face and then manipulated it with all the resources of human intelligence.[62] James began with a nuclear anecdote and elaborated it into a novel through the examination of subtly changing states of awareness; Wells started from a polemical assertion and, employing a pattern of logical cause and consequence, amplified his tale by mockery and contradiction. While James nurtured, Wells pruned and offered a new leaf for turning. Although he admitted to being a careless craftsman and preferred anarchy to form, Wells knew very well what he was doing.[63] His misfortune may have been that he ceased doing it well.

Much of the energy in Wells's early tales arose from his polemical responsiveness to the literature of his own day. While other writers were concentrating on fashioning novels that were complete in themselves, Wells was openly inviting whatever external information his readers could manage to bring to his stories.[64] I believe that this quality in his early stories often served him well; but about the time that he published *Boon*, something seems to have changed. For some years his works had been taking on a schoolmasterish tone, as in *The New Machiavelli* (1911), *Marriage* (1912), *The Passionate Friends* (1913), and *The Wife of Sir Isaac Harman* (1914). After *Boon* it becomes more and more difficult to distinguish Wells's fiction from his journalism. With some few exceptions, he seems to be less playful. Wells subtitled *Bealby* (1916), the last of his sprightly novels, *A Holiday*. It was a valedictory to that manner. He would permit himself few such holidays again. Hereafter Wells was inclined to drill his readers in his own familiar opinions.

Wells did not cease to borrow. Sometimes he had recourse to traditional sources (*The Undying Fire, All Aboard for Ararat*); sometimes he imitated himself (*Mr. Blettsworthy on Rampole Island, The Camford Visitation*); but most often he alluded to the writings of his contemporaries. *Meanwhile: A Picture of a Lady* (1927), for example, may be read partly as a response to James's *Portrait of a Lady* (1881 and 1908), and *Star-Begotten* (1937) surely owes much to George Du Maurier's *The Martian* (1897).[65] When he draws thus upon contemporary writings in the later novels, there is a difference. The source is no longer the focus of Wells's examination but an excuse to repeat his familiar messages. He is not rebutting, but pronouncing.

When Mr. Preemby in *Christina Alberta's Father* (1925) suddenly decides that he is the reincarnation of Sargon, Wells may have been alluding to the strange case of Joséphin Péladan, the French author who claimed to be descended from a Babylonian king. His most famous novel, *Le Vice suprême* (1884), features a mage called Merodack who represents an exaggerated version of Wells's idea, for he is a man of iron will capable of subordinating all of his desires. Péladan's series of novels, *La Decadence latine*, of which *Le Vice suprême* was the first, concluded posthumously in 1925, the year Wells published his novel. Publicity surrounding Péladan's work might have recalled that bizarre figure to Wells's mind. The purpose of Péladan's series was to demonstrate that decadence follows upon the decline of religion. Péladan himself sought to revive a form of religiosity.[66] The parallel with Preemby is clear and the circumstance favors Wells's intention of promoting a revival of the ideal of service in a high cause. But the connection is oblique, not contradictory.

Similarly, though *Mr. Blettsworthy on Rampole Island* seems to owe something to narratives of exploration like Darwin's *Voyage of the Beagle* or Thomas Huxley's *Diary of the Voyage of H.M.S. Rattlesnake*, the resemblances are general, as far as I can determine, and merely provide a convenient mode for Wells's didactic fable.[67] I think that it is more obvious that Wells borrowed from Huxley for some of the dialogues in *The Happy Turning* (1942). Chapter seven of Wells's tale is called "Miracles, Devils and the Gadarene Swine" and reads as though Wells had just put down Huxley's *Science and Christian Tradition*, in which several essays deal with miracles in general and the Gadarene swine in particular.[68] But here again the material is condensed and incorporated into Wells's playful attack upon conventional thinking. There is no responsiveness to Huxley's position, simply assimilation.

One final example of this Wellsian practice is an especially illuminating one. Not only does it reveal the change in his use of the device but it shows how subjective he had become in his privacy. *Babes in the Darkling Wood* (1940) was published twenty-two years after Rebecca West's novella *The Return of the Soldier* (1918). West began her story about the time that she and Wells were living together on Monkey Island, which she used as a setting for an idyllic youthful romance in her story, concerned for the most part with the return of Christopher Baldry, suffering from partial amnesia, from the war to his estate in England. He has lost all memory of the last fifteen years, including any knowledge of his wife, Kitty. He recovers instead his early love for Margaret Allington, from whom he had been separated. A psychiatrist concludes that Chris has unconsciously wanted to forget the life he has led since then. It is Margaret, now married but still sharing Chris's love, who must revive his memory by mentioning his dead son, thus sacrificing his pleasant illusion of regained love to a cruel reality.

*Babes in the Darkling Wood* opens with an account of the youthful free-love romance of Gemini and Stella, an idyll that is ended by relatives who separate the liberated youngsters. During this period of separation, Gemini is almost accidentally unfaithful to Stella and leaves on a trip to Russia. While he is abroad, Gemini is caught in the war and is psychologically damaged by his experiences. He rejects a world that appears loathsome to him, though part of his suffering originates in his own sexual guilt.[69] Under the care of Stella's wise Uncle Robert, Gemini recovers sanity, but only when Stella manages to revive his sexual desire is he fully cured.

Both stories center upon the return of a psychologically damaged young man to a woman for whom he no longer can experience desire. According to his earlier practice, Wells reverses the circumstances. Chris Baldry returns to his first love through a rejection of an intolerable existence which he must later resume; Gemini similarly rejects an intolerable world, but his psychological cure reanimates his old love and thereby his love of life. It is as though Chris Baldry were given his Margaret back again.

Superficially, one might think that Wells is doing here what he did in *The Sea Lady*, but I think not. In the early novel Wells was smuggling a polemic into a romantic tale. His story was a revision of Ibsen's lesson. In *Babes in the Darkling Wood*, Wells's revision of West's narrative is incidental to the purpose of his novel. Like so many of Wells's later books, this novel is a call to mankind to take up its duty in the service of the World State. The allusion to West's novel does not prompt this message, which by this time is programmatic. Instead, plot borrowing is a form of self-indulgence. By 1940 Wells was once more on cordial terms with Rebecca West. The allusion to her early novel may have been a private joke between them or simply nostalgia on Wells's part. The romance of Gemini and Stella certainly seems to be a rendering of those splendid days at Monkey Island when he shared physical and intellectual excitement with his new love. The energy behind this borrowing is strictly personal and could not have been appreciated by an ordinary reader. What Wells had often done for others by his allusiveness, he now was doing privately for himself.

Wells's early stories are secret debates, but his later novels are pronouncements from the chair. At the beginning of his career he was genuinely committed to a scientific outlook even for literature. He assembled interesting and related details and worked them out in a controlled experiment. It was a lively inductive method. Later he tried to marshal his details in the service of a preconceived hypothesis. Wells told the truth when he asserted that he was a journalist and not a novelist. He was an alert reporter of the contemporary world, and his fiction reflected his responses to recent attitudes in science, education, politics, and literature. Upon the armature of such contemporary data he formed his tales. But when he passed beyond reportage and substituted himself as the root of his fiction, when antithetical sources ceased to be lively occasions for dispute and became instead foils for his opinions spoken by surrogate voices, his art suffered. Wells's later works are as interesting as his early ones insofar as ideas are concerned; but whereas the early tales so often crystallized around some central event or thought, often borrowed from a contemporary literary work or event, the later works followed almost in diary fashion the unconsolidated reflections of Wells's own "persona." He was an author who throve upon debate; when he yielded this weapon, the force went out of his fiction. Without a target, his aim faltered. He looked in his heart and wrote.

Throughout his career Wells borrowed from other writers in little as in large things. We have mentioned some of his debts to the great, but Wells could create a masterful work from trivial sources as well. For example, he claimed that *The Invisible Man* owed its inception to W. S. Gilbert's comic poem "The Perils of Invisibility."[70] Wells may have acquired the idea for the historian of a future time, used simply in *In the Days of the Comet* (1906) and more elaborately in *The Shape of Things to Come* (1933), from Gabriel de Tarde's *Underground Man*, to which he had written a preface in 1905. But these borrowings were just one element of what amounted to a game of composition. As I have already suggested, Wells liked to include sly and even private jokes in his stories. The vessel that discovers Prendick adrift at sea, and by which he arrives at Moreau's island, is called the *Ipecacuanha*. That substance is a drug used to induce vomiting. The name suggests what Wells figured he was administering to his audience with this potent novel. Wells may have had something similar in mind when he named the monster of *The Invisible Man* after a fabulous beast. It is Griffin himself who remarks his oddity when he identifies himself to Kemp as "almost an albino, six feet high, and broad, with a pink and white face and red eyes" (*Inv. Man*, chap. XVII). He is well on his way to strangeness before he takes his concoction.

Wells was forever toying with names. Sometimes they were just ludicrous sounds, but often they were suggestive. He passed judgment on Rud Whitlow the moment he named him, for a whitlow is a boil or inflammation of the skin. Rud, on a vaster scale, is a pustule in the social body.[71] In *You Can't Be Too Careful* Wells offered a rich sampling including the minister Burlap (whose business it is to cover up the facts of life), the schoolmaster Mr. Myame (who *maims* and distorts the characters of children in his charge), and Edward Albert Tewler himself (who is, despite the slangy suggestion of his name, inept in sexual matters). More ominously, the setting for the disturbing experiences of Dr. Finchatton is called Cainsmarsh, a locale haunted by the murderous inheritance of Cain.

Sometimes the jokes are more obscure. I shall offer just one of this sort. Wells seems to have had a good opinion of William Cadbury as a decent businessman. He speaks of him approvingly in *The Work, Wealth and Happiness of Mankind* as the organizer of an investigation of abuses on cocoa plantations (*Work*, chap. XIII: 2). He praised Cadbury's Bournville in *In the Days of the Comet*, and in *First and Last Things* he described the Cadburys as "an energetic and public-spirited family, their social and industrial experiments at Bournville and their general social and political activities are broad and constructive in the best sense" (*Things*, bk. III: 8). Now it so happens that Linnaeus' name for cocoa, the major raw material for the Cadbury company, was *Theo broma*, "the food of the gods." This might be viewed as a mere coincidence if a book entitled *The Food of the Gods: A Popular Account of Cocoa* by Brandon Head had not appeared in

1903, the year before Wells published *The Food of the Gods*. Head praised the Cadburys for their far-sightedness, especially concerning the model town of Bournville. It is entirely possible that Wells was incorporating in his paean to change, growth, and progress, a subtle compliment to the Cadbury organization.

Many of Wells's jokes include himself. I have already mentioned his use of the novelist Wilkins as a simplification of himself in his novels. He often referred to his own writings, sometimes within the very work mentioned, as when he alludes to the serial appearance of *The War of the Worlds* in the book version. When Bedford wants a pseudonym in *The First Men in the Moon*, he chooses "Wells"—"which seemed to me," he says, "to be a thoroughly respectable sort of name" (*Moon*, chap. XX).[72] At the end of his fanciful tale "The Queer Story of Brownlow's Newspaper" (1932), the narrator asserts that he is as convinced of the existence of a newspaper from forty years in the future "as I am convinced that my own name is Hubert G. Wells."[73] Sometimes the jokes were for a very restricted audience. In *'42 to '44* (1944), he remarks that "Jane Austen is one of my dearest aunts, Rebecca West when she is mocking and happy, another" (*'42*, pt. II: 17). Only someone who knew that West, in describing Wells and Bennett as uncles in *The Strange Necessity*, had stolen a playful appellation that they had for one another would have got the joke.

It would be fun to go on and on with details of this sort, but I hope that I have made my point that Wells's concept of fiction was much broader and more open than most of his contemporaries'. It caught up all of life and assimilated it—sometimes efficiently, sometimes not. To judge it adequately, it is necessary to recognize why elements appear in his novels as they do. Recognizing their functions often reveals a richer accomplishment than critics have been willing to allow. Wells's narratives are not Jamesian achievements, but many—right up to the end—are exciting romps.[74] But Wells was not merely a novelist. Like Shaw he praised himself as a journalist because he felt his obligation was to put his skill with language to work.[75] It is not surprising that sometimes his fictional and didactic techniques interwove.

Wells was a gifted, complex master of the language with well-defined ideas about how best that language should be employed for the benefit of mankind. In almost all of the political, social, and economic areas he wrote about, Wells classed himself as an amateur—his judgment on his shadow, William Burroughs Steele, in *The Anatomy of Frustration* makes this clear. In one thing only he claimed excellence. He was a professional writer and thereby an effective educator. Nothing could be more important, he felt. And, as we have already seen, one thing above all others was the cardinal topic of education—the story of mankind. It was to this effort—the education of men about man—that Wells devoted himself at first incidentally, but ultimately entirely.[76] Behind this effort was a rooted belief that the story of individual life and the story of man were similar and furthermore that the "story" of history was no more the absolute truth about humanity than the "story" of many a fable or realistic novel. Narrative, to him, was not recapitulation, but creation. It was the greatest of educational skills. It was the unique gift of men. It was Wells's great contribution that he sought to write the unenacted history of the race. He helped to teach men "the greatest importance of the anticipatory aspect of life" (*Homo*: 9).

In 1920 Wells did mankind the courtesy of telling it the story of its life. The story of *The Outline of History* was familiar in most details, but the general shape was new, for human events were not bound together by the decisions of great men or the accidents of national conflict, but by the increasing self-consciousness of human communities through the development of communications.[77] Wells's purpose in fashioning his narrative of man's history was not to offer a panorama of memory, but to free man from his past and to guide him toward the future. Modern civilization, he explained, was merely the working out of relationships inherited from the earliest cultures. "It is only by the attentive study of their origins that we can detach ourselves from the prejudices and immediate ideas of the particular class to which we may belong, and begin to understand the social and political questions of our own time" (*Outline*, chap. XVIII: 4). By telling men what they had been, he hoped to persuade them to make themselves what they might be.

Long before he wrote *The Outline of History*, Wells had developed the habit of viewing history as mutable and open to rearrangement. Two of his early science-fiction successes exploited the most alterable part of history, the future; he considered himself the inventor of futurology with his remarkable *Anticipations* (1901), a book studded with keen predictions about the future. Because he did not view history as a fixed line, he felt no embarrassment in describing it as a continuum including not only what had been but what was yet to be. The present was not the end of a process or story, but a juncture; hence, he treated all historical accounts as provisional, though in general he inherited the Victorian assumption, stated to his taste in Winwood Reade's *Martyrdom of Man* (1872) and Thomas Huxley's many essays and lectures, that human history was progressing in an evolutionary, ascending, or improving manner. Nonetheless, like Huxley, he never supposed that this improvement was guaranteed. His many books hint or openly state that the future of man is in man's hands. Consequently, it was important that man should have an accurate picture of where he had been and where he might go. To understand the history of his race, man could begin with the rudimentary proving ground of his own nature. Imitating the biologists' maxim that ontogeny recapitulates phylogeny, Wells assumed that the life of the individual followed a process of growth and maturity similar to that of the race. If a man could examine his own life and, by will and discipline, shape its course, then mankind could do something similar. The main purpose of Wells's career was to tell men this simple truth and to persuade them to act on it.

Wells felt that his personal history reflected the history of his time. He saw himself as an experimental subject and insisted that his autobiography was an account, open to modification, of a "very ordinary brain." He pictured his life as representative. Although he had described individual histories in such novels as *Love and Mr. Lewisham* (1900), *Kipps* (1905), and *The War in the Air* (1908), it was not until *Tono-Bungay* (1909) that Wells struck upon a method that he would return to time and again—the pseudo-memoir or autobiography. In *The Passionate Friends* (1913), which employed this technique, Stephen Stratton exclaims near the end of his record, "I begin to realize for the first time how thin and suggestive and sketchy a thing any novel or biography must be. How we must simplify!" (*Friends*, chap. XII: 1). With this fictional form Wells hoped to convey the realism of autobiography with the freedom and control of fiction. Because he selected types whose lives were meant to be representative in the same manner that he believed his own to be, Wells's characters inherited his tendency to view himself as a specimen worth examination. As a consequence, Wells's fiction became powerfully autobiographical and his characters educational devices whose purpose was to liberate Wells and his readers by offering proof that each individual can shape his life into a personal history that helps to shape the larger story of the race. Even the failures reinforce the point.

George Ponderevo says that he is trying to render "nothing more nor less than Life—as one man has found it. I want to tell—myself" (*Tono*, bk. I, chap. I: 2). He feels his life is worth recording because he has transcended the normal patterns; he has not lived "true to the rules of [a] type" but has been jerked out of his stratum and has lived crosswise to various planes of existence (*Tono*, bk. I, chap. I: 1). His life is peculiarly indicative of his times. Moreover, his slow acquisition of consciousness about the nature of society parallels, in microcosm, the human race's developing consciousness. Although he claims to be offering, not a "constructed tale," but "unmanageable reality," George records a life shaped from disorder and confusion into order and purpose (*Tono*, bk. I, chap. I: 2). He calls his guiding purpose Science or Truth. George had felt that men were "creatures of change and impulse and unmeaning traditions" and himself "without an object to hold [his] will together" until he came to idealize science. Then, he says, "I discovered myself for the first time" as a being with a direction and a purpose (*Tono*, bk. II, chap. IV: 10). Once the pattern of his own life has taken form in George's imagination, science teaches him to subordinate his individual life to the larger life of man.

That George's incomplete life story is meant to recapitulate a larger history is most evident at the end of the novel when he makes his night journey down the Thames. "To run down the Thames so," he says, "is to run one's hand over the pages in the book of England from end to end" (*Tono*, bk. IV, chap. III: 2). The pages of George's book offer a similar experience, and at their close he feels that he can see himself and his country without illusion. He moves beyond the monuments of human success and failure toward the sea, the illimitable mystery of the future. "We are all things that make and pass," he says, "striving upon a hidden mission, out to the open sea" (*Tono*, bk. IV, chap. III: 4). He says this at the boundary between land and sea, past and future—the provisional point where he can give life a shape because he believes it is open to change.

*Tono-Bungay* was an early attempt to present a private history as a model for mankind's story. In creating this model, Wells was also inventing his personal history. Through fiction he offered himself an alternative design for his own life. He repeated this test time and again in his fiction and in his *Experiment in Autobiography* (1934) as well. The practice is fully apparent in *The New Machiavelli* (1911). George Ponderevo, claiming amateur standing, demonstrated the individual's ability to order his life by recording his "story"; Richard Remington goes a step further in treasuring as well the ordering power of language.

Like the original Machiavelli, Remington wishes to be an architect of history, though he is concerned principally with what history *will* be, not with what it has been. In telling his story, Remington gives his life a shape that is governed, like Ponderevo's, by an abstract ideal. The pattern of his life exhibits a similar progression from impulsive disorder to intellectual command. However, Remington's lawless nature conflicts with the conservative regulations of society, and he is unable to put his plans for a New Republic into effect. Nonetheless, he discovers that just as he gives his own life a design by documenting it, he can also compose the future by fixing its outline in print. He believes that he has found his place in the larger destiny of mankind.

I was as it were one of a little swarm of would-be reef builders looking back at the teeming slime upon the ocean floor. All the history of mankind, all the history of life, has been and will be the story of something struggling out of the indiscriminated abyss, struggling to exist and prevail over and comprehend individual lives—an effort of insidious attraction, an idea of invincible appeal. (*Machiavelli*, bk. III, chap. I: 5)

Remington's book represents the embodied will of man, the forcing into reality of what was only dream.

Like other Wells characters, Remington discovers that any writer is a historian, since he records what passes in man. A writer conveys substance to an idea through an act of will. His power is the paradigm of what Wells desired for mankind. The truest act of human will is to change circumstantial nature, which can best be done by altering man's concept of Nature first. History is an attempt to create a new picture; for Wells, it was the story of man struggling toward comprehension and control. Remington's book, while serving as the history of an individual life, also provides a model for the life of the race. Out of ignorance and power, mankind comes to self-consciousness and purpose by shaping the story of its past and giving a direction to its future.

But history is not complete. In "The Labour Unrest" Wells explained, "We want to have your young people filled with a new realisation that History is not over, that nothing is settled, and that the supreme dramatic phase in the story of England has still to come" (*Forces*, "The Labour Unrest": 6). The story of man must always be retold because it is always in progress. Its broad outline is clear—a movement toward one common human destiny from one common human origin, but its outcome can only be guessed, for it depends upon an understanding of the story so far (*Outline*, chap. XXXIX: 3). "History," Wells declared, "is the beginning and core of all sound philosophy and all great literature" (*Outline*, chap. XXXI: 8). He did not mean the factual table of dates and events. The real business of history "is to get down below these outer forms to the thoughts and lives of individual men" (*Outline*, chap. XVI: 1). The progress of the race was in the accumulated experience of mankind. Because man's unique quality was the ability to reason and to share the fruits of his experience, Wells believed that "all human history is fundamentally a history of ideas" (*Outline*, chap. XXXIX: 7).

Wells did not have a mere abstract of great thoughts of mankind in mind. To him history was a record of discoveries. These ideas were important ideas that aided man in adapting to his circumstances, especially through increased racial cooperation. Certain great teachers provided these ideas, but personal accounts of common men were important too. "*The Travels of Marco Polo* is one of the great books of history," Wells cheered. "It opens this world of the thirteenth century . . . to our imaginations as no mere historian's chronicle can do" (*Outline*, chap. XXXIII: 3). This is a curious and complex statement, though it seems straightforward. Wells means two things when he calls Polo's record a great book of history. It was great in its day, for it described the opening of a new world and new realms of experience to its contemporary readers; but more important to Wells, it was a human, authentic document that recorded its time with vividness of life.

In the same manner, Wells chose increasingly to develop his fictions as accounts of individual men whose experiences typify their times. They are imitation Polos, modern adventurers of the mind. Seldom do they achieve their high goals. As representatives of mankind, they cannot since mankind is only midway in its story. Most are frustrated. Lewisham recognized his defeat and passively submitted to a larger design. Kipps and Mr. Polly freed themselves from the chaos of the past but did not strive eagerly toward the future. After Ponderevo and Remington, however, aspirants such as Trafford, Stratton, Benham, and Clissold suffer enormous tensions as they labor to create an order for mankind while simultaneously ordering their personal lives.

Many of Wells's novels from the time of *Tono-Bungay* to *The Outline of History* concentrate upon the theme of individual life emerging out of ignorance and chaos to some form of command and focus. Some, such as *Marriage, The Passionate Friends, The Wife of Sir Isaac Harman,* and *The Soul of a Bishop*, are mainly concerned with the relationships between individuals, while others more clearly merge individual and racial interests in the same pattern, as in *Mr. Britling Sees It Through* and *Joan and Peter. The War in the Air* and *The World Set Free* actually carry human history from present chaos into an altered or improved future. All of these works reveal a consistent pattern that Wells offered more vigorously as time passed. The First World War convinced him that mankind's need to consolidate its racial will toward a coherent social system or World State was more urgent than he had supposed. He became more evangelistic, reminding men to observe the lessons provided by the past and to seize the time to make a better future.

From the turn of the century Wells had been devoting himself to the creation of a new picture of human history. His writings chronicled the great change that had come upon the race with the improvement of communications and the development of technology. The titles of his nonfictional books indicate that his interest is more in the shape of the future than in the record of the past: *Anticipations* (1901), "The Discovery of the Future" (1902), *Mankind in the Making* (1903), *The Future in America* (1906), *New Worlds for Old* (1908), *What is Coming?* (1916), *The Salvaging of Civilization* (1921), and so on. History is the past chaos out of which a design may come into being. But it is man who evokes that design. And it is the writer who is master of that evocation.

Mankind's desperate need to understand its story impelled Wells to offer his *Outline*. But before he published that work, he presented in his modernization of the story of Job, *The Undying Fire* (1919), a manifesto summarizing what he and Job Huss, the martyr-like protagonist of the novel, wished to achieve. Huss says that when he discovered that Nature had "a face of boundless evil," he realized that man had to control Nature if he was to know a better world (*Fire*, chap. III: 9). "There is nothing beyond man," he says, "unless men will that something shall be" (*Fire*, chap. V: 4). Sir Eliphas disputes Huss's view, arguing that "this life is only the first page of the great book we have to read" and implying that the rest of the volume is already composed and only remains to be read (*Fire*, chap. IV: 3). Huss is less hopeful and less passive, for he feels that the future is a changing mystery. "We have a vision of the opening of the story, but the first pages we cannot read" (*Fire*, chap. IV: 1). Man must write that story, not expect to sit back and be carried along by a preexisting narrative. Huss, who believes that man must know history to create the future, succeeds in transmitting his vision to others. One of his former students, writing from the battle-fields of France, says, "*You made us think and feel that the past of the world was our own history; you made us feel that we were in one living story with the reindeer men and the Egyptian priests, with the soldiers of Caesar and the alchemists of Spain; nothing was dead and nothing alien; you made discovery and civilization our adventure and the whole future our inheritance*" (*Fire*, chap. VII: 2).

Although Wells created stories about man's history—future to distant past—he did not use the story metaphor immediately, but developed it gradually. One early use of the metaphor demonstrates what Wells wished to accomplish with it. When as a boy Lionel Wallace accidentally discovers his wonderful garden in "The Door in the Wall" (1906), he meets some charming playmates and then an enchanting woman who shows him a book. "The pages fell open. She pointed, and I looked, marvelling, for in the living pages of that book I saw myself; it was a story about myself, and in it were all the things that had happened to me since ever I was born." The book brings him up to the moment he discovers the door. Lionel is eager to see the next page, but the woman demurs. He insists and she submits, but the page shows no enchanted garden, only a grey street in West Kensington. Suddenly he is there in reality. The tale shows that the story of our life is always in process of composition. It will not have the order of a well-made book until we have come to our end.

This short story explains one impulse in Wells's Utopias—they represent the book of man's life more fully written so that we may read the climax before it arrives. In *A Modern Utopia* (1905), Wells emphasizes the fact that his story is being told in the subjunctive.[78] What he describes is what *would be*, not what is. He becomes more specific, clearly exploiting his dual-purpose metaphor, in *In the Days of the Comet* (1906), which opens with an unnamed narrator discovering an old man writing. He begins to read the old man's manuscript—William Leadford's autobiographical account of the transformation of mankind, which begins, "I have set myself to write the story of the Great Change" (*Comet*, bk. I, chap. I: 1). Wells is more playful and more explicit in *The World Set Free* (1914), where much of the information for the narrative is drawn from the scientist Holsten's diary and from Frederick Barnet's autobiographical novel *Wander Jahre*. In *The Dream* (1924), Sarnac's story of his dream is the story of mankind told from the perspective of the distant future; and in *The Shape of Things to Come* (1933), the narrative consists of a history from the distant future made available in the present by means of an ostensibly prescient dream. Within this history, history is seen as a document or narrative in the process of composition. Addressing the assembled representatives of world revolution, Arden Essenden says, "What are we now and what do we intend to do? The days before us begin a new chapter in human history. It is for us to choose the heading and plan that chapter now" (*Shape*, bk. III, chap. VIII). Each person who contributes to the progress of the race is a composer of the story of mankind. Furthermore, each individual is that story in miniature. When Arden Essenden is obliged to commit suicide for the good of the State, we are told that he probably took his pill while sitting in his garden, "then sat dully in the sunshine staring at those flowers which make the colophon of his story. Then the book closed for him" (*Shape*, bk. IV, chap. II).

Wells indicated in his fantasies that the desire to know the future, to read the end of the story before the end has come, is futile except in fables and dreams. In his realistic tales he made the companion point that whereas life is a story, it is not a conventional novel. The novelist White in *The Research Magnificent* (1915) cannot escape the influence of his profession and thinks of Benham's life in terms of the kinds of novels he writes. White struggles with the analogy. We are all, in living, "writing long novels," he thinks. But Benham's life was mainly ideas; and thus, to treat that life as it was "does not make a book. It makes a novel into a treatise, it turns it into a dissertation." He realizes that the traditional novel is simply a love story that takes ideas for granted (*Research*, chap. I: 13). Later, White concludes that the oldest novel in the world "was a story with a hero and no love interest worth talking about," the story of Tobias, a young man emerging from "the shelters of his youth into this magic and intricate world" (*Research*, chap. II: 1). Conditioned by the simplications of popular fiction, White cannot handle the complexity of real life. It is left to the unnamed narrator to recount Benham's life and make of it a novel that is like life instead of creating a life that approximates the hackneyed conventions of fiction.

"Whether he be original or a plagiarist," wrote Ortega y Gasset, "man is the novelist of himself."[79] This could be Wells's maxim. He said and showed it many ways. Accepting Jung's gift of the concept "persona" eagerly, he adapted it to his own terms. "It is the story we tell about ourselves in relation to the outer world," he has Steele write in *The Anatomy of Frustration* (1936) (*Frustration*, chap. XIX [c]). Mankind, he said elsewhere, was "continually doing its best to make a plausibly consistent story of its behaviour both to itself and the social world about it," but this need to order existence can lead to a false story (*Careful*, bk. III, chap. I).[80] Theodore Bulpington is a portrait of the type who cannot endure the truth and gives himself up to a fabrication of his life as romance. Wells struggled against the impulse toward self-dramatization in himself and found such posing ridiculous in his friends. Bulpington he described as a caricature of "the irresponsible disconnected aesthetic mentality," and from his description of Ford Madox Hueffer as "a great system of assumed personas and dramatized selves," it is possible he used that friend as his model (*Autobiography*, chap. VIII: 5).

Wells's story metaphor was his salvation. Man's life was a narrative in process of composition and so was the individual's. Each was made up of pages and chapters and recounted adventures, romances, and ideas. Since true history was the record of ideas, true narratives should be narratives of ideas. Looking into his personal or racial past, man read an account of passions and ideas. The passions remained the same; the ideas grew and developed. Wells found confirmation of this scheme in his own life, and he tried to transfer what he considered a typical personal history to mankind at large, believing that just as he had found freedom through the willed control of random passions and the expression of his ideas, mankind could control the beast in himself and transform the world from jungle to garden through improved communications.

Two realistic novels written after the *Outline* illustrate Wells's conception in a more complicated and intriguing fashion. In his short narrative "The Grisly Folk" (1921), which begins as a historical account and subtly transforms itself to a short story, Wells wrote:

> This restoration of the past is one of the most astonishing adventures of the human mind. As humanity follows the gropings of scientific men among these ancient vestiges, it is like a man who turns over the yellow pages of some long-forgotten diary, some engagement book of his adolescence. His dead youth lives again. Once more the old excitements stir him, the old happiness returns. But the old passions that once burnt, only warm him now, and the old fears and distresses signify nothing.[81]

Wells went out of his way to demonstrate the connection between racial and personal history in *The Secret Places of the Heart* (1922), where the restoration of the past becomes a therapeutic device. Sir Richmond Hardy, seeking a cure for nervous distress, makes a tour of England's most important archeological sites and discovers that "archeology is very like remembering" (*Heart*, chap. V: 4). He helps a young American woman "remember" the racial past; they feel that they are sharing the adolescence of the race and sense that they have given history a more intimate meaning. Thus, when they visit Glastonbury Abbey and, ironically, Wells Cathedral, it is "like turning over the pages of the history of our family to and fro" (*Heart*, chap. VII: 6). Sir Richmond set out on this excursion because he felt that his will was failing. Having traveled into the little-known regions of his own nature by examining the racial past and opening his heart to another human being, he returns to practical life reassured about himself and the purpose of human endeavor, which he is in a position to guide. During his therapeutic holiday, Sir Richmond has read over human history up to the present and recovered the vision of a future open to modification by man. Unfortunately, he dies while laboring to give that future shape.

*The Secret Places of the Heart* is a slight attempt compared to the elaborate examination of these same themes in *The World of William Clissold* (1926). Clissold openly acknowledges that even though men have made valiant attempts "to impose a coherent and comprehensive story" upon life, there is actually "no plot nor schema nor drama nor pattern in the flow of events as they are apprehended by human minds" (*Clissold*, vol. I, bk. I: 9). Consequently, the design that man gives to history—the story he tells about mankind—is a fabrication, but a fiction with a purpose, for if man can picture a better world, he may be able to live into it. Clissold sees his life divided into chapters and says that "thinking of one's childhood is like opening a great neglected volume hap-hazard and reading in it"; yet, he knows that there is no story to individual or racial history until man wills that there should be one (*Clissold*, vol. I, bk. I: 4). In telling his story, Clissold gives it form. Likewise, if one tells the story of mankind, one creates a believable shape that mankind may approximate.

Although Wells generally used the analogy of writing and history positively, he also foresaw its darker possibilities. He had consistently warned against the traditionalist, conservative view of history which was backward looking and given to consolidation and repetition instead of innovation and adaptation. In *The Autocracy of Mr. Parham* (1930), he presented his version of what this attitude—most clearly represented at the time by fascist ideologies—might lead to. The university don Mr. Parham is transformed into the Master Spirit or Lord Paramount, a figure resembling Sir Oswald Mosley, England's most prominent fascist. Mussolini is referred to by name and appears as the character Paramuzzi as well. David Low's illustrations make the connection unmistakeable.

Parham is utterly conservative, with a desire to play some part, through journalism, "in the story of the Empire and the world" (*Parham*, bk. I, chap. V). He values the Great Men of history, and his notion of historical tradition emphasizes "the military organization of the Empire, national and imperial ascendancy, flags, armies, frontiers, love of the Empire, devotion, sacrifice, and having a damned good go at Russia" (*Parham*, bk. III, chap. VII). He is everything that Wells deplored, and his actions when he takes power lead to disaster. As the Lord Paramount, he views history as a story unfolding. He sees himself as the successor of Napoleon, Caesar, Alexander, and Sargon, and feels that his mission is to make history.

> As he made it he wrote it in his mind. He saw his own record, the story of his war, towering up at the end of the great series of autobiographic war histories from Thucydides to Colonel Lawrence and Winston Churchill. *Parham De Bello Asiatico.* That he would do in the golden days of rest, after the victory. It was pleasant to anticipate those crowning literary hours amidst the stresses of present things. He would find himself making character sketches of himself and telling in the third person of his acts and decisions in the recognized style of such records.
>
> It was queer at times how strongly his anticipations of this record imposed themselves upon his mind. There were phases and moments when he did not so much seem to be doing and experiencing things as relating them to himself. (*Parham*, bk. III, chap. V)

Like other Wellsian visions of the future, Parham's turns out to be a dream, but it is an evil dream. Hints abound to suggest that the Lord Paramount's reading of history is aberrant. Like Sir Eliphas in *The Undying Fire* (1919), he sees history as a book already written, with a predetermined narrative that he approximates in reality. Momentarily unsettled by Sir Bussy, the Lord Paramount is "like a reader who has lost his place in a story and omitted to turn down the page" (*Parham*, bk. III, chap. VIII). Later, the news of a disastrous sea battle between England and America unfolds before him relentlessly "as if it were history already written" (*Parham*, bk. IV, chap. I). In attempting to revive the past, the Lord Paramount has imitated its blunders and crimes. As a version of the old history repeated, it resembles those familiar chronicles of war and bloodshed.

Wells concisely indicates what is wrong with the Lord Paramount's view of history in an amusing and crafty metaphor. At the moment the Lord Paramount usurps command of the English government and dissolves Parliament, "It seemed already history, and for all the length of that pause it was as if the Lord Paramount were rather witnessing what he had done than actually doing it. It became flattened but bright like a coloured picture in a child's book of history" (*Parham*, bk. III, chap. II). The Lord Paramount's vision of history, in short, is puerile. It is a simplified and

falsified conception lacking the important realities of change. The Lord
Paramount's revolution is not an advance, but a giant step backward. All
of the good features of his scheme—the call for discipline and self-denial—
are in the service of a wrong-headed policy.

When the Lord Paramount is frustrated by a group of scientists working to free England from his control, he fears that the human story has
come to a pause. He has identified the story of man with his own circumstances. What he perceives as a pause might be viewed by others as an
advance—the heading of a new chapter, let us say. The Lord Paramount's
egoistical practices bring the same threat to mankind that Wells had frequently described elsewhere. It's quite possible, General Gerson, the brutal
militarist, remarks on the eve of an attack upon scientists who possess a
lethal gas, that the book of history is about to close with a bang. That, says
Wells, is precisely what will happen if Gersons and Parhams are permitted
to govern men. They are uninventive, looking to the devices of the past.
They cannot imagine a history that is different; hence, future history
stretches out as a terrifying tale of the old horrors repeated. Wells sought to
convince men that history past and to come was nothing more than a story
they were telling themselves. They could give the plot a happy turn if they
chose.

One of Wells's fundamental requirements was that men know their
history and have a common ground of information which would bind them
together. Religions had shaped images of the future in the past; a new,
secular religion could achieve this again. Wells and his characters such as
Clissold and Wilbeck called for a World Brain, a New Encyclopedia, a new
Sacred Book to replace the old unifying texts. In *The Salvaging of Civilization* (1921), Wells said that what modern civilization needs is "a revised and
enlarged Bible . . . to restore a common ground of ideas and interpretations." The original Bible had given man

> a Cosmogony. It gave him an account of the world in which he found himself
> and of his place in it. And then it went on to a general history of mankind. It did
> not tell him that history as a string of facts and dates, but as a moving and
> interesting story into which he himself finally came, a story of promises made
> and destinies to be fulfilled. It gave him a dramatic relationship to the schemes
> of things. It linked him to all mankind with a conception of relationships and
> duties. It gave him a place in the world and put a meaning into his life. It
> explained him to himself and to other people, and it explained other people to
> him. In other words, out of the individual it made a citizen with a code of duties
> and expectations. (*Salvaging*, chap. IV: 1)

Treating the subject humorously many years later, Wells had God say in
*All Aboard for Ararat* (1940), "That Book of mine is wonderfully trust-

worthy. You will never get a better universal history." Despite its faults, he claims that the story remains fundamentally convincing (*Ararat*, chap. I: 3). Wells agreed about the Bible's power but believed that science had invalidated its scheme and consequently modern man needed a new story of this order. He coyly admitted that for lack of such a Bible the reading public had "taken my *Outline* very eagerly" (*Salvaging*, chap. IV: 1).

Wells did not suggest that the Bible was a true record. Its account of the world was no more than a fiction, a hypothesis according to which men could organize their lives and give their society purpose until a new hypothesis was required. Wells urged that that time had come; man needed a new story by which to shape his life, even if it was a fiction that would be replaced in its turn. Behind this conviction was Wells's belief that the true direction of man's progress is from selfish individualism to communal cooperation. This was the movement he hoped for in himself and which he described in the *Outline*.

Wells's fiction and journalism after *The Outline of History* was designed to create that new Bible, that new cosmogony for modern man, who, he hoped, would imitate the novelist by imagining an alternative reality and then bringing it into being. He petitioned men to believe that they were capable of this high endeavor, but they did not seem to comprehend. Joseph Davis in *Star-Begotten* (1937) decides to tear up his universal history entitled *The Pageant of Mankind* in order to make way for the new, enlightened race he believes is coming into being. His wife reasons that he cannot tear up the past, but he replies, "You can tear up every lie that has ever been told about it. And mostly we have lied about it. Mythology, fantasy, elaborated misconceptions. Some of the truth is coming out now, but it is only beginning to be told" (*Star*, chap. X: 3). Wells reckoned that he was asking very little of his fellow men. He sums up the basic requirement in *Star-Begotten* when Davis asks his intellectual friend Keppel if he is sure that the world, "after a few more troubled decades, a troubled age or so at most, will go sane," and Keppel has to answer no. But then Davis asks, "Do you *disbelieve* it?" And Keppel answers no again "with equal conviction. 'And that also,' said Dr. Holdman Stedding, after a moment's deliberation, 'is my position' " (*Star*, chap. IX: 5).

Wells wanted this open-mindedness, this willingness to attempt the adventure of a more splendid future. How it must have baffled him that men could not offer so much. "Our history is just a story in space and time, and to its very last moment it must remain adventure," he wrote succinctly in *The Work, Wealth and Happiness of Mankind* (*Work*, chap. XVI: 3). It had all been so simple in his own case! He told the story of his own growth and success time and again in his fiction, and even disguised it as the story of the race, but though the race bought the book by millions, they did not get the message. I have said that it was simple for Wells. That is not entirely true. Perhaps it is more correct to say that it always seemed to be turning out well, for along the way the struggle was not easy. In *The Anatomy of Frustration* (1936), for example, Wells felt it necessary to apologize for the asperity of the explorers and pioneers of the future, like himself, and explained that their labors to fashion a new world created a stress unknown to those who subside unquestioningly into the apparent security of conventional life (*Frustration*, chap. XII). Dr. Finchatton presents a slightly different explanation for the frustration of the imaginative in *The Croquet Player* (1936). Men are breaking the Frame of their Present, he says. "We lived in a magic sphere and we felt taken care of and safe. And now in the last century or so, we have broken that. We have poked into the past, unearthing age after age, and we peer more and more forward into the future. And that's what's the matter with us" (*Croquet*, "The Skull in the Museum").

At last the strain wore upon Wells himself. Yet in his decline he continued to read his own story into that of the race; and as he faded, he foresaw in *Mind at the End of its Tether* (1945) the *Götterdämmerung* of mankind.[82] He had believed in the possible triumph of rationality in the world. "He did his utmost to pursue the trends, that upward spiral, towards their convergence in a new phase in the story of life, and the more he weighed the realities before him the less was he able to detect any convergence whatever," he wrote of himself (*Tether*, chap. I). The narrative had no real direction. The tales he had told now seemed idle dreams. What story there was, was over. Any intelligent observer realizes, he concluded, "that the human story has already come to an end and that *Homo sapiens*, as he has been pleased to call himself, is in his present form played out" (*Tether*, chap. II). Within a year the book of *Homo Wells* closed forever.

It has been said that Wells sacrificed his fictional powers to propaganda, but he had never believed that fiction should be separated from its context and shorn of practical purpose. His triumph was his attempt to identify fiction with the broadest of contexts—the history of the race. His tragedy was that the story he offered did not capture the imagination of his audience. It was his own story that he wrote—his own dream and his own fear. In the end, he would have said, that is all that history or literature can ever be.

# Conclusion

In recounting her experiences as a champion of birth control, Margaret Sanger praised Wells as an intellectual influence and as a man. "He has not only brains, but a capacity for loving both individuals and humanity at the same time. He can be amusing, witty, sarcastic, brilliant, flirtatious, and yet profound at once. He is quick, sensitive, alert to the slightest meaning, or intonation, or feeling. To be with him means you must pull yourself up, keep alive every second, or you miss the Wells as he reveals himself to you in his writings."[1] Knowing Wells personally, she was able to appreciate in his writing what has escaped many readers. Wells lived and wrote with zest. He was considered a brilliant talker, not in the Shavian manner, but in the back-chat and conversational style.[2] His writing style often approximates that form of verbal expression and is rich in wit, apt phrases, personal jibes, private jokes, caricature, teasing, and seriousness all together. Exposition runs side by side with poetic evocation. Under serious harangues rides an undercurrent of corrective humor. Very often it seems that Wells's books are not novels, but playgrounds.

Wells has not been sufficiently credited with being conscious of his own qualities, both good and bad, yet he is among the most self-conscious artists—it is my word, not Wells's—of fiction and polemic that his age produced. He was also fully aware of his manner and techniques. Take this description of the style of his surrogate, William Burroughs Steele, in *The Anatomy of Frustration* (1936).

> Having thrown this paradoxical quality over his discussion, he feels able to go on to his detailed study of our general frustration. Through the shimmer of a varying idiom he is able to make his vision appear sometimes the vision of a prophet and sometimes the flattest commonsense. It is—to vary the image—stereoscopic, this double style—and to my mind at any rate it exposes his subject rounded and living as no hard, consistent terminology and logical idiom could do. (*Frustration*, chap. VII)

Wells knew what he was doing, but that did not make it good or always appropriate. Tact, for example, was not something of which he had an abundance. Energy was. And organization. Only a disciplined, energetic man could write *The Outline of History* in one year or publish the number of books and articles that he did in his lifetime. His liveliness was contagious. Even the Webbs, who were his polar opposites, found him attractive. Beatrice Webb, always shrewd, was one of his shrewdest observers. At the beginning of the relationship, she noted that he was "extraordinarily quick in his apprehensions" and recognized that he was "a good instrument for popularising ideas." "Altogether," she concluded, "it is refreshing to talk to a man who has shaken himself loose from so many of the current assumptions, and is looking at life as an explorer of a new world."[3] This characterization was of the young Wells, but even much later, when their quarrels were behind them, Beatrice Webb's judgment on Wells was still favorable. "There is something likeable in his frankness and lack of solemnity about his own life, his bubbling egotism, his comradeship with the younger scientists, his insistent determination to educate his fellow man on all aspects of life."[4] Elsewhere she noted, "I have never ceased to respect his work."[5]

Those who knew Wells as their senior admired him. Rebecca West praised him for his "wild and surpassing generosity" as a writer.[6] Leonard Woolf, whose relationship with Wells was not always smooth, wrote that "looking back over the last 45 years I still see [Shaw, Wells, and Bennett] as a remarkable trinity—not negligible men or writers."[7] And Margaret Cole, who valued him from a different perspective, described him as a "vivid, many-gifted, generous, cantankerous personality." She read *New Worlds for Old*, she said, "and tumbled straight into Socialism overnight."[8]

Wells moved these young people deeply first in his writings but also as a man. Those who were on familiar terms with him were constantly surprised by his power. Bennett, perhaps Wells's closest literary friend, having already published *Clayhanger* and well into *Hilda Lessways*, paused to read *The New Machiavelli*. "This book makes a deep impression on me," he writes to himself in an awed tone, "and even causes me to examine my own career and to wonder whether I have not arrived at a parting-of-the-ways therein, and what I ought to decide to do after the book—after *Hilda* is finished."[9] Even his literary antagonists admired and appreciated him.

But Wells was not all roses. He was an extremely complicated man. No doubt his dedication to frankness and honesty made him seem even more so. His sincere commitment to order, self-renunciation, and world revolution cohabited with a disruptive, lustful, egotistical, and naughty impulsiveness. He was contrary. Margaret Cole, who admired him nonetheless, saw this trait from a political point of view.

Of course, no group of people was ever right in his eyes, particularly if they were trying to make plans for the Planned Society which he so ardently advocated; if they were Fabians they had horrid mean insect souls like Sidney Webb; if the Labour Party, they were hidebound stupid Nonconformists who wouldn't even preach birth-control; if Communists, blind worshippers of a bearded, disagreeable old dyspeptic called Karl Marx. I doubt whether there is any organisation which H. G. ever joined from which he did not resign in a rage; the rage *may* always have been well-founded, since organisations are apt to be exasperating, but the result was a trifle anarchical.[10]

W. Somerset Maugham remembered different features of Wells's contradictoriness. "H.G. had strong sexual instincts and he said to me more than once that the need to satisfy these instincts had nothing to do with love." He was too alert to the absurdities of love objects to feel genuine love, Maugham says.

> He was incapable of the idealisation of the desired person which most of us experience when we fall in love. If his companion was not intelligent he soon grew bored with her, and if she was her intelligence sooner or later palled on him. He did not like his cake unsweetened and if it was sweet it cloyed. He loved his liberty and when he found that a woman wished to restrict it he became exasperated and somewhat ruthlessly broke off the connection.[11]

In a letter to his wife in 1914 Wells said, "The brute fact is that I am not and never have been—if there is such a thing—a passionate lover. . . . I want a healthy woman handy to steady my nerves and leave my mind free for real things."[12]

I have written a section of this book on Wells's use of the double. He wrote from knowledge, for he was a profoundly divided man, not simply into dualities, but into fragments like Hesse's Harry Haller in *Steppenwolf*. He could be both the Time Traveller adventuring into a dismal future and the narrator who preserves hope, the imperious Moreau and the patient Prendick. He was both idealistic voice and earthy biologist in *A Modern Utopia*. There was enough of the fascist in him to create Mr. Parham and Rud Whitlow, while being fully identified as well with the persons who stand as their correctives.[13] He was enough tempted to self-indulgent dreaming to know the slipperiness of a Theodore Bulpington while being convinced of his relationship to the Broxteds. Moreover, he was humble and honest enough to jeer at both aspects in himself. He used himself as a guinea pig. Maugham commented wittily that "Trafford in *Marriage* is indeed the portrait of the man H.G. thought he was, added to the man he would have liked to be."[14]

If Wells was a divided man, he was also the product of a divided time. He saw himself as representative of that time and so did others.[15] H. V.

Routh oversimplified when he said that Wells was notable as a thinker of other men's thoughts and a good publicist of them. Still it is true that little that Wells recommended was entirely new. Very little ever is. His interest in education approximated a widespread interest of the time. The Webbs, for example, had already put forward many suggestions for reform and Sidney Webb published *London Education* as early as 1903.[16] Samuel Hynes observes that the aims of the National Council of Public Morals were not much different from Wells's, one of which was the idea that sex was something more than personal gratification.[17] Wells's friend Graham Wallas shared many of his interests, including revision of representative democracy and governance by a trained elite. Some of these ideas were stated in *Human Nature in Politics* (1908). And in *The Great Society* (1914), Wallas also called for the organization of human will towards the Great State of the future. Even Wells's idea for a history of the future had been preempted by Lövborg in Ibsen's *Hedda Gabler* (1890), though that book never appeared in print. Wells's did—more than once.

Many of the ideas that Wells took up were in the air. That is why he took them up. He liked the free exchange of ideas. Sometimes he and his friends sounded remarkably alike because they exchanged so many ideas. In "Man's Destiny" J. B. S. Haldane wrote that he was inclined to suspect that the human will was to some degree free and therefore there is "no such thing as a destiny of the human race. There is a choice of destinies."[18] Like Wells he insists that the process of civilization depends upon science and that there is no limit to man's intellectual and spiritual progress if man can control his own evolution.[19] He sees the same ghastly alternative if man cannot. Even Beatrice Webb sounds much like Wells in her private reflections on metaphysics and the Will to Believe, though she gives science a second place. "I am thrown back on my Intuition—on my emotional Will to Believe." Her belief that the heart of man will rise to higher things rested on no more evidence than Wells's did.[20]

If he was not original in his ideas, Wells was original in his manner of presenting them. *Anticipations* (1901) was an astonishing book, and even trained philosophers admired the directness and clarity of *First and Last Things* (1908).[21] He quickly became the acknowledged master of a new kind of scientific romance, he created a new brand of utopian fiction, and he reinvented the novel for his own day. He boasted that his outlines, such as *The Work, Wealth and Happiness of Mankind* (1932), were experimental. Even his autobiography was an experiment. He was not successful in all of his experiments, but the experiments themselves were worthwhile. To my mind he was authentically modern, for like Nietzsche, he valued those moments of genuine humanity when intellect leaps forward and all anteriority vanishes, when the past is expunged in order that the present may become a staging point for a new departure. Paul de Man has explained that Nietzsche recognized the problem of modernity as man's fabrication or invention of a past from which he would have liked to have descended instead of the past from which he actually has descended. Modernism becomes conscious of its strategy and recognizes that it is part of a generative scheme and therefore of history. Only through history is history conquered; modernity is the horizon of a historical process that has to remain a gamble.[22]

Nietzsche, too, was in the air. Wells could not help being influenced by his ideas, for his inclination was in that direction already.[23] Sometimes he did not fully digest his Nietzsche. Mencken called *The Research Magnificent* "a poor soup from the dry bones of Nietzsche."[24] Several currently more fashionable contemporaries of Wells proffered ideas very similar to his. Ortega y Gassett, to whom Wells dedicated *The Shape of Things to Come*, despite the younger writer's antagonism for utopias, advised man that he must liberate himself from himself.[25] "Man is an infinitely plastic entity of which one may make what one will, precisely because of itself it is nothing save only the mere potentiality to be 'as you like.' "[26] Much of "History as System" reads like a gloss upon Wells's program. Consider this, as a last example: "The past is not yonder, at the date when it happened, but here, in me. The past is I—by which I mean my life."[27]

Wells did not expect his books to last.[28] But he hoped that his propaganda would "take." He complained to Maugham that he had been telling people the same thing for thirty years and they wouldn't listen. It is just that, Maugham comments acutely, that led to his failure.[29] But perhaps he failed because he was too faithful to his own impulses. He was a dreamer, realist, idealist, philanderer, socialist, elitist, artist, and propagandist—all at the same time. Being true to himself meant risking confusion or outrage in his readers. No one doubts that he was honest. But was he wise? He was more enamored of self-analysis than of self-control, and the many contradictions and vacillations of his character appear unmodified in his work. Believing that man was determined, he lived in the dream of freedom; believing that man was barbarous, he lived in the hope of Utopia; knowing that Nature led nowhere, he fostered a faith that men could give Nature a story and make of eternal change continual progress. In his life and in his writings, Wells was a divided nature whose segments lived on dissimilar planes of experience. Many of the apparent contradictions in his writings are comprehensible if seen from the proper perspective. One such perspective is philosophical. Though Wells was not a rigorous thinker, his views were consistent and were rooted in a few fundamental assumptions. These assumptions shaped his art, for I shall insist on calling it that. They arose from deep psychological sources and exhibited themselves in recurrent images that were certainly spontaneous but which Wells exploited self-consciously. Despite what many friends and antagonists believed, Wells's career as a novelist did not end with *Mr. Britling Sees It Through* (1915). His very last novel may be peculiar, even outrageous, and it is not what traditional theorists of The Novel would accept, but it is nonetheless an entertaining and lively fiction.

Robert M. Philmus has noted the element of private myth in Wells's science fiction.[30] But there is a private myth that extends throughout and energizes all that Wells wrote. It began in emotion and ended in thought. The circumstances of his own life taught Wells to crave freedom. The MacKenzies suggest that the underworld of *The Time Machine* "is an echo of the life of the 'Downstairs Persons' at Up Park. The shafts above the tunnels leading to the lair of the Morlocks recall those which open into the Up Park drive."[31] These primal images conveyed broad social and political implications, but they began deep in Wells's personal experience. The Wells house in Bromley was the Neolithic cave from which Bertie Wells struggled through the chaotic social jungle, through time to the spacious upland and stars of the future. It is not difficult to imagine that Moreau's House of Pain owes as much to Mr. Covell the butcher who lived next to the Wellses in Bromley and in whose yard "pigs, sheep and horned cattle were harbored violently, and protested plaintively through the night before they were slaughtered" as it did to any literary source or philosophical speculation (*Autobiography*, chap. II: 1).

Wells's childhood experience of the basement kitchen became an image of physical and mental entrapment; hence, his desire to see a world of well-housed people was a rejection of an error-ridden past, not merely a city planner's abstract scheme. But it was not merely deformity of body and mind that Wells wished to escape. Man's emotions too were still trapped in a barbaric past. Often Wells likened that basement kitchen to a Neolithic cave, but the usual analogue was the jungle. There the sexual and aggressive forces in man still raged. Wells wished to clear a path in that jungle and to bring men onto the windblown uplands of reason.

That Wells, in his Schopenhauerian moods, considered sex a troublesome impediment to man's progress did not prevent him from eagerly seeking its consolations. But the youth who deplored his prematurely ruined body always dreamed of a human beauty that made nudity a grace rather than an enticement and his picture of a desirable woman was heroic. It was Britannia or Michelangelo's sibyl—an image very different from those simpering Griseldas or cruel Judiths and Salomes that peopled the literature of his formative years. In serious relationships he sought a heroic companion of bold and dependable character. Only rarely did he find such companions. Too often he capered after the nymphs of the primeval forest.

Wells's preferred impulses were mainly a vigorous rejection of the disorderly past and a reaching toward an orderly future. Order was man's gift. He imposed design upon nature; but to do so, he had to see nature for what it was—his antagonist, not his soothing parent. And he had to see himself for what he was—without vain disguises. When man could take this objective view of his inner complexity and the mysterious world around him, he could apply the principles of science and map out a plan for the future. He would see himself as a part of a larger entity. He was an individual, but also a unit of mankind, itself a part of the whole Bios.

Once he had achieved this objective or scientific outlook, he would see that all of existence is provisional, that man cannot determine anything absolutely but creates the environment that shapes him. Thus Wells warned men not to trust to any automatic improvement in their condition, no progress or beneficent evolution. Instead he taught them to seize every lucky accident and turn it to account. Even the apparent disaster of war might prove the necessary event to take man forward to a better world. In the same way, man could learn to harness the powerful emotions in him in the service of a new world order.

Unlike unconscious nature, conscious mankind could design the beauty to which he aspired. Wells loved the precise beauty of the crystal and took it as a leading image of the process he wished men to master. The inchoate mental energy of man could suddenly crystallize upon one guiding idea, bringing a sudden, awesome order. The act of writing itself was just such a process available to the individual. Books could be gems conveying, not merely beauty, but salvation; for it was through books, rather than the schools and universities, that Wells looked for the real education of mankind.

Finally, Wells's faith in mankind's ability to refashion itself rested on his conviction that men need only exert the power of their wills to guide the inevitable process of change. Men, he said, must become artists of life, a strange and serious mutation of Oscar Wilde's advice, derived from Walter Pater, that men should make their lives works of art. And Wells believed that writers were the front line of these artists. He believed as well that the crystals he shaped were meant not merely to be admired but to be put to daily use cutting away the rags and tatters of the past and shaping the patterns and models of the future. Ultimately, he hoped to rewrite man's history, which was no more, he knew, than the story man told itself at any given point in the long narrative. Wells told men that life was a glorious risk in which each individual, with a grand scheme to inspire him, must nonetheless live with the tension of knowing that all life is provisional and that each day was an adventure of failure and lucky chance in which men moved from moment to moment in chaos while dreaming of a transcendent order.

Norman and Jeanne MacKenzie said that Wells selected literary models that matched his own psychic preoccupations or cosmic obsessions.[32]

He compelled all grist to the mill of his fiction, using everything that came to hand, from his own experiences through to the thoughts and writings of others. The dynamic of his fears and hopes conferred a sustaining form upon all that chaos. Wells was an obsessive writer. This obsession was his strength and his weakness.

It is ironic that while Wells is booming as the author of science fiction, he is neglected as a novelist. This neglect may be a question of quality or it may be a matter of fashion. Colin Wilson—himself a diverse, renegade author—complained, "Most of my contemporaries seem to feel pretty strongly that the activities of thinking and novel-writing are incompatible, and that to be interested in ideas reveals a deficiency in the creative faculties. And since the critics also like to foster this idea—perhaps out of a kind of defensive trade-unionism—it seems to have achieved the status of a law of contemporary literature."[33] Well, fashions change. In a time that seems amenable to the nonfiction novel, Wells may be due for a more sympathetic hearing. His books are topical. That is a problem. But so were Swift's. And men, alas, do not seem to have changed markedly since Wells wrote or for that matter since Swift did. I have tried to show that Wells introduced into fiction a great deal that was new and surprising—more than most people suppose. And he continued to experiment freely throughout his life. He was considered a giant in his day, and there was cause. Very likely he will never be one again, but we cannot therefore pretend that he is a dwarf.

# Notes

First references appear in the notes that follow with complete entries in each chapter division with one exception. All references to *H. G. Wells: The Critical Heritage*, ed. Patrick Parrinder (London and Boston: Routledge and Kegan Paul, 1972) will appear simply as *Heritage*, followed by the specific page references. Materials from the University of Illinois Library H. G. Wells Collection are designated simply by the word "Illinois."

## INTRODUCTION

1. Martin Calinescu examines the idea of modernity thoroughly in *Faces of Modernity: Avant-Garde, Decadence, Kitsch* (Bloomington and London: Indiana University Press, 1977). At one point he offers this definition: "Modernity, then, can be defined as the paradoxical possibility of going beyond the flow of history through the consciousness of historicity in its most concrete immediacy, in its presentness." Separated from tradition, artistic creation becomes an adventure and a drama (pp. 49-50). With the proper expansion to include history and philosophy, this definition is a good picture of what Wells represented.

2. Kenneth Young, *H. G. Wells* (London: Longman Group, 1974), p. 11.

3. The H. G. Wells Society has continued to promote interest in Wells in all respects and publishes an irregular *Wellsian* and a newsletter.

4. David Lodge was among the first to remind modern readers of Wells's skill with language in " 'Tono-Bungay' and the Condition of England," *Language of Fiction: Essays in Criticism and Verbal Analysis of the English Novel* (New York: Columbia University Press, 1966), p. 221.

5. Christopher Caudwell, "H. G. Wells: A Study in Utopianism," *Studies in a Dying Culture* (New York: Dodd, Mead, n.d.), p. 83.

6. Richard Hauer Costa determined that Wells's ideas were nothing and that his imagination was everything in *H. G. Wells* (New York: Twayne Publish-

ers, 1967), p. 49. Anthony West claims that Wells was an unclear and an undisciplined thinker ("H. G. Wells," *Encounter*, 8 [1957], 54). And Wilbur L. Cross in "Herbert George Wells," *Four Contemporary Novelists* (Freeport, New York: Books for Libraries Press, 1966 rpt.) dismisses Wells completely as a thinker (p. 187). These are merely samplings of the numerous critics who have had little respect for Wells's ideas.

7.    Conrad Aiken, reviewing *The World of William Clissold* in the *Atlantic Monthly* in November of 1926, credited Wells as "a skillful tractarian" but gave him less credit as a novelist (*Heritage*, p. 276).

8.    Frank Swinnerton, *Swinnerton: An Autobiography* (Garden City, N.Y.: Doubleday, Doran, 1936), p. 173.

9.    Recently, Allan Conrad Christensen has made a persuasive effort to revive Bulwer in his *Edward Bulwer-Lytton* (Athens: University of Georgia Press, 1977).

10.    Theodore Dreiser, Introduction to *Tono-Bungay*, Volume I of the Sandgate Edition (New York: Duffield, 1927), p. vii.

11.    Edward Shanks, "The Work of Mr. H. G. Wells," *First Essays On Literature* (London: Collins, 1923), p. 167. Robert Lynd, reviewing *The Passionate Friends* for the *Daily News and Leader* of 12 September 1913, objected that Wells's work belonged to the "about" school of literature. He was always writing about something (*Heritage*, p. 213). Jorge Luis Borges, full of praise for Wells's early fantasies, remarked that "God must not theologize," meaning that Wells should not have prosed about his philosophical positions (*Heritage*, p. 331).

12.    Pelham Edgar observed in 1933 that there was no artistic satisfaction in Wells's novels any longer. "He is merely the victim of his own ideas: he is no longer a public entertainer" (*The Art of the Novel: From 1700 to the Present Time* [New York: Russell and Russell, 1966 rpt.], p. 226). In making this remark, Edgar revealed his extremely restricted and demeaning notion of what a novelist was.

13.    The early chapters of William Coleman's lucid *Biology in the Nineteenth Century: Problems of Form, Function, and Transformation* (London: Cambridge University Press, 1971) summarize the state of knowledge at that time. See Rosylnn D. Haynes's *H. G. Wells: Discoverer of the Future* (New York and London: New York University Press, 1980) for an account of Wells's relationship to the science of his day.

14.    Huxley was both friend and antagonist of Herbert Spencer and was critical of the limitations of Comte's theories (Leonard Huxley, *Life and Letters of Thomas Henry Huxley* [New York: Appleton Co., 1900], II, 322 ff., 415, et passim).
Young Wells seems to have had a genuine admiration for Spencer, if his letter to A. M. Davies of 1894 is an accurate indication. In it Wells commends Davies's conversion to a positive view of the philosopher (Illinois).

An anonymous reviewer of *Mankind in the Making* for the *Academy and Literature* for 26 September 1903 advised Wells to go and read Spencer, who had first stated some of the ideas presented in the book (*Heritage*, pp. 92-93). He might rather have assumed that Wells had come upon these ideas after reading Spencer.

15.     Wells did not always present the same face to interrogators. In a letter of October 1942 to Siegfried Sassoon, he complained, "There you were up there, free to get every drop of juice out of England and at the same time I was having the most ferocious struggle to have my way with life and escape frustration and falsification by the very system that" benefited Sassoon (Illinois). The tone was much different in a letter of 1908 to Mrs. Tooley, obviously a reply to a sort of questionnaire: "No 'early struggles' of any sort. My life has been easy & uneventful" (Illinois).

16.     Wells makes this point throughout *The Science of Life*. In fact, in a letter of 29 January 1933 to Corliss Lamont, Wells criticizes Lamont's book, *Issues of Immortality*, for failing to deal with the question of individuality. He refers Lamont to his own *Science of Life* and also to chap. II: 2 of *The Work, Wealth and Happiness of Mankind* (Illinois).

17.     The quotation is from "A Memorandum on the Relation of Mathematics, Music, Moral and Aesthetic Values, Chess and Similar Intellectual Elaborations to the Reality Underlying Phenomena" ('*42*, Appendix II).

18.     Gertrude Himmelfarb, *Darwin and the Darwinian Revolution* (New York: Norton, 1968), p. 297.

19.     Ibid., p. 420.

20.     Many theorists on human progress posited stages for the growth of reason, especially among the French and particularly with Comte. J. W. Burrow mentions this subject in *Evolution and Society: A Study in Victorian Social Theory* (Cambridge: Cambridge University Press, 1970), p. 9.
Wells seems to have respected another work of this kind, the American John William Draper's *History of the Conflict between Religion and Science* (1894), which describes a progression of stages in civilization. (New York: Appleton & Co., 1874).

21.     See '*42 to '44*, where Wells calls Reade a "great and penetrating genius" ('*42*, pt. II: 21).

22.     *Arnold Bennett and H. G. Wells: A Record of a Personal and a Literary Friendship*, ed. Harris Wilson (London: Rupert Hart-Davis, 1960), p. 66. The letter is dated 23 November 1901.

23.     See Bernard Bergonzi's *The Early H. G. Wells: A Study of the Scientific Romances* (Toronto: University of Toronto Press, 1961) and *Early Writings in Science and Science Fiction by H. G. Wells*, ed. Robert Philmus and David Y. Hughes (Berkeley: University of California Press, 1975), for detailed accounts of the development of *The Time Machine* from story to successful novel.

24.     In his preface to the fourth volume of the Atlantic Edition of his Works, Wells recalled how consciously he set himself to do the opposite of what his contemporaries were doing. They were busy summing up the events of the past century; he wished "to work out the probabilities of contemporary tendencies as thoroughly as possible, and instead of a story make a genuine forecast" (*The Works of H. G. Wells*, IV [New York: Scribner's, 1924], ix).

25.     This remark from an unsigned review in the *Daily Chronicle* for 14 June 1900 is typical of what many commentators on Wells's writing felt—or felt obliged to say. "When he brings to bear upon human character the close, accurate observation which has been cultivated by his scientific studies, he produces first-class work" (*Heritage*, p. 80).

26.     "The Moth," for example, resembles Sheridan LeFanu's "Green Tea"; "The Hammerpond Park Burglary" is a spoof of crime stories; and "The Temptation of Harringay" is an obvious takeoff on Wilde. Parodies of this nature were common at the time. One need consider Wilde himself, or Max Beerbohm, for some of the best.

27.     Arnold Bennett said that Wells was inescapably a reformer (*Bennett and Wells*, pp. 124 ff.). T. de Wyzewa, writing in 1907, was already tempted to divide Wells's works into those written before and those written after his conversion to socialism (*Heritage*, pp. 142 ff.). But Wells's didactic strain was there from the start and so, to a great extent, was his socialism.

28.     This letter is in the Illinois collection.

29.     In his introduction to W. N. P. Barbellion's *The Journal of a Disappointed Man* (London: Chatto & Windus, 1919), Wells said that Barbellion had offered himself as a "specimen, carefully displayed and labelled," of modern unhappiness resulting from egotism (p. viii). He respected the book as a "scientific" document.

30.     I have discussed the role of dreams in Victorian Literature in *Victorian Conventions* (Athens: Ohio University Press, 1975), pp. 448-52 et passim. Wells was intrigued by J. W. Dunne's use of dreams to investigate time in *Experiment with Time* (1927). He gives an account of his acquaintance with Dunne in the introduction to *The Shape of Things to Come*.

## CHAPTER ONE: LIBERATION

1.      Frank Swinnerton, *Swinnerton: An Autobiography* (Garden City, New York: Doubleday, Doran, 1936), p. 161.

2.      Van Wyck Brooks says that Wells's main experience was that of disentangling himself (*The World of H. G. Wells* [New York: Mitchell Kennerley, 1915], p. 144). Patrick Parrinder discusses the importance of the motif of release in Wells's work (*H.G. Wells* [Edinburgh: Oliver and Boyd, 1970], p. 5). And Robert P. Weeks treats the theme briefly but well in "Disentanglement as a Theme in H. G. Wells's Fiction," *H. G. Wells: A Collection of Critical Essays*, ed. Bernard Bergonzi (Englewood Cliffs, New Jersey: Prentice-Hall, 1976), pp. 25-31.

3. G. K. Chesterton, *The Autobiography of G. K. Chesterton* (New York: Sheed & Ward, 1936), p. 228.

4. V. S. Pritchett, "The Scientific Romances," *The Living Novel* (New York: Reynal & Hitchcock, 1947), p. 123.

5. Chesterton, *Autobiography*, pp. 25 and 107.

6. The opposition of Up Park and Wells's early settings has become a commonplace of Wells criticism, especially in regard to Bladesover in *Tono-Bungay*. Young Wells saw the drapers' emporiums to which he was more than once sent for employment as prisons that he was lucky to escape (*Autobiography*, chap. III: 4; chap. IV: 1).

7. Among others, the following critics take up this point: David Lodge, " 'Tono-Bungay' and the Condition of England," *Language of Fiction: Essays in Criticism and Verbal Analysis of the English Novel* (New York: Columbia University Press, 1966), pp. 225 ff.; Alfred Borrello, *H. G. Wells: Author in Agony* (Carbondale and Edwardsville: Southern Illinois University Press, 1972), p. 8; Richard Gill, *Happy Rural Seat: The English Country House and the Literary Imagination* (New Haven and London: Yale University Press, 1972), pp. 100 ff.

8. *Autobiography*, chap. IV: 1. Wells calls attention to Caradoc Evans's *Nothing to Pay* as a realistic account of the lives of drapers' assistants.

9. Wells's aversion to confined places led him to miscalculate the usefulness of submarines because he could not believe that many men would be found willing to accept the "chilly confinement" beyond the assistance of other men which such service would require (*Shape*, bk. I: 7).

   See also Wells's early story about a diving bell, "In The Abyss" (1896). "The Red Room" (1896) may owe something to James's far superior story about a man's confrontation with his own fear, "Owen Wingrave," which was first printed in the *Atlantic Monthly* for April 1892.

10. At the time, many people were concerned about the labor unrest in England of the late nineteenth century. Barbara Tuchman gives a vivid account of some of this activity in *The Proud Tower: A Portrait of the World Before the War: 1890-1914* (New York: Bantam Books, 1967), especially in her chapter on the socialists. Samuel Hynes approaches the subject from the reformers' point of view in *The Edwardian Turn of Mind* (Princeton: Princeton University Press, 1968); and Donald Read deals mainly with labor disorders in the years before the First World War, particularly in his chapter on the trade unions in *Edwardian England 1901-15* (London: George G. Harrap 1972).

11. I cannot agree with those critics who have pictured the artilleryman as a figure of wisdom and conviction. It seems to me that Wells is satirizing him as a big talker who will never accomplish anything but will dally with what amusements and luxuries he has been able to preserve. Wells's narrator leaves the artilleryman in a mood of repulsion, calling him a "strange undis-

ciplined dreamer of great things" (*War*, bk. II, chap. VII). Compare instead Mr. Polly's willingness to fight Uncle Jim in the open. One can imagine how truly repulsive trench warfare must have been in Wells's eyes.

12.    See Gill's *Happy Rural Seat* and, more recently, Mark Girouard's *Life in the English Country House: A Social and Architectural History* (New Haven: Yale University Press, 1978). The tradition of open and healthy housing was well established in utopian or utopianlike writing. Some good examples are William Morris's *News from Nowhere* (1890), W. H. Hudson's *A Crystal Age* (1887), and even Henry David Thoreau's *Walden* (1854).

13.    It must be pointed out that the Magic Shop is not without danger. There is a minatory air about the shop, and it is not clear to what extent the real things brought from their imaginary sources are beneficial.

14.    Gilbert K. Chesterton, *Heretics* (New York: John Lane, 1919), p. 77, and *Autobiography*, pp. 224 ff.

15.    Frustration as the central experience for thinking men was, of course, the connecting motif of *The Anatomy of Frustration* (1936). See Robert M. Philmus's "Revisions of His Past: H. G. Wells's *Anatomy of Frustration*," *Texas Studies in Literature and Language*, 20 No. 2 (Summer 1978), 249-66, for a clear summary of the book.

16.    J. Kagarlitski calls attention to this feature of Wells's thinking and quotes Wells's preface to a collection of his works in Russian. Writing, he says there, is a modern form of adventure that opens doors for you; you can go to the sources of human deeds and endeavours (*The Life and Thought of H. G. Wells*, trans. Moura Budberg [London: Sidgwick & Jackson, 1966], p. 101). Vincent Brome also noted that "expression was often the first way of escape" for Wells (*H. G. Wells: A Biography* [London: Longmans, Green, 1951], p. 195).

17.    Brome declares without hesitation that "if for nothing else Wells will be remembered as the man who liberated the mind of a whole generation with the passion of the artist" (*H. G. Wells*, p. 116).

## CHAPTER TWO: NATURE

1.    G. K. Chesterton, *The Autobiography of G. K. Chesterton* (New York: Sheed & Ward, 1936), p. 143. See Rosylnn D. Haynes, *H. G. Wells: Discoverer of the Future* (New York and London: New York University Press, 1980) for an account of Wells's scientific training.

2.    Thomas H. Huxley, "Evolution and Ethics," *Evolution and Ethics and Other Essays* (London: Macmillan, 1894), p. 83.

3.    Robert Philmus and David Y. Hughes summarize Wells's relationship to Huxley's work in *Early Writings in Science and Science Fiction by H. G. Wells* (Berkeley: University of California Press, 1975), pp. 179 ff. Several commentators on Wells's career have stressed his pessimism. Anthony West

asserts that his optimism was a self-deception to mask an underlying despair ("H. G. Wells," *Encounter*, 8 [1957], 53; a briefer version of this essay appeared in *Harper's Magazine*). R. H. Costa claims that Wells's misanthropy was lifelong (*H. G. Wells* [New York: Twayne Publishers, 1967], p. 137). Jack Williamson concludes, in *H. G. Wells: Critic of Progress* (Baltimore: Mirage Press, 1973), that Wells was more pessimist than optimist (p. 28). Both Bernard Bergonzi and J. Kagarlitski stress the deep strain of pessimism in the young Wells (*The Early H. G. Wells: A Study of the Scientific Romances* [Toronto: University of Toronto Press, 1961], p. 22; *The Life and Thought of H. G. Wells*, trans. Moura Budberg [London: Sidgwick & Jackson, 1966], p. 48). My own view is that even though young Wells was appalled by man's failings and his likely fate, he had aspirations to change the human condition. Throughout his life his moods fluctuated between despair and hope. At different phases of his career, one or the other seemed to be more insistent, but he never lost courage.

4. In *The Science of Life* Wells said that "there is not the slightest reason for supposing that the powers, intellectual, spiritual, and emotional, which we human beings happen to possess, are the highest of which this planet is capable." Further great strides in mental possibility may occur; certainly things will not remain as they are (*Life*, bk. III, chap. V: 3).

5. *Evolution and Ethics*, pp. 51 ff. Huxley knew Tennyson's works well and his wife was a devoted fan. He quotes "ape and tiger" in the passage I refer to here and uses other passages from Tennyson later in the lecture. William Irvine discusses Huxley's interest in Tennyson in *Apes, Angels, and Victorians: Darwin, Huxley, and Evolution* (Cleveland and New York: World Publishing Company, 1955), pp. 234, 342, et passim, and Gertrude Himmelfarb mentions Tennyson's place in the emergence of evolutionary thought in *Darwin and the Darwinian Revolution* (New York: Norton 1968), pp. 227 ff. David Y. Hughes treats the Tennysonian connection in "The Garden in Wells's Early Science Fiction," *H. G. Wells and Modern Science Fiction*, ed. Darko Suvin and Robert M. Philmus (Lewisburg: Bucknell University Press, 1977), p. 53. Although Wells recognized the vicious aspects of Nature, he urged imitation of its more positive traits. In *The Work, Wealth and Happiness of Mankind* (1932), he said, "Nature is a great friend of co-operation; it is a gross libel upon her to say she is always 'red in tooth and claw.' On the contrary, she has something like a passion for making living things interdependent. She elaborates and confirms every disposition to associate" (*Work*, chap. I: 4). This idea underlies much of *The Science of Life* as well.

6. Wells probably read Huxley's *Man's Place in Nature*, which contains a far more fearsome picture of a gorilla. One can imagine Wells as a young man coming upon this picture and being reminded of his youthful fear. Ultimately, he may have confused the two images.

7. *Evolution and Ethics*, passim. Voltaire writes at the end of *Candide*, "Cela est bien dit, respondit Candide, mais il faut cultiver notre jardin." William Morris used the garden metaphor to describe his Utopia in *News from Nowhere*. Wells exploited it playfully in *The Happy Turning* (*Turning*, chap. VIII). See below.

8.   Social Darwinists used the metaphor of the jungle to picture the conditions of life, but they did not normally suggest a pathway out of the jungle. Patrick Parrinder discusses fatalism among Social Darwinists of the 1890s in *H. G. Wells* (Edinburgh: Oliver and Boyd, 1970), p. 18.

9.   Wells liked to use cleansing fires in his fiction. There is a good deal of silliness in Henry Arthur Jones's *My Dear Wells* (London: Eveleigh Nash & Grayson, 1921), but Jones exposes an interesting truth when he harps upon Wells's remark that as a young clerk he wished to burn down his employer's shop. If Wells did not do that in reality, he often relieved his desire to do so by having his characters set or witness such liberating conflagrations.

10.  In his early story "The Stolen Bacillus" (1894), Wells used the theme of the baboon disease as a possible threat to mankind. See chapter three for a brief examination of the connection between the two works.

11.  David Y. Hughes has examined the metaphor in "The Garden in Wells's Early Science Fiction."

12.  Mr. Barnstaple is like a savage in the garden of Utopia (*Gods*, bk. III, chap. II: 1). The world of the future is a garden in *The Shape of Things to Come* as well (*Shape*, bk. V: 1). Alfred Borello mentions the edenic quality of the Utopia of *Men Like Gods* in *H. G. Wells: Author in Agony* (Carbondale and Edwardsville: Southern Illinois University Press, 1972), p. 87.

13.  Wells is having some fun with the names in this novel. Terragena probably suggests conception of the earth, or earth's beginning, and perhaps, by extension, Eden. Vinciguerra suggests victory in war, hence promising that the Italian patriot's values will triumph. Wells frequently used names in this way. See chapter eleven for a brief discussion of the practice.

14.  In his old age Huxley developed a strong affection for gardening. (See Leonard Huxley, *Life and Letters of Thomas Henry Huxley* [New York: Appleton, 1900], II, 469 ff., and Irvine, pp. 337 et passim. Irvine entitled his last chapter "Il Faut Cultiver Notre Jardin.")

15.  Wells may have read Leonard Huxley's life of his father where T. H. Huxley refers directly to Voltaire's use of the garden in *Candide* (*Life and Letters*, II, 469).

16.  Philmus and Hughes say, "The heavens always had a poetic intensity of meaning for Wells" (*Early Writings*, p. 182). See also p. 186, where they discuss Wells's version of Platonism. Parrinder also comments on the symbolism of stars in Wells's work (*H. G. Wells*, pp. 21 and 28).

17.  This essay has been attributed to Wells by Philmus and Hughes in *Early Writings*, p. 243.

18.  Wells developed his metaphor amply in describing his purpose for writing *The Work, Wealth and Happiness of Mankind* (1932). Of himself he says, "He is attempting a book, a survey of the world, a scheme and map of *doing,*

which will enable him to say to anyone whatever: 'This is the whole world of work and wealth, of making and getting and spending, and here at this point is your place, and this is where you come in. The map is not a very large-scale map, and consequently you and your sphere of activity may not loom very large, but here and not elsewhere is where you are" (*Work*, Introductions: 6).

19. Wells gave an extreme example of the bird's-eye view in the upward flight away from the body described in "Under the Knife." He liked to think of widening mental horizons (*Outline*, chap. XXXIII: 4). But this was a trait common to reformers and planners. Beatrice Webb had a dream of a bird's-eye view of past and present (cited in J. W. Burrow, *Evolution and Society: A Study in Victorian Social Theory* [Cambridge: Cambridge University Press, 1970], p. 91). Colin Wilson, one of the few novelists today to express admiration for Wells's late novels, also craves a bird's-eye view of life in *The Philosopher's Stone* (New York: Warner Books, 1974), passim.

20. Frequently it is organized air power that guides the world to a new order, either by destruction of the old system or by a more efficient new one. See such stories as *The War in the Air, The World Set Free, The Shape of Things to Come*, and *The Holy Terror*, for example.

21. Wells often discusses the possible delights of flying in some of the early stories and mentions his own pleasure in the experience in "My First Flight" and "The Present Uselessness and Danger of Aeroplanes. A Problem in Organization" (*Forces*, "My First Flight"; *Going*, chap. XI) See also "The Beauty of Flying" in *A Year of Prophesying*, where he prefers open planes.

22. "Panther and Jaguar were far more than mere affectionate nicknames. They stood for the whole attitude towards life evolved by Rebecca and Wells, who continued to use these names as long as their love lasted. They emphasized the ruthless withdrawal from society that the relationship entailed, the fact that Rebecca and Wells were not part of the pack and did not acknowledge its law. Instead they were 'carnivores' living apart in their hidden 'lair,' going forth to 'catch food,' and meeting 'at the trodden place in the jungle'" (Gordon N. Ray, *H. G. Wells and Rebecca West* [New Haven: Yale University Press, 1974], p. 36). Since theirs was a passionate as well as an intellectual relationship, no doubt Wells had in mind that impulsive quality of animal life that played so important a part in his imagery.

## CHAPTER THREE: FLESH AND BLOOD

1. Alfred Borello notes that the characters in Wells's science fantasies discover that their fiercest enemy is the nature of mankind (*H. G. Wells: Author in Agony* (Carbondale and Edwardsville: Southern Illinois University Press, 1972), p. 55.

2. This idea is perennial, but see Koenraad W. Swart's *The Sense of Decadence in Nineteenth-Century France* (The Hague: Martinus Nijhoff, 1964) for an examination of the revival of this sentiment in nineteenth-century France. In England at the turn of the century, decadence was associated

with physical degeneracy as well (Donald Read, *Edwardian England 1901-15: Society and Politics* [London: George G. Harrap, 1972], pp. 155 ff.).

3. Geoffrey West says that Wells had himself under control sexually in the early days but later had to struggle vigorously against sex (*H. G. Wells* [New York: Norton, 1930], pp. 46 and 179).

4. There was a great furor over what many people felt was Wells's advocacy of free love in this novel, but Arnold Bennett correctly asserted that there was nothing indecent in Wells's writings (*Books and Persons: Being Comments on a Past Epoch 1908-1911* [New York: George H. Doran, 1917], p. 115).

5. Rosylnn D. Haynes gives a clear and thorough account of what Wells aspired to in his appreciation of a scientific outlook on life (*H. G. Wells: Discoverer of the Future* [New York and London: New York University Press, 1980], pp. 39 ff.).

6. There are many accounts of Wells's boasting about his sexual exploits or imposing sex as a conversational topic. Frederic Warburg recounts such an experience in *An Occupation for Gentlemen* (London: Hutchinson, 1959), p. 249. C. P. Snow also comments on this trait in Wells and adds that he searched for women and pleasure "with remarkable efficacy" (*Variety of Men* [New York: Scribner's, 1966], p. 78).

7. Ingvald Raknem comments on Wells's increasing attention to sex in *H. G. Wells and His Critics* (London: George Allen & Unwin, 1962), p. 154 ff. Jean-Pierre Vernier devotes two sections—"sentiment et sensualité" and "expériences matrimoniales" of *H. G. Wells et son temps* (Publications de l'universite de rouen, 1971)—to Wells's attitudes and experiences concerning sex (pp. 65 ff.).

8. Wells seems to have felt a constant need to try to seduce women. The early examples of Amber Reeves and others are familiar. More recently, Enid Bagnold has reported how she avoided seduction (*Autobiography* [Boston: Little, Brown, 1969], p. 173). And Gloria G. Fromm has related Dorothy Richardson's relationship with Wells in *Dorothy Richardson: A Biography* (Urbana, Chicago, London: University of Illinois Press, 1977). There were many others, of course.

9. In the typescript of *The Sea Lady*, Wells had given his mermaid the name Doris Cytheraea Waters, suggesting her lusty origins. Cytheraea is lined out (Illinois).

10. Wells said, however, that Marjorie returned from Labrador much the same as when she went out (Preface to *The Works of H. G. Wells*, Volume XV, [New York: Scribner's, 1925].

11. In *The Work, Wealth and Happiness of Mankind*, Wells asserted, "Progress is encumbered by the relative barbarism of women, but even among women education is spreading" (*Work*, chap. X: 5).

12.   Women did not always agree with Wells's sympathetic views, especially feminists such as Freda Kirchway (*Heritage*, p. 309).

13.   Wells owed a good deal of his thinking about sex relations, the family, and cultural assumptions to J. J. Atkinson's *Primal Law* and Andrew Lang's *Social Origins*. G. A. Connes in *Étude sur la pensee de Wells* (Paris: Hachette, 1926) and Raknem cite other sources for Wells's ideas (pp. 141 ff.).

14.   See Raknem, pp. 225 ff. Vernier also discusses Wells's depiction of women, pp. 300 ff.

15.   Wells did not consider the traditional love story a good ground for fiction. He claimed that his treatment of love was something entirely different. In an interview with Robert van Gelder, he remarked that love should not sell stories ("H. G. Wells Discusses Himself and His Work," *Writers and Writing* [New York: Scribner's, 1946], p. 129). Reassessing *When the Sleeper Wakes*, Wells apologized for the sin of treating Helen Wotton as a conventional "love interest" (Preface to *The Works*, II [1924], ix).

16.   Michaelangelo's sibyl is reproduced as the inner cover design of the first edition of the novel.

17.   Freedom in love is an important feature of *Men Like Gods* as well. Stuart P. Sherman reveals his own superficiality in his charge that Wells created Utopias that were convenient for philanderers (*On Contemporary Literature* [New York: Holt, 1917], p. 72). Wells was neither that trivial nor that foolish.

18.   I have discussed the matter of sexuality in the schools in *Old School Ties: The Public Schools in British Literature* (Syracuse: Syracuse University Press, 1964). See also Jonathan Gathorne-Hardy's more recent *The Old School Tie: The Phenomenon of the English Public School* (New York: Viking Press, 1978).

19.   Various studies of Victorian sexuality mention books of this kind. Eric Trudgill's *Madonnas and Magdalens: The Origins and Development of Victorian Sexual Attitudes* (New York: Holmes and Meier, 1976) is one of the best.

20.   Lovat Dickson offers a dispassionate examination of Wells's attitude toward his treatment of love and sex in his fiction, and adds his own shrewd estimates as well in *H. G. Wells: His Turbulent Life and Times* (Harmondsworth: Penguin Books, 1972), pp. 231 ff. Gordon Ray provides an intimate picture of some of Wells's personal aspirations and difficulties concerning sex in *H. G. Wells and Rebecca West* (New Haven: Yale University Press, 1974), passim. Helen Thomas Follett and Wilson Follett convincingly defended Wells against charges of loose and fluent sensuality. They wrote that he was honest with himself and society, which is better than timid chastity ("H. G. Wells," *Some Modern Novelists: Appreciations and Estimates* [New York: Holt, 1918], pp. 256 ff.).

21.    See my chapter on disguise in *Victorian Conventions* (Athens: Ohio University Press, 1975). Wells was aware that clothing could reveal a great deal by pretending to hide it. See "The Refinement of Humanity" (1894) in *Early Writings in Science and Science Fiction by H. G. Wells,* ed. Robert Philmus and David Y. Hughes (Berkeley: University of California Press, 1975), pp. 71-75.

22.    Wells recognized, of course, that external appearance was a secondary virtue in men, and he even deplored the overvaluing of sound physique to the neglect of intellectual and other gifts (*Forces,* "Of the New Reign"). He gave an example of the ugliness of the body in the bad old days in *In the Days of the Comet* (*Comet,* bk. I, chap. IV: 3).

23.    This is a good summary of what Wells yearned for all of his life. He was entirely up to making fun of his own predilections, though; and in *The Conquest of Time* he remarked that *Men Like Gods* was a bother to the illustrator of the serialization in *Hearst's International* because the Utopians did not wear clothes (*Conquest,* Appendix II).

24.    See David Lodge, " 'Tono-Bungay' and the Condition of England," *Language of Fiction: Essays in Criticism and Verbal Analysis of the English Novel* (New York: Columbia University Press, 1966), p. 219, and so forth.

25.    See chapter one of Bernard Bergonzi's *The Early H. G. Wells: A Study of the Scientific Romances* (Toronto: University of Toronto Press, 1961).

## CHAPTER FOUR: IDENTITY: SELF AND RACE

1.    Wells dwells on the changeability of the human species in "Man Becomes a Different Animal. Delusions about Human Fixity" in *The Way the World is Going* (*Going,* chap. I: 1). Human mutability is assumed throughout *The Science of Life* (1930). In *You Can't Be Too Careful* Edward Albert Tewler mouths the old cliché, "You don't change human nature," but Wells had already responded to that in *The Work, Wealth and Happiness of Mankind*: " 'Human nature,' they said, 'never changes.' In truth, it never ceases to change" (*Careful,* Introduction; *Work,* chap. I: 1).

2.    Wells had duality on his mind even in daily matters. He wrote to Maurice Baring on 6 November 1908, "There are two of you the same as me. There is a wise expressive man who writes works and there is an individual in the flesh who is either sly or drunk" (Illinois).

3.    J. Kagarlitski points out Wells's attention to man's divided nature and his examination of the rational and biological elements in man (*The Life and Thought of H.G. Wells,* trans. Moura Budberg [London: Sidgwick & Jackson, 1966], p. 147).

4.    F. H. Doughty focuses on Wells's concept of frontage and hinterland in *H.G. Wells: Educationist* (New York: George H. Doran, 1927), pp. 94 ff.

5.    Letter of 5 July 1900 (*Arnold Bennett and H. G. Wells: A Record of a*

*Personal and a Literary Friendship*, ed. Harris Wilson [London: Rupert Hart-Davis, 1960], p. 47).

6.    Geoffrey H. Wells felt that Wells failed to satisfy readers finally because he was so deeply divided against himself (*Heritage*, pp. 290 ff.). John Middleton Murry suspected that "the contradiction between his intellectual passion for 'a new order' and his irrepressible irreverence was probably unresolved to the end" (*Heritage*, p. 326). In contrasting Wells with Dorothy Richardson, Gloria Fromm says that Richardson knew what she was doing, but "Wells, unable to decide who he wanted to be, repudiating identity after identity, suffered from his 'fugitive impulses.' He built selves as well as houses and cast them (in his own words) 'as a snake casts its skin' " (*Dorothy Richardson: A Biography* [Urbana, Chicago, London: University of Illinois Press, 1977], p. 200). I believe that Professor Fromm has oversimplified Wells and not recognized his abiding consistency. After all, when a snake sheds its old skin, it does not grow something entirely novel; the new skin replicates the old one but is more suited to the new dimensions of the creature. Matilda M. Meyer was warned, as soon as she took service in the Wells household, about the master's abrupt changes of mood, but she adds that she rarely had occasion to complain (*H. G. Wells and his Family as I Have Known Them* [Edinburgh: International Publishing, 1955], pp. 22-23).

7.    This device resembles the technique of *A Modern Utopia*, including the confrontation of two contrasting character types at the conclusion of the narrative. There is a playful irony here, though, in that the optimistic voice is that of the untrustworthy Graves, who, with his sexual misconduct, initiated Blettsworthy's difficulties in the first place. His name is not entirely reassuring either. If one considers the relationship with *Candide*, to which Wells dedicated this novel, there may be a further irony in Graves's confident optimism.

8.    From documents at Illinois.

9.    Van Wyck Brooks observed that Wells treated two basic types of human nature in his fiction, and Patrick Parrinder has stressed the same point more recently (*The World of H. G. Wells* [New York: Mitchell Kennerley, 1915], p. 33, and *H. G. Wells* [Edinburgh: Oliver and Boyd, 1970], p. 40). When he was younger, Wells offered a more playful version of the contrast presented in *Apropos of Dolores* in the sprightly tale *Bealby* (1915), where the resolute juvenile Bealby is contrasted with the mean caravan driver, William. "About Bealby there was ever an imaginative touch; he was capable of romance, of gallantries, of devotion. William was of a grosser clay, slave of his appetites, a materialist. Such men as William drive one to believe in born inferiors, in the existence of a lower sort, in the natural inequality of men" (*Bealby*, chap. IV: 10). This description might appear no more than a simplified opposition of romantic and realist temperaments, but it is also a version of Wells's contrasting of the apelike and angelic in man.

10.    Ingvald Raknem, like other critics, draws attention to Wells's presentation of diametrically opposed types of characters, though he examines them in

terms of their sexual natures (*H. G. Wells and His Critics* [London: George Allen & Unwin, 1962], pp. 210-11).

11.    Arnold Bennett felt that the politically creative part of this novel was less convincing than the politically shattering part (*Books and Persons: Being Comments on a Past Epoch 1908-1911* [New York: George H. Doran, 1917], p. 298).

12.    William Bellamy offers an interesting interpretation of this tendency, placing it in the larger context of the Edwardian period. First he observes that the fin de siècle brought on a polarization of subjective and objective ways of viewing life. Then he describes the way writers dealt with this. "Such a phenomenological 'Utopianization' of everyday reality is the primary mode in the fiction of Wells, Bennett and Galsworthy; the degree to which the 'raw material' of life was felt to be susceptible to cognitive recreation increased as their careers progressed. While 'compromise' was the general mood of the pre-1900 fiction, the fiction of the years between 1905 and 1910 increasingly explores the potential of the self's ability to become 'cosmic' by a process of knowing which takes the individual beyond pathological self-consciousness, and heals the apparent schizophrenia of *fin-de-siecle* man. 'Cosmic consciousness' is not an odd luxury to be indulged by people more mystic than the average; it is, in the mature work of the three Edwardians, the only workable solution for the post-cultural self in crisis" (*The Novels of Wells, Bennett and Galsworthy: 1890-1910* [New York: Barnes & Noble, 1971], pp. 42-43).

13.    Wells mentions Myers's writings in *When the Sleeper Wakes* (*Sleeper*, chap. XVII). It is likely that Wells would have continued to read Myers's later work.

14.    Gertrude Himmelfarb discusses Darwin's assertion of the value of suffering in some higher design for man in *Darwin and the Darwinian Revolution* (New York: Norton, 1968), p. 347. W. Warren Wagar says that Wells saw history as challenge and response, and thus as struggle, after the manner of Spencer and Huxley (*H. G. Wells and the World State* [New Haven: Yale University Press, 1961], p. 55). Wells seems to have believed that striving would replace struggle, and effort, pain.

15.    Even in relaxation Wells was given to contentious amusements such as vigorous athletic contests, games such as demon patience, and the sorts of diversions recorded in *Floor Games* and *Little Wars*.

16.    Wells had little appreciation for Hegel because of the inevitability implicit in his scheme. Nonetheless, Wells's picture of history as man's slow development of a World State might be described as Hegel out of uniform and with his shirt sleeves rolled up.

17.    This is Edwin E. Slosson's perception of Wells's character in 1917: "The interesting point to observe is that temperament and training have combined to give him on the one hand a hatred of this muddled, blind, and inefficient state of society in which we live, and on the other a distrust of the

orderly, logical, and perfected civilization usually suggested as a possible substitute. He detests chaos, but is skeptical of cosmos. Set between these antipathetic poles, he vibrates continually like an electrified pith ball" (*Six Major Prophets* [Boston: Little, Brown, 1917], p. 99).

18.  In October of 1907 Wells sent a draft of his "Credo" to Harold Monro. Section 5 of this document summarizes much of what I have quoted from *First and Last Things*. "I am disposed to believe and I do believe that my Ego is as it were derived from my species and detached from it to the end that I may gather experience and add to the increasing thought and acquisitions of the species. I believe that the species moves forward unconsciously to a consciousness of itself and to a collective being, and that love is an emotional realization of this collective being however partial and that right action is what forwards it. I am a Socialist because to me Socialism is a practical material aspect of this awakening through will of the conscious collective being of humanity" (Illinois).

19.  John Theodore Merz, in *A History of European Scientific Thought in the Nineteenth Century*, Volume I (New York: Dover Publications, 1965), refers to various figures, such as Hegel, Comte, Lotze, and Spencer, who described the increasing unity in the inner life of mankind. He said of his work, first published between 1904 and 1912, that he could not have undertaken the study had he not believed in the unity of all human interest and that all mental efforts combine to produce and uphold the ideal possessions of the race (p. 33). J. W. Burrow has a sound evaluation of Spencer's social evolutionism in *Evolution and Society: A Study in Victorian Social Theory* (Cambridge: Cambridge University Press, 1970), chap. 6.

20.  F. H. Doughty wrote, "If, as Butler suggested, Darwin banished mind from the universe, Mr. Wells may be said, to a great degree, to have recalled it" (*H. G. Wells: Educationist* [New York: George H. Doran, 1927], p. 48).

21.  There were many persons during Wells's lifetime who promoted similar beliefs. Henry Salt was one example. Like Wells, he desired a universal brotherhood, and his Creed of Kinship extended to the subhuman as well. See George Hendrick's *Henry Salt: Humanitarian Reformer and Man of Letters* (Urbana, Chicago, London: University of Illinois Press, 1977). Wells presents his position more objectively in his *Thesis* ('42, Appendix I: 2).

22.  Samuel Butler, *Life and Habit, Works*, ed. Henry Festing Jones and A. T. Bartholomew (New York: Dutton, IV, [1923] 104), and "God the Known and God the Unknown," *Works*, XVIII, (1925) 46. The pieces appeared in 1877 and 1879 respectively.

## CHAPTER FIVE: PROGRESS

1.  This notion concerning human solidarity was in the air at the end of the nineteenth century. Comte's positivism was perhaps the most obvious example. But, as Zeev Sternhell points out, the generation of 1890 in Europe took as its point of departure, not individual, but social and political collec-

tivity ("Fascist Ideology," *Fascism: A Reader's Guide. Analyses, Interpretations, Bibliography*, ed. Walter Laqueur [Berkeley and Los Angeles: University of California Press, 1976], p. 322).

2.     Ingvald Raknem says that the idea of a World State was commonplace at the time (*H. G. Wells and His Critics* [London: George Allen & Unwin, 1962], pp. 266 ff.). William Morris, for example, had been championing a World State for some time, and Wells knew about that.

3.     In this same discussion, Wells stipulated his objections to Marx's prescriptive plan for the future. J. B. Bury's *The Idea of Progress: An Inquiry into its Growth and Origin* (1932) is still the best basic history of the concept, but there are many recent studies of progress. Walter Houghton takes it up as a part of his study of Victorian culture in *The Victorian Frame of Mind 1830-1870* (New Haven and London: Yale University Press, 1957). More common now is a spirit of disenchantment with the idea of progress, specifically scientific progress, represented by such works as Gunther S. Stent's *The Coming of the Golden Age* (New York: Doubleday, 1969) and *Paradoxes of Progress* (San Francisco: Freeman, 1978).

4.     See especially Huxley's "The Struggle for Existence in Human Society," *Evolution and Ethics and Other Essays* (London: Macmillan, 1894), pp. 195-236. Huxley noted that progress and evolution were two different things and were neither pessimistic nor optimistic by nature.

5.     George Orwell unfairly charged Wells with a total commitment to science in "Wells, Hitler and the World State," *Collected Essays* (London: Secker & Warburg, 1961). In fact, Wells simply said that science helps, not that it is automatically good.

6.     See Wells's essay on Pavlov and Shaw in *The Way the World is Going* (*Going*, chap. XXV).

7.     Ivor Brown, *H. G. Wells* (London: Nisbet, 1923), pp. 35-36.

8.     Augustin Filon, *Heritage*, p. 100.

9.     Van Wyck Brooks, *The World of H. G. Wells* (New York: Mitchell Kennerley, 1915), discussed Wells's contrasting of the competing views of society as governed either by chance or by design (pp. 50 ff.).

10.    *Heritage*, p. 86. Henry Arthur Jones informed Wells that there are wicked men in the world and that therefore Wells's theories would not work in *My Dear Wells: A Manual for the Haters and England* (London: Eveleigh Nash & Grayson, 1921), p. 54.

11.    Frederic Ozanam, among others, had made this point in the 1890s, as Koenraad W. Swart points out in *The Sense of Decadence in Nineteenth-Century France* (The Hague: Martinus Nijhoff, 1964), p. 86.

12.    G. K. Chesterton thought he was correcting Wells when he insisted that

everything does not change, but Wells himself warned conservatives that those unchanging features of existence were hurtful to them (*Heretics* [New York: John Lane, 1919], pp. 81 ff.). Redwood, viewing Caterham as a strong but foolish reactionary, thinks, "He did not know there were physical laws and economic laws, quantities and reactions that all humanity voting *nemine contradicente* cannot vote away, and that are disobeyed only at the price of destruction. He did not know there are moral laws that cannot be bent by any force of glamour or are bent only to fly back with vindictive violence" (*Food*, bk. III, chap. IV). Henry Arthur Jones also failed to see this and boasted of his own belief in changeless principles of economics and law, as though Wells saw none of it (*My Dear Wells*, pp. 92-93).

13.  Critics seem to have agreed that *Tono-Bungay* is Wells's best novel, and they have concentrated upon it for analysis. Two who have noted the importance of the theme of change in the book are Kenneth B. Newell, *Structure in Four Novels by H. G. Wells* (The Hague and Paris: Mouton, 1968), p. 73 et passim, and David Lodge, *Language of Fiction* (New York: Columbia, 1966), pp. 240-42.

14.  Wells expressed his disgust over the Sacco and Vanzetti case in an article reprinted in *The Way the World is Going* (*Going*, chap. XXII).

15.  Edwin E. Slosson, *Six Major Prophets* (Boston: Little, Brown, 1917), p. 63.

16.  Geoffrey West describes Wells's youthful activities in a debating society that took up lively issues of the day (*H. G. Wells* [New York: Norton, 1930], p. 51).

17.  Ibid., p. 99.

18.  Bennett made these observations in his review of Wells published in the *Cosmopolitan Magazine* in August of 1902 (*Arnold Bennett and H. G. Wells: A Record of a Personal and a Literary Friendship* [London: Rupert Hart-Davis, 1960], p. 269). In a letter of 1905 Bennett drew a distinction between himself and Wells, explaining that he recognized that progress was inevitable and could be achieved only through a passion for justice, but that he was objective about justice as he was about everything (p. 123).

19.  See, for example, St. John G. Ervine, *Some Impressions of My Elders* (New York: Macmillan, 1922), p. 253; Havelock Ellis, *Heritage*, pp. 96 ff.; E. M. Forster, *Heritage*, pp. 248 ff.; and Richard Hauer Costa, *H. G. Wells* (New York: Twayne Publishers, 1967), p. 85.

20.  Jack Williamson, *H. G. Wells: Critic of Progress* (Baltimore: Mirage Press, 1973), p. 27.

21.  Ibid., p. 47. This is also the basic argument of W. Warren Wagar's "H. G. Wells and the Radicalism of Despair," *Studies in the Literary Imagination*, 6, No. 1 (1973), 1-10.

22.  C. P. Snow, *Variety of Men* (New York: Scribner's, 1966), p. 80.

23.    John Middleton Murry, *Heritage*, p. 328.

24.    H. L. Mencken, *Prejudices. First Series* (New York: Knopf, 1923), p. 28. Theodore Dreiser, Introduction to *Tono-Bungay*, Volume I of the Sandgate Edition (New York: Duffield, 1927), p. v.

25.    Koenraad W. Swart mentions some early optimists with ideas resembling Wells's. French theocrats and others in the early and middle nineteenth century, for example, believed that a catastrophe had to precede the establishment of a better community. Much of Proudhon's thinking sounds like Wells, too. In 1868 an anonymous novel entitled *La Cité nouvelle* pictured a mechanized, but decivilized, world of 2000 A.D. Socialists, for the most part, believed that improvement would come through sudden change, such as a revolution or widespread disaster. Wells may have derived some of this attitude as well from William Morris and Shelley.

26.    Dillon Johnston calls attention to the theme of fortunate accident in Wells's autobiography in "The Recreation of Self in Wells's 'Experiment in Autobiography,' " *Criticism*, 14, No. 4 (Fall 1972), 350 ff.

27.    Robert Philmus and David Y. Hughes note that Wells was concerned with the accidental character of mammalian evolution in his earliest published writings (*Early Writings in Science and Science Fiction by H. G. Wells* [Berkeley: University of California Press, 1975]. p. 8). In *The Outline of History* (1920), Wells described evolution as a matter of chance (*Outline*, chap. V: 4). He reasserted the point with more authority in *The Science of Life* (1930) (*Life*, bk VIII, chap. III: 4).

## CHAPTER SIX: ORGANIZATION, ORDER, AND EDUCATION

1.    Wells was self-conscious about the crystal image from very early in his career and used it playfully in his correspondence. In a letter to his friend A. T. Simmons in February of 1889, he wrote, "Neither attempt to find things too clearly crystallized in words for the phenomenon of crystallization is too often the follower of evaporation or cooling" (Illinois).

2.    John Dixon Hunt, *The Pre-Raphaelite Imagination 1848-1900* (Lincoln: University of Nebraska Press, 1968), pp. 56 and 141. See also plate 14.

3.    Ibid., p. 149.

4.    Rebecca West, *The Return of the Soldier* (New York: Century, 1918), pp. 132-33.

5.    F. H. Doughty's *H. G. Wells: Educationist* (New York: George H. Doran, 1927) is not satisfactory, but then it was published before Wells had written some of his major statements on education. Other critics such as W. Warren Wagar, *H. G. Wells and the World State* (New Haven: Yale University Press, 1961), p. 123, and Alfred Borrello, *H. G. Wells: Author in Agony*

(Carbondale and Edwardsville: Southern Illinois University Press, 1972), pp. 36 ff, have stressed the importance of education in Wells's writing. Rosylnn D. Haynes discusses Wells's educational interests in *H. G. Wells:Discoverer of the Future* (New York and London: New York University Press, 1980), pp. 63 ff. and elsewhere.

6.   This assumption pervades *The Science of Life*, but see also *The Outline of History* and *'42 to '44* (*Outline*, chap. VI: 2; *'42*, Appendix I: 2).

7.   Patrick Braybrooke thoroughly misunderstands Wells, perhaps for glibness' sake, when he says that Wells would like to see a multiplication of professors of education and then declares that this would solve nothing (*Philosophies in Modern Fiction* [Freeport, New York: Books for Libraries Press, 1965 rpt.], p. 73). No multiplication of professors would please Wells if they were turned out of the same old mold.

8.   Beatrice Webb said that Wells disagreed with her and her husband's tolerant view of education and insisted that one must exclude what one believes harmful and put forward one's own creed vigorously (*Our Partnership*, ed. Barbara Drake and Margaret I. Cole [London: Longmans, Green, 1948], pp. 307-08). The entry is for 11 May 1905.

9.   See Edward C. Mack's *Public Schools and British Opinion, 1780-1860* (New York: Columbia University Press, 1939) and *Public Schools and British Opinion Since 1860* (New York: Columbia University Press, 1941). My own *Old School Ties: The Public Schools in British Literature* (Syracuse: Syracuse University Press, 1964) deals mainly with literary figures' treatment of the schools in fiction. More recently Jonathan Gathorne-Hardy has ventured a history of the public schools that includes a good deal of judgment on the schools through the years (*The Old School Tie: The Phenomenon of the English Public Schoo¡* [New York: Viking Press, 1978]).

10.   Wells is quoting Macaulay in this passage. He refers to the deterioration of ruling class education in *The Fate of Homo Sapiens*, too (*Homo*: 17).

11.   Wells gives a condensed description of his basic plan of education in his autobiography. "I am convinced that the informative framework of a proper education should be presented as the three sides of the triangle I have drawn in them; Biology, History and Human Ecology. A child should begin with Natural History, a History of Inventions, Social Beginnings and Descriptive Geography, that should constitute its first world picture, and the treatment of these subjects should broaden and intensify before specialization" (*Autobiography*, chap. IX: 7). See also *The Way the World is Going* (*Going*, chap. XIV).

12.   Wells admired efficient indoctrination as an educational method. He likened the nuclei described in *The Shape of Things to Come* to the effective devices employed by the National Socialists, the Kuomintang, and other similar organizations.

13.   Remington's training resembles George Ponderevo's in *Tono-Bungay*.

Ponderevo also gained his real education from private reading, though the books he read were more lively and fanciful than Remington's (*Tono*, bk. I, chap. I: 5). He was not so unhappy with his education at private school, especially because the headmaster had some command of mathematics, but he recalls that "one inestimable privilege at that school was spiritual neglect" (*Tono*, bk. I, chap. I: 6). In other places, Wells points out that most educational institutions fail to build character through a knowledge of the world and offer platitudes or religious threats instead. From this point of view, neglect may seem a genuine boon.

14.    C. P. Snow comments warmly on Wells's greatness as an educator in *Variety of Men* (New York: Scribner's, 1966), p. 73. With a less extensive perspective, Doughty lamented what he considered Wells's lapse from educator to propagandist (pp. 133 ff.).

15.    Wells described this type in his short story "The Lost Inheritance." It is possible that there is an irony in the title, for the young man who would have inherited his eccentric uncle's fortune fails to do so because he never bothers to read the book that his dying uncle gives him. Had he really listened to his uncle's preachings and read his books, he would have inherited not only wealth but reason.

16.    Wells no doubt had critics like Christopher Caudwell in mind. Caudwell sniped that Wells "took the role of popular 'thinker', writer of the novel 'of ideas' and of 'outlines' of science and history, because he had been unable to pursue real art and had been forced to forsake real science" ("H. G. Wells: A Study in Utopianism," *Studies in a Dying Culture* [New York: Dodd, Mead, n.d.], p. 83).

## CHAPTER SEVEN: THE WILL

1.    Van Wyck Brooks noted that the "idea of the relationship between free will and determinism is the underlying assumption of Wells" (*The World of H. G. Wells* [New York: Mitchell Kennerley, 1915], p. 22). He remains conscious of this theme throughout his study, deciding finally, though Wells's career had a long way yet to run, that Wells would not sacrifice an "unimpeded free will" even for the collective consciousness he so desired (p. 122). Geoffrey West quotes Wells's letter of 1888 to his friend Simmons in which the young enthusiast adjures his correspondent, "Make your brain and body a cunning instrument in the hand of your will, and dissociate your mind from sympathy with the weapon" (*H. G. Wells:* [New York: Norton, 1930], p. 84). In "Liberty: A Study in Bourgeois Illusion," Christopher Caudwell lectured Wells on the subject of free will. Basically he asserted the ancient view that true freedom is in the understanding of iron determinism (formerly divine providence). Caudwell tells Wells that free will and causality are not opposed, but the one is the recognition of the other (*Studies in a Dying Culture* [New York: Dodd, Mead, n.d., pp. 205-06). Wells was not confused on this point. He opposed Caudwell's communist determinism because, like other dogmatic political views, it assumed an inevitability in events that released men from the necessity of struggling to improve their condition.

2. See Wells's early essay "The Limits of Individual Plasticity" (1895) (*Early Writings*, chap. II). In *Nietzsche, Henry James, and the Artistic Will* (New York: Oxford University Press, 1978), Stephen Donadio shows that James too was conscious of, and dedicated to, the reshaping of material existence. But he wished to do this by focusing on the artist, not on the material world. He wished to give a sense of man perceiving, not of man acting. Both writers shared this desire to shape existence with Nietzsche, though he was not the only philosopher holding such an attitude.

3. Henri Bergson, beginning with a distinction drawn by Spinoza, argued that there was a difference in kind between the external world of causality and the internal psychic world. In the one, causation was credible because points, after moving, could return to their former positions. In the psychic system this was not so. Return to a former condition was impossible because changes in perception changed the psyche itself. Bergson's argument is very sophisticated, but simply put, it says that we have two selves—the external projection, or spatial self, that must act in space, and the inner becoming self, which is measurable only in duration (*Time and Free Will: An Essay on the Immediate Data of Consciousness*, trans. F. L. Pogson [London: George Allen & Unwin, 1910]). Bergson's study was first published in French in 1889.

4. Robert Philmus and David Y. Hughes discuss this point in *Early Writings in Science and Science Fiction by H. G. Wells* (Berkeley: University of California Press, 1975), noting that " 'the absolute standpoint' does not impinge on the human sense of freedom, nor does it impugn as delusive a human consciousness of change" (p. 53). See also pp. 48, 50 ff.

5. Wells touches upon this question again briefly in *The Work, Wealth and Happiness of Mankind* (*Work*, chap. II: 3-4). There is an interesting passage in Samuel Butler's *Notebooks* dealing with the free will of atoms that is worth quoting in this context. "The element of free-will, spontaneity, individuality, so omnipresent, so essential, yet so unreasonable and so inconsistent with the other element not less omnipresent and not less essential, I mean necessity—this element of free-will which comes from the unseen kingdom within which the writs of our thoughts run not, must be carried down to the most tenuous atoms, whose action is supposed most purely chemical and mechanical; it can never be held as absolutely eliminated, for if it be so held there is no getting it back again, and that it exists even in the lowest forms of life cannot be disputed. Its existence is one of the proofs of the existence of an unseen world, and a means whereby we know the little that we know at all" (*Samuel Butler's Notebooks*, selections edited by Geoffrey Keynes and Brian Hill [London: Jonathan Cape, 1951], p. 197). I have no idea if Wells ever encountered this passage from Butler's thoughts, but it shows what kind of speculation remained active during Wells's lifetime.

6. Wells presented these ideas somewhat differently in his Credo of 1907: "In order to steady and determine my life, which otherwise remains aimless and unsatisfactory, I declare that this ultimately incomprehensible Universe about me is systematic and not chaotic and that I and my will and the determinations I make, and likewise all other things are important in that

scheme. I cannot prove this. I make this declaration as an Act of Faith" (Illinois).

7.     In an article entitled "The Blob That Ate Physics," *Science News*, 108, No. 2 (12 July 1975), 28-29, Dietrick E. Thomsen recorded the opinions of Stephen W. Hawking of Cambridge University which indicated that the absolute causality required by classical physics may not be defensible. If these matters are still open to dispute, Wells's position was not untenable.

8.     Wells complained about Marxist thought frequently, but two prominent objections occur in *The World of William Clissold* and *The Work, Wealth and Happiness of Mankind* (*Clissold*, vol. I, bk. II: 8; *Work*, chap. VIII: 2).

9.     W. Warren Wagar says Wells saw will as a cure for the maladies of man (*H. G. Wells and the World State* [New Haven: Yale University Press, 1961], p. 79).

10.    Dillon Johnston's "The Recreation of Self in Wells's 'Experiment in Autobiography,'" *Criticism*, 14, No. 4 (Fall 1972), 345-60, is an excellent venture at explaining Wells's intentions and strategies in his autobiography. Essentially Johnston argues that the autobiography itself is a sample of willed development.

11.    Jean-Pierre Vernier examines the highly personalized form of Wells's socialism in *H. G. Wells et son temps* (Publications de l'universite de rouen, 1971), pp. 250 ff.

12.    Wells was to make similar assertions about the developing will of the Allies against the mere organization of the enemy in World War II (*Autobiography*, chap. IX: 6).

13.    Before the war, Wells had announced to the nation, "We have come to a phase in our affairs when the only alternative to a great deliberate renascence of will and understanding is national disorder and decay" (*Forces*, "The Labour Unrest": 5).

14.    Wells urged that boys be educated to a recognition of the function of the will. In "The Schoolmaster and the Empire" he said, "They must have an idea of will prevailing over form" (*Forces*, "The Schoolmaster and the Empire": 3).

15.    In *God, The Invisible King* the spirit that guides man, his growing will, remains the same, except that Wells calls it God: "He is the undying human memory, the increasing human will" (*Inv. King*, chap. III: 2 and elsewhere).

16.    In *The Fate of Homo Sapiens* Wells remarked that if democracy means among other things a social community with an educated will like that of a team of cooperating individuals, then there might be hope for it (*Homo*: 6). Beatrice Webb commented on Wells's lack of confidence in government "by the 'man in the street'" in her notes to herself (*Our Partnership*, ed. Barbara Drake and Margaret I. Cole [London: Longmans, Green, 1948], p. 231).

17.    Ingvald Raknem is wrong in saying that Wells was interested only in the will of the exceptional man ( *H. G. Wells and His Critics* [London: George Allen & Unwin, 1962], p. 271). Wells believed that a very small number of human beings had achieved command of the will, but he wished to extend the capacity for that control as widely as possible.

18.    I cannot agree with Van Wyck Brooks that *Kipps* represents waste without free will or with R. H. Costa, who says that the lives in *Kipps, Tono-Bungay*, and *The History of Mr. Polly* are rigidly determined (Brooks, p. 56; Costa, *H. G. Wells* [New York: Twayne Publishers, 1967], p. 27).

19.    Wells, like many of his critics, was not satisfied with the structure of the novel. The novel was planned to be larger and fuller, he said. "But it became unsatisfactory technically, it ran to monologue, the writer could not bring himself to rewrite it, and for all structural purposes he brought it to an end with Ann Veronica's elopement" (Preface to *The Works of H. G. Wells*, XIII, [New York: Scribner's, 1924], ix).

20.    Wells responded warmly to Alfred Adler's theories of the inferiority complex and the compensating superiority complex, which he commented upon in *The Science of Life* and used in *You Can't Be Too Careful* (*Life*, chap. VII: 12). Wells seems always to have associated sexual passion with domination.

21.    Wells mentions the feelings that impelled him to write *Anticipations* in *Experiment in Autobiography* (*Autobiography*, chap. IX: 1). It is possible that Wells picked up some of his ideas from striking new experiments, such as the moving sidewalk at the Paris Exposition of 1900. Moving sidewalks appear, however, in *When the Sleeper Wakes* and *Anticipations*, the first published in 1899, the other during 1900.

22.    William Coleman provides a concise statement of the change in scientific attitudes during these years in *Biology in the Nineteenth Century: Problems of Form, Function, and Transformation* (London: Cambridge University Press, 1971), pp. 160 ff.

23.    William Winwood Reade, *The Martyrdom of Man* (New York: Truth Seeker Company, n.d.), p. 510. George Connes discusses the influence of Reade and others upon Wells's thinking in *Étude sur la pensée de Wells* (Paris: Hachette, 1926).

24.    Samuel Hynes, *The Edwardian Turn of Mind* (Princeton: Princeton University Press, 1968), pp. 23 ff. and 45.

25.    See "The Limits of Individual Plasticity" and other early pieces. Philmus and Hughes indicate that Wells did not immediately accept new theories of heredity (*Early Writings*, p. 10n.). But by the time he collaborated on *The Science of Life*, he had settled on the Mendelian theory (*Life*, bk. IV, chap. IV: 1-12).

26.    Gertrude Himmelfarb, *Darwin and the Darwinian Revolution* (New York:

Norton, 1968), p. 425. Mark H. Haller gives a concise background of the beginnings of eugenics in *Eugenics: Hereditarian Attitudes in American Thought* (New Brunswick: Rutgers University Press, 1963).

27.    Haller, p. 18. Eugenics was a vexed issue during the twenties and thirties. Some informed people had curiously ambivalent feelings about the subject. For example, J. B. S. Haldane, after speculating on the control of breeding in humans, comes to this oddly stated conclusion: "To sum up, the rational programme for a eugenist is as follows: Teach voluntary eugenics by all means; but if you desire to check the increase of any population or section of a population, either massacre it or force upon it the greatest practicable amount of liberty, education, and wealth. Civilization stands in real danger from over-production of 'undermen.' But if it perishes from this cause it will be because its governing class cared more for wealth than for justice" (*Possible Worlds and Other Papers* [New York and London: Harper & Brothers, 1928], p. 206).

28.    Wells examines Galton and cites him extensively in his thesis ('42, Appendix I: 6).

29.    Margaret Sanger, *My Fight for Birth Control* (New York: Farrar & Rinehart, 1931), p. 137, and *An Autobiography* (New York: Norton, 1938), p. 186.

30.    Peter Fryer, *The Birth Controllers* (New York: Stein and Day, 1966), pp. 220-30.

31.    Ibid., pp. 240 and 267.

32.    Sanger, *My Fight*, p. 276.

33.    Fryer, p. 259.

34.    Many did believe quite simply in selective breeding. George du Maurier was vigorous in promoting the idea, and it even found its way into his last novel, *The Martian* (Leonee Ormond, *George Du Maurier* [Pittsburgh: University of Pittsburgh Press, 1969], p. 488).

35.    Wells's forceful, modern characters are in favor of birth control. See the young American women in *Secret Places of the Heart*, for example (*Heart*, chap. VI: 5).

36.    Unfortunately for my argument, Wells refers to Graham's death in his preface to Volume II of *The Works*, (1924) p. ix, thereby confirming the serial version of the story in which Graham is found dead.

37.    Walter Lippmann said of Wells's position among Utopians, "He seemed to live in that dangerous region where freedom is being tried and vision embodied. He seemed to be buffeted from both sides, challenged by his dreams which revolted at the compromises of reality, and assaulted by reality which denounced the emptiness of all dreams" (*Heritage*, p. 221). It is an acute observation.

38.    But the dream becomes real in the new world after the comet (*Comet*, bk. III, chap. II: 3). William Gaunt says of Morris, who used the dream device freely, "To turn a dream into a reality it was necessary to make everyone dream" (*The Pre-Raphaelite Tragedy* [London: Jonathan Cape, 1975], p. 176).

39.    Vincent Brome calls attention to Wells's use of the metaphor of awakening in relationship to the operation of the will in *H. G. Wells: A Biography* (London: Longmans, Green, 1951), p. 141.

40.    See "A Vision of the Past" (*Early Writings*, chap. V). A quick glance at some of Wells's titles and headings shows how often dreams were on his mind. There are the obvious ones, such as *The Dream* and *The Happy Turning: A Dream of Life*, but one must keep in mind "The Dream Book of Dr. Philip Raven" in *The Shape of Things to Come*, "The Dream" that is chapter one of *The Soul of a Bishop*, and so forth. See the Introduction for further comments on Wells's use of the dream motif.

41.    *The Dream* employs the nice Morrisian trick of having a Utopian dream himself back to the past; it is another turn of the screw upon "A Dream of John Ball."

42.    E. D. H. Johnson shows the relationship between providential belief and fictional structure in Dickens's novels (*Charles Dickens: An Introduction to His Novels* (New York: Random House, 1969), pp. 101 ff., and chapter six of David Goldknopf's *The Life of the Novel* (Chicago and London: University of Chicago Press, 1972) discusses the change from a providential to a socio-technological view of life and the effect of that change on fictional form.

43.    One thinks of two such similar yet opposite figures as Thomas Hardy and W. B. Yeats. See Maurice Larkin's *Man and Society in Nineteenth-Century Realism: Determinism and Literature* (Totowa, N.J.: Rowman and Littlefield, 1977) for a treatment of this subject.

44.    Alan Sandison, *The Wheel of Empire: A Study of the Imperial Idea in Some Late Nineteenth and Early Twentieth-Century Fiction* (New York: St. Martin's Press, 1967), p. 26.

45.    Ibid., p. 15.

46.    Ibid., pp. 20-26. Needless to say, personal matters played an enormous part in authors' attitudes as well. See, for example, Angus Wilson's *The Strange Ride of Rudyard Kipling: His Life and Works* (New York: Viking Press, 1977); Frederick R. Karl's "Conrad, Wells, and the Two Voices," PMLA, 8, No. 5, pp. 10 49-65; Jerome Hamilton Buckley's *William Ernest Henley: A Study in the "Counter-Decadence" of the 'Nineties* (Princeton: Princeton University Press, 1945), for information about the way in which personal attitudes affected the philosophical views of various writers. David Daiches's *Some Late Victorian Attitudes* (New York: Norton, 1969) is a concise rendering of some common influences and ideas of the period.

47.     Bernard Bergonzi in *The Early H. G. Wells: A Study of the Scientific Ro-mances* (Toronto: University of Toronto Press, 1961) and John A. Lester, Jr., in *Journey Through Despair: 1880-1914. Transformations in British Literary Culture* (Princeton: Princeton University Press, 1968) specifically take up the relationship of the fin de siècle spirit to the other currents of writing at the time.

48.     See Lionel Stevenson's *Yesterday and After*, Volume XI of *The History of the English Novel* (New York: Barnes & Noble, 1967), for an estimate of Wells's place in the tradition of the novel (pp. 58-59).

49.     *George Gissing and H. G. Wells: Their Friendship and Correspondence*, ed. and intro. Royal A. Gettmann (Urbana: University of Illinois Press, 1961), p. 25. Gissing had his characters utter similar sentiments. For example, Osmond Waymark in *The Unclassed* (1884) rejects the idea of living life for its own sake. "But life as the source of splendid pictures, inexhaustible material for effects—*that* can reconcile me to existence, and that only" (*The Unclassed* [New York: AMS Press, 1968], p. 117).

50.     *Gissing and Wells*, pp. 48-49.

51.     Ibid., pp. 203-04. Jacob Korg says that Gissing's basic opinion implicit in his essay "Hope of Pessimism" written in 1882 was "that the order of the universe is intrinsically evil and that human idealism can do little to change that fact" (*George Gissing: A Critical Biography* [Seattle: University of Washington Press, 1963], p. 52).

52.     Korg, p. 115.

53.     George Gissing, *The Nether World*, intro. Morley Roberts (New York: Dutton, n.d.), pp. 94-95.

54.     Ibid., pp. 312 and 60.

55.     Ibid., p. 103.

56.     George Gissing, *The Emancipated: A Novel* (Chicago: Way and Williams, 1895), p. 108.

57.     Ibid., p. 365. Elgar repeats the view to his sister later (p. 371).

58.     Ibid., p. 115.

59.     Ibid.

60.     George Gissing, *Demos: A Story of English Socialism*, 3 vols. (London: Smith, Elder, 1886] vol. 3, p. 92.

61.     Michael Collie, in *The Alien Art: A Critical Study of George Gissing's Nov-els* (Hamden, Conn.: Archon Books, 1979), touches upon Gissing's debt to Schopenhauerian views, his conviction of social and psychological deter-

minism, and his feeling that heredity counted for more than will could (pp. 50, 57, 86). Still he, like John Goode, who also notes Gissing's loyalty to Schopenhauer, suggests that Gissing had no systematic ideology concerning determinism (*George Gissing: Ideology and Fiction* [New York: Barnes & Noble, 1979], pp. 198 and 186).

62. Letter of 20 December 1897 quoted in Jocelyn Baines's *Joseph Conrad: A Critical Biography* (London: Weidenfeld and Nicolson, 1960), pp. 200-01.

63. Paul L. Wiley discusses failure of will and the chain of fatality as themes in Conrad's fiction in *Conrad's Measure of Man* (Madison: University of Wisconsin Press, 1954).

64. Joseph Conrad, *Nostromo* (New York: Random House, 1951), p. 405. Conrad uses the imagery of games, farce, and play throughout the novel. Michael C. Kotzin traces another fantasy pattern in the novel in "A Fairy-Tale Pattern in Conrad's *Nostromo*," *Modern British Literature*, 2 (1977), 200-14.

65. Conrad, *Nostromo*, pp. 305-06.

66. Joseph Conrad, *Chance: A Tale in Two Parts* (New York: Norton, 1968), p. 128. J. B. Priestley felt that *Chance* captured the pervading sense of chance in life in 1914 (*The Edwardians* [New York: Harper & Row, 1970], p. 277). Looking back on the period, he concluded that things were determined and recognized as such. "But this surely is determinism, denying the free will we have? We do not know enough to settle and then be rid of this age-old argument. Some things are determined, so far as individuals are concerned, and though we are not without free will, it is more limited than we usually imagine it to be. Time and scale come in here, but not into this book" (*Edwardians*, p. 282).

67. Arnold Goldsmith, "Henry James's Reconciliation of Free Will and Fatalism," *Nineteenth-Century Fiction*, 13, No. 2 (September 1958), 109-26.

68. Donadio, p. 9.

69. Wells frequently testified to the importance of William James to his thinking. An out-of-the-way example is in his introduction to James Harvey Robinson's *The Mind in the Making* (London: Jonathan Cape, 1923), where Wells wrote, "For me, I think James Harvey Robinson is going to be almost as important as was Huxley in my adolescence and William James in later years" (p. 7). Anthony West notes Wells's admiration for James and for pragmatism in "H. G. Wells," *Encounter*, 8 (1957), 56.

70. See Georges Lafourcade's *Arnold Bennett: A Study* (London: Frederick Muller, 1939) for an estimate of Bennett's "philosophy" (pp. 220-28).

71. Stuart P. Sherman, *On Contemporary Literature* (New York: Holt, 1917), p. 108.

72.    Ibid., p. 113.

73.    Walter F. Wright, *Arnold Bennett: Romantic Realist* (Lincoln: University of Nebraska Press, 1971), p. 8.

74.    Arnold Bennett, *Clayhanger*, Volume I of *The Clayhanger Family* (London: Methuen, 1925), p. 426.

75.    Ibid., p. 182. In *Mental Efficiency And Other Hints to Men and Women* (New York: George H. Doran, 1911), Bennett says that when he encounters some difficulty, he says to his mind, "Mind, concentrate your powers upon the full realization of the fact that I, your master, am immortal and beyond the reach of accident" (pp. 115-16). His novels do not depict this kind of strength. It sounds like Benham confronting the jungle of existence, but it is mere puff.

76.    Comparing Wells and Bennett, an anonymous reviewer compliments Bennett as the foremost contemporary exponent of the great art of representation. "To him life passes as a show, to which he, as a spectator, is determined to apply his utmost powers of memory, observation, choice, and comparison" (*Heritage*, 195). Wells, on the other hand, puts himself heartily into his narrative. Mencken objected that presenting mere spectacle was Bennett's weakness; "when there is no organization of the spectacle at all, when it is presented as a mere formless panorama, when to the sense of its unintelligibility is added the suggestion of its inherent chaos, then the mind revolts no less" (*Prejudices. First Series* [New York: Knopf, 1923], p. 44).

77.    G. K. Chesterton, *The Autobiography of G. K. Chesterton* (New York: Sheed & Ward, 1936), p. 173.

78.    Ibid., pp. 181 ff.

79.    Theodore Dreiser, Introduction to *Tono-Bungay*, Volume I of the Sandgate Edition (New York: Duffield, 1927), p. ix.

80.    In this Wells resembled James, especially as Stephen Donadio has pictured him.

81.    William C. Frierson credits Wells with the development of subjective fiction, especially in the form of the life-novel (*The English Novel in Transition 1885-1940* [Norman: University of Oklahoma Press, 1942], pp. 130 ff.). Throughout his study of Wells, Raknem discusses Wells's originality or imitativeness and notes that Wells was always willing to assist innovative young writers, even claiming that he was the discoverer of Joyce (p. 326).

82.    Ford Madox Ford, "Conrad on the Theory of Fiction," *Conrad: A Collection of Critical Essays*, ed. Marvin Mudrick (Englewood Cliffs, N.J.: Prentice-Hall, 1966), p. 172.

83.    Collie, p. 69.

84. Ibid., p. 57.

85. Ibid., p. 53.

86. Virginia Woolf says in "George Gissing," *Collected Essays*, Volume I (London: Hogarth Press, 1966), that for Gissing as for Remington in *The New Machiavelli* writing becomes a means of ordering life, but whereas Gissing had no pretension to extending that ordering, Remington—and Wells—did (p. 300).

87. Goode, p. 28.

88. Ibid., pp. 143 and 178.

89. Donadio quotes this passage from *The Spoils of Poynton* and discusses its significance (p. 202).

90. Arnold Bennett, "The Author's Craft," *The Author's Craft and Other Critical Writings of Arnold Bennett*, ed. Samuel Hynes (Lincoln: University of Nebraska Press, 1968), p. 9.

91. For example, he subtitled *The World of William Clissold* "A Novel at a New Angle," often wrote introductions to explain his innovations (as with *A Modern Utopia*), clearly labeled some of his works experimental (as he did with *The Work, Wealth and Happiness of Mankind*), and sometimes became very testy about preserving his new departures—as when he complained to the editors at the Cresset Press in August of 1935 that he did not want photographs in *The King Who Was a King*. "I know what I am doing in this business," he snapped, "and I will not have this new and important experiment in publication let down, through any neglect on my part" (Illinois).

92. Wells's negative judgment on James and others for seeking perfection in literary style extended to their outlook on life. In an interesting letter of 13 August 1940 to the young writer Mark Benny, Wells wrote, "On his hall table at Rye [James] had a dozen sets of hats or caps, sticks, gloves, so that whenever he went abroad he should have the real right thing. And he believed, as Gissing did most painfully, that somewhere hidden away in society was *the* Lady and *the* Gentleman. It's a legend. No more will you find them than the Holy Grail. But he went through a world haunted and mocked by the sense of this unseen standard of perfection" (Illinois).

93. "A man, in Wells's opinion, brings his own will to bear in a chaotic world that knows no moral laws and only in this sense does he become real. Art is another demonstration of human will. Man creates it, it is human by nature and purpose, it carries a moral aim unknown to the outside world. It is the means of man's assessment of the world and of himself. Were it to submit to the chaos of the outside world it would lose the element of man's organising will. Therefore for Wells in the end art remains a separate and vitally important form of man's activity, one of the forms of mankind's existence *as a whole*" (J. Kagarlitski, *The Life and Thought of H. G. Wells*, trans. Moura Budberg [London: Sidgwick & Jackson, 1966], p. 208).

# CHAPTER EIGHT: WRITING

1.   Instances where he recommends English as a universal language are *Anticipations*, chap. VII; *Mankind*, chap. IV: 2, and chap. VI; *Free*, chap. IV; and *Shape*, bk. III, chap. V.

2.   Wells gives as an example of written assertions succeeding over realities the biblical account of Solomon, which he considers a grave distortion of the facts (*Outline*, chap. XIX: 2). Wells takes up the importance of language in the education of humans, emphasizing the marked change of method from other creatures, in *The Science of Life* (*Life*, bk. VIII, chap. III: 7). More broadly, *The Work, Wealth and Happiness of Mankind* recounts the various ways in which humans are taught to perceive the world into which they are born and the role anticipated for them (*Work*, chap. VIII: 2 and elsewhere).

3.   Beatrice Webb praised Wells for his clever phrases, whereas Randolph Bourne considered them clever but shallow (*Heritage*, pp. 88 and 240). Wells himself showed how a world movement such as Communism could fall victim to its own calcified slogans (*Work*, chap. VIII: 2).

4.   In *The Work, Wealth and Happiness of Mankind* Wells considered the question of the accuracy of words as it related to the central issue of the Realism/Nominalism controversy (*Work*, chap. II: 2). This is a matter that concerned Wells throughout his career. He had dealt with it directly as early as *First and Last Things* (*Things*, bk. I: 12-13).

5.   In an early review of Wells's work Arnold Bennett contended that "his strongest points are his clear vision and his intellectual honesty" (*Arnold Bennett and H. G. Wells: A Record of a Personal and a Literary Friendship*, ed. Harris Wilson [London: Rupert Hart-Davis, 1960], p. 275). Wells was frequently praised for his sincerity and his honesty (*Heritage*, pp. 64, 123, 219).

6.   This pursuit of truth was what he admired so greatly in Roger Bacon. (*Work*, Introduction: 3; chap. II: 2; chap. VIII: 4). C. P. Snow said that Wells liked to compare himself to Roger Bacon, Comenius, and Machiavelli (*Varieties of Men* [New York: Scribner's, 1966], p. 82).

7.   Vincent Brome puts the case for Wells as an aggressive word-master thus: "The stock case-book history of the mother-babe trail was plainly blazed for the least experienced eye to see, and words for Wells had so obviously become a means to power, which granted him in the end verbal omnipotence. He had manipulated people and worlds in writing as he could never manipulate them in real life. Rational analysis had become the big stick for beating the lights out of his enemies, and behind his enemies the society which had forced on him the squalor of his early days." Brome adds that this interpretation leaves out of account Wells's noble thoughts and the fine language that graced his books (*H. G. Wells: A Biography* [London: Longmans, Green, 1951], p. 199).

8.  Stephen Donadio develops a similar point about Henry James, beginning with a quotation from Theodora Bosanquet: "When he walked out of the refuge of his study into the world and looked about him, he saw a place of torment, where creatures of prey perpetually thrust their claws into the quivering flesh of the doomed defenceless children of light" (*Nietzsche, Henry James, and the Artistic Will* [New York: Oxford University Press, 1978], pp. 9-10).

9.  Various persons commented on Wells's practice of writing in the small hours (Arnold Bennett, *The Journals* [Baltimore: Penguin Books, 1971], p. 394; Matilda M. Meyer, *H. G. Wells and His Family* [Edinburgh: International Publishing, 1955], pp. 32 and 95). Brome gives a more detailed account of Wells's writing habits (p. 73).

10. That Wells treated his characters as though they were scientific specimens has become a commonplace in writing about him. See, for example, Van Wyck Brooks, *The World of H. G. Wells* (New York: Mitchell Kennerley, 1915), p. 31; Richard Hauer Costa, *H. G. Wells* (New York: Twayne Publishers, 1967), p. 135; Patrick Parrinder, *H. G. Wells* (Edinburgh: Oliver and Boyd, 1970), p. 37; Alfred Borrello, *H. G. Wells: Author in Agony* (Carbondale and Edwardsville: Southern Illinois University Press, 1972), p. 113.

11. Gordon N. Ray examined Wells's attitudes in "H. G. Wells Tries to Be a Novelist," *Edwardians and Late Victorians*, ed. Richard Ellmann (New York: Columbia University Press, 1960), pp. 106-59. Jean-Pierre Vernier discusses Wells's theory of the novel in *H. G. Wells et son temps* (Publications de l'universite de rouen, 1971), pp. 285 ff. Paul Goetsch offers a sound assessment of Wells's views on fiction in *Die Romankonzeption in England 1880-1910* (Heidelberg: Carl Winter Universitätsverlag, 1967), pp. 249-83.

12. Wells had the preacher's tone in his early science essays and speculative pieces such as "The Man of the Year Million." In "A Slip Under the Microscope," he pictures his Wells-like student as a youth eager to learn, but also to teach the world.

13. In February of 1902 Wells wrote to Bennett, "There is something other than either story writing or artistic merit which has emerged through the series of my books, something one might regard as a new system of ideas— 'thought' " (*Bennett and Wells*, p. 74). Wells was not discovering this feature of his work, but expounding it.

14. William Morris expressed a willingness to let much of the accumulated art of the world be lost. He did not like a world turned museum ("The Aims of Art," *Signs of Change* [London: Reeves and Turner, 1888], p. 132). Jean-Pierre Vernier says that Wells moved from a visionary to a didactic approach in his fiction ("Evolution As a Literary Theme in H. G. Wells's Science Fiction," *H. G. Wells and Modern Science Fiction*, ed. Darko Suvin and Robert M. Philmus [Lewisburgh: Bucknell University Press, 1977], pp. 85 ff.). It is certainly true that after beginning with some challenging

essays, Wells "lapsed" into light pieces and fiction, but a letter of Wells to A. M. Davies in the summer of 1894 explains why this was so. "You are a true friend to warn me of my literary falling off. The bother is I have got to live and during my period of excellence not an editor would look at my stuff. This decadent style seems to have caught the fancy" of the editors from whom Wells required money (Illinois).

15.     In *The Wife of Sir Isaac Harman* Wells says of the nineteenth century, "Literature was to have its once terrible ferments reduced to the quality of a helpful pepsin. Ideas were dead—or domesticated" (*Harman*, chap. IX: 1). He presented a similar picture in *The Shape of Things to Come*, where he again recorded literature's withdrawal into its peculiar Bohemia concerned with elaborate style in the twenties and thirties (*Shape*, bk. III: 7). Theodore Bulpington is an extended sketch of the type.

16.     Wells might have intended a *Punch*-like quality, since his narrator actually offers the moralist in this story a copy of that magazine.

17.     Geoffrey West quotes a letter of Wells's printed in the *English Review* for August 1920: "Literature is not jewellry, it has quite other aims than perfection, and the more one thinks of 'how it is done' the less one gets it done. These critical indulgences lead along a fatal path, away from every natural interest towards a preposterous emptiness of technical effort, a monstrous egotism of artistry, of which the later work of Henry James is the monumental warning. 'It,' the subject, the thing or the thought, has long since disappeared in these amazing works; nothing remains but the way it has been manipulated" (*H. G. Wells* [New York: Norton, 1930], p. 253).

18.     Wells recommended *The Ambassadors* to Bennett, who couldn't take it (*The Journals*, p. 118). Wells praised Conrad's *Mirror of the Sea* as extraordinarily good (*Bennett and Wells*, p. 142). Later he complained of Conrad's style ('*42*, pt. II: 17). There is no doubt some irony in Wells's mention of the "high mystery" of the novel as taught by Henry James in *The Work, Wealth and Happiness of Mankind* (*Work*, chap. XV: 8).

19.     Gordon N. Ray, *H. G. Wells and Rebecca West* (New Haven: Yale University Press, 1974), p. 191.

20.     Beatrice Webb, *Our Partnership*, ed. Barbara Drake and Margaret I. Cole (London: Longmans, Green, 1948), p. 366. In the preface to *The Works of H. G. Wells*, Volume X (New York: Scribner's, 1924), Wells said that it could be argued that *Comet* was a novel.

21.     Frank Swinnerton, *Swinnerton: An Autobiography* (Garden City, N.Y.: Doubleday, Doran, 1936), p. 171.

22.     Enid Bagnold describes Wells's dislike for his own early writings in her *Autobiography* (Boston: Little, Brown, 1969), p. 176.

23.     The story "Through a Window" (1894) may be an early fable of this attitude, for Bailey, an invalid who enjoys watching the spectacle that passes

outside his window, one day discovers that there is no real separation of his room from the world when a fugitive Malay enters his room. Bailey is forced to act and kills the man.

24. Wells says further of Shaw, "But certainly he is the greatest living artist in expression, in self-expression, and he does it so excellently that it seems ungracious to raise the question whether he has ever had anything but himself to express" (*Going*, chap. XXV).

25. St. John G. Ervine felt that Wells's written style was precisely like his talk (*Some Impressions of My Elders* [New York: Macmillan, 1922], p. 241).

26. Bennett and Wells, p. 124.

27. Examples of such charges occur in *Heritage*, pp. 175, 180, 198. Two are unsigned and one is by Mencken. Robert Philmus and David Y. Hughes show the development of *The Time Machine* in detail (*Early Writings in Science and Science Fiction by H. G. Wells* [Berkeley: University of California Press, 1975]). The manuscripts of *The Island of Dr. Moreau* at the University of Illinois Library reveal what a great deal of rewriting and reconsideration Wells put into the novel. Swinnerton comments on the appearance of Wells's manuscripts after his revisions had been added (*Autobiography*, p. 170), and Brome offers similar comments on Wells's revising practices (p. 73).

28. In *You Can't Be Too Careful* Wells exploits the comic possibilities of malapropisms in the French language quite effectively (*Careful*, bk. III, chap. VIII, et passim).

29. Robert Bloom discusses Wells's use of metaphors in *Anatomies of Egotism: A Reading of the Last Novels of H. G. Wells* (Lincoln and London: University of Nebraska Press, 1977), pp. 96-97 and 159-60.

30. Swinnerton, *Autobiography*, p. 158.

31. R. Thurston Hopkins, *H. G. Wells: Personality, Character, Topography* (New York: Dutton, 1922), pp. 28, 94 ff.

32. *Bennett and Wells*, pp. 114-15.

33. W. Somerset Maugham, *The Vagrant Mood: Six Essays* (London: William Heinemann, 1952), p. 214.

34. Mark Schorer's "Technique as Discovery," *Forms of Modern Fiction: Essays Collected in Honor of Joseph Warren Beach*, ed. William Van O'Connor (Minneapolis: University of Minnesota Press, 1948), pp. 9-29, is the principal modern challenge to Wells's standing as an artist of the novel.

35. In *You Can't Be Too Careful* Wells said that he followed in the tradition of Hogarth and Fielding (*Careful*, bk. VI, chap. III). Ingvald Raknem discusses Wells's early interest in realism and romance (*H. G. Wells and His*

*Critics* [London: George Allen & Unwin, 1962], pp. 289 ff.). Sidney Dark praises Wells for reviving the parable (*An Outline of Wells: The Superman in the Street* [New York and London: G. P. Putnam's Sons, 1922], pp. ix-x). Helen Thomas Follett and Wilson Follett likened Wells's fiction to that of Defoe (*Some Modern Novelists: Appreciations and Estimates* [New York: Holt, 1918], p. 241). Lionel Stevenson denoted Wells as clearly falling within the nineteenth-century tradition of the novel (*Yesterday and After*, Volume XI of *The History of the English Novel*. [New York: Barnes & Noble, 1967], p. 59).

36.    R. A. Scott-James wrote of Wells in his review of *Ann Veronica* that he was "a man whom rules are not big enough to hold—one who makes rules and defies them, because nature, and especially human nature, does so too" (*Heritage*, p. 157).

37.    Jean-Pierre Vernier discusses Wells's narrators in the early romances in "Evolution As a Literary Theme," pp. 75 ff.

38.    Many critics have noted Wells's tendency to behave like a scientist (*Heritage*, pp. 179-80). Van Wyck Brooks regarded the detachment of the early tales as both scientific and artistic (pp. 25-26). Rosylnn D. Haynes concentrates on this theme in *H. G. Wells: Discoverer of the Future* (New York and London: New York University Press, 1980).

39.    Robert M. Philmus, *Into the Unknown: The Evolution of Science Fiction from Francis Godwin to H. G. Wells* (Berkeley and Los Angeles: University of California Press, 1970), pp. 100 ff.

40.    Patrick Parrinder describes this change as a movement from the hero as victim to the hero as prophet (p. 98).

41.    Various critics have suggested that Wells ceased to be an artist after 1920. Brome (pp. 83, 113, 200) and Bergonzi (p. 171) have this view. Raknem discusses the decline of his reputation after that date (p. 150). But Dreiser was willing to accept *Clissold* as a major novel (Introduction to *Tono-Bungay*, Volume I of the Sandgate Edition [New York: Duffield, 1927], p. xi). Arnold Bennett admired that novel (*The Journals*, p. 517; *Bennett and Wells*, p. 236). There were mixed responses to *Clissold*, as the entries in *Heritage* show, but H. L. Mencken and John Maynard Keynes both considered it a fine achievement (pp. 282, 289). Bennett was still championing Wells in 1928 when he praised *Blettsworthy* to Lord Beaverbrook as "the best novel Wells has written for years" (*Letters of Arnold Bennett: Volume III: 1916-1931* [London: Oxford University Press, 1970], p. 310). Robert Bloom has recently shown the value of the late works.

42.    Samuel Hynes gives a full account of the matters surrounding Woolf's composition of "Mr. Bennett and Mrs. Brown" in "The Whole Contention Between Mr. Bennett and Mrs. Woolf," *Edwardian Occasions: Essays on English Writing in the Early Twentieth Century* (New York: Oxford University Press, 1972), pp. 24-38. There were many charges that Wells was unable to create believable characters (see *Heritage*, pp. 162, 251, 275; Ra-

knem, pp. 178 ff.; Follett and Follett, p. 258; J. D. Beresford, *H. G. Wells* [New York: Holt, 1915], p. 59). But there were those who praised Wells as a fine creator of characters: see *Heritage*, p. 158, and Ivor Brown, *H. G. Wells* (London: Nisbet, 1923), pp. 40 ff. In this, as in so much, Wells was the subject of considerable controversy.

43.    Beatrice Webb noted to herself in 1909 that Wells had put a good deal into *Tono-Bungay* that he had picked up from her but had woven it into his text in such a jumble that it came out all wrong (*Heritage*, p. 150).

44.    Raknem comments on Wells's use of real persons in his fiction and adds that he did not always present them as themselves, but as distortions (p. 202). R. A. Scott-James objected to Wells's use of real Fabians' names in *Ann Veronica* (*Heritage*, p. 158). Wells approved of the practice of using real names for public persons as well as of depicting characters manifestly resembling real personages in other writers' novels too. He praised the practice in his introduction to Sir Harry Johnston's *The Gay-Dombeys* (New York: Macmillan, 1919), pp. vi and viii.

45.    Sidney Colvin appreciated the contribution that real names made to the realism of Wells's novels but still was critical of Wells's use of them in a letter of 8 July 1902 (Illinois).

46.    On the other hand, Wells did object to comment upon him in Mary Austin's *Earth Horizon*. She wrote a letter to him in November of 1932 explaining that she had intended nothing libelous (Illinois). And in a letter of 19 June 1935 to Methuen and Company, Wells objects that George Doran's *Chronicles of Barabbas 1884-1934* is libelous (Illinois). These, however, were nonfiction.

47.    See Gloria G. Fromm, *Dorothy Richardson: A Biography* (Urbana, Chicago, London: University of Illinois Press, 1977) for a discussion of Richardson's use of Wells (pp. 187 ff.).

48.    Henry James objected to the autobiographical element in fiction and said so to Wells (*Heritage*, p. 200). Arnold Bennett argued that "first-class fiction is, and must be, in the final resort autobiographical" ("The Author's Craft," *The Author's Craft and Other Critical Writings of Arnold Bennett*, ed. Samuel Hynes [Lincoln: University of Nebraska Press, 1968], p. 24). In the preface to Volume XIV of *The Works*, Wells complained that reviewers of his work had insisted on identifying autobiographical elements in almost all of his characters, no matter how diverse they were. He conceded that there was an element of truth in the claim. "It is only by giving from his own life and feeling that a writer gives life to a character," he explains (p. x).

49.    Bernard Bergonzi notes Thomas Seccombe's observation in 1914 that features of *Gulliver's Travels*, *Frankenstein*, and *Jekyll and Hyde* are detectable in *The Island of Dr. Moreau* (p. 106).

50.    Raknem, pp. 354 ff. Raknem also mentions the influence of Flammarion on *Anticipations* (p. 60n). Borello discusses the derivative quality of the early

stories (p. 71), and Peter Haining presents a good sampling of material that Wells used or might have used in his early writings in *The H. G. Wells Scrapbook* (New York: Clarkson N. Potter, 1978).

51.    This connection is examined in Robert L. Platzner's "H. G. Wells' 'Jungle Book': The Influence of Kipling on *The Island of Dr. Moreau*," *Victorian Newsletter*, 36 (1969), 19-22. The typescripts indicate that Wells added the Saying of the Laws section at a later stage of composition (Illinois).

52.    G. West, p. 108. Bergonzi notes this connection as well and also discusses many other possible influences, such as C. H. Hinton's *Scientific Romances* (1888), though Hinton's "romances" do not greatly resemble anything that Wells wrote. Bergonzi also mentions the influence of Nietzsche on Wells's thought.

53.    In the typescript of *In the Days of the Comet* Wells wrote above the reference to James's "The Great Good Place"—"verify?"—indicating that he had made the reference casually and was directing himself to make certain that the reference was accurate (Illinois).

54.    In a footnote to Wells's epistolary reference to Le Gallienne's *The Quest of the Golden Girl*, Grant Richards remarks that Le Gallienne was one of Henley's *bêtes noires* and thus, no doubt, a special target for Wells at the time (*Memories of a Misspent Youth 1872-1896* [New York and London: Harper & Brothers Publishers, 1933], p. 330). Wells reviewed Le Gallienne's novel in the *Saturday Review*. See *H. G. Wells's Literary Criticism*, ed. Patrick Parrinder and Robert M. Philmus (New Jersey: Barnes & Noble, 1980), pp. 124-28.

55.    There are numerous references to Boccaccio in Le Gallienne's novel.

56.    Kenneth B. Newell, *Structure in Four Novels by H. G. Wells* (The Hague and Paris: Mouton, 1968), p. 87.

57.    Norman and Jeanne Mackenzie in *H. G. Wells: A Biography* (New York: Simon and Schuster, 1973) dismiss *The Sea Lady* as "a poor piece of work" (p. 178). Little had been written on *Babes in the Darkling Wood* before Robert Bloom discussed it at length.

58.    Miriam Alice Franc, *Ibsen in England* (Boston: Four Seas, 1919), pp. 66, 90-91.

59.    Henrik Ibsen, *The Lady from the Sea,* trans. James Walter McFarlane in the Oxford Ibsen, Volume VII, ed. James Walter McFarlane (London: Oxford University Press, 1966), p. 120 (act 5). Subsequent indications of acts appear in the text.

60.    The chapter had been titled "Moonshine" and "Moonshine In Excelsis" before "Moonshine Triumphant" was selected (Illinois).

61.    Borello condenses Wells's position thus: "In involving himself personally,

the author becomes one with the reader and the two jointly explore the problem at hand" (p. 115). Gordon N. Ray has shown how alert Wells was to the novel of his day in "H. G. Wells Tries to Be a Novelist." He argues in that essay that Wells did, for a time, become a novelist in the Jamesian sense, with such novels as *Love and Mr. Lewisham, Kipps, Tono-Bungay*, and *The History of Mr. Polly*. I can accept this argument while maintaining that Wells's fundamental outlook was less aesthetic than argumentative, less artistic than journalistic. *The Sea Lady*, however, shows how strongly he was attracted to the aesthetic position.

62.  Leon Edel and Gordon N. Ray, *Henry James and H. G. Wells: A Record of their Friendship, their Debate on the Art of Fiction, and their Quarrel* (Urbana: University of Illinois Press, 1958), pp. 18-19.

63.  Ibid., pp. 169, 176-77, and 160. In "H. G. Wells Tries to Be a Novelist" Professor Ray illustrates in detail how consistent Wells's views on the novel were. He knew precisely what he did not like in the fiction of his day and had a clear, if not formulaic, view of what he wanted from good fiction, including his own. When Bennett suggested that Wells permit the documents in the controversy with James to be published in 1919, Wells declined, saying, "I wrote carelessly in that correspondence, feeling I was dealing with an old man and being anxious to propitiate him—without too much waste of epistolary effort on my part. The publication of the correspondence therefore as it stands might entirely misrepresent my attitude towards our 'art' " (*Bennett and Wells*, p. 204). When Wells argued with James about the novel, he granted the "existence of such a thing as The Novel, a great and stately addendum to reality, a sort of super-reality with 'created' persons in it, and by implication [he] admitted that [his] so-called novels were artless self-revelatory stuff, falling far away from a stately ideal by which they had to be judged" (*Autobiography*, chap. VII: 5). It is obvious why Wells would not want these sentiments, which were clearly not his fundamental beliefs, circulated.

64.  William Golding uses the same technique in *The Lord of the Flies*, which is a negative comment upon R. M. Ballantyne's *Coral Island*. Golding's *The Inheritors* is an open corrective to Wells's "A Story of the Stone Age" and "The Grisly Folk." This technique, and the specific connection with Wells, are discussed in Bernard Oldsey and Stanley Weintraub's *The Art of William Golding* (New York: Harcourt, Brace and World, 1965), Mark Hillegas's *The Future as Nightmare: H. G. Wells and the Anti-Utopians* (New York: Oxford University Press, 1967), and Mark Kinkead-Weekes and Ian Gregor's *William Golding: A Critical Study* (New York: Harcourt Brace and World, 1967).

65.  William Scheick calls attention to this relationship in "The Fourth Dimension in Wells's Novels of the 1920's," *Criticism*, 20, No. 2 (Spring 1978), 183.

66.  A. E. Carter, *The Idea of Decadence in French Literature 1830-1900* (Toronto: University of Toronto Press, 1958), pp. 100 ff.

67.  The diary of the *Rattlesnake* voyage was not published in a complete form

until 1936, but the story had been partially recorded in Leonard Huxley's *Life and Letters of Thomas Henry Huxley*, 2 vols. (New York: D. Appleton, 1900). Of course, there is the obvious influence of the kind of journey depicted in Voltaire's *Candide*, acknowledged in Wells's dedication.

68.    T. H. Huxley, *Science and Christian Tradition* (London: Macmillan, 1894). Huxley and Gladstone squabbled over this issue for months in 1889-1891. See William Irvine, *Apes, Angels, and Victorians: Darwin, Huxley, and Evolution* (Cleveland and New York: World Publishing, 1955), pp. 321 ff., for an entertaining account.

69.    Wells was benefiting from the information collected for the discussion of shell shock in *The Science of Life* (*Life*, bk. VIII, chap. VII: 10).

70.    *Scrapbook*, p. 60.

71.    In *The Science of Life* Wells and his collaborators describe the actions of the body in terms of communal or political activity (*Life*, bk. I, chap. II: 7-8). It is not a great step to turn the analogy around and suggest that the troubling body in the community becomes a pustule. "Whitlow" also means felon.

72.    Wells makes reference in the novel to the serial publication of his story (*Moon*, chap. XXI). J. Kagarlitski points out that while Wells was making fun of Spencer in his satire on overspecialization in this novel, he was also satirizing his own suggestions in *Anticipations (The Life and Thought of H. G. Wells*, trans. Moura Budberg [London: Sidgwick & Jackson, 1966], p. 88).

73.    *Scrapbook*, p. 97.

74.    Bloom has suggested that there is greater merit in the late works than critics have allowed. See also R. D. Mullen, " 'I Told You So': Wells's Last Decade, 1936-1945," *Wells and Modern Science Fiction*, pp. 116-25. Peter Quennell says that Wells's later books can be read with pleasure, but not as aesthetic wholes, an attitude that reveals his commitment to a specific aesthetic code that Wells would not have accepted (*The Singular Preference: Portraits and Essays* [London: Collins, 1952], p. 173).

75.    Bernard Shaw wrote in *The Sanity of Art* (1895), "Journalism is the highest form of literature; for all the highest literature is journalism. The writer who aims at producing the platitudes which are 'not for an age, but for all time' has his reward in being unreadable in all ages" (New York: Boni and Liveright, 1907), p. 4.

76.    "It happens to have been my role throughout life to assemble facts and interpretations of fact, bearing upon man's power of controlling his future," Wells writes in *The Fate of Homo Sapiens*. He goes on to recount his progress in this interest from *The Time Machine* onward (*Homo*: 9).

77.    See also chapter nine on education. This is a constant theme in *The Work*,

*Wealth and Happiness of Mankind.* In his future history, *The Shape of Things to Come*, Wells has his writer of the future assert, "The history of mankind, as we unfold it to the contemporary student, is a story of ever increasing communication and ever increasing interdependence" (*Shape*, bk. V: 9). Similarly, in *The Fate of Homo Sapiens* he says in his own voice, "Any attempt to make a general outline of human history falls almost uncontrollably into the form of a story of developing communication, learning and co-operation between the primordial ape-man family groups" (*Homo:* 4).

78.     Robert C. Elliott is unappreciative of Wells's device in *The Shape of Utopia: Studies in a Literary Genre* (Chicago and London: University of Chicago Press, 1970), pp. 113 ff.

79.     José Ortega y Gasset, *History as a System and other Essays toward a Philosophy of History* (New York: Norton, 1962), p. 203. There are strong resemblances between Ortega and Wells, but they differed on many points as well. Wells acknowledged the resemblances by dedicating *The Shape of Things to Come* to the Spanish philosopher.

80.     In *'42 to '44* Wells puts it this way: "Conduct systems of reaction require a story or stories of what we are in order to hold our *selves* together and to put our *selves* over to other people" (*'42*, Appendix I: 1).

81.     Clissold has an affection for prehistory in part because it is a period that allows for free speculation (*Clissold*, vol. I, bk. II: 12).

82.     The MacKenzies treat the connection between Wells's own condition and his attitude toward mankind in *Mind at the End of its Tether* in *H. G. Wells* (p. 444).

# CONCLUSION

1.     Margaret Sanger, *My Fight for Birth Control* (New York: Farrar & Rinehart, 1931), p. 274. In *An Autobiography* (New York: Norton, 1938) she comments on his capacity for making fun of himself (p. 271).

2.     Many of his contemporaries commented on Wells's abilities as a talker. Among them were Arnold Bennett, *The Journals* (Baltimore: Penguin Books, 1971), p. 108; Frank Swinnerton, *Swinnerton: An Autobiography* (Garden City, N.Y.: Doubleday, Doran, 1936), p. 120, and *The Georgian Literary Scene 1910-1935* (London: Hutchinson, 1969), p. 53; St. John G. Ervine, *Some Impressions of My Elders* (New York: Macmillan, 1922), p. 242; and Beatrice Webb, *Beatrice Webb's Diaries 1924-1932*, ed. Margaret Cole (London: Longmans, Green, 1956), p. 241.

3.     Beatrice Webb, *Our Partnership*, ed. Barbara Drake and Margaret I. Cole (London: Longmans, Green, 1948), p. 231.

4.     Webb, *Diaries 1924-1932*, p. 241.

5.    Beatrice Webb, *Beatrice Webb's Diaries 1912-1924*, ed. Margaret I. Cole (London: Longmans, Green, 1952), p. 201.

6.    Rebecca West, *The Strange Necessity* (Garden City, N.Y.: Doubleday, Doran, 1928), p. 215.

7.    Leonard Woolf, *Beginning Again: An Autobiography of the Years 1911-1918* (New York: Harcourt, Brace & World, 1964), p. 124.

8.    Margaret Cole, *Growing Up into Revolution* (London: Longmans, Green, 1949), p. 42.

9.    Bennett, *The Journals*, p. 339. Kenneth Rexroth tells of the powerful impression *The Research Magnificent* made on him in *An Autobiographical Novel* (Garden City, N.Y.: Doubleday, 1966), pp. 37 and 95.

10.    Cole, *Growing Up*, p. 147.

11.    W. Somerset Maugham, *The Vagrant Mood: Six Essays* (London: William Heinemann, 1952), pp. 211-12.

12.    The letter is in the collection of the University of Illinois Library.

13.    Many persons have recorded Wells's effort to take direction of the Fabian movement. Samuel Hynes comments on Wells's desire to appear as a prophet and a leader (*The Edwardian Turn of Mind* [Princeton: Princeton University Press, 1968], pp. 108 ff. Ford Madox Ford saw Wells as wanting to be Arbiter of the World (*Portraits from Life* [Boston: Houghton Mifflin, 1937], p. 116).

14.    Maugham, p. 216. H. V. Routh says in *English Literature and Ideas in the Twentieth Century: An Inquiry into Present Difficulties and Future Prospects* (London: Methuen, 1948) that the central characters of Wells's social and political novels were usually what Wells might have remained, what he would have wished to be, or what he was (p. 28).

15.    R. A. Scott-James said that Wells was representative of and symbolic of the life of his times (*Personality in Literature 1913-1931* [New York: Holt, 1932], p. 58. David Low, Wells's friend and collaborator, also saw him as a symbol of his age (*Low's Autobiography* [London: Michael Joseph, 1956], p. 282).

16.    Webb, *Our Partnership*, p. 279.

17.    Hynes, pp. 285 ff.

18.    J. B. S. Haldane, *Possible Worlds and Other Papers* (New York and London: Harper & Brothers Publishers, 1928), p. 300.

19.    Ibid., pp. 302-05.

20.    Webb, *Diaries, 1912-1914*, p. 40.

21.    William James said it was philosophy without humbug. He praised Wells's "power of contagious speech" and said, "This book is worth any 100 volumes on Metaphysics and any 200 of Ethics, of the ordinary sort" (*The Letters of William James*, ed. his son Henry James, [Boston: Atlantic Monthly Press, 1920], II 316). There were many books speculating about the future around the turn of the century. Charles H. Pearson's *National Life and Character: A Forecast* (London: Macmillan, 1893) is an example. His predictions for the future are generally accurate, though quite modest. To turn from a work of this kind to Wells's *Anticipations* is like turning from a sepia photograph to a motion picture.

22.    Paul de Man, *Blindness and Insight: Essays in the Rhetoric of Contemporary Criticism* (New York: Oxford University Press, 1971), pp. 147-51. I wish to thank Professor Clarence B. Lindsay of the University of Toledo for calling my attention to de Man's essay in this connection.

23.    Bernard Bergonzi mentions the influence of Nietzsche in Wells's early years in *The Early H. G. Wells: A Study of the Scientific Romances* (Toronto: University of Toronto Press, 1961), pp. 9 ff. David S. Thatcher's *Nietzsche in England 1890-1914: the Growth of a Reputation* (Toronto: University of Toronto Press, 1970) and Patrick Bridgwater's *Nietzsche in Anglosaxony* (Leicester: Leicester University Press, 1972) offer extensive examination of Nietzsche's influence in England in general and on Wells specifically.

24.    H. L. Mencken, *Prejudices. First Series* (New York: Knopf, 1923), p. 24.

25.    José Ortega y Gasset, *History as a System and other Essays toward a Philosophy of History* (New York: Norton, 1962), p. 195.

26.    Ibid., p. 204.

27.    Ibid., p. 223.

28.    Maugham, pp. 214, and elsewhere.

29.    Ibid., p. 219.

30.    Robert M. Philmus, *Into the Unknown: The Evolution of Science Fiction from Francis Godwin to H. G. Wells* (Berkeley and Los Angeles: University of California Press, 1970), p. 34.

31.    Norman and Jeanne MacKenzie, *H. G. Wells. A Biography* (New York: Simon and Schuster, 1973), p. 123.

32.    Ibid., p. 119.

33.    Colin Wilson, *The Philosopher's Stone* (New York: Warner Books, 1974), p. 17. Wilson says that he suspects that "H. G. Wells is probably the greatest novelist of the twentieth century, and that his most interesting novels—if not necessarily the best—are the later ones" (p. 18).

# Index

It has not been possible to include all references to authors, titles, and subjects in this index. I have tried to include those items most directly related to Wells and to the themes I have treated in this book.

285

WELLS, (*continued*)
245n.16, 249n.4-5, 254n.1, 260n.27,
261n.6, 265n.20 and 25, 272n.2,
280n.69-71; "Scope of the Novel, The,"
see "Contemporary Novel, The"; *Sea
Lady, The*, 6, 27, 54, 76, 202, 213-15,
218, 252n.9, 278n.57, 279n.61; "Sea
Raider, The," 35; *Secret Places of the
Heart, The*, 25, 37-8, 55, 60, 76-7, 142,
153, 161, 174, 207, 228-9, 266n.35; *Select Conversations With An Uncle*, 7,
24, 83; *Shape of Things to Come, The*,
8, 26, 39, 67-8, 70, 85, 101, 105, 109,
125-6, 140-1, 148, 175-6, 180, 188, 191,
204, 227, 239, 246n.30, 247n.9,
250n.12, 251n.20, 261n.12, 272n.1,
274n.15, 281n.77 and 79; "Slip Under
the Microscope, A," 5, 7, 97, 272n.12;
*Social Forces in England and Ameri-
ca*, viii, 17, 61, 63, 68, 123, 162, 180,
191, 203, 224, 251n.21, 254n.22,
264n.13-14; *Soul of a Bishop, The*,
213, 225, 267n.40; "Star, The," 32, 96;
*Star-Begotten*, 44, 51, 78, 80, 99, 117,
121-2, 162, 200, 203, 216, 232; "Stolen
Bacillus, The," 67, 250n.10; "Stolen
Body, The," 45, 73; *Story of a Great
Schoolmaster, The*, 37, 50, 121, 127;
"Story of the Days to Come, A," 19,
52, 60, 198; "Story of the Late Mr.
Elvesham, The," 63, 73-4; "Story of
the Stone Age, A," 8-9, 35, 38, 44, 60,
152, 162, 198, 201; "Sun God and the
Holy Stars, The," 43-4; "Temptation
of Harringay, The," 193, 246n.26; *Thesis on the Quality of Illusion*, 74, 161,
266n.28; "This Misery of Boots," 138;
"Thoughts on Cheapness and My
Aunt Charlotte," 193; "Through the
Window," 274n.23; *Time Machine,
The*, 4, 18, 33, 35, 37-8, 40, 43, 54, 69,
73, 85, 96, 102-3, 105, 132, 145-6, 150,
152, 155, 190, 198, 205-6, 237, 240,
245n.23, 280n.76; *Tono-Bungay*, viii,
6, 17, 19, 46, 53, 57, 68, 83, 97, 102,
109, 142-3, 150, 152-3, 171, 173, 183-4,
204, 222-3, 225, 247n.6, 259n.13, 261-
2n.13, 265n.18, 277n.43, 279n.61;
"Treasure in the Forest, The," 36;
"Truth About Pyecraft, The," 182;

"Under the Knife," 51, 63, 251n.19;
*Undying Fire, The*, 25, 32, 44, 103,
127-8, 141, 153-4, 158-9, 216, 226, 230;
"Visibility of Change in the Moon,
The," 87; "Vision of the Past, A," 32,
267n.40; *War in the Air, The*, 25, 100-
1, 105, 123, 146-7, 156, 222, 225, 247-
8n.11, 251n.20; *War of the Worlds,
The*, 18, 32, 52, 96, 107, 152, 155, 204-
6, 220; *Way the World is Going, The*,
45, 69, 89, 91, 107, 116, 119, 146, 185,
191, 197, 208-9, 254n.1, 258n.6,
259n.14, 261n.11, 275n.24; *What is
Coming?* 60, 225; *Wheels of Chance,
The*, 6, 24, 57-8, 109, 121, 142, 150,
152, 206-7, 211; *When the Sleeper
Wakes*, viii, 46, 85, 101, 105, 146, 152,
159-60, 194, 206-7, 253n.15, 256n.13,
265n.21, 266n.36; *Wife of Sir Isaac
Harman, The*, 17, 57-8, 101-2, 109,
142, 149, 163, 184, 194-5, 203, 213,
216, 225, 274n.15; *Wonderful Visit,
The*, 6, 23, 64, 75, 202, 211; *Work,
Wealth and Happiness of Mankind,
The*, 45, 79, 98, 107, 125, 156, 158,
164, 179, 182, 189, 196, 219, 232, 238,
245n.16, 249n.5, 250-1n.18, 252n.11,
254n.1, 263n.5, 264n.8, 272n.2-4 and 6,
274n.18, 281n.77; *World Brain*, 114,
184-5; *World of William Clissold, The*,
25, 33, 45, 52, 57, 66, 83-5, 103-4, 115-
16, 121, 124-5, 142, 149, 151, 154, 158-
9, 162-3, 175, 183-4, 186-7, 192, 204-7,
225, 229, 244n.7, 264n.8, 271n.91,
281n.81; *World Set Free, The*, 44-5,
51, 54, 97, 101, 109, 124, 144-5, 150,
174, 225, 227, 251n.20, 272n.1; *Year of
Prophesying, A*, 251n.21; *You Can't
Be Too Careful*, 21, 53, 57, 61, 100,
105, 120, 132-3, 147, 175, 200, 205,
208, 219, 228, 254n.1, 265n.20, 275n.28
and 35
West, Anthony, 244n.6, 249n.3, 252n.3,
269n.69
West, Geoffrey, vii, 106, 211, 255n.6,
259n.16, 262n.1, 274n.17
West, Rebecca, 46, 118, 193, 217-18, 220,
236, 251n.22
Wilde, Oscar, 51, 193, 241, 246n.26
Wiley, Paul L., 269n.63